The British Heroic Age

ALSO BY FLINT F. JOHNSON
AND FROM MCFARLAND

*Hengest, Gwrtheyrn and the Chronology
of Post-Roman Britain* (2014)

*Evidence of Arthur: Fixing the Legendary King
in Factual Place and Time* (2014)

*Origins of Arthurian Romances: Early Sources
for the Legends of Tristan, the Grail
and the Abduction of the Queen* (2012)

The British Heroic Age
A History, 367–664

FLINT F. JOHNSON

McFarland & Company, Inc., Publishers
Jefferson, North Carolina

LIBRARY OF CONGRESS CATALOGUING DATA ARE AVAILABLE

Names: Johnson, Flint, author.
Title: The British heroic age : a history, 367–664 / Flint F. Johnson.
Description: Jefferson, North Carolina : McFarland & Company, Inc., Publishers, 2017. | Includes bibliographical references and index.
Identifiers: LCCN 2016052874 | ISBN 9780786495221 (softcover : acid free paper) ∞
Subjects: LCSH: Great Britain—History—Anglo-Saxon period, 449–1066. | Great Britain—History—To 1066.
Classification: LCC DA152 .J669 2017 | DDC 942.01—dc23
LC record available at https://lccn.loc.gov/2016052874

BRITISH LIBRARY CATALOGUING DATA ARE AVAILABLE

ISBN (print) 978-0-7864-9522-1
ISBN (ebook) 978-1-4766-2611-6

© 2017 Flint F. Johnson. All rights reserved

No part of this book may be reproduced or transmitted in any form or by any means, electronic or mechanical, including photocopying or recording, or by any information storage and retrieval system, without permission in writing from the publisher.

Front cover photograph of Whitby Abbey in North Yorkshire, England © 2017 Steve Geer / iStock

Printed in the United States of America

McFarland & Company, Inc., Publishers
Box 611, Jefferson, North Carolina 28640
www.mcfarlandpub.com

Thanks to those whose patience has led me to this point.
Thank you to my muse.

Acknowledgments

I would like to thank the members of the King Arthur Facebook page for their help in avoiding several "clankers," and especially Stephen Holden for his questions and concerns as this monolithic work has progressed. Whatever problems remain are solely my own responsibility. As always, I would like to thank my personal muse, Marina.

Table of Contents

Acknowledgments vi
Preface 1
Introduction 5

Interpretations and Sources

1. A Political History 9
2. The Evidence: Roman Sources 13
3. The Evidence: Native Sources 25
4. The Evidence: The *Northern Memorandum* and the *Kentish Source* 47

Britannia

5. Roman Society 61
6. Britain: 367–410 66
7. Picts, Irish and the Germanic Raiders 71

410 Through the Early Sixth Century

8. The Romano-Britons 77
9. The Germanic *Foederati* in the Fifth Century 84
10. The Irish in the Fifth Century 86
11. The Picts 90
12. The Rise of British Kingships 92
13. Heroic Age Politico-Economic Dynamics 96

14. The Early Kings	100
15. The Germanic-Controlled Territories	114

Sixth Century Celtic Kingships

16. Growing Pains of British Kingship	117
17. The New Economic System	119
18. Arthur	122
19. 530–600: An Expanding View	126
20. Rhun son of Maelgwn	129
21. Battle of Arfderyð	132
22. Urien's Alliance and *Y Gododdin*	135
23. Gwrtheyrn	138
24. 530–580: The Setting for the Rise of Germanic Kingships	144
25. 550–575: Columban Dal Riata	147
26. The Decline of the British Kingdoms	151

Rise of the Germanic Kingships: Late Sixth Century to 664

27. Germanic Kingship	155
28. The Southumbrian Theater	158
29. The Northumbrian Theater	165
30. Between the Thames and the Humber	171
31. An Interwoven History: 600–664	174

Religion in Post-Roman Britain

32. The Age of Saints	193
33. Religion as a Political Tool	196
34. Native Religions	200
35. The Dark Ages	204

Appendix: The Vortigern Figure	209
Chronology: 367–664	212

Table of Contents

Glossary   215
Guide to Period Sources   217
Chapter Notes   222
Bibliography   249
Index   267

Preface

In a way, our understanding of British history has developed a lot like a person matures from a small child into adulthood. During the nineteenth century everything about Britain during the Dark Ages was understandable and most issues were seen as black or white. Gildas had provided a list of events from the Late Roman occupation up to his birth. Bede had added accurate details for that period and continued the history up to the eighth century. Nennius' *Historia Brittonum* filled in what few blanks there were of the period along with many British events and names while *The Anglo-Saxon Chronicle* gave a detailed history of the English kingdoms' development. Geoffrey of Monmouth provided an overview—themes and fluidity. There were of course discrepancies between all these sources, but it was believed they were nothing more than simple and straightforward misunderstandings between honest historians of the distant past.

The focus of historical studies then was to find better ways of understanding the materials so that all of them made sense together. With that in mind, scholars spent their careers poring over the same four basic sources. Meanwhile, archeologists continued to improve their methods for uncovering the past. The revelation that carbon disintegrated at a steady rate helped with dating, as did the study of tree rings. Progressively more careful ways of digging and recording information helped as well.

The trouble was that the more scholars learned about history and archeology, the more obvious it became that the four traditional sources of the period were related to and inspired by each other. Once that was recognized their agreement really did not mean anything useful. In fact, it just meant that Gildas was the only one who knew anything about the fifth century unless it could be proven that Bede, *Historia Brittonum*, and *The Anglo-Saxon Chronicle* had used other sources.

Optimistic caution followed their revelation; experts claimed to know less and their studies became more specific as they made in-depth studies on each of the basic four, learning about their sources and eventually the motivations for their writing. The studies revealed more and more bias and less and less real knowledge of the period.

Dr. Dumville brought post–Roman studies to an extreme during the 1970s with a series of articles pointing out the basic oversights in the most-used sources. It was Ninnius, not Nennius, who claimed to have written the *Historia Brittonum*.[1] His authorship was debated. The work had been written and rewritten for very political reasons and was not necessarily accurate.[2] Similar accusations were thrown at Bede and *The Anglo-Saxon Chronicle*.[3] Dumville flatly stated that any events which occurred between the departure of Roman troops in 409 and the beginnings of contemporary recordkeeping in the mid-sixth century were irrecoverable.[4]

Historical and archeological scholars had largely pulled away from Dumville's stance by the 1990s. Several literary experts began studying the individual sources at length. Professor Koch even attempted to reconstruct several sixth-century poems—*Y Gododdin*, "Marwnad Cunedda," "Trawsganu Cynan Garwyn," "Moliant Cadwallon," and "Marwnad Cynddylan."[5] Professors Marged Haycock and Jenny Rowland have studied many other poems in-depth to provide context and meanings for them line by line.[6] The important recent works of Thomas Charles-Edwards and a new generation of historians have revealed new ways of looking at the sources and the period.[7]

The modern era of Arthurian studies began on shaky foundations as well. Arthur and his twelve battles had after all been named in the *Historia Brittonum*. Studies by Jessie Weston and Alfred Nutt speculated that the Holy Grail was based on Romanian and Turkish religious observances or alternatively Celtic mythology.[8] Nutt's work continued with Roger Loomis, who connected Arthur to a sun god and his war-band with various figures in Irish Mythology.[9] His thoughts held the field until the 1960s, promoting translations of Arthurian works from medieval Welsh, English, French, German, Italian, Danish, and Spanish with his popularity.

The 1960s saw scholars trained in Celtic literature approaching Arthurian studies with different and more disciplined approaches to the subject. Rachel Bromwich ended all doubt about the origins of Arthur's name while continuing work by her and other experts researched how and when the materials had transferred to the continent.[10] John Morris' *Age of Arthur* was a book written by a widely knowledgeable expert in the area, but its unestablished theories were in the short term viewed as a step back in the area.

Since then, Arthuriana really continued on in two veins. One group of scholars and good capitalists have written book after book finding different ways of saying the same things about Gildas, *Historia Brittonum*, the *Annales Cambriae*, Bede, and *The Anglo-Saxon Chronicle* with varying levels of academic knowledge and economic success.[11]

At the highest levels, the work of disentangling sources, influences on

Arthurian literature, and character name histories has been at the forefront. Intensive studies have been accomplished on the continental romances,[12] the Welsh stories,[13] and their relationships. Peredur, Lancelot, and Gawain have been the subjects of several papers as well.[14]

Several changes have occurred on both fronts over the last few years. As Professor Koch recently pointed out, the last of Professor Ifor Williams' students died. Williams was a brilliant scholar but his reputation and charisma stifled the growth of an entire generation of scholars. With their decline and deaths progress has come in leaps and bounds; new and innovative work has been done on every major work of literature from this period. This has led to new approaches in the way historians have interpreted the period. It has also guided new methodologies. In 2012, the author developed a new and more accurate means of extracting historical information from historical, pseudo-historical, and literary sources through intensive studies of the materials followed by a strict application of the results. The immediate results were a better understanding of the traditional Guinevere abduction and the Holy Grail legend. More far-reaching uses were found in a study of Arthur's historicity and an exploration of Hengest and Gwrtheyrn's place in history. It was found that, stripping away all the materials we know to be biased, the history of Britain between 410 and the end of the sixth century is very different from any picture we have yet developed.[15]

In a very real way, what is laid out below is simply a continuation of the author's previous work in context supplemented with the latest scholarly works. Approached from another perspective, the present monolith is a summary and rationalization of everything that has been accomplished in the subject of post–Roman Britain up to this point. Note that when dealing with relative (as opposed to specific) chronologies I've used an x to indicate range, e.g., Inabwy (515x565), indicates he was born between 515 and 565, whereas a dash would suggest birth and death years.

What follows below has several goals. First, to demonstrate a pattern of disintegration in Roman Britain that reached a climax in the decades after the Britons overthrew Constantine's government and were refused Roman rule. In addition, I will demonstrate that the breakdown of Roman social, political, and economic order occurred with the re-emergence of the British social structure.

Second, the *Britannia* section will demonstrate the continuation of political and linguistic *romanitas* at the local level. Third, historical and archeological evidence will show the nature of Romano-Germanic culture. This evidence will be used to demonstrate how the Germanic tribes were divided during their service as *foederati*. The same evidence will show that they continued to function as separate entities after Rome left Britain, during their initial revolt, and throughout the rest of the fifth century.

Fourth, several chapters will be devoted to explaining how the Picts and Irish immigrants to Britain had the political stability and military strength to overwhelm the Britons wherever they attacked. Concurrently, they will demonstrate why both culture groups were unable or unwilling to exploit their advantage through a permanent conquest. Fifth, chapters devoted to the sub-Roman period will walk through the process by which both the Germanic tribes and the British villages developed from isolated groups into full and integrated kingships in less than two centuries.

Sixth, evidence will be presented that demonstrates Christianity was not a thriving religion among all the Britons. Instead, evidence will be presented to show that it survived the fifth century along the borders of the old Roman province of *Britannia* and only developed into the dominant religion after all semblance of Roman culture had dissipated from everyday life. It is also hoped that the data will present Anglo-Saxon Christianity as a product of economic pressure, which was used for the spread of political power. Finally, the author hopes to explore the theory that the Germanic conquest of British lands was inevitable.

A great deal has been learned and unlearned since the modern study of post-Roman Britain began in the nineteenth century. However, as complex as the sources and a study of the history has become there is still much that can be learned about the period, many underlying themes and controlling factors to understand, and new ways and more useful methods of looking at the few historical sources at our disposal. Post-Roman Britain is no longer as easy as Geoffrey of Monmouth portrayed the subject in his famous 1136 work, but neither is it beyond our comprehension, either.

Introduction

After two disappointments, in 407 the Roman troops stationed in Britain declared a low-ranking officer named Constantine emperor. As had become custom during the late fourth century, Constantine replaced the governor and his entire administrative staff with a government loyal to him. That was not enough for his troops, however, and in 409 he gathered every soldier Britain could spare and sailed for the continent.

Constantine's intent was to fight his way to Rome and overthrow the legitimate emperor. He landed in Gaul and sent many of his men into Hispania under his lieutenant Gerontius. They fought successfully against Honorius' generals during that time. Eventually, though, Gerontius betrayed Constantine and had him killed in 411.

The citizens of Britannia had given up before then. Zosimus tells us that in 410 they overthrew his government and requested a governor from Rome. The Romano-Britons had every right to expect one, too. In the decades leading up to 410 many provinces had defected from the empire to be ruled by generals or tyrants only to be welcomed back when their leader died.

But 410 was a signal year in the Roman Empire, it was the year the Visigoths under Alaric sacked Rome. The city was left largely intact so there was little long-term damage done. The real casualty was to the mythos of Rome; it was no longer the bastion of security in an empire that was being fought over every few years. Instead, it was now perceived as vulnerable. Rome would be vulnerable for the rest of its life as the capital.

Honorius saw this immediately. He settled with Alaric before turning around to bolster Rome's defenses and bring the legions closer to the capital. He must have received the request from Britain during his reorganization. Their message would have presented him with a straightforward problem; protect Rome and its immediate provinces or send troops to a troublesome province with a history of revolts. He chose to focus on the heart of the empire. Of course he had not given up on reacquiring Britain in the future, though, so he told the Romano-Britons that they, as Roman citizens or *civitates*, would have to look to their own defenses.

That left the Romano-Britons in the worst of all possible situations. In trying to give themselves the best possible chance of surviving the assaults by Picts, Irish, and Germanic peoples they had eliminated the stable government of a usurper to make way for a legitimate Roman leadership. But they never received that leadership, leaving them without a regional government in the face of attacks from three groups.

Nor could the Britons recall Constantine's governor or staff; if they had not been killed as part of the coup, then they had run back to the continent where there was more safety and security. That left Britain with no legitimate governor, no illegitimate governor, and no bureaucracy to support a province. Britain was effectively alone.

The island was not just left to fend for itself, though—it was largely forgotten. Religious rejects like the Pelagians migrated there because it was isolated by the English Channel. For the same reason no emperors or generals ever sailed to Britain in search of recruits or even foodstuffs. After 410, official histories of the Roman Empire rarely even mentioned the island or its inhabitants.[1]

Nor should the lack of Roman interest surprise us. Britain had no island-wide ruler who could threaten the continent,[2] nor did it have resources that could only be obtained through occupation.[3] For a Rome being attacked on all sides, Britain was a former province that could be safely ignored while it focused on more immediate problems.

Britain was not even a major trading interest in the period. The English Channel made commerce that much more difficult even in the best of times, but during the fourth century the entire area was infested with Saxon pirates and in the fifth century, after Honorius officially abandoned Britain, the Roman Navy had no further reason to keep patrolling the area at all. Even if an historian of the era had taken an interest in Britain there was precious little information to be had on the subject.

The first such source would have been Constantius, who wrote about two visits by St. Germanus to strengthen the church in his *Vita Germanii*.[4] The first occurred in 429[5] and rooted out the Pelagian heresy while the purpose of the second is unknown. It was written several decades after the fact, when his source was a very old man.

A second is the two Gallic Chronicles. We know nothing about where they received their information about Britain, but they do say that the entire island was looted by the Germanic tribes in 441. They also say that all communication was cut off. This cannot be entirely true because we know that waves of people left Britain after 450 and that at least one British bishop attended a synod, but it does tell us what we could already guess—that we know so little because there was very little information coming out of Britain.[6]

In Britain during the same era, the closest thing to an historian is Gildas. He was not an historian, though. Gildas was writing a sermon and a legal argument; he had no interest in recording a holistic British history. Instead, he was only concerned about humiliating kings and holies while warning them that God had punished them in the past and would in the future.

Beginning in the late sixth century and continuing into the seventh century is the hypothetical *Northern Memoranda*. The history is no longer extant, but it can be reconstructed from its later derivatives like *Annales Cambriae* and *Historia Britonnum*. Current theory is that it was originally written by a religious man within Cumberland during the sixth or early seventh century, possibly by Pasgen son of Urien as a sort of family history until taken up by a seventh-century Northumbrian prince hoping to use Urien's fame to reinforce his own political position.[7] Alternatively, it could have been written by someone hoping to use Pasgen's royal family to strengthen the holiness of Pasgen's religious houses, though its use as political tool in the seventh century seems certain.

The *Kentish Source* was probably written within decades of the first Christian missionary in Kent (c. 580).[8] The only remnants of that history are to be found in Bede's eighth-century writings about sixth- and early seventh-century Kent and the ninth century *Anglo-Saxon Chronicle*. Since we know, though, that it could not have been written before 580, anything much earlier than 530 has no historical value.

Other sources are also extant, many literary sources as well as several unique documents like the tribute list the *Tribal Hidage*, the mnemonic *Welsh Triads*, and the church grants known as the *Llandaff Charters*. Each manuscript offers tantalizing clues as to the nature of post–Roman history and occasionally gives us a larger picture of what might have been happening in Britain during the period. They are not histories, though; they are the raw materials necessary to write a history. And there are not enough of them to provide a clear picture.

Why? The Romano-Britons definitely had the ability to write a history; Gildas alone is proof that Latin schools were still active and that the British people were thinking of the past.[9] But he is also serves as an explanation of why more were not written; writing nearly a century and a half after 410, Gildas still considered himself a Roman. The Roman mentality had been that the empire was a united entity, so that there were remarkable few regional histories written during its entire existence. Gildas might have pushed through that thinking around 540, but he was an extremely intelligent individual and he did still consider himself Roman. It should come as no surprise that anyone living before him never have considered a British history.

Even if they had we might not know about it. Most of the Romano-British lands were conquered during the period under discussion. Those that remained independent were politically unstable during most of the fifth century. Later kings were more worried about their family history than a history of the British people.

The Irish who settled along the western coast would only occupy the area for decades before either returning to their homeland or becoming absorbed in the British culture.[10] The Picts did not write about themselves, or at least did not write on surfaces that preserved easily. The only native evidence we have of them are two late origin stories and the symbol stones that today dot the Highlands.[11]

As for the Germanic peoples, they would not be literate until the late sixth century and would not bother with historical writing until at least the early seventh century with the *Kentish Source*.

Added to the problem of numbers is the influence of the most popular historical figure in the world, Arthur, on them. By Geoffrey of Monmouth's time (1136) his name had spread across the island, displacing local legends or altering them so that Arthur or his men had become the leading figures in many of them.[12] In ways that the historical Arthur never could have, the literary Arthur has erased or marginalized his less talented and less fortunate contemporaries.

At first glance he has affected history only from the late fifth century up through the careers of Urien and his son Owain (c. 600). An examination of *The Welsh Triads* provides us with a better perspective though. He is prominent in the first twenty-six triads, the oldest stratum.[13] However, triads twenty-seven through the end of the series are dominated by Arthur and his men. The histories have the same difficulty; much of the earliest material is free of Arthur's influence—Gildas, Bede, the *Northern Memorandum*, and the *Kentish Source*. Unfortunately, the earliest historical information is often out of context. It was given a context by Geoffrey of Monmouth, who tended to put Arthur at the center of all things.

What can be learned about Arthur has been largely discussed in the author's previous works. He rose to kingship in or near the first generation of British kings in former Roman territories. He was likely based in or around Old Carlisle. He may have used Hadrian's Wall as a sort of border for his own kingdom. But that was the extent of his actual power during his lifetime. If he was lucky, his entire career as a king lasted twenty years.

The facts of Arthur's life mean that a figure who did not dominate the period has come to dominate histories of the period. That is a problem for any examination of post–Roman Britain, one that can be best addressed by examining the source materials in the methodology the author has developed.

Interpretations and Sources

1

A Political History

Even without many primary sources, writing a book on the history of Britain from 367 up to 664 seems like a massive undertaking at first glance. Any serious study should involve at least looking at all the histories, literature, and archeological research from the period. One would think that the archaeology alone would require a separate study and the extant literary sources—from poetry to folklore and even personal letters—would be just as expansive and would require the mastery of several different areas of study.

As the island was occupied by the Irish, Picts, and Germanic tribes as well as the Britons, common sense would dictate that four entirely different traditions of history and literature would exist and would need to be individually studied if a scholar were to have any chance of making sense of the subject.

All these assumptions are only partially true, though. There are not as many sources as one would hope for to properly study the period, but what there are is so difficult to interpret that there is just as much work involved. The involvement of four different cultures complicates the examination, but the fact that scholars from each ethnicity made use of their counterparts' history and literature makes the work much simpler. As will be seen in the pages below, many of the most important extant histories are closely related to each other.

Probably the most difficult aspect of this study, in fact, is in understanding how the historians of every culture made use of each other for their own ends or for the ends of their patrons. This problem will not only apply to the broad histories of Gildas, *Historia Brittonum*, *Annales Cambriae*, Bede, and *The Anglo-Saxon Chronicle* but also to more isolated or localized works such as dynastic pedigrees and monastery documents.

The biases of the sources is not the only problem, though. Much of the information given is not extant in a form we would recognize as historical, like a newspaper reporting events. Instead, everything we know of is given in a deeply cultural context. This fact makes understanding the materials they present especially difficult for several reasons. For one, what little we know of the fifth, sixth, and seventh centuries is consistent in presenting cultures vastly different from our own in terms of personal and public values. For another, there are four different cultures to consider. At times, many of the sources have passed from one culture to another, adding another layer of interpretation.

The manuscripts themselves present more difficulties. Scholars know from references by medieval authors that there were many more works during the Middle Ages. Those that have survived have not done so because they were the best or the most historically accurate, however. Manuscripts that were interesting were borrowed by different monasteries, whose monks would make copies while they read it. Those that no monks were interested in were not copied.

Now, manuscripts were written in vellum, a particularly durable writing material. However no form of paper, no matter how tough, could hope to last for a thousand years. If only a couple monks found a manuscript interesting in all that time, then only two copies would have been made. And, if both of those monasteries were attacked by Anglo-Saxons, Irish, Picts, Vikings, or the French at any time after that, their manuscripts might just be destroyed. To put it in context, Geoffrey of Monmouth's *Historia Regum Britanniae* was a bestseller during the Middle Ages, and more copies have been found of it than of any other lay manuscripts. With all of that popularity, 215 manuscripts have been found.

Another problem with the manuscripts is the meticulous science of determining which copy most closely resembles the original. Studying the development of scribal errors for only a dozen manuscripts often requires months of some of the most painstaking work in the field and the most obvious line of descent can be disrupted with the finding of another manuscript or the discovery of some new element in an old one.

Historians' prior assumptions are also a problem. Even the most neutral of learning environments starts with a simple reading of the four basic "historical" sources—Gildas, Bede, *Annales Cambriae*, and *The Anglo-Saxon Chronicle*—as interpreted by Geoffrey of Monmouth. There is nothing to say that Geoffrey had any better idea about post–Roman Britain than we do, and a great deal suggests that most of his writings were tempered by the desires of the people he wrote for and his own fancy. It is delicate and time-consuming to be aware of that bias without assuming it is simply wrong.

A sixth obstacle to a study of the period is the limited archaeological remains. Through traditions and information from various other sources, scholarship and digs have come upon many of the chief sites occupied in Wales and several in Cornwall/Devonshire and the north, while similar luck has helped Anglo-Saxon scholars determine many of the occupied sites in England, but they represent only a small proportion of the total occupied sites—for instance there is no certain site or sites for a ruler or rulers in modern Cumberland up until the early seventh century when Mercia controlled it. Though it has now been determined there must have been several kingships in early Pictland, only one has been certainly located.[1]

There is also the simple fact of oral history to consider. The native customs of all the culture groups of Britain put a great deal more stock in oral history than written records. Celtic bards and their Germanic equivalent *skops* were some of the most respected members of their respective societies. Several of the bard's mnemonic devices have been preserved in manuscripts, while we have a number of stories and legends that could only have survived by word of mouth.

However, oral history is often not as useful to historical studies as the written word because it has a habit of growing and adapting to new surroundings.[2] Under the best of circumstances, oral materials must be handled with extreme care. In the constant turmoil that was Early Medieval Britain, it must be highly suspect. In short, this leaves the historian with a very small number of historical sources and the awareness that most of the information they contain may be inaccurate.

Keeping all this in mind, suddenly a topic with so few sources and those from such varying viewpoints, one must change perspectives in addressing the history of post–Roman Britain. The passed century may have seen a thorough discussion of every source relating to the Arthurian period from many different perspectives and by people with diverse backgrounds. However, the author has seen a number of breakthroughs over the last decade and by experts who have never seen fit to tie all the findings together in one overarching history. That is what the present volume is intended to do.

All of the above is why the present offering is primarily a political history. The choice is also one the author is well qualified for. He has dabbled in the cultural and social history of the period in his previous works, but his efforts cannot compare to Dr. Charles-Edwards on the subject, Dafydd Jenkins' work in Welsh law, or David Binchy in the importance of family.[3] Nor would he claim to be an expert in the art of the British, Picts, Irish, or Anglo-Saxons.[4] With all the recent work done on the literature by various experts and the linguistics themselves by Professor John T. Koch, the author would not even entertain the thought of contributing in that particular field.[5] He has touched on the religion and of the period as well, but nothing to compare with the religious studies of D. Simon Evans.[6]

Instead, the author laid the groundwork for such a study by dating many of the key people of the period in *Hengest, Gwrtheyrn, and Fifth Century-Britain*. Before then, he had alluded to many of the key concepts and questions of the period in the author's former work as well as *Evidence of Arthur* and *Origins of Arthurian Romances*. These writing choices have made the generation of the present volume a next logical choice. It provides the opportunity for responding to some of the logical questions that should follow his work. For example, if Gwrtheyrn was a sixth-century king and Hengest was a figure of the fourth century, what exactly happened in the decades between 410 and the rise of the first generation of kings in the late fifth century? How did fifth-century politics work if a king could not expect to reach forty?

2

The Evidence
Roman Sources

As with all sources, those listed below have their individual limitations. Historians who study Rome, Greece, Egypt, Mesopotamia, later Medieval Europe, or any subject in the modern world readily accept that fact and treat them accordingly because they literally have hundreds of available sources. In the modern world especially, the study of nearly every person or event has the advantage of multiple perspectives. An historian is never forced to rely on just one item to derive any accurate information.

British studies are not as fortunate. Often there is only one source that discusses any particular incident, person, or chronology—and almost always its bias renders its information questionable. This leaves the scholar with a dilemma; to accept the source as accurate and make use of its easily digestible information or to stop and question every aspect of that source for flaws and limitations and then only use the untainted information no matter how little or useful it might be. The former option is easier, and was used by nearly all scholars until the 1970s. However, the approach can only yield inaccurate and conflicting information. In British studies it brought experts to the conclusion that the fused royal history of three dynasties as found in the *Historia Brittonum* was historical. In Anglo-Saxon studies it led otherwise sensible scholars to believe that the first Germanic invaders arrived in 449. It was only through the simpler approach that Gwrtheyrn and Hengest were ever believed to be contemporaries in the mid-fifth century.

In the high-pressure world of academia there are ready-made reasons for cheating on the more thorough approach; it is time consuming and unlikely to yield definitive results. It is also exhausting to keep track of what details are likely colored by bias, which are inaccurate due to lack of information, and which can be verified.

However, it does have the advantage that whichever results are arrived at are likely to be accurate. There should be no certainty in our conclusions because there is so much about the materials at our disposal that is entirely unknowable. At least by conducting an exhaustive study on each source there is less uncertainty.

With this in mind, modern scholars have chosen a middle path. When writing broad histories of the period, they have labeled individual sources as either wholly accurate, a good support for information found elsewhere (or their own theories), or entirely dubious. The best scholars have then used each source consistently from there on. The approach balances the time element of the critical approach with the blatant inaccuracies of the naïve analysis. The results have still been unreliable though. Most of the period sources have some useful and reliable information but none of them can be believed without question. By treating all sources as two-dimensional pieces in the three-dimensional puzzle of post–Roman Britain, many scholars have done no justice to themselves or the period they study.

To put it another way, the study of post–Roman history began much like a child's construction of reality; simplistic and fully understandable. As the study of post–Roman Britain has matured, so our child's understanding of the world has become more complex. To extend the metaphor, our hypothetical child became a cynical man in his late twenties during the 1970s, and now has finally reached a rational middle age.

Key to that deepening understanding has been a realization that the sources are more complex than a simple label of accurate or inaccurate. To be used properly, each one must be understood as the multifaceted work it is; a compilation of multiple sources often handled multiple writers, each of whom had their own limitations and biases for writing. We must also keep in mind that each source was composed by a person or persons with limitations and an agenda of his own. For instance, the chapters of *Historia Brittonum* run the entire gambit between historical truth and blatant lie, with folklore and myth taking up significant portions of several chapters.

Understanding that new reality, the next few chapters will be devoted to listing and then describing each source's particular idiosyncrasies—reasons for being, points of origin, authors, patrons, and so forth. In chronological order, the works that will be discussed are Ammianus Marcellinus, the praise poems of Claudian, Prosper of Aquitaine's annals, the letters of Sidonius Apollonaris and St. Patrick, Constantius' *Vita Germani*, Zosimus, Gildas's letters, Taliesin's poems, Aneirin's *Y Gododdin*, Gregory of Tours' personal diary and contemporary history, *Vita Samsoni*, the *Code of Æthelberht*, *The Tribal Hidage*, the letters of Columbanus, *Vita Kentigerni*, the *Laws of Ine*, the *Codes of Wihtred*, *The Code of Hlothere and Eadric*, Adomnán's *Vita Columba*, the anonymous *Vita Cuthberti*, Eddius Stephanus' *Vita Wilfridi*, Bede's writings, *Historia Brittonum*, *The Anglo-Saxon Chronicle*, *Fer 'n' Alban*, Germanic, British, Irish, and Pictish genealogies, *The Welsh Triads*, saga poetry, various englynion and oral memories, and of course archeology. Together, this unassuming and short list of materials will be used to reconstruct the three hundred years of British history which Arthur's name dominates. To do so best, the individual sources will be studied in the next two chapters. The two hypothetical sources, *Northern Memorandum* and the *Kentish Source* will be explored in a third chapter.

This chapter will begin with the Roman, or more accurately the continental, sources. The Roman Empire was an extremely centralized government. This is obvious at the top, where emperors had absolute power over every aspect of the government and were worshipped as gods by the citizens. One aspect of their control was that many governors were selected from among their personal friends and business partners. Another was that by law governors could only manage a province for a fixed number of years before returning to Rome and being replaced by another friend or associate of the emperor.

Each new governor brought along his own group of friends and trusted assistants to fill the highest echelons of the province's bureaucracy, allowing state-educated people from poor families to hold the lower positions in the government.[1] The system was ideally designed to maintain loyalty because all the people in higher stations owed a personal debt to the governor, while he was personally obligated to the emperor for his position. Every person involved could best help themselves by serving the empire.

This connection to Rome was felt by the other citizens as well by the fifth century. Apart from Germanic mercenaries along its borders and slaves, every inhabitant of a Roman province was considered a Roman citizen. That meant that all laws applied equally to people in Israel and Rome, to the provinces of Britain and Italy. In its earliest days, Rome had connected its deities with the local gods but had allowed freedom of religion without penalty. With the institution of Christianity after 300, even that regional separation had disappeared. In all cultural and societal respects, a person from Greece or Syria was not a Greek or a Syrian, they were Romans. With this in mind it should surprise no one that there were no British historians in the empire, only Roman historians who mentioned Britain when it was prominent in Roman affairs. It is because of this mentality that our continental sources on Britain are so limited.

The mindset worked both ways. Rome may only have fallen in 476 with the city being sacked in 410, but the empire had been rotting from the inside for centuries. And Britain had been suffering with it. The renewed threat of invasion, now by Germanic tribes, in the late third century had produced a series of successful generals who had been declared emperor and had instigated a series of short civil wars. The twin changes of external threats and internal instability would fundamentally alter the stability of the empire.

To combat the problem, the empire was often divided in two during this period. That solution did simplify the defense of the empire, but the improved external security only inspired more internal conflicts. It became more and more commonplace for Roman soldiers on the borders to proclaim their general as the emperor. Once they had accepted the title tradition demanded that they return to Rome so that the Senate could ratify them. For many years in the third and fourth centuries, the emperor might be a usurper who had followed a usurper. Often these men spent a majority of their careers trying to stabilize the government while at the same time putting down revolts by other emperor hopefuls.

As was mentioned in the Introduction, elections in 406 and 407 led to the rise of Constantine. However, that was not the first instance in Britain. Carausius had been in Britain when he was declared the emperor in 286. So was Maximus in 367.

The constant internal struggles generated their own problems. When the Germanic tribes had first come in contact with Rome during the third century they had been awed by its cultural achievements. That, as much as Roman successes in battle, had kept them from attempting an all-out invasion of the empire. Instead, the Romans had hired many of them to serve as *foederati*, mercenaries who patrolled the borders in exchange for food and supplies. However, watching their employers squabble among themselves only lessened Germanic awe for them. Internal conflicts also meant that free trade among the provinces was more difficult. Eventually, it led to the tribes receiving less and less of the food and supplies they had been promised.

They could only respond with force. The Visigoths sacked Rome in 410 and the Vandals in 455, but both tribes would leave the city out of respect. It was only in 476 that the Ostrogoths would subjugate the city. Even then their leader, Odoacer, would give the emperor a large pension.

There were also more hostile chieftains. Attila the Hun, "The Scourge of God," would take tribute from the Eastern and Western Roman Empire during the 440s and 450s, when he was not pillaging Europe. Less successful chieftains raided the European borders of the empire throughout the period.

During the fourth century newly accepted and still developing Christianity was also a major force. The last few decades of the fourth century and the first few of the fifth would see the rise of two mutually exclusive philosophies in the religion—the concepts of Free Will and Predestination. The former was championed by a British lawyer named Pelagius who would spend most of his career in Rome speaking about his ideas. He was opposed by St. Augustine of Hippo, a powerful speaker and the writer of several books, including *City of God*. Their dispute, fought between themselves and drawing in all the Christian leaders of the period, would only end with the Council of Carthage in 418 and the declaration of Pelagianism as a heresy.

2. Roman Sources

With the external pressures of roving chieftains, the internal issues of so many upstart emperors, revolts by Germanic *foederati*, and the controversy of Rome's one religion, it should not be surprising that Britain's security and stability were not of great concern to the continent. Nor did Roman historians find what happened in Britain as worthwhile as the events on the continent. However, a few did mention the province of Britannia occasionally. But first, a brief critique of archeology.

With all of the literary and historical sources, we have pieces of information that were generated and recorded because someone in the past wanted the future to know about it. Without a doubt we have the information given to us by the craftiest, wealthiest, and luckiest people of post–Roman Britain. With archeology there is no intent in what we find. No warrior wanted to leave his sword behind; he wanted to either use it in the next life or hoped his son would use it. Farmers did not want their homes abandoned; they wanted their descendants to live in it. In that respect, archeology deals with less bias than any other historical study.

The study does have some serious drawbacks, though. For one, every potentially useful site cannot be excavated. Even if they could find the funding to feed and shelter sometimes dozens of volunteers, many places of interest are in the middle of private or heavily traveled areas. In Britain, permission is only given for some excavations when a site might be destroyed by new construction. Even then it is limited by time, money, and the area of study.

On more accessible sites, modern archeological methods take a more conservative approach. Experts examine the soil using sonar and other techniques and use the information to pick out the sections most likely to produce useful artifacts and then only dig there. Usually, it is only a small portion of the structure. This approach is less intrusive but gives fewer artifacts and allows for less surprise. It is only when a broad range of excavations return similar results that a pattern may be roughly determined and any one object's nature might be understood. Even then, looking at the materials without the perspective of modern eyes is one of the more difficult aspects of archeology.[2]

Another area of difficulty is interpreting the results of an individual dig without placing it against a context of already accepted truths. In British studies, the pseudo-historian Geoffrey of Monmouth has long been known as a poor historian who took from whatever sources he could find to create a coherent history. However, his work was the first attempt to write a full history of the period, and its storyline has proven to be a seductive place from which to reconstruct the fifth and sixth centuries.

Dating, too, is notoriously difficult among artifacts—usually nothing closer than a range of several decades is even possible. That is not a consistent problem. A large number of a specific brooch or type of pottery might allow scholars to guess a tighter date-range. On rare occasion, an artifact is even found in context with a relatively unused coin and a specific year can be determined. At other times tree ring dating (dendrochronology) of a large number of similar items can reveal a narrow range of years for a building.

However, such a tight dating is not generally the rule. Expensive or beautiful items often became heirlooms. Good armaments or even plows might be used for some generations after they were made. This can throw off the dating by as much as a century. The reality of archeology is that it is useless for absolute chronology and often difficult in establishing a relative date. It is of greatest use in understanding the culture of the people, and can only be done safely with the assistance of written sources. Any use of the field beyond that must be purely speculative.

Ammianus Marcellinus is the first person to write about Britain after 367. He was born in Antioch around 365 and spent the first part of his life as a soldier. After he retired he came to Rome where he wrote his history, which ended in 378. Ammianus could not have written before 400 and probably started a few years after.

Ammianus' background suggests a thorough knowledge of Roman tactics as well as a limited understanding of Rome's larger military strategies.

His problem is that he had a limited knowledge of Britain. For instance, his first relevant mention is of two Germanic chieftains coming to Britain as *foederati*. They are the only two *foederati* he names in Britain during the second half of the fourth century. His testimony is contrary to what can be constructed from the archeology of the period and several official Roman records. The other evidence shows that Germanic posts were set up along the southern and eastern coasts of Britain. Standard *foederati* practice was that each post was settled by an entire tribe—chieftain, warriors, women, and children. Each *foederati* station in the archeological record means a different tribe under a distinct chieftain.

Foederati activity was so intense in the late fourth century because their cousins, other Germanic tribes, were preying on ships coming to and from Britain. That is probably why Ammianus knew so little about Britain. What Ammianus does not have in volume, however, he more than makes up for in quality. He comes across as neutral every time he mentions the province of Britain.

Claudian was a poet working for Emperor Honorius in the years around 400. His favorite subject was Stilicho, the most powerful and successful general of the era. Claudian makes no secret of his partisanship.[3] On the other hand, he could not outright lie about Stilicho and his activities, either. He was a contemporary to both his hero and Honorius, and Honorius may well have known about the events he praised. If he had misrepresented the truth and Honorius had found out about it he might have been executed for it. Stilicho was executed in 408.

Prosper of Aquitaine wrote his *Epitoma Chronicon* in the decades following 400 through 455. He was a staunch supporter of Augustine and Predestination in the Christian debates of his time.[4] For this reason he might have made a paper tiger out of some of Free Will's arguments and in speaking of St. Germanus, the hero who went to Britain to end Pelagianism, he might have been expected to exaggerate his exploits there. However, his only contribution to this study is his date of 429 for the visit. As he was a contemporary to the event he must have been accurate; he had access to the information and if he had altered the date it would have affected his credibility in areas that were more important to him, and more subjective.

Prosper is followed by the *Gallic Chronicles*, two simple annals likely written by a pair of holy men from Gallia Narbonensis.[5] Both chronicles continue the history begun by Eusebius (776 BCE–325 CE) and continued by his son Jerome (325–379) beginning in August of 378 BCE They are known by the year in which they end, giving the *Chronicle of 452* and the *Chronicle of 511*.

Both chronicles are considered fairly accurate about the continental information they report.[6] However, Britain would have been a different story. As has been seen, the English Channel was being pirated by Saxon tribes during the fifth century. St. Germanus was able to cross it, but he was a former general and a political leader who had unusual resources at his disposal. For merchants and other less prominent travelers the journey would have been too dangerous to risk, which meant that commerce and with it information coming out of Britain would have been trickling out of Britain at this time. There would have been no way of measuring the accuracy of whatever data they were given, either. Even if Ian Wood is right and a Briton named Faustus of Riez did compose the *Chronicle of 452*,[7] these writers were recording rumors and the information they give should be treated as such.

The one unique piece of information they give about Britain is that the island was overrun by the Germanic tribes in the 440s. *The Chronicle of 452* dates the event to 441/2 while the *Chronicle of 512* says it occurred in 440.[8] We know they are wrong because British and Pictish kingdoms would exist later in the fifth century. The Germanic tribes did not even make an island-wide raid because there is no evidence of it in the archeological record. Knowing the limitations of the source, Dr. Miller suggested it was a ghost event, though most scholars have assumed the entry must have been based on some real incident and have suggested that this 441 was the year all communications with Britain went dark, probably the time of Gildas' mercenary revolt.

The next historian to mention Britain was Zosimus, a pagan who held a position at the royal court of Anastasius I (491–518) in Constantinople. That is where he wrote his *Historia Nova*, which contains our most thorough explanation about the events at the end of Roman Britain. There are two unique things to know when reading Zosimus. The first is that he was a pagan, making him the only non-Christian source for the end of the Roman Empire. The second is that he relies exclusively on one source per period—to the extent that his tone and the choice of facts given when he changes from one source to another. When his source has no information he offers none.[9]

For the years after 407 that source was Olympiodorus of Thebes. However, with Olympiodorus he was less faithful than with previous sources. Very little of his writings have survived, and those only as fragments. What we do know from those fragments is that Zosimus often disagreed with him. Nor is Zosimus' absolute chronology very strong; on the rare occasion that he gives a date for any Western European event more reliable sources normally give different years.

On the other hand, Zosimus is generally more even-handed than his Christian contemporaries when discussing the politics and personalities of the Eastern Roman Empire.[10] He could be overly harsh on the Christian emperors, but he has never been accused of an outright falsehood.

Zosimus' relative chronology of the West seems reasonably accurate even if his absolute chronology is unreliable so that in light of his (or Olympiodorus') general precision otherwise, it seems likely that other factors were involved. When speaking of Britain in particular, distance must have been a significant dynamic. The Eastern Roman Empire had no interest in reclaiming it, nor had any Western Roman ruler since Honorius. For that reason, it seems likely that any errors in his work were due more to an inability to obtain correct information or a lack of interest in his subject (as he did not gather information himself) than to any sinister motivation.

The *Vita Germani*, probably written between 480 and 490 but definitely before 494,[11] is the first personal account of a continental visit to post–Roman Britain. As the name suggests, the book comes from a biography of St. Germanus of Auxerre; it was designed specifically to stress the religious authority of its hero while minimizing any negative aspects of his life.

In the later Middle Ages, the writing of *vitae*, the biographies of holy people, would develop into an entire genre full of recurring miracles and other supernatural elements. Written at the very beginning, though, the *Vita Germani* has none of that. It has little more than a few exaggerations of events. We also know that Constantius, the author, used St. Lupus as his primary source for the British information. Lupus was Germanus' companion on his first trip to Britain.

Several authors have noted that Constantius is extremely precise in his continental details.[12] This is contrasted with his extremely vague reporting on Britain. For instance, he only names Elafius specifically and never gives the villages, cities, regions, or provinces that Germanus visits. Because of his disparity on this point, his lack of information about Britain is likely more a measure of an old man's memory and the fact that communications with Britain were difficult than to any intentional deception on the part of the author.[13]

Constantius writes about two voyages to Britain. The first, naturally, contains the most details and includes a miraculous calming of the sea, a chief citizen named Elafius, the "Halleluiah" victory, and a debate between Predestination and Free Will. The second trip has many similarities to the first. Several scholars, primarily Thompson, have provided good evidence that it did happen.[14] There is always the possibility, though, that Lupus provided Constantius with just enough mutually exclusive materials for Constantius to conclude that there had been two distinct voyages to Britain.

Though Procopius is the next source for the period, he provides some information about Britain from the early fifth century up until his own time. Procopius was born in Caesarea, Palestine around 490—the same era the *Vita Germani* was written. An intelligent and well-educated scholar, he served under Belisarius for most of his career.

Procopius admired Belisarius, and wrote about his campaigns in his *Wars of Justinian* in 551 or shortly after. He also wrote a *Secret History*, in which he attacked both Belisarius and the emperor Justinian. His history is what is of interest to scholars. Despite its obvious bias, it contains useful inside information about the goings-on of the Byzantine Empire.[15]

However, when dealing with Western Europe, and especially with Britain, Procopius is neither reliable nor does he have inside information. During his career, which spanned most of the first half of the sixth century and into the second, Belisarius managed to conquer Italy for a short time. However, no further conquests were attempted to the West. Nor were there any secure trade routes between Italy and Britain. The only information Procopius had access to was the occasional diplomat who might have been in or near Britain and other second or third-hand sources.

The sparsity of his sources shows in the few times Procopius mentions Britain. He seems to have been unaware that Constantine had been immediately preceded by two other usurpers.[16] He thinks that Britain is ruled by three over-kings—of the Britons, the Angles, and the Frisians.[17] He is not even sure about what to call Britain, Britannia or Brittia.[18] His information has been qualified as hearsay and will be treated as such.

With Gregory of Tours we come again to a more reliable source. Gregory was born in what is now modern France in about 538. He was descended from a Roman patrician family that had survived the Frankish conquest and retained its status through its work in the church. Gregory lived his entire life as an aristocrat in a stable kingdom.

His family was especially prominent in Tours, where his relatives had been several of its bishops. His mother moved him there after the death of his father. He was consecrated to the office of bishop in 573.

As a bishop and a member of one of the most prominent families in Gaul, Gregory was exposed to political and ecclesiastical information throughout the kingdom. He also would have had a limited awareness of happenings in Britain. Because of his prominent family and his 21-year tenure as a bishop he would have had first-hand knowledge of every significant event in the region for the last half of the sixth century. He is as close to a firsthand account of Britain in the sixth century as could be hoped for.

He is also an ideal historian. Gregory never formed a themed history in which he put down one religion in favor of another or bent historical facts to meet his priorities. What he wrote instead was an extended chronicle, which he updated after every significant event in Gaul. The only editing he made was to interpolate materials he found important in retrospect.[19] There is also strong evidence that he occasionally used his writings to set the record of his own relationships straight.[20] Previous authors have also mentioned a number of simple mistakes. However, he has never been accused of giving false information intentionally.[21]

Gregory is of greatest use as a recorder of Breton affairs, a people foreign to the Franks but who had forged small kingdoms on the western coast of the kingdom. The Bretons gave their allegiance to the Frankish kings but did not take part in Frankish politics or religious affairs whenever possible. Instead, their leaders fought amongst themselves in endless rivalries. Gregory clearly enjoyed reporting on them, using their bickering as a sort of comic aside to his writing because they were such a small and inconsequential group in the greater scheme of Frankish politics. It is even feasible that he has omitted episodes when they were lacking in this respect.

The next continental source is the *Vita Samsoni*, which is possibly the oldest surviving British saint's life. In the past, it was assumed that the biography was written in the ninth century, when most of the other Breton *vitae* were published.[22] However, that position has lost ground. Ninth-century Breton *vitae* focus on Breton independence from France; in the *Vita Samsoni*, the Frankish kings are occasionally the saint's allies and not his enemies. The author claims to have been the great-nephew of Samson and to have consulted with a very old contemporary in writing the book. Nothing in the work contradicts that claim, and in fact the name-forms and other details in the extant manuscripts support a seventh-century date.[23] The fact that it is generally free of fantastic elements also favors an earlier rather than later date.

Accepting it was written in the early seventh century the *vita* still has its own particular problems. For one, it was written in Brittany so that the writer could not have had easy access to any of the sites Samson had been active at.

Secondly, even if the author was his grand-nephew and used a contemporary for some of his information, there was still an entire lifetime between the events of the *vita* and the time they were written down. During those intervening decades many important details may have been forgotten or rationalized for any of a number of unforeseen reasons.

Still, as a near-contemporary source the information it provides is invaluable. The events and issues of Samson's life, as well as the saint's perspective on contemporary events and personalities, is a useful supplement to the information to be gleaned from annals and histories.

The Ravenna Cosmography is the last of our continental sources. Written in the seventh century by an anonymous Ravenna cleric, the work lists all of the Roman units in Europe along with their current locations. It also gives sources for each region, though they are all otherwise unknown. Because of this, it was traditionally believed to have been taken from a Roman itinerary. The problem with the cosmography is that we know some of its information is inaccurate. For instance, many of the locations where it says there are soldiers had been long abandoned by 700. More importantly for this book, the preamble names the Saxons as newcomers to Britain whereas traditional history has placed that event at around 450 and an overwhelming amount of evidence has shown that Germanic migrations began in the late fourth century. In the past, it was assumed that in not claiming to use a known scholar the *Ravenna Cosmography* was more credible. It now seems more likely that the sources were invented.[24]

The safest assumption to make is that the cleric who composed *The Ravenna Cosmography* gathered the most recent information he had and synthesized it. Realizing that without sources his work would look like fantasy he created them. The result was a haphazard picture of Europe that was current in some places but hopelessly outdated in others. Unfortunately, both are the case with Britain, making it useful in some ways and misleading in others.

If we can accept that the *Vita Samsoni* was written in the seventh century we have a single continental source that gives more information than one or two dates or the third-hand explanation of one or two events in Britain.

The rest are exactly that, two-dimensional sources of information for the period. Not that they have not been useful together in the reconstruction of the fifth century and the change in dynamics during the sixth and seventh centuries, but they are not as useful as they could be if even one of them could give a context for the events they record.

This lack of perspective is not surprising. As we have seen even with the limited continental source materials, communication with Britain was very difficult during this period. The English Channel was flooded with Saxon pirates during the late fourth century and this continued till the late fifth century. By the time that era was over, the Germanic peoples controlled the entire eastern and most of the southern coastline, separating the British from the continent. The Germanic peoples who stood as the barrier were not yet formed into kingdoms that might have welcomed communications and even trade. They were instead non–Christians more interested in cattle-raiding among each other than in anything the continent had to offer. It was their lack of awareness more than anything that limited the continent's knowledge of Britain during the period.

3

The Evidence
Native Sources

As has often been noted, post-Roman Britain has very few native sources of information. But when the reader goes over what we already know about the period, that reality makes perfect sense. It is a fact of history that in 409 the last Roman organization in Britain was dismantled. We also know that Rome would revive again in the 420s and 450s but it would never again send a governor to Britain. Looking back at the fifth century from an historical perspective, we not only know this, we know that what followed was inevitable.

It was not so clear to any person living in that era, though. The Britons of 409 had been educated in Roman culture. Legend had it that Rome had existed for over 1000 years with Romulus and Remus. The empire had been in the middle of at least one war for as far back as oral memory stretched while civil wars and insurrections had been commonplace for centuries. Through it all, Rome had survived and thrived. For any person growing up in the Latin culture, the idea that the Roman Empire could fall was simply unthinkable. As far as the people of Britain were concerned Rome had simply entered a period of difficulties. Once a strong emperor was on the throne he would stabilize the empire and bring the legions back to Britain. That had always happened before.

That certainty influenced every aspect of Roman life in Britain. Since Rome would return, there was no need to adapt to the barbarian threat. There might be no Roman bureaucracy and no official contact with the empire, but that did not mean that the Britons should stop living, learning, eating, and even worshipping like the Romans. Nor was there any motivation to install an island-wide government. In fact, alone among the provinces, Britannia had dismantled its rebel government in anticipation of the Roman return.

It was that absolute faith in the Roman Empire that doomed Britain. With the political superstructure gone, no person or group had the moral authority to install a new leader. There is no record of a successful Romano-British general trying to carve out a Roman kingdom there, either, even though it was common on the continent and many scholars have assumed it happened in Britain.[1] Without them, the chances of a British leader emerging to unite Britain would have been slight, even if the thought of breaking away from Rome had not been unthinkable.

Without a single leader or a government capable of repelling raiders through the collection of taxes and the maintenance of forts and soldiers, there was no means of keeping control over the English Channel raiding. As a result, there was no reliable line of communication to the continent during the fourth century and into the fifth.[2] It also meant that there was no patronly funding for would-be historians and no retirement plan set up so that an old soldier or a government employee had the time and money to write any sort of history as was happening on the continent with Ammianus Marcellinus or Procopius.

Even if one or two wealthy families had remained in Britain, it would have made no real difference to historical writing. Because of the dissolution of Roman government and the evacuation of the Roman Army under Constantine, the Britons of the early fifth century had no sense of security from the Irish, Picts, or Germanic tribes. There were probably still enough soldiers to man Hadrian's Wall and a few forts along the western frontier, but only skeleton garrisons; they could not have repelled any serious raiding parties and would have been overwhelmed by any real invasion. All wealthy families that had stayed behind would have been more worried about personal security than anything frivolous like poetry or history.

The political and military instability alone would have limited historical writing, and the Romano-British belief that they were still Roman would have prevented any regional British histories. Religion was also a factor though. When the people overthrew Constantine's government and begged Rome to return, Roman Christianity was not the single overwhelming religion it would become during the "Age of Saints." In 410, it was only one of many religions. If the reader will recall, Pelagian Christianity was so powerful that a special mission would be sent to Britain in 429. Mithradaism was practiced by the few remaining soldiers, as well as their families. The Celtic religion was followed by most of the people who had not been under the direct control of Rome during the last century or so. There was also an underground religion that focused on the respect of nature and regeneration.

With so many other religions active at the time, Christianity did not possess the universal respect it would take on in later times, nor did the monks who practiced it or the monasteries where they lived. Probably, this meant that the records of a monastery were not sacred. It has long been known that *Annales Cambriae* and the Irish annals developed from notes written on Paschal or Easter Tables.³ The tables themselves could have easily been copied and passed from one monastery to another regardless of the number of other religions or the relative prestige of Christianity. However, there would have been no point in recording the many battles and royal deaths of the fifth century if the monks had known that whatever they wrote down might be destroyed next week. It should come as no surprise, then, that the first written Insular records of the fifth century come in two letters; one addressed to a king from a long-lived dynasty and the other to a gathering of British ecclesiastics, and by one of the most famous religious people of the time—St. Patrick.

We are certain the letters were written in the fifth century. Every study that has ever been made on them has confirmed that the language and grammar belongs with other Latin writing of the period.⁴ We also know that Patrick wrote them and that they were intended for people who would have known about any factual errors. All three of these pieces of information have given scholars confidence that they contain valuable information on Patrick's period. What we cannot be so sure about is the relationship, or even the order, of the letters to each other. The *Confessio* may have been written within months of Patrick's arrival in Ireland and his letter to Coroticus a decade or so later. Or, Coroticus might have pressured his local clergy into challenging Patrick after they had exchanged letters, thus inspiring the *Confessio*.

Knowing that, the author will arbitrarily start with the letter to Coroticus. Coroticus, from the context of the letter, was a chieftain of Aloo who had recently abducted several of Patrick's freshly converted Christians.⁵ Patrick had already written one letter requesting their return but his presbyter, a man he had trained from a young boy, was laughed at. The letter has been mainly useful for suggesting the development of British kingship during this time. The fact that he had trained a presbyter "from a young boy," also suggests that Patrick had been in Ireland for several years by the time of the raid. The mention of Coroticus "of Aloo" has also strongly suggested to many people the Strathclyde king Ceredig, whose capital would have been at Alt Clud, modern Dumbarton.

In his *Confessio*, Patrick responded to an accusation about an indiscretion he had made before his promotion to deacon. His letter is not, as we might think, a confession of his guilt, but more like a short autobiography of his life. This is where we learn the most about fifth-century Britain. He was born into a wealthy family and learned Latin until the age of about twelve when he was captured by Irish raiders. He eventually escaped from Ireland and returned home, where he finished his studies, took religious vows, and returned to Ireland in order to evangelize the people.

What he does not provide is any information about the political structure he was raised in. He names no king, no region, not even a board of elders.

The reader is left not knowing if his village was an isolated community or one of a coalition. Nor is there any suggestion of a wider political situation. Patrick might have been born at the violent end of the Roman period, raised during the Germanic revolt of 441, or seen the rise of the British kingdoms decades later.[6]

On the weight of John Koch's argument we look at *Marwnad Cunedda* next. Koch provides strong reasons why it may have been composed on Cunedda's death or shortly after. Working backwards in time:

It was definitely not written down in the twelfth century. The name-form of Cunedda is wrong for someone from the fifth century who was remembered orally in Gwynedd before being written down then. The *Ystoria Taliesin*, on which Haycock believes *Marwnad Cunedda* is based,[7] contains nothing that resembles it in form or content. Third, if *Marwnad Cunedda* was written in the twelfth or thirteenth century it should have a better-copied text than *Armes Prydein*. It does not. Finally, the tradition that Taliesin humiliated other bards was common by the eleventh century but is absent here.

In fact, bards are portrayed so positively that the poem looks like it might be pre–Gildas. Along that line of thinking, Cunedda's activities are only placed in northern Berneich. If the poem had been written when Cadwallon was in Northumbria or later (632), he would have been alluded to.

Koch places the poem specifically in the fifth century for three reasons. First, the poem mentions no future events. Second, none of Cunedda's ancestors are named in the poem. Considering how important lineage would become by the sixth century, this suggests that it was written at a time before Cunedda's official family lineage had been established. Third, the poem mentions nothing Christian, which again suggests a fifth century date.

Gildas wrote the next two documents, an open letter known as *De Excidio Britanniae* and a letter of advice to an abbot named Uennianus. *De Excidio* is the more useful of the two documents because he provides an historical context for his present as a preface to his letter. The problem lies in the fact that he wrote for a specific purpose; to demonstrate that the British people were being punished and rewarded by God based on how well behaved they were. He ends his letter by listing off individual kings and naming their sins as well as broadly noting the clergy's indiscretions and warning them of the inevitable retribution by God.

Gildas' strategy of giving an historical background before listing crimes was a standard practice in Roman courts. That is clearly his purpose, too[8]; the entire design of the letter is actually a carefully crafted argument, which he uses to prove that the British people will be punished by God's hand if they do not behave like proper Christians.

Gildas was clearly a well-educated writer; scholars have noted that he used none of the linguistic patterns which would indicate he was a native speaker of Latin and yet seems to use all of the unusual words in his repertoire correctly.[9] It is his legal approach, though, that is of the most interest. The learning of courtroom techniques was part of the normal education given to the wealthy and most intelligent Romans. For the latter it was so that they could defend themselves. For others, it was to prepare them for life as a public servant. It was the most advanced education available in the Roman world, so that Gildas tells us in his writing exactly how much was still available in Britain during his childhood. Gildas' education is evidence that not only was he taught by a grammarian, *grammaticus*, but also by a *rhetor*, a specialist in rhetoric.

Gildas was also an excellent student. Recent study has demonstrated Gildas was one of the best writers of his age, more resembling the most accomplished Roman writers of the classical period than any other post–Roman scholar.[10]

As he was so intelligent, we must assume that when he wrote in Latin to a lay audience there must have been people in the halls who could understand the language. Considering the limited life-span of the age, roughly thirty years, that means the same education may have been available as little as ten years before he wrote.

When he wrote is a little less certain. The annals date his death to about 570. If he lived to as old as eighty, that would put his writing in the middle third of the sixth century. Columbanus, an abbot whom we will learn more about below, mentioned *Uennianus* in one of his letters in about 600. This also suggests that Gildas was active during the sixth century. Internal evidence is also consistent; his use of the term *iudices* in De Excidio Britanniae ranges from judge to ruler, which is exactly as it should have been defined during that era.[11]

More focused studies have cleared things up a little. The first and literal interpretation is that he wrote an open letter in the forty-fourth year following his birth and the Battle of Badon. Following Dumville in working through Gildas' *historia* section from the letter to Aetius (433–456) and working forward that gives a range of about 485x515 for Badon and 525x560 for *De Excidio Britanniae*.

The author's use of date-guessing around Gildas' known relations to the Irish and Welsh saints, his obit as found in the *Annales Cambriae*, and the internal chronology of his work suggests a range of 521x535 for his work and 478x491 for his birth.[12]

An alternate theory proposed by McCarthy and Ó Cróinín is that when Gildas mentioned forty-four years he was speaking about the year in the Easter table and not the year after his birth.[13] The date of Easter moved around on an 88-year cycle. The only Easter table Gildas could have meant started in 438, meaning that he wrote in 482.

It is his historical prelude that has always been of the most interest, though. He begins in the fourth century with detailed information about the last years of Roman Britain—Maximus' career. The narration goes on with the building of two walls (Antonine's and Hadrian's), followed by what is probably the Honorian Rescript of 410 in which Rome officially abandoned the island.

What most people have not considered yet is that Gildas' spelling of Aetius shows us he only had access to oral knowledge for the mid-fifth century and before. But in a time when fifty-five was the maximum life-span of an average person and eighty for a member of the clergy, Gildas could not have heard anything earlier than 408 (if he had been told something at five by a seventy-five year old man who just happened to remember what was going on in the world when he was five himself) and, considering that civilization was falling apart and communications with the continent had been shut off by the Germanic tribes, we can only be safely certain he had actually heard about the events of maybe 433 and after (a sixty year old man recounts events that occurred when he was five and over to a fifteen year old Gildas).

Our date-guessing is supported by Gildas' narrative.[14] Working in reverse order, Gildas mentions Aetius (433–456), followed by what has been assumed was the Honorian Rescript (410), the building of two walls, and Maximus' career as an emperor (383). In all of the pre–Aetius material, though, only Maximus' career is certain. This Maximus would become a cult figure in Welsh lore, developing into the founding father of several prominent dynasties as his legend grew.[15] His status as the last link to the Roman Empire ensured he would be remembered, in the sixth century and throughout the medieval period. The next three items, the two returns of the Roman Army each time followed by the building of a wall and the Honorian Rescript, are not history. Hadrian's Wall and Antonine's Wall were created centuries before Gildas was born, and we know historically that the Roman Army only returned one more time after Maximus. That ended with the emperorship of Constantine who eventually left for the continent as well.

In the past it has been argued that Gildas may have lived in the North and been privy to improvements in the walls that we are not.[16] Alternatively, a few scholars have suggested he might have been talking from the south about Hadrian and Antonine's Wall or even about a southern wall.[17] The fact is that he could not have known when the walls were built. It is even possible that he used them to create a theme; the Romans had twice returned because they believed the Britons were worthy of being protected. The implication was that they might one day be worthy again.

The Honorian Rescript is also a stretch. From Zosimus, whom we have met above, we learn that Honorius sent his infamous letter on the heels of Rome being plundered. For Gildas, there was no emperor involved; the

Romans simply told the Britons that they were tired of traveling to Britain so they should just protect themselves. In short, nothing before Aetius is actually historical.[18]

There is one more item to mention about Gildas before moving on. Many scholars have commented on how sparing he is with his names (and how irritating that is with the question of Arthur's historicity, for instance). He had a purpose here, though, too. He has only employed that information which helped him further his purpose. Details about historical activities or the people who were involved in them would have created a tangent to his purpose, which was to prove to the British people that they needed to act like good Christians or God was going to punish them. Everything that Gildas wrote, and omitted, must be seen only in the light of his goals and his rhetorical abilities.

Trawsganu Cynan Garwyn is a praise poem in honor of a sixth-century Powysian king of the Cadelling dynasty. It references the Wye River, Gwent, Anglesey, the Menai Straits, Dyfed, Cornwall/South Wales, and Herefordshire—which is similar to areas Gildas named in *De Excidio Britanniae*. The Selyf from the same dynasty would have been born around the same time as Gildas' work, and Gildas mentioned Solomon often. Professor Koch has suggested that Gildas might have been writing from there,[19] in which case the poem may represent a contemporary work. Koch has also noted that it was updated till the tenth century, when it was probably considered too insulting to other British kingdoms for public use.[20]

Taliesin was a British bard of the sixth century who wrote for, in order, Cynan Garwyn and Urien, with a pair of poems for Gwallog during his time under Urien. Bards held a unique place in Celtic society. They were trained in mythology, legend, and history (all three being one in the same) and given a multitude of motifs and presentation techniques. This allowed bards to tell wonderful stories that could vary from audience to audience. It also gave them the rudiments for creating poetry and in particular praise poetry for kings. Additionally, their historical knowledge made them ideal royal genealogists.

Their last two uses made the bard a useful tool for the newly made kings of post–Roman Britain. Their praise poetry gave them entertainment value for the kings and their men, but on a more subtle level it could be used to reinforce their rule. As genealogists, bards were ideal for learning about the great local kings of the past and attaching them to their king's genealogy to give him further credibility. And since the bard's knowledge of history was considered absolute, his official history was considered beyond question as well.

The biases of a bard's work are easily seen. As someone in the king's employ, a bard had every reason to magnify his lord's successes while minimizing failures. And, while his audience might already have known the reality, they might have accepted some spin on reality. The truth is, we cannot discern reality from propaganda. We can only take very small portions of it.

Bards could also make large changes to a king's family tree. His king might have known his grandfather, or he might not have. He would have had no idea of any ancestor before that. Logically, if he had no idea his people would not remember, meaning a bard could attach any local chieftain to the family tree before that generation and add to the prestige of the dynasty.

Twelve poems are generally regarded as Taliesin's. Their language contains enough archaic words to ensure that they were written during the sixth century. The social setting and the warrior's mindset all match the period smoothly. They even progress in sophistication, with the Cynan poems very basic and the Urien works becoming more developed. By their development and by information given in the poems it is clear that Gwallog's patronage interrupted Urien.

As the centuries passed, Taliesin would take on the persona of the ultimate bard, traveling back in time to every crucial event. In the sixth century though, he was just a very good bard

Aneirin was also a British bard of the sixth century. He worked for the King of Gododdin, though exactly when or with whom he was active has never been resolved.[21] Aneirin wrote one extant poem, *Y Gododdin*, which is a series of elegies about the warriors who died on a joint campaign he claims to have participated in to the South. The uncertainty about Aneirin's dating led to a long-held belief that the battle took place around 600.[22]

There are two surviving versions of the poem. The first was written down in about 700,[23] after over a century in an oral environment. As a result, many stanzas are badly damaged. Successive manuscript copyings have given the edition additional errors.

The other account continued to evolve in an oral environment and was only written down in the ninth century. Before then, *Y Gododdin* was regularly used by bards wishing to showcase their talents to potential patrons. The combination of an extended stay in an oral environment and its popularity among a class of entertainers noted for their spontaneity and endless modification has, by common sense and by manuscript evidence, resulted in a much greater variation than the earlier version.

The result is two greatly devolved versions of an ancient poem. The work has attracted a large number of scholars over the years who have attempted to collate the two versions into an accurate representation of the original. This has been most notably accomplished by Professor John T. Koch, who has attempted to restore the language through his own extensive linguistic background and innovative techniques.

The Irish Annals have been little studied and less agreed upon.[24] They may have been based off *Isidore's Chronicle* or *Rufinus' Chronicle*.[25] Contemporary writing started at middle of the sixth century,[26] the last half of the century,[27] or Bangor, Iona, Lismore, and Clonmacnoise began in about 600[28] the 680s,[29] 700[30] and 740[31] respectively.[32]

At some point during the eighth century the Bangor, Iona, and Lismore annals were compiled into a hypothetical text known as the *Chronicle of Ireland*. The chronicle was probably maintained in County Louth or eastern Meath until 913 because the annals that were later based off of it contained a continuous Uí Néill history as well as a continuing interest in the descendants of Aed Sláine during that time.

After 913, the monastery at Innisfallen, a second site in Ulster, and the monastery at Clonmacnoise each took a copy of the *Chronicle of Ireland* and began writing independent entries again. It is at this point that earlier entries were made. We know this for a couple reasons. First, the orthography or spelling for events before 640 is late, stretching nearly to the ninth century at times. Also, Kathleen Hughes noticed that the common core of information between the three annals was 50% between 488 and 585, but 67% between 650 and 700 when contemporary dating started. That statistic only makes sense if the earlier entries were added after the *Chronicle of Ireland* was in use at different sites.

The only extant annal that did not contribute to the *Chronicle of Ireland* was the *Annals of Clonmacnoise*. It did, however, add the chronicle's entries to its own. *The Annals of Clonmacnoise* survived independently until at least 1627, when Connall Mag Eochagáin translated it into English. It has since been lost, taking with it any orthographic evidence. However, copies remain and the entries seem to focus on the families around Clonmacnoise.

According to the preface of the only surviving copy, *The Code of Æthelberht* was commissioned by the king of Kent, suggesting it was written some time during Æthelberht's reign,[33] most likely during his ascendancy over the Germanic kings south of the Humber River between 596 and 616. As will be seen in the chapters below, Kent had first been unified during his reign. The law code was possibly designed to imitate the Romans and solidify that unification.[34] Alternatively, it is possible that Augustine of Canterbury urged it so that Kent could follow contemporary continental kingdoms.[35] Whatever the reason, it would have made a good tool in drawing his subject kingdoms closer to him as well.

Æthelberht's code focuses on standardizing payments for personal and property injuries and touches on matters of trade.[36] This suggests that the law code was also created as a way of making the law consistent throughout his kingdom, and in fact there is good evidence that the code was based on oral customs.[37]

The law code breaks up society by classes—churchmen, the king and his dependents, an *eorl* and his dependents, a *ceorl* and his dependents, the semi-free, women, servants, and slaves. It focuses on the amount of compensation given for various offenses based on the offending party and the social status of the victim. It gives certain values for specific goods and so gives their relative worth among the sixth-century Germanic peoples. As with all the Kentish law codes, the *Code of Æthelberht* is found only in the *Textus Roffensis* manuscript, a book written down by a single scribe between 1122 and 1124 under the supervision of Ernulf, Bishop of Rochester.[38]

The two codes that followed Æthelberht's in Kent were the *Code of Hlothere and Eadric* (676–685) and *The Code of Wihtred* (c. 695). *The Code of Hlothere and Eadric* is unique in that it never directly deals with the church.[39] While it does focus on compensations for injuries and damage to property, it also lays out procedures for making proper accusations and making land purchases in London. It has proven most useful for showing scholars how the legal process worked in seventh-century England.

The Code of Wihtred deals almost exclusively with the church, how the state dealt with religious matters, and theft.[40] It has proven useful for demonstrating the growing power of the church in the period. For instance, a bishop's word was considered the equal to a king and any slave forced to work on the Sabbath was to be freed.[41] Each concession to the church's authority also included some admission to the king's authority however, e.g., praying for and honoring their king.[42]

Between the two Kentish codes Ine of Wessex commissioned his own *The Laws of Ine*, probably as an act of prestige in order to reestablish stability after a long period of inter-kingdom warfare in the South.[43] Frederick L. Attenborough dated the code to between 688 and 694 based on its similarity with a code of laws issued by Wihtred of Kent.[44]

The Laws of Ine demonstrates several aspects about Ine and the period in which he lived. Many of the laws reveal the growing power of church[45]— in a few instances it is superior to the king. Other laws show us the growing importance of trade by speaking directly about it and by focusing on the treatment of theft and foreigners. Scholars have often looked on the laws to show the importance of the *ceorl* in English society.[46] However, Richard Abel seems to have come closer to the truth with his realization that the law code was not so much a reflection of society as it was of Ine's hopes for his kingdom and the kingdoms he ruled. As Professor Abel demonstrated, Ine was hoping to centralize his power. He was also hoping to put into law for all warriors what had been tradition among a lord's personal household; ultimate loyalty was to lie with the king and not his lord.[47] In that regard, and in any way relating to it, *The Laws of Ine* will have to be ignored.

The Pictish Chronicle was composed between 971 and 995, by Gaelic-speaking monks under Kenneth II's supervision. We know this because Kenneth II (971–995) is the last king mentioned and the chronicle does not know when he died. There are also a few Gaelic words in the sections on kings and the rest of the text is in Latin.

There are several versions of the chronicle, but the best is probably the "A" text as it seems to have the fewest errors. The document is divided into in three parts: The origins of the Picts, a Pictish king-list, and a chronicle of the kings of Alba (Scotland). We will not dwell on the first section here because all of its information dates to before the post–Roman period. The third section is about the kings of a united Scotland from Kenneth MacAlpin to Kenneth II; it is of no interest because all of them lived well after the period we are looking at.

The second section, about Pictish kings, begins in prehistory and extends through the era we are examining into the ninth century. Thanks mainly to Dr. Molly Miller we have learned much about this king-list. For instance we know that the living history horizon, that is the point at which events were still remembered by a living person, is 662–668.[48] Contemporary writing began during the time of Abbot Failbe (669–679),[49] and retrospective entries, that is all kings who were active much before 600, were made between 712 and 726.[50]

Miller pointed out that the reign of Drest I, who was assigned 100 or 45 years or a life-span of 100 years (depending on the version) was a legendary figure. She also noticed that the reigns of every one to four kings prior to Drest I always added up to some multiple of fourteen, the number of years in one partial cycle of Easter dating during the medieval period.[51] Realizing the significance of the number, she continued her calculations forward. It was only when she came to the two Drests who took the crown in 526 that the trend finally ended.[52] From this she concluded that the historical horizon, the year from which all dates were accurate, was 526. That horizon seems unlikely if living history began in 662x668, which means that *The Pictish Chronicle* must be cross-referenced with the Irish annals, the *vita* of Columba, and Bede, and these are only accurate about four decades later.

The *Vita Columba* was probably composed by Adomnán in 697 to mark the centenary of Saint Columba's death. It is believed to be based on oral memories and an earlier collection, *De uirtutibus sancti Columbae*, which was written around 640 by Cummene Find, who was later the abbot at Iona (656–668/9).[53] The work is generally reliable. The exceptions are miracles (of course) and Columba's participation in secular affairs. Adomnán tended to minimize his offenses or sidestep them altogether. The main difficulty with the source in studying British affairs is that the author's purview was so narrow that the reader can get no idea of the wider political world. Adomnán is not even forthcoming about the politics within Dal Riata.

Though we do not know the anonymous writer of the *Vita Sancti Cuthberti*, we do know it was written by a single Lindisfarne monk because of his possessive pronouns and consistent use of the first person singular.[54] Several posthumous miracles set the earliest date of composition at 699, the year after Cuthbert was interred. The fact that it mentions Aldfrith reigning peacefully tells us it was written before his death in 705.[55] We also know it was commissioned by Bishop Eadfrith of Lindisfarne,[56] was heavily influenced by St. Martin's activities,[57] borrowed stories from Gregory's *Dialogi*, Sulpicius Severus' *Vita Sancti Martini* and *Vita Sancti Antonii*, Evagrius' translation of Athanasius' biography of Anthony the Great,[58] and that the author had read *Epistola ad Hilarium* and *Actus Silvestri*.[59] Most of the information in the *vita*, though, came from the oral information of the Lindesfarne monks,[60] and is therefore well within oral memory.

The *Tribal Hidage* is a simple list with Germanic and British kingdoms. Each entry is followed by its *hidage*. *Hidage* was what the Anglo-Saxons used as a measure of land for tax purposes. One hide meant that if a person cut the hide of an average cow into thin strips and spread them end to end around the perimeter of a square they would encompass an area of about 120 acres.

Along with the size of a kingdom, *hidage* was used to determine how much tribute a kingdom owed. The *Tribal Hidage* is a tribute list, with Mercia at the top having by far the largest *hidage* of the group. In the past, scholars had assumed it was issued by Mercia,[61] but a careful look at the list shows two details out of place. For one, neither Northumbria nor any of its original kingdoms (Pennawc, Berneich, Deur, and possibly Dent and Perym) are present.

The second is that Mercia is listed as having a much higher *hidage* than any other kingdom, much higher than it is known to have had in any other historical source. *Hidage* lists were made for tributary kingdoms, while a king was likely to collect his hereditary kingdom's tribute personally.

If the reasoning is sound, then the *Tribal Hidage* was most likely composed in Northumbria. The question then becomes one of when. One other detail is useful in that regard; Elmet is listed. Edwin would make Elmet a part of Northumbria in 626. Since he became king in 616 and was the first known Northumbrian to rule over Mercia, the *Tribal Hidage* was probably written in the window of 616x626.

The Letters of Columbanus were written by an outspoken Irish abbot of around 600. Columbanus began his career as a monk at Bangor, where his personal charisma and faith attracted a large following. Instead of traveling around Ireland or even Scotland as previous Irish holy men had done, though, Columbanus went to the continent with his disciples. In Gaul he founded several monasteries before his outspoken views on the Frankish royal family made him unwelcome there.

At this time he also started writing letters of advice to the pope; these are mainly what have been preserved. In the short run, they drew the pope's attention, which would lead to the scrutiny of Celtic Christianity's unique approach to the faith,[62] and its eventual elimination at the Synod of Whitby (664), which effectively ended the period under study in the next few pages. For the modern scholar, Columbanus mentions Gildas in the past tense as the writer of both the *De Excidio Britanniae* and a letter to Uinniau. Columbanus' letters show that Gildas was dead by 600 but was a highly respected churchman.

Marwnad Cynddylan had confused historians of the period because Cynddylan is securely dated to the first half of the seventh century, when the British kingdoms were allied with the Mercian Penda, and while the poem speaks about many raids into Mercia. Recent work by Professor Koch has offered a solution to the problem. His subtle and plausible corrections to the poem's key words change its meaning from raiding on to raiding with Penda.[63] From there the rest of the poem makes sense. It mentions the Christian Northumbrian king's massacre of monks near Chester because it is a justification for allying with the pagan Penda. It also discusses concern for the soul, marriages to pagans, and pagan magic out of guilt for that alliance.[64]

This new interpretation is important for several reasons. In the context of this book it is a personal record of the British relationship with Penda; history says that the Mercian king fought against the Germanic kingdoms throughout his career but he was remembered as an honorable ally by the British. The poem also helps to date Cynddylan more securely. If he was in league with Penda then he probably fell at Winwæd/Hatfield Chase (655) and not Maserfelth (642) as has always been believed.[65]

The *Senchus Fer n'Alban* has several extant copies, all found in Ireland, all in Irish, and none dating from before the fourteenth century. Bannerman concluded these all came from a Latin original and this has never been disputed.[66] Most versions begin with the legendary landings of Eochaid Muinremar and the sons of Erc through the reign of Conall Crandomna (obit c. 660). One version traces the Dal Riata line back to Cairpre Riata of the first or second century BCE but all variants go up through the reign of Conall Crandomna in about 660. The Senchus also provides a census of the Dalriadic regions. It has been presumed that the document dates to the seventh century but the question of why has never been answered. It seems to the author that there are two possibilities.

In about 574, Columba oversaw the inauguration of Áedán son of Gabrán as the first king of a united Dal Riata. Áedán would go on to be one of the strongest kings in Britain for decades. This would have provided him with the perfect opportunity for recording and enforcing an official dynastic history. Once created, the history would have been maintained up to Conall Crandomna, continuing for nearly fifty years under the Northumbrian rules of Edwin, Oswald,[67] and Oswiu.[68]

The second possibility is that at some point during Conall Crandomna's reign he rebelled from Northumbria and took the opportunity to record a family history in order to generate loyalty for his movement and his family. In this theory, there would be no need to theorize how a legendary history had survived nearly a century of Northumbrian rule.

Dr. Bannerman favored a seventh-century origin-legend.[69] The author would, too. As was demonstrated in *Hengest, Gwrtheyrn, and the Chronology of Post-Roman Britain*, the Senchus manipulated the mid-sixth century history of Dal Riata; it plucked the most famous and powerful leaders of the early Irish settlement from all available historical sources and formed them into a readily understandable united family history. Áedán would have had difficulty changing history that was within the living memory of his people but Conall Crandomna, living decades later, would have had no such problems.

One further note; Bannerman noted that the extant text has tenth-century grammar.[70] As the initial draft was written before 660, this must represent a revision. Possibly, it may have been translated into Irish at that time.

There are two extant versions of the *Vita Kentigerni*, both written in the twelfth century. The first was prepared between 1147 and 1164 for Bishop Herbert and the second for Bishop Jocelyn (1175–1199). They both list a Baldred as Kentigern's successor to the bishopric of Strathclyde. This detail tells us that their common original was written in 800 or before.

The only Baldred to be found in Strathclyde's religious records is an Anglo-Saxon abbot from Northumbria who died in 757, some 145 years after Kentigern. This Baldred could not have been Kentigern's successor. However, a person who died in 757 would have had access to the name of Kentigern's mother and the British place-names of Lothian as well as several contemporary religious and political facts. All this suggests that Baldred might have had a reason to write a life of Kentigern.

Between 744 and 756, Northumbria was fighting a back and forth war of conquest with Strathclyde. For years after the kingdom had given up, the kingdom might still have claimed ownership over the region. This is probably the era when Baldred was made a bishop of Strathclyde. A Northumbrian installed as the leading ecclesiastic would have made an intelligent political move, and once installed it would have been difficult to depose him.

The reason a Northumbrian bishop is important to the writing of the *Vita Kentigerni* stretches back almost a hundred years. In 664 there was a great debate between proponents of Celtic and Roman Catholic Christianity. The continentals had won. Since that time, Northumbria had been attempting to spread the religion. Kentigern had lived decades before that decision and so had followed the Celtic practices. However, he was the patron saint of Strathclyde and, as the Bishop of Strathclyde, Baldred would have had access to more information about him than was present anywhere else. He might have seen writing a *vita* about Kentigern as an opportunity to use the greatest Strathclyde saint as an early follower of the Roman practice.

Once looked for, the bias is easy to spot in the *vita*. Kentigern stays with David briefly before going on pilgrimage to Rome. There the reader is informed that Kentigern had originally been created a bishop by the wrong (British) method. Having learned this, he is immediately re-consecrated according to canon. The episode really has no other purpose; the patron saint of Wales informs the patron saint of Strathclyde that the Celtic practice is wrong and the two use the Roman practice to install Kentigern as a proper bishop. In a matter of several lines, Strathclyde's most revered holy man was made an ally of the Roman church in Britain.

The rest of the *vita* has a few miraculous events, but none of the standard motifs that plague later *vitae*. There are no other passages where the Roman version trumps over the Celtic, and the people and incidents it mentions are, where checkable, perfectly plausible.

Apart from this clear evidence of bias, the *vita* looks extremely valuable to the present purposes because of its accurate information about Kentigern and his era. Both accounts begin with Kentigern's birth in Lothian. By the middle of the seventh century the Northumbrians controlled Gododdin so there was no way of getting local legends by the eighth century.

Kentigern's grandfather, Lleudun, is called the ruler of Dunpelder in both lives. Dunpelder, also known as Traprain Law, was a major royal residence up through the fifth century and possibly into the sixth. Judging by the hoard that has been found there, it was the home of very wealthy kings, too. However, this was not common knowledge when the two extant versions of the *Vita Kentigerni* were written down in the eleventh century. By that time only Din Eidyn, modern Edinburgh, was remembered as a Gododdin king capital; toponymic studies have also demonstrated that native place-names are forgotten after about a century when an area is conquered by a different culture, which means that it would have gone out of use much after 750.[71]

A third clue can be found in the personal name of Kentigern's mother; Thaney in the Herbertian life and Taneu in the Jocelyn version. These are from Archaic British *Täneü*, which in written form was obsolete by about 800.[72]

If the original version was written in or before 800, then the *Vita Kentigerni* could be a valid source for the period. I say could because each source that has been studied above has been riddled with layers of personal bias, passages where the author has guessed to create a scene or story out of missing knowledge, and the thinking of the time. Even if the original *vita* was old enough, to simply accept everything in it without knowing the background would be naïve. However, as it stands, the *Vita Kentigerni* seems like a near-contemporary source of useful information.

The *Llandaff Charters* are a collection of diplomas and charters that are related to the Llandaff monastery. They begin in the sixth century and terminate in the twelfth, but it is clear from the handwriting and other details that the earlier documents have been rewritten. They were probably not just recopied, either; there are several clear and unavoidable chronological inconsistencies between the extant documents that are the result of this later editing.[73]

As the last charters date to the twelfth century, that is the most likely time to find some form of explanation about the discrepancies in the charters. In 1107, Urban was consecrated bishop of Glamorgan in southeast Wales. For whatever reason, by 1119 he was styling himself the Bishop of Llandaff and took a personal interest in the development of the monastery's prestige in order to enhance his diocese's importance. To that end he involved himself in property disputes between Glamorgan and the St. David and Hereford monasteries from 1115 until his death in 1134.

The *Llandaff Charters* were extremely useful for his designs. Several of the documents predated any claims by St. David's or Hereford and supported his claims. To the modern eye they are clearly forgeries, though. Though covering many decades, they were all written in the same hand, suggesting they were rewritten long after the fact even if the word forms themselves are much older.[74] There are also the several chronological inconsistencies mentioned above; issues that would not exist if the documents had not been altered.

It makes the most sense that the *Llandaff Charters* went through a second draft at some time after 1115, when Urban could have made the most use of the changed documents. If that is what happened, then the Llandaff documents' chronology as well as their land grants must be treated with suspicion.

That said, the otherwise unknown witnesses and archaic language in the charters are definitely ancient, making clear that the original documents were probably created contemporarily with the people mentioned.[75] Recognizing this useful fact, Professor Wendy Davies has generated a relative chronology based on the witnesses found in the charters that have not been biased by Urban's claims.[76] Her results have shown that the charters do not date back as far as they claim, but that the charters do give us a reasonable political landscape for the Arthurian period in southeast Wales.

The Pillar of Eliseg is a monument near modern Valle Crucis Abbey, which is near medieval Dinas Bran. It states that it was erected by Cyngen son of Cadell in honor of his great-grandfather Elisedd son of Gwylog; Dinas Bran was probably his capital. We know almost nothing about Cyngen or the events of his reign—only that he had three sons, that he died in 855, and that his maternal nephew Rhodri Mawr annexed his kingdom when he died. It stands to reason that either he had bad luck with children or his kingdom was unstable during his adulthood. If that is so, the monument might have been created to give the kingdom and his dynasty some historical stability.

The Pillar of Eliseg claims that Elisedd was descended from Gwrtheyrn through his son Brittu. As the author demonstrated in *Gwrtheyrn, Hengest, and the Chronology of Post-Roman Britain*, Gwrtheyrn and his dynasty were connected to the Severn valley and not northern Wales,[77] making this official pedigree unlikely. Besides, as we will see below, Gwrtheyrn was one of the great heroes of Wales before the tenth-century revision of the *Historia Brittonum*, which makes the pillar a clear example of ninth-century Powysian propaganda.

Stephanus' *Vita Wilfridi* was written by a man who journeyed with Wilfrid on at least one of his trips to the continent,[78] between about 709 and 719 or up to a decade after Wilfrid's death. On the other hand, Eddius Stephanus idolized his subject, often presenting him as a hero who was mistreated by his fellow ecclesiastics.[79] Bede wrote a biography as well and though written later and without the personal knowledge Stephanus enjoyed, Bede did not share the same opinion of Wilfrid. This makes the two sources useful in tandem.

The attitude of the anonymous *Life of Ceolfrith* was in many ways similar to Stephanus in his Wilfrid biography. The writer was a monk of Wearmouth or Jarrow who accompanied Ceolfrith on his last trip to Rome. He was therefore both more knowledgeable than Bede on his particular topic, but not on the subject of Ceolfrith himself, whom Bede had known since early childhood. In addition, it is clear that this anonymous writer produced his work within a very short time after the saint's death in 716 but probably after Bede wrote as Bede does not mention the work. Ceolfrith was not the controversial figure that Wilfrid was, and because of that fact the anonymous life had no serious discrepancies with other histories of the period.

The *Canu Heledd* cycle was traditionally believed to be a group of poems written by Heledd, princess of a Powys kingdom. Its main theme was the conquest of her birth kingdom and the death of her family. The tragedy in the cycle is that Heledd was married to the Mercian king who caused all the destruction. Because the area she speaks of was conquered in the middle of the seventh century the poems were traditionally dated to that period. However, recent study by Jenny Rowland has demonstrated that the poems could not have been written until at least a century later. Her research suggests the poems were most likely written in the last two-thirds of the ninth century.[80] Nor is the story they portray credible; the area was not conquered outright it was gradually assimilated.[81]

However, the personal names seem to be accurate; they match the kingdom's extant genealogy and the facts as found in the *Marwnad Cynddylan*. As we have seen, it was created contemporary to the loss of the kingdom.

Even the choice of Heledd as the poem's voice suggests that some elements of the cycle might be ancient. Historically speaking, a daughter married to a potential rival would have been the most likely survivor if that rival ever conquered her native kingdom. And, once she had lost her political value, he would have abandoned her as Heledd has been abandoned in the cycle.

Alternatively, the choice of narrator could have been taken from Celtic myth. Part of the symbolism surrounding kingship was that the wife was the personification of the kingdom; she was young and fertile with each new king and grew haggard and barren as he aged or when he died to be renewed with the next king. As the lone surviving representative of the Powysian family, Heledd might have taken on that role.[82] She is described much like the personification of the land between rulers. Regardless of the reason Heledd was used as the narrator, there seem to be some original elements in *Canu Heledd*, but any materials which do not make sense when laid beside the earlier *Marwnad Cynddylan* cannot be used for historical purposes.

In 911, Hywel Dda inherited his father's kingdom in a joint rule with his brother Clydog.[83] Through marriage, inheritance, and political maneuvering he had taken control of all Wales except for Morgannwg and Gwent by 942.[84] With so many kingdoms under one king, and possibly under the influence of his contemporary Athelstan's law code,[85] it was only natural that he decided his people needed a standardized law code as well. According to the extant prologues he held a conference of leading legal experts and had Welsh law codified into *The Laws of Hywel Dda*. This may well have been a legend he propagated, but the fact remains that the laws are associated only with him.

As with the *Code of Athelstan*, *The Laws of Hywel Dda* was created during a time of cultural unity under one king in order to help standardize law and centralize authority in Hywel's new empire. Because of this motive there was no serious bias against any of the Welsh kingdoms; the laws are fairly representative of Welsh society.

The most famous surviving version of this law is contained in the *Black Book of Chirk*. This is also the oldest version of the law code and has been shown to contain historical information.[86] It is possible that there are historical segments which favor Gwynedd or the dynasty Hywel was a part of in order to demonstrate its fitness to lead the Welsh kingdoms.[87] If so, the most likely place to find that sort of bias would be in any historical information to be found there.

Saga poetry is the next major category of source material. Technically, the poetry of Taliesin and Aneirin fall into this group but they have been dealt with separately because they are central to any study of the period. Here I would like to deal mainly with the works focusing on the loss of Powys, basically the Llywarch Hen poetry.

The "Pen Urien" group of poems is a part of the Llywarch Hen collection and is named after its most important elegy, "Pen Urien." For many years it was thought that they might have been created by Llywarch Hen himself because of their personal nature; e.g., in "Pen Urien" the subject is Llywarch's sorrow over having to take his cousin (Urien)'s head on the battlefield. Thanks to Dr. Rowland's research, though, we can now be confident that they were actually written by several bards who added them over an extended period of time.

Rowland has focused on the internal inconsistencies in the greater Llywarch Hen collection. The most glaring contradiction is that most of the poems work around the theme that Llywarch is too old to fight (*Hen* is Welsh for "old") and must convince his sons to fight for him. That is not the case with the "Pen Urien" poems, though. In one, Urien gives Llywarch's youngest son Gwên a horn as a gift, indicating that during Urien's lifetime Llywarch's sons were already adults. In the title poem, Llywarch participates in a battle before decapitating his cousin. If the poems were internally consistent, then these two details would mean that Llywarch was still a fighting man when his children were themselves warriors. This is in direct contradiction to Llywarch's standing as a retired warrior.

A modern reader might see in this and the later poems a collection intended to cover the breadth of Llywarch's life. However, as Dr. Rowland has rightly observed, a complete life story is not what bardic poetry was about. A poet would focus on one period—a king's dealings with another king, a warrior's campaign, or even an old man's regrets—but not an entire lifetime.[88]

There are further indications that the cycle had different authors with access to alternate information. Some of the Llywarch Hen cycle has Latin and religious influences that indicate a later date more in line with the fall of Powys in the ninth century,[89] while the "Pen Urien" materials seem almost contemporary with the events.

Another difference is the change in who is the enemy. Llywarch asks the kings Dunawd and Brân for aid in the poem "Gwahodd," yet in the "Pen Urien" group of poems these two are opposed to Urien and therefore Llywarch.[90] In "Gwahodd" there is no explanation of the changed loyalties, either. As we will see in the next chapter, Welsh materials from the ninth century on would view all the British as allies and the English as the enemy. Historically that was not the case, which is why the older group of poems describe some Britons as allies and others as enemies.

One of the major questions about the Llywarch Hen cycle is the taking of Urien's head after he died. The subject is treated directly in "Pen Urien," "Celain Urien," and "Efrddyl" but the context of the act is never explained; we do not even know why it was taken.[91] The answer is really not important in determining how useful the poems are, or even how old they might be.

There is a clear conflict of loyalties for the beheader that is never fully explained, suggesting an old perspective. There are also no explicit connections to "Marwnad Cynddylan," and the place-names in the "Pen Urien" group of poems are either independent of "Marwnad Cynddylan" or in perfect accord with those in authentic Taliesin poems. All of these clues also suggest that the "Pen Urien" collection is very old. It is only the orthography and language of the extant poems themselves that suggest their date might be as late as the late eighth to the middle of the ninth centuries.[92]

The concern for the treatment of Urien's head is not important in understanding how the "Pen Urien" group of poems is interrelated, either. Each poem has a different approach to the same scene. The barrage of perspectives has sometimes been seen as demonstrating that different authors contributed to the poems.[93] However, there are strong verbal links between the poems that suggest they only had one author. Each one also seems to perform a different function within the cycle. It seems reasonable that their different perspectives are simply poetic devices used to more fully explore the scene.[94]

As to the other examples of the group, "Unhwch" and "Dunawd and Urien" seem consistent with the three poems named above. Unhwch is the main subject in them, but they have the same conflict of interests, which the other three poems demonstrate. "Aelwyd Rheged," the last poem, is retrospective. It was possibly created as a transition to the later Llywarch Hen poems which feature Llywarch as an old man. Stanzas 37 through 41 seem to take an ironic viewpoint towards Urien, and therefore do not belong in the collection proper. Stanzas 32 through 35 most likely refer to a Run other than Urien's son, and are probably later additions as well.

Although the "Pen Urien" poems seem to be at odds with many details in *Historia Brittonum*, both sets of material are clearly derived from a common source or at least a shared perspective. This suggests that all the materials may have derived from the *Northern Memoranda* at one stage or another. If they have, then this collection of poems becomes valuable as an opposing viewpoint to the information to be found in *Historia Brittonum*.

The next source we will examine is *Culhwch ac Olwen*, an Arthurian story originally brought to its current form around 1100,[95] but found in *The White Book Mabinogion* dated to about 1350 and *The Red Book of Hergest* written between 1382 and 1410.[96] The story itself is a variation of "Six Go Through the World,"[97] with Arthur and his court superimposed on the original story. Added to the tale were famous individuals up through the early twelfth century—St. Sulien of St. David's, "Sberin" son of Alan Fergant, and possibly William the Conqueror. It is a menagerie of myth, legend, historical figures, and several different kinds of stories combined together by someone with a bard's education and specialized knowledge of Christianity. No editor or commentator has ever suggested any hidden motives behind the story.

3. Native Sources

The last three insular sources—the Welsh Triads (*Trioedd Ynys Prydein*), the royal genealogies, and the king-lists—were all dependent on the bards and skops of the Celtic and Germanic peoples, respectively. It was these two groups of people who acted as the historians as well as the entertainers in their respective cultures. Very little is known about their training but we can understand them best through their surviving writing.

In our present age, history is composed of dates, events, and people which remain constant. For instance, in 1066 William the Conqueror won the battle of Hastings. The why and the how are fluid, changing with each new era or historian, e.g., in the decades following 1066, the English would have recorded William as an invader and the language he insisted on, French, as an abomination. In the 1300s, his victory at Hastings meant that England had lands in France from which to pursue the French crown. Nowadays, any grade school child will tell you that the real history of England does not start until 1066.

Not so for the early medieval Celts and Germanics. Arthur was always a hero pitted against the Germanic peoples. Cú Chúlainn was always the loyal warrior of Conchobar. On the other hand, they had no use for dates, only relative years in the case of king-lists (which is why so little is known even after writing was introduced). They knew the main participants of battles, but tended to add in others as the years went (which is why the participants of Ardferydd in the 570s are not certainly known even now). They retained key events in their history such as the invasion of the Milesian gods or the Battle of Camlann, but these only served as backdrops for what they considered important—the survivors, the most loyal warriors, and the most generous kings. They made little or no real effort to remember when they happened.

Whereas any good modern history class will pursue an understanding of a subject—who killed John F. Kennedy and why? Was Hitler a brilliant sociopath or just an angry man?—the Celts never worried about it. They memorized what they considered the important facts of myth, legend, and history and remembered them using pneumonic devices. We know this because *The Welsh Triads* are just such a device.

In the forty-six triads from *Peniarth 16* and the *Black Book of Carmarthen*, Arthur is already present more often than other characters, but he has not overwhelmed the triad system just yet.[98] The orthography of all the triads dates them to the thirteenth century, though several of the *Peniarth 16* triads are were written as late as the fifteenth century.[99] These probably came from an early twelfth century written source.[100] All triads from other sources have been clearly influenced by Geoffrey of Monmouth's *Historia Regum Britanniae* and are not trustworthy where Arthur is concerned.

The historians of the early Middle Ages were not just historians but also entertainers. As such, they learned hundreds of motifs to help them craft their stories and rhyme to give them cultural power. They were also trained in how to adjust a story to their audiences—size, demographics, and even personal tendencies. As such, their opinions on the personal motivations of kings and queens were not just based on their own thoughts but were shaped by the political atmosphere within which they worked; they changed from king to king and session to session which is why a neutral source for information like the triads was so useful and, generally speaking, so consistent even if they were only written down hundreds of years after the period under study here.

As the author established in *Hengest, Gwrtheyrn, and the Chronology of Post-Roman Britain*, the British kingdoms took shape in the last years of the fifth century and the Germanic tribes not until the middle sixth century. In all cases their first rulers were mercenaries, angry young peasants, and maybe a wealthy landowner or two. None of them would have had royal lineages. That was practical; with kingship abandoned for centuries among the British, the bloodlines had been lost. Similarly, there is no sign of kingship among the Germanic tribes until the middle of the sixth century,[101] suggesting that their bloodlines may have been forgotten or at least obscured by then.

New dynasties were also inconvenient. Without a history of family kingship, any new king had to deal with the question of legitimacy; why did they deserve to be the king? What exploits had they and their ancestors accomplished that set them apart from every other warrior?

The burden of those questions was handed off to the bards and *skops*. Using their knowledge and training, they scavenged local legends to manufacture a pedigree that gave the kings credibility. Their "court historians" absorbed the most famous kings and warriors of the local regions and occasionally from old legends into one lineage or king-list, like the ones that are extant. Then they simply appended the additional names to the beginning of the king-list or genealogy. The technique not only added status to the current king, but lengthened his dynasty in the process. It is because of the bard's and *skop*'s resourcefulness that a good historian cannot trust any official dynastic history before a more historical source starts naming the kings within an historical setting.

Apart from the sources in the next chapter, the above is a fairly complete if terse discussion on all the pertinent insular sources of early British history. As with all social studies, very few of the conclusions outlined above are without their critics, but the consensus of scholars is in agreement with what has been put forward. As has been seen, we already know a good deal about the primary sources' influences. We are fortunate in that, as whatever history of post–Roman Britain is to be constructed must be based upon them.

4

The Evidence
The *Northern Memorandum* and the *Kentish Source*

The author will suppose that any academic readers must have cringed when they saw a chapter devoted to two sources that are not extant—no fragment of either document has ever been recovered. Yet, the one-time existence of both the *Northern Memorandum* and the *Kentish Source* has been largely accepted in academic circles,[1] so it remains only to extrapolate as much as possible from them.

History buffs are probably asking why this chapter comes after an essay on later materials. Both the *Northern Memorandum* and the *Kentish Source* have complex and intertwined histories. They have also most affected some of the last and most detailed source materials on post-Roman Britain.

We will begin with *The Northern Memorandum* for reasons that will become obvious as the essay goes on. Only two extant histories directly accessed it—*Historia Brittonum* and the *Annales Cambriae*.[2] The earliest event they have in common is Badon, which can be safely dated to the range 478x491.[3] It is also probably the earliest piece of information from the original source; in both works the Battle of Badon is led by the same person and accomplishes the same result.

There are figures in one or both sources, but they need not have been in the original. Patrick was a universal figure throughout the British Isles. Ambrosius is in *Historia Brittonum* but not *Annales Cambriae* and his presence in the history was as much to serve the book's anti-Powysian theme as it was to serve as a resistance leader.[4]

The original *Northern Memorandum* covered as much as a century and a half of history. It was not a fluid history though, before the Urien alliance, northern figures and events are mentioned sporadically and often inaccurately. For instance, the section on Arthur immediately precedes Urien even though there were probably decades between their careers. The history makes no effort to segway the two figures, either.

There is no question the main figure was Urien. Speaking of Arthur we can be sure it either gave a battle list, which has been shown to be a composite from several different kings,[5] or mentioned Badon as Arthur's decisive battle along with a single personal detail about his actions there.

With Urien the information becomes more detailed and personal. As we will see below, the *Historia Brittonum* author had his own propagandistic reasons for making Urien such a prominent part of his history. That might explain why we are given his allies, a specific and likely battle site, and an enemy. However, there is an independent body of poetry (Taliesin), which confirms these facts were connected to Urien. Even better, the details of Urien's death focus on him specifically and are also consistent with the bardic tradition.

The clear interest in Urien tells us three more details about the history. First, only a contemporary or near-contemporary author would have had access to such details. Second, that the original historian was partisan toward Urien, whether because he was related, was patronized by Urien or a relative, or simply admired him is unclear.

Finally, we know that the memorandum was drawn up in a monastery at some time during the era covered in this monolith. It could only have been written in a monastery because only bards and religious people had the training to record history during this era and of the two groups bards would not have remembered so much easily accessed historical information.[6]

Next question, when was the *Northern Memorandum* written down? As the author and others have demonstrated, the memorandum is unreliable when it speaks about Arthur and Ambrosius, figures of the late fifth and early sixth centuries. In fact, the historical horizon in the *Historia Brittonum* and *Annales Cambriae* is roughly 575.[7] If the events from that date on are accurate, then the *Northern Memorandum* must have been written down within living memory of them. To determine exactly when the document might have been written, though, we must first understand exactly where it might have been written.

In the *Historia Brittonum* Rhun, an otherwise unknown son of Urien, is mentioned in conjunction with baptizing Edwin. It is not odd that a son of Urien might have gone into religion; as the author has demonstrated later sons were commonly put into monasteries to avoid inheritance conflicts and as a safety in case all of a king's eldest sons were killed in combat.[8] Nor is it unlikely that Rhun might have baptized Edwin; Edwin spent his youth running from one kingdom to another and might well have spent time in Reged.[9]

What is noteworthy is that a Reged prince is connected to such a prominent Germanic king's baptism. That Rhun's granddaughter would marry

4. The Northern Memorandum *and the* Kentish Source   49

Oswiu, also mentioned in the *Historia Brittonum*, is another interesting detail. It suggests that the Rheged dynasty was significant well into the seventh century.

Just as obvious, whoever was recording the *Northern Memorandum* thought that both Rhun and his granddaughter were important enough to mention. That bears repeating and expanding; in an era where only the most famous ecclesiastics figured in histories and the English were the enemy, an otherwise unknown man named Rhun is credited with baptizing one of the most powerful Germanic kings of the time. At a time when women were only useful for the political alliances they represented, Rieinmellth is not only named, but her lineage is listed back to Urien.

What those two unlikely credits mean is that a monastery associated with Rhun recorded all the information in the *Northern Memorandum*; no other foundation would have had a reason to make them. Because we know the document was associated with Rhun we can approximate its date of creation. Rieinmellth was married to Oswiu, who was born in 611/2 and was a prince in exile from 616 to 633. Assuming he married young, a political marriage with Reged between 625 and 633 might have been beneficial. This means the *Northern Memorandum* must have been written at or after 625. Oswiu remarried early in his own reign of 642–670, so that by maybe 650 he was no longer with Rieinmellth and the notice would have been out of date. This gives us a range of roughly 625x650 for the date of the original *Northern Memorandum*.

The author has elsewhere speculated that 75 years is the maximum that any first-hand information could have survived in an oral environment among ecclesiastics (an 80 year-old informing a youth about something that happened when he was 5), while 60 years (a 60 year-old telling a youth about something that happened when he was twenty) is much more probable.[10] If those calculations are correct, then the *Northern Memorandum* is accurate back to 590 and possibly 550. So the limited information to be found in *Historia Brittonum* about Urien is probably accurate. It also explains why the events associated with Arthur (c. 480–520) and Ambrosius are probably not very accurate.

As significant as the range of 625x650 is, though, neither the *Historia Brittonum* nor the *Annales Cambriae* accessed it directly. We know this because of the sudden interest in things Anglo-Saxon after 650. In *Historia Brittonum*, there is a body of Anglo-Saxon genealogies. The *Historia Brittonum* also mentions sporadic islandwide events up to the Battle of Nechtanesmere in 685. *Annales Cambriae* has three Anglo-Saxon oriented additions after 650—the Battle of Cogfry between Northumbria and Mercia (644), Penda's death (655), and the first celebration of Easter by the Roman method among the Saxons (665). Most of this information could have been added when Alhfrith worked with the history between 664 and 671 during his bid to usurp his father, Oswiu's, Northumbrian throne.[11]

The second highly influential but hypothetical source for the period is the *Kentish Source*. It is important to understand it because Bede, the original author of the *Historia Brittonum*, and the tenth-century composer of *The Anglo-Saxon Chronicle* both relied on it for their early post–Roman history.[12]

We can be sure that the *Kentish Source* was created in Kent; though we know from archeology and Roman documents that there were *foederati* all along the eastern and southern coast of England from the fourth century Bede, *Historia Brittonum*, and *The Anglo-Saxon Chronicle* all claim that only Kent was initially occupied, and that it was occupied around the middle of the fifth century. This assertion would have given Kent the claim of primacy over all the other Germanic kingdoms and would have benefited no other kingdom.

Knowing the place of origin helps us with dating the *Kentish Source* too. The earliest possible year that it could have been written is about 580. That is about when Bertha, Æthelberht's wife, arrived from Frankia.[13] She came with her personal priest. At the time, the pair were the only two Germanic Christians on the island. Before Bertha, no person in Kent would have had the knowledge of Latin necessary to write it. That early a date seems unnecessary though. As the author has shown elsewhere, Kent's history doesn't become historical until the time of Eormenric, Æthelberht's father, and he may have been ruling in 580 and possibly up to 593.[14]

Theoretically, the latest possible date for the history would have been 731, the year Bede wrote his *Historia Ecclesiastica*. Of course, that date would require that Bede sent to Kent for information and that Kent responded by writing up the entire Kentish origin-story before Bede had the chance to get suspicious. The author can say from personal experience that histories take years. Also, the name-forms seem more seventh than eighth century.

A more likely date range can be found by using what we have learned about the *Northern Memorandum* and the law codes. The original version of the *Northern Memorandum* was probably written by Rhun, the son of the history's main hero Urien. It may have been written after Urien was dead but was clearly inspired by him. Meanwhile, the laws of Æthelberht, Ine, and Wihtred were all written when a uniquely powerful king was at the height of his powers and had the political strength to reshape history to his needs.

In Kent, Æthelberht was far and away the most powerful king in that kingdom's history. He had reached the height of his power by 597 (when he accepted a formal Christian delegation from Rome) and had probably faded by the time he died in 616. His son apostatized when he succeeded to the throne, making 597x616 the most likely range for the *Kentish Source*.

If it was written in that period it would explain the historical horizon

4. *The* Northern Memorandum *and the* Kentish Source

starting around 590 and the fact that only his father Eormenric's name is remembered. At a time when the maximum reasonable life-span for a layman was fifty-five, Æthelberht might have been the only person alive who still remembered anything about his father by the time of his death at fifty-six,[15] and for many years before then.

Alternatively, it has been seen in addressing the historical horizons of Gildas and the *Northern Memorandum* that living memory among layman can survive up to 50 years (a 55 year-old man telling a five year-old) while an ecclesiastic would be in a position to hear history at roughly twenty and might live till 80. If Æthelberht (born c. 560) relayed history about himself and his paternity to ecclesiastics in 616, that information might have been available until roughly 676. Though Kent was independent and strong rarely up until that point it is reasonable that it could have written a history during any point in those decades.[16]

Much more can be learned of the sources by studying the individual extant histories that used them. Bede is the logical first step here. He is the earliest historian to have used either the *Northern Memorandum* or the *Kentish Source*; his *Historia Ecclesiastia* contains elements of the *Kentish Source*. As luck would have it, he is also the most widely used and influential source for early Britain. What he wrote was considered absolutely factual among all later historians of the period because of his impeccable Latin and the precision of his language; qualities of training and a disciplined mind. In the modern era these talents have also fooled many generations of scholars into believing the information that he gives is trustworthy as well. It has only been in the last half century that his motives and the materials he used have been carefully scrutinized. It is because of these efforts that he has been assigned a more realistic standing among British historians.[17]

Bede's first source was Gildas, the angry British ecclesiastic we have already met. If you will remember, he wrote an open letter to several kings of Britain warning them that their immorality had caused God to bring the Germanic people to the island and that, if they returned to that behavior, God would again punish the British people through the invaders. As a prelude to his warning he narrated a history of Roman Britain which was vague in names and time from the beginning but was entirely inaccurate much beyond the middle of the fifth century, the edge of living history when he wrote.

Gildas was not the only place Bede found his information. He also acknowledged that Albinus, Abbot of the Monastery of St. Peter and St. Paul, gave him access to Kent's early history through Archpriest Nothhelm,[18] the *Kentish Source*.

This is where he found Hengest and Horsa. We know this because from his landing at Thanet until he disappears from history, Hengest remains in Kent. Only a campaign by his son and nephew take place outside of the kingdom.

Hengest also served the *Kentish Source*'s purpose, which was to raise Kent above the other kingdoms. We know this because Hengest was either a mythical figure or a person of legend and therefore an illustrious addition to Kent's house.[19]

It is also where he found Vortigern, the powerful king who managed to unite Britain under one leader after the Romans left and the fool who was manipulated by Hengest into allowing the Anglo-Saxons into Britain. *Vortigern* is the Anglo-Saxon translation of Gildas' *superbus tyrannus*, or proud sovereign.[20] *Vortigern*, and *superbus tyrranus*, are also forms of Welsh *Gwrtheyrn*. As we will see, Gwrtheyrn was a powerful ruler in the south during the early sixth century; whoever wrote the *Kentish Source* either mistakenly or intentionally confused him with the villain of *De Excidio Britanniae*.[21]

Bede was also provided some information about Octha and Oisc. According to most extant versions of the *Historia Ecclesiastica* Octha was the son of Orric surnamed Oisc who was the son of Hengest,[22] while in the Cotton Vespasian manuscript Oct(h)a was the son of Hengest and the father of Oisc. The origins of Octha and possibly Orric are unknown, but Oisc is a linguistic descendent of Ansehis.[23]

Nothhelm also gave Bede information on Kent beginning a few years before the Archbishop Augustine landed in 597 and up to Bede's present. In that he was not simply a vehicle for Kent's official dynastic history, relaying Æthelberht's accomplishments and the superiority of Kent, he was a servant of the church. The fact that Notthelm was made Archbishop of Canterbury only four years after the *Historia Ecclesiastica* was finished in 731 is evidence he accomplished both tasks. He was careful to show that Kent, and Canterbury in particular, was the first bastion of the Christian church in Britain; Augustine's official sanction by the pope is made much of as is his landing and first establishment at Canterbury. Bede voiced some concerns over the information he received from the *Kentish Source* on occasion, but from what is to be found in his *Historia Ecclesiastica* he did not edit its contents.

In addition to Gildas and the *Kentish Source*, Bede used information from Cyneberht, Esi, and the Lastingham communities, but only in order to fill out the more recent history and not without reference to other written and oral sources all over Northumbria.[24]

Bede not only copied from Gildas, Notthelm, and the historical records of several monastic communities, he also had his own biases and these influenced how he wrote history as well. As Dr. Miller long ago made note, Bede edited the information he had in three ways—by omission, interpretation, and style.[25] He omitted items that did not fall into his own themes, interpreted the data in light of his English perspective on Britain's history, and changed words to fit his own priorities. Bede was not a neutral historian; he was just as prejudiced as all of the sources at his disposal.

4. The Northern Memorandum and the Kentish Source

First and foremost, Bede was a Bernician. Whenever the opportunity arose he elevated Bernicia's importance, preferably at the expense of her enemies, mainly Mercia and Deira. He called religion into his book as well; Bernician military defeats were described in terms of divine anger for a king's actions, while successes were due to the divine support of Bernician supremacy. By attributing Bernicia's fortunes to God he was implying that Bernicia was divinely sanctioned in the same way the Hebrews had been in the *Torah*. The finished history was offered to the Bernician king, a man he clearly respected and admired.

Bede was also biased toward his religion, Roman Catholicism, over the archaic Celtic version practiced by the British and Irish. He made no effort to hide his leanings any time religion came into play in his history—from Edwin's stay with the Britons, through the massacre of Briton monks after the Battle of Chester, to the Council of Whitby. In the first instance he ignored the Celts. In the second he rationalized that they prayed against the Northumbrians and had deserved to be massacred. The Council of Whitby, revolving around the controversy between the Celtic and standard practices of the church, is given a full chapter and dealt with fairly but only because by popular agreement the results showed the misguidance of the British peoples; they had failed to modernize with the rest of the church and so were completely in the wrong.

Even though the Irish also practiced the Celtic version of Christianity Bede managed to avoid attacking them, though. He might have ignored their fault because the Irish had originally brought Christianity to Northumbria. Alternatively, Celtic Christianity might have just been a vehicle for attacking the Britons, who had been Northumbria's enemy for hundreds of years by his time. There is no way to tell what guided Bede there.

The Britons were Bede's last prejudice, and Gildas was a perfect tool for his assaults. As the reader will recall, Gildas had spent the first part of his letter explaining how the British had repeatedly sinned against God and been punished by renewed Anglo Saxon attacks—because like Bede, he had seen his people as God's chosen. All Bede had to do was eliminate the sermonizing and update the history to his century and his message came across clearly. The Britons were morally inferior to the Germanic peoples and deserved to be conquered.

His altered history made the Germanic peoples the natural focus for the remainder of his work. When he introduced Hengest and Horsa into his history he almost forgot about the British in favor of his own people. He does mention the Battle of Badon in passing and promises to return to the subject, but even that acknowledgment of British history was too much to follow up on.[26]

The next historical source is the *Historia Brittonum*, compiled in roughly

829 by an unknown author.²⁷ Mervyn Frych had established a new dynasty in Gwynedd when he had claimed the throne through a female line in 825. His patronization of the *Historia Brittonum* was an attempt to use his family history to strengthen his family's royal legitimacy. He hoped that his ancestry from the great British hero Urien would help him to unite the British kingdoms against the English so they could drive the invaders into the sea. To that end he collected all information on British history he could find, including *Northern Memorandum* and, through Bede, parts of the *Kentish Source*. Then he edited it to suit his purposes.²⁸

Anything negative about the other British kings would have been counterproductive, so he only used the positive materials and the materials that could be made positive. Arthur and Gwrtheyrn were famous kings so their victories against the English were told with whatever details were at Gwynedd's disposal. The foundation story of Powys' dynasty, the family Merfyn had married into, was also given a place. Garmon, a famous saint, was included in the Cadell story some time after 840 as a result of Gwynedd's contact with Charles the Bald,²⁹ and confusion with the more famous St. Germanus.³⁰

Back in Gwynedd, Merfyn merged the previous dynasty with an even earlier native one that had Roman ties, that of the Roman officer Padarn. He connected it to a third dynasty which was from the North,³¹ imitating his own migration and suggesting that his dynasty would be just as powerful and long-lived as it had been.

Urien was doubly important in Merfyn Frych's scheme. First of all, he was the most famous ancestor in Merfyn's lineage. As the founder of a new dynasty in Gwynedd, advertising Urien's exploits was a good way for Merfyn to sell his own legitimacy. Second, Merfyn found information in the *Northern Memorandum* about Urien being a part of a loose but successful British coalition. He recognized the usefulness of the history and made use of it. Though the alliance's main enemy had probably not been the English,³² Merfyn had the history altered so that the English were the only enemy. Whether or not Urien was the leader in the *Northern Memorandum*, Merfyn had the history written as though he was. Urien as the confederacy's leader paralleled his own aspirations—to lead the British kingdoms against the English.

In the tenth century Merfyn's descendant Hywel Dda, the Dyfed king responsible for *The Laws of Hywel Dda*, had the *Historia Brittonum* rewritten. This is probably where more of the *Kentish Source* materials were added. Hywel was, after all, in regular contact with Athelstan and acknowledged him as an overlord. It only makes sense that Athelstan would have made the English historical records available to him, especially as they were historical evidence of English superiority and showed how they had legitimately gained power over the British, as Athelstan was legitimately superior to Hywel Dda.

The Dyfed king had other uses in mind, however. He had his sights set

4. The Northern Memorandum *and the* Kentish Source

on conquering Powys, and Kent's origin-story was the perfect vehicle for undermining that dynasty's credibility. It would not have mattered to him that Gildas had invented an over-king to explain the Germanic presence, or that Kent had fused that figure with the recent king Gwrtheyrn, latinizing them both to Vortigern, to prove Kent's primacy over the other Germanic kingdoms. All Hywel Dda cared about was that Gwrtheyrn by his time was associated with Powys and he wanted to demonize Powys' dynasty. In attacking one of the kingdom's earliest and most famous rulers he could do just that, and the *Kentish Source*'s portrayal of Vortigern was exactly what he was after. He followed the *Kentish Source*'s lead in translating *superbus tyrannus* as Vortigern and translating that to British as Gwrtheyrn. He accepted the story that Gwrtheyrn was an islandwide ruler who was guilty of inviting the Germanic peoples and then allowing them to take control of the English lands whole, portraying him as a weak-minded man who was easily manipulated by others.

The editor even embellished, repeatedly portraying scenes where Gwrtheyrn was taken advantage of or acted immorally—his seduction by Hengest's daughter, his dowry of Kent, the ambush that left his nobles dead, and his humiliation at Dinas Emrys by Gildas' hero Ambrosius. As a *coup de tat*, he wrote that Gwrtheyrn had slept with his own daughter who had borne him a son; St. Germanus (Garmon) summoned God's wrath as a result. It is Hywel Dda's version that became the foundation for Geoffrey of Monmouth's history of Britain, and from there became the traditional way of seeing post–Roman Britain.

The second British source to use the *Northern Memoranda* was *Annales Cambriae*. It was kept as a contemporary annal kept at St. David's between 795 and 954,[33] because of the annals focus on Maredudd and his descendants as well as Hyfaidd and Llywarch, five St. David's bishops, and the record that a city near St. David's had burned.

The information up to 795 was added between 795 and 954.[34] Before 613 the entries are based mainly on *Isidore's Chronicle* and the Irish Annals but also include events of local and islandwide importance that are not found there like the birth of David and Camlann.

After 612, the *Annales Cambriae* becomes more interested in British events.[35] Hughes believed this section had been derived from a *Northern Chronicle* because it seems to focus on Cadwallon and the other Gwynedd kings as they fought with Penda and Mercia against Northumbria. However, as we have seen with the Irish Annals, the *Northern Memorandum*, and the later section of *Annales Cambriae*, contemporary record keeping is usually accompanied by a record of local abbots and bishops; there are no Gwynedd abbots mentioned here, nor is it clear from the language that the entries are even contemporary.

This section cannot have come from the *Northern Memorandum*, either, because it does not even mention the history's central figure Urien.[36] Nor does it agree with *Historia Brittonum* on the year Ceretic was expelled from Elmet during Edwin's reign, *Annales Cambriae* places it in 616 while *Historia Brittonum* says 617. *Historia Brittonum* also places the restoration of Iddeu, the Battle of Gai, and the death of Penda in that year while the annals name the Battle of Gai, the death of Penda, and the installment of Oswiu in three consecutive years. *Historia Brittonum* says Cadwaladr died during Oswiu's reign while the annals say he died fourteen years afterward. There is no doubt that the two sources are similar, even in their biases, indicating an original common source. Most likely all the northern British information came from the *Northern Memoranda*. Because of this connection, the British historical horizon of *Annales Cambriae* may well stretch back to the late sixth century.[37]

The motivation for adding in the entries before 795 is unknown. Hywel Dda was interested in rewriting history, so the work theoretically could have been done during his reign (904–950). If he had authorized it, though, why did he authorize a notice for Ambrosius and two for Arthur but not mention his ancestor Urien? It seems more likely to this scholar that *Annales Cambriae* before 795 represents an alternative to *Historia Brittonum*'s history that made use of the same Cambro-Irish community as the *Historia Brittonum*.[38] Though it did not directly oppose the propaganda of Gwynedd-created *Historia Brittonum*, it did omit any mention of Urien or his sons Owain and Rhun. This was most likely done to eliminate the very credibility Merfyn had been using them for. If *Annales Cambriae* was written by some party opposed to Merfyn's family, the pre-795 information was added between 829 and 904, the year in which Merfyn's descendant Hywel inherited Dyfed.[39] At that point, he would have ensured that all writings coming out of the kingdom were pro-Urien.

Written only decades later, *The Anglo-Saxon Chronicle* is the last historical work that certainly accessed the *Kentish Source*. The document extends up to 1110, but was originally written during Alfred of Wessex's kingship (871–899), most likely in 891 when the original records end.[40] When Alfred inherited the throne, Wessex was the only English kingdom that had not been conquered by the Danes yet. He spent most of his first few years as king in hiding from the Danes.

Alfred, or at least someone with the same goals as Alfred, wrote *The Anglo-Saxon Chronicle*.[41] We know this because it records a pro-Wessex view of English history, but never at the expense of the other kingdoms. Whoever wrote the first part of *The Anglo-Saxon Chronicle* did it in the hopes of using the individual accomplishments of the English people weaved into a common history to unite the English people against the Danes.

The Anglo-Saxon Chronicle accepted the history as found in the *Kentish Source* and Bede and followed the most reasonable extrapolations to be made

4. *The* Northern Memorandum *and the* Kentish Source

from both sources. In it, Hengest and Horsa landed in Britain, outwitted Vortigern, and fought battles against the British. The only real changes it made in the original settlement story was in reordering Hengest's battles against the British so that they appeared to be English victories instead of British ones, and in providing an exact chronology for the events *Historia Brittonum* had added.

The real genius was what came next. Bede had said that Ælle of Sussex had been the first of the English over-kings. The patron of *The Anglo-Saxon Chronicle* went one step further, providing Sussex with an origin legend that followed Kent's as the second earliest landing.[42]

Bede had said that Ceawlin of Wessex had followed as the third over-king, so only then was Wessex's founding written in.[43] The early Wessex entries were managed delicately. The chronicler was obviously careful about respecting the other existing English kingdoms. Perhaps more importantly, it was an opportunity to rewrite the kingdom's history. In *The Anglo-Saxon Chronicle*, there is strong evidence that the most active members of at least three early Wessex dynasties were blended into a single family history.[44]

Only then was Bernicia's origin given, in 547. It should also be noted that *The Anglo-Saxon Chronicle* did not date the establishment of Deira, East Anglia, or Essex—a fact that has never been pointed out let alone speculated on.

For East Anglia and Essex, the reasoning seems fairly straightforward. East Anglia may not have been Christian and dominant long enough to generate an origin story of its own, and of all the English kingdoms Essex was never in a dominant position over the others.

As to Deira, the situation is a little more complicated. *The Anglo-Saxon Chronicle* did have access to the *Historia Brittonum* or the *Northern Memorandum* because it uses the synchronization of Maelgwn's death and Ida's foundation of Bernicia to date the latter event to 547. However, the *Historia Brittonum* also says that Soemil "separated Deur from Berneich." Further on, the Anglian collection of genealogies shows that this Soemil was five generations earlier than Ælle of Deira, and Bede had already synchronized him with the ninth decade of the sixth century using his story about St. Gregory seeing Anglian slaves in a Roman slave market before he was made pope in 590. This would have placed Soemil in the fifth century. It has previously been demonstrated that the author of the chronicle was more than capable of such synchronization with Kent's foundation and the weaving of the Sussex and Wessex foundation myths, so, why was Soemil not put in *The Anglo-Saxon Chronicle*?

It seems simple enough to the present writer. Even if the chronicle writer had been able to manipulate dates so that all the foundation myths still agreed with Bede, the only real accomplishment would have been to create a third kingdom that had existed before Wessex. If that were not deterrent enough, validating Soemil would have caused the additional problem of possibly reinvigorating that age-old conflict between Deira and Bernicia by providing evidence that the conquered kingdom had a greater antiquity than its conqueror Bernicia.

In other respects, the chronicle was thorough. It gave all the major kingdom's king-lists and genealogies, along with a common history of the English people—its victories, defeats, alliances, and wars, the obits of its bishops and other notables. The intention was to help readers to remember their common origin and instill them with a national pride that would be necessary to finally defeat the Danes. It used additional information from the *Kentish Source* in providing information about Æthelberht's early battles and possibly the Battle of Dyrham.[45]

Bede gives us the least diluted version of the *Kentish Source*. It was originally a history created for the purpose of showing the dynasty of Kent as the first and foremost Germanic dynasty in Britain. With his own idiosyncrasies, Bede connected Hengest's son and nephew with Northumbria, but the majority of the text remained focused on the South.

Historia Brittonum recorded the most accurate version of the *Northern Memorandum*, and with the help of the Taliesin and Aneirin poems we can see an even clearer version of the work as a history of the north centered around Urien's career but including bits of the legendary past like Ambrosius, Arthur, and Ida. *Historia Brittonum* also used the *Kentish Source* secondhand through Bede, with the Hywel Dda edition adding in enough details about the dynastic rival Gwrtheyrn to illustrate him as an incompetent fool who had no right to rule Powys, and as the dynasty's founder his crimes only magnified the dynasty's flaws.

Annales Cambriae omitted everything about Urien and materials related to him (like Catraeth?), possibly in an attempt to circumvent or ignore the Gwynedd dynasty that was descended from him. In doing so, though, it gives us a glimpse of other items in the *Northern Memorandum*—Ambrosius and Arthur are still present, but the Battle of Ardferydd and the obit years of several important northern kings make their first appearance here. The dates for these events are probably guesses, but they are educated guesses.

The Anglo-Saxon Chronicle tried to rationalize the information in Bede and expounded upon his stories, putting them into a specific chronology in order to show the development of the English people and the hierarchy of its kingdoms. With its additional information regarding Dyrham and Æthelberht, it clearly accessed the *Kentish Source* directly as well.

What does this tell us about the *Northern Memorandum* and the *Kentish Source*? It reinforces the idea that they have been the basis for our perceptions of post–Roman history. Their main points remain the main points of any study of the period. Their biases can be found in every extant history we possess and was accepted and integrated into every modern history until historians first started to understand their underlying motives.

4. *The* Northern Memorandum *and the* Kentish Source

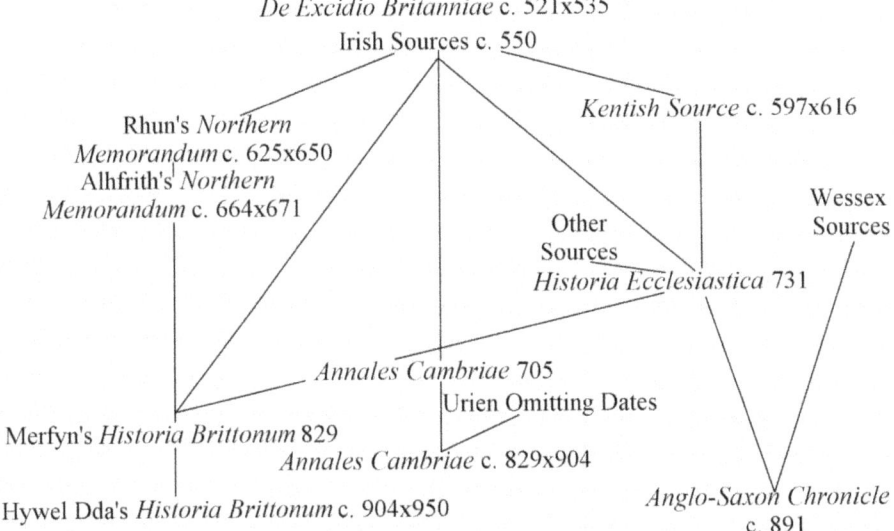

A timeline for the *Northern Memorandum* and the *Kentish Source*.

The essay should also have demonstrated that neither the *Northern Memorandum* nor the *Kentish Source* were stagnant works. The original writer of the *Northern Memorandum* would have had no reason to record information about the foundations of Bernicia and Deira because it would not have been of any interest to him or the British community he was writing for. When Alhfrith compiled and updated the memorandum as part of his campaign against Oswiu,[46] though, he would have used that information to generate support among the nobles and warriors of both regions.

The same can be said of the *Kentish Source*. In Bede's time, the important secular events of the post–Roman past revolved around Hengest and his manipulations of Vortigern because it was still important to justify the Anglo-Saxon's possession of England. To Bede, and probably to the composer of the *Kentish Source*, the introduction of Christianity was much more important than Æthelberht's accomplishments. However, Alfred needed a common history of success against a common enemy and so he chose to include more of Æthelberht's career as well the Battle of Dyrham.

Could the events that are only found in the later histories have been in the originals? Of course, we cannot pretend to know all the author's biases or interests. However, the known motivations were only present later and both histories had strong motivations for creation. This suggests that the materials were added. That is a revelation that will serve us well in trying to understand post–Roman history.

BRITANNIA

5

Roman Society

In order to get any sense of what was lost and retained through the turbulent period of 367–410, it is first necessary to understand a little more about the origin point—Roman Britain. The island was never fully conquered, but by 43 CE part of Britain already had a governor. During the course of the second century of the Common Era the rest of modern England came under Roman rule. At the time this book opens, Britain had been influenced by Rome for three hundred years and indoctrinated into Roman government for over another two hundred. That is easily long enough for Roman conventions to become British conventions and for Roman traditions to become British traditions.

Roman influence should have been a stroke of fortune for the suddenly independent Britons. The Roman Empire had lasted for five hundred years, and its predecessor the Roman Republic for several centuries as well. Both organizations had survived so long because of the carefully laid foundations of Roman government and society.

At the core of society had been the Roman education. Romans did not follow the motto of "no child left behind." In fact, they were just the opposite. Like most civilizations up until the nineteenth century, the Romans did not believe in public education. The wealthy were able to buy tutors and the poor were not. In adulthood, the poor worked as farmers or craftsmen and the wealthy were expected to run businesses and participate in the government. An education equivalent to a high school diploma was a mark of distinction, a sign of elite status.

And this is where the writers of the Roman laws were brilliant. Knowing how valued schooling was, the government also offered state-funded education to the most intelligent children of poorer families. These children were given the same teachers and shared an identical curriculum with the wealthy children; the *trivium* of grammar, logic, and rhetoric until the age of twelve. If they did well enough, these students were then taught the *quadrivium* of arithmetic, geometry, music, and astronomy to complete their instruction.

Rough appearance of Britain before the attacks of 367.

Free education raised a child's social status from laborer to white collar (or white toga) worker. In return for the enhanced prestige, these individuals were expected to spend their careers as government employees. Giving free education to the intelligent poor ensured that the lower government positions were always run by a competent group of persons whose loyalty was to the state.

The upper government positions were also left in the hands of the capable, though not necessarily to the most loyal; public service was also expected of the wealthy. The village/town/city elders were responsible for many of the same concerns as elders in our century; they allotted money for maintaining roads and buildings, ensured continuing trade, and organized all matters of education.

The difference between ancient Rome and the modern world was that a wealthy Roman concerned with public service was also expected to help pay for the building and maintenance of all public areas—including buildings, roads, and sanitation. This service, of regularly donating money for the common good, probably relaxed class tensions between the wealthy and the poor; there were few if any peasant revolts during the entire Roman existence.

Public service helped Rome more directly, too. Aqueducts kept Roman cities clean enough to avoid plagues. Roads were the lifeblood of the nation's communications, trade, and military and because of this kept Rome closely connected in peace and war.

The Romans were especially attentive of their highways. Every fifteen to twenty kilometers (nine to thirteen miles) there was a *mutatione* or changing station. At a *mutatione* a traveler could hire a wheelright, cartwright, or veterinarian to service their transportation. Every twenty-five to thirty kilometers (sixteen to nineteen miles) there was a *mansione* or full-service motel. These required the passport of a government employee to use. Non-official travelers could use nearby *cauponae*, or inns. The prices for all accommodations and services were fixed to avoid gouging. Having official stations allowed for the efficient movement of traders throughout the empire, permitting even the most isolated provinces to have access to exotic items.

Their transportation system was part of the reason for Roman military success. Well-maintained roads allowed for the rapid movement of legions, supplies, messages, and information throughout the empire. No matter how large and unwieldy the empire became, it was always possible to move enough troops to a troubled area in time to neutralize a threat.

The military had its own advantages as well, of course. Roman armor was better than the legendary hoplites had enjoyed; it was lighter but just as durable because of an improved smelting process. Swords were a little better too because of the introduction of iron. Roman shields were designed to interlock much like hoplite phalanxes. Time and again this foresight proved useful against cavalry charges.

Improved smelting and the introduction of iron were benefits that some of Rome's enemies had too. What gave Roman armies their best advantage on the battlefield was their adaptability. In the earliest armies, the smallest units had been legions of thousands. Roman Legions had originally been of 6,000 soldiers. They were divided into six cohorts, each divided into three maniples. Each maniple was under the direct authority of three centurions, who each commanded a century. It was these smaller units which gave the legions the flexibility to adapt instantly on the battlefield.

The centurion was what made the smaller divisions work. Chosen from among veterans of fifteen to twenty years' service these intelligent, loyal, natural leaders were equivalent to modern captains. In battle they were responsible for maintaining order and discipline through example. Those who continued to prove themselves could be promoted to maniple and cohort commander.

One of the formations the Romans invented was the *testudo*, or tortoise. The configuration protected the front, sides, and top of a unit against bowmen or flammable weapons. The *testudo* also provided enough cover to attack a fortified stronghold. Other, more tactical arrangements made possible by the legion's flexibility were the wedge formation, the Cannae tactic that had an intentionally weak center and strong wings, and the Zama tactic, which could neutralize elephants.

Once the Romans were in control of a region, they made themselves easy to accept. Through trade they brought the most exotic items from throughout the empire to it. They built Roman roads, aqueducts, and baths. Incoming Romans brought wealth to the economy. Roman soldiers were legendary throughout the ancient world for their success in battle; their presence meant security.

They were also accepting. Roman governors not only kept whatever customs and traditions the natives had, they had a special officer whose sole purpose was to keep relations with the natives healthy and open. Provinces were also encouraged to accept Roman rule through a system of rewards that granted the province varying levels of status within the empire. The ultimate goal was to award a province's people the title of full citizens. To help smooth the process, veteran Roman soldiers would be offered grants of land in frontier provinces as a reward for their service. Later, the same offer would be given to foreign soldiers as a part of their Romanization. The presence Romans in a population kept the empire from becoming a nameless entity and made it more interactive.

Rome's biggest tool was its acceptance of religion. As far as the Roman Empire was concerned, all faiths were equal. The worshippers of Mars, Ra, and British Belatacudros were all just as welcome; taxed equally and without any form of punishment. In fact, one of the first things the Romans generally did when they were learning about a new culture was to equate the local gods with their own.

This policy changed a little in the early empire, when it became standard practice to deify emperors upon their deaths. It was then expected that all Romans would worship them in addition to whatever religions they followed. When the monotheistic Jews refused to obey, they were attacked and forced to disperse. They were the first case of religious intolerance.

The second instance was possibly the druids. We do not know enough about them, though, to be sure. They might have refused to worship Roman emperors on religious grounds, or their disobedience could have been a part of larger political insurrection. There might have been personal or political factors we are unaware of. We may never know.

The third time a religion was officially attacked was with Christianity. Like the Jews, Christians were unable to worship former emperors. Also like the Jews, they were hunted down and forced into hiding. How captured Christians were treated after that could be the subject of an entire book.

The Romans had a well-designed and beautifully executed government and social arrangement. By limiting education to the most intelligent and capable they made the best use of their resources. By providing those individuals with status throughout the empire along with a secure means of generating income they created a bond of loyalty with its best and the brightest citizens. It was these intelligent, publically funded individuals who ran the Roman government and kept it functioning through centuries of wars and inconsistent rulers.

By expecting and insisting that the economically elite contribute time and personal funds to local needs, Roman policy muted internal dissension. Rome's policy of religious tolerance made the assimilation of new cultures smooth by demonstrating respect to each conquered people.

Rome's system of advancement and its flexibility made the legions the most adaptable and intelligently lead military units in the ancient world. By putting so much of Rome's resources into the formation, maintenance, and ease of travel along its roads, the Roman people created the framework for an extensive trading network and the amazing mobility of its armies. By establishing such a solid foundation of government, education, military, and trade, Rome molded itself into one of the most stable, most influential cultures of the ancient world. If not for the limited technology of the time and centuries of internal conflicts, the Roman Empire might still exist today.

6

Britain
367–410

The Roman province of Britannia had been dominated by two unique facts during its entire existence—a large tin deposit in Cornwall and the English Channel. Tin, a difficult metal to find in large quantities and a necessary element in Roman iron, had originally made the entire island an appealing conquest and continued to make it one of the most desirable provinces in the empire until the end of the fourth century.

The narrow gap of twenty-some miles that was the English Channel, on the other hand, was nothing but trouble. Back in the first century BCE, the channel had kept Julius Caesar from conquering it along with Gaul. During Britannia's entire career as a Roman province, it created nothing but problems for the Roman military. In Europe, Africa, and Asia Roman roads allowed for quick and precise tactical movements that no invader could match. Even sending soldiers across the Mediterranean was no great risk since the last pirates had been killed in Julius Caesar's time. The English Channel was something different, though. It was not bounded on every side by Roman provinces, making it easier to access from outside the empire and because of that more open to attack.

From the beginning the channel had been one of the most vulnerable parts of the Roman Empire. During the chaos of the fourth and fifth centuries that shortcoming was exposed when Germanic tribes settled along the coasts just above the Roman Empire and learned seamanship so that they could prey on the British shipping lanes.

Their attacks made perfect sense. On land, the Roman army was unparalleled and the boundaries of the empire carefully and consistently guarded. On the sea the situation was different. Water meant none of the natural obstacles that made guarding easier; as a result pirates could attack anywhere. Add to that that the Romans were not born seamen. It was only natural that the Germanic invaders would exploit the weakness.

In response, the British governors did something that was common in the Late Roman Empire. They hired Germanic tribes to protect their shipping lanes. In exchange for food, supplies and steady pay and under the official direction of a Roman unit, a chieftain agreed to patrol one section of the English Channel. His entire tribe—men, women, and children—would immigrate to a "hot spot" along the southern or western coast of Britain. From there, he and his warriors would protect the shipping lanes from piracy. During the course of the fourth century, several tribes were hired as *foederati* and stationed along the northern and southern coasts of Britain. It seems to have worked because information and Romano-British goods continued to flow into Europe, while coins continued to flow into Britain.

The *foederati* system was not an indicator of weakening Roman power it was simply another example of Roman adaptation; in this instance a new technique to adjust to the threat posed by aggressive Germanic tribes. Under the *foederati* system, Germanic peoples settled along the Roman Empire's boundaries, supervised by Roman officers and supported by Roman troops.

They were also immersed in Roman culture; the Roman officers they interacted with spoke only Latin, as did any nearby villagers they might trade with. The nearest Germanic tribes might be several miles further away and the Romans made certain there was no need to contact them for food or supplies. In a scenario like that, the first generation of migrants might keep their language as the primary communication, but their children were bilingual and by the third generation Latin was the main language and Germanic something that was spoken only at home. When it emerged in the third century, the *foederati* system was an effective means of Romanizing the Germanic tribes.

However, over the next two hundred years the Roman Empire declined. Internally, dynasties became shorter and less stable; as the fourth century wore on it became uncommon for an emperor to pass on his title. Externally, Roman borders were tested in Europe and Asia by dozens of tribes and kingdoms. Roman Britain's threats were Irish raids along its western coast, Pictish and northern Briton attacks across the northern border, and of course Germanic pirating along the English Channel. All of these changes weakened Rome's economy and the strength of its culture. Its degrading culture, along with less direct control over the *foederati* caused by Roman units regularly moving across the empire to defend its borders, made Romanization of the Germanic tribes less effective.

In the year 367, Ammianus Marcellinus recorded an alliance between the Picts, Irish and Germanic tribes in a joint attack on the province. The assault overwhelmed Roman defenses, exposing their inadequate numbers by attacking simultaneously from the west, north, and east. Unlike previous attacks, the allies took what they wanted and withdrew immediately so that

Roman units could not meet the threats one at a time. Ammianus tells us that the villages of Roman Britain burned to the ground.

In response, the emperor promoted Theodosius the Elder to *comes*, or general, and sent him to Britain in 368. Theodosius probably realized there were not enough Roman troops to protect the entire province. There is a good chance that he transferred most of the northern and western garrisons to reinforce the southeastern coast while he created buffer kingdoms in northern England and Wales. Once he had reestablished Roman order and ensured the tin supply was protected, he returned to the continent. The emperor rewarded him with the title of *Comes Britanniarum*.

Theodosius had countered the attacks but had done nothing to change the circumstances which had led up to them. As a result, the Picts and northern Britons continued to raid below Hadrian's Wall, never conquering the area for reasons that will be developed below but never slowing their attacks either.

The Irish, their younger princes driven by the ithagenic or cousinly succession of their culture, would continue raiding the western coast. Portions of Cornwall, southern Wales, and the island of Anglesey would be under their control before 400. They would establish kingdoms in the next few decades that would last for up to a century. Other Irish groups, likely raiders of British, Pictish, and Irish settlements alike, would move into Argyll and probably used the unique geography of the area to hide from their victims. Its pirating groups would eventually develop into the kingdom of Dal Riata, which would in turn become the core for Scotland.

However, as Theodosius had hoped, his alterations to Britain's defenses allowed Roman Britain to survive. Because of his efforts, Cornwall continued to produce tin and transport it to the continent.

In 383, the Irish, Picts, and Germanic tribes came together again and overwhelmed the province of Britannia with a second joint attack. This time Rome sent Magnus Maximus to restore order. Roman records say that he defeated all the attackers quickly and effectively. Welsh oral and genealogical memory credits him with founding several dynasties. This could mean that he installed kingdoms in Wales and Cornwall to act as buffers against future attacks. More likely, his successes in battle touched a nerve with the British and they remembered him as a great hero.[1]

Having restored order to the province, his legions proclaimed him the new emperor. An intelligent man, Maximus either found a new and loyal Britannia governor or satisfied himself that the old one was loyal. He then drained the northern and western frontiers of legionnaires and probably took units from the Saxon Shore command before sailing to the continent to fight his way to Rome. If he had managed it, Britannia would have remained an integral part of the empire. But Maximus was killed in 388. Just as bad, his soldiers never returned to the island. Rome had suffered a devastating loss in 387 at the Battle of Adrianople, so his troops were likely absorbed by the victor's army to help recoup some of the losses.

In Britannia the loss was not just military but political and economical; it effectively left the province with a governor loyal to a dead traitor and no currency to pay either government employees or the few soldiers who remained. It was a dangerous situation in the face of Germanic, Irish, and Pictish attacks and with the *foederati* as loyal to the Roman culture as they were to their pay, so the Romano-Britons must have deposed their Maximian governor and all of the people he had appointed—most of the bureaucracy and any regional officials—before begging Rome to accept the province back into the empire. To their relief, Rome accepted Britannia and a governor was sent to them along with additional Roman troops. In 388 Britannia probably had fewer soldiers on the island than before Maximus, but at least there was enough to maintain order and man the necessary fortifications.

There were not enough, though, to protect the borders from raiders. Soon the province was being attacked again on all sides again. The only real difference now was that the three groups did not need to work in tandem any more to take what they wanted.

As soldiers and officers were in short supply, there were probably fewer posted to the *foederati* than before which would have meant less control over them. The Germanic tribesmen must have noticed the change. They could not have missed the fact that raids were becoming more frequent either. All this meant that they were being assimilated into Roman culture more slowly, if at all.

Even with Britannia's reintegration back into the Roman Empire, the increasing raids of the late fourth and early fifth centuries meant that shipments of gold, supplies, and pay for the soldiers were much less consistent. This must have irritated the legionnaires and the *foederati*, but there are no records of them complaining. Instead it was the wealthy that reacted first. Reduced trade also meant less of the Roman culture was brought to them— pottery, art, literature, wine, oil, and fashions. Letters from friends and connections with the empire's politics only went through haphazardly. With the increased raiding, even they and their families were no longer safe if a raiding party happened upon their estate. As a result, many of the wealthiest Romano-Britons left Britannia during the late fourth and early fifth century for the comparative safety of the continent, leaving their villas abandoned and eventually replaced by much smaller farmsteads.[2]

The departure of the upper class weakened Britannia's economy. More importantly, it crippled the political and social structure; without the wealthy there was no group with the funds and the social expectations to repair buildings and roads. Roman Britain can be said to have begun its process of decay during this period.

It was only in the fifth century that the legionnaires finally came to realize that they were essentially isolated from the rest of the empire and rebelled themselves. Beginning in 406, the Roman Army in Britain selected three men in succession to be the emperor. The first two proved to be disappointments when they refused to leave Britannia and fight their way to Rome. The third man, Constantine, was not so squeamish. He departed for the continent in 407. More important for the island, he first installed his own governor of Britannia,[3] and probably drained the province of most of its regular troops to swell his army.

Constantine probably planned to send soldiers back to Britannia once he was crowned in Rome. Unfortunately for the island he was killed in 411 and his soldiers were not returned to Britannia. They were needed too; the province was being overrun by 410. Desperate for help, the Romano-British went with a formula that had worked in the past. They deposed Constantine's entire government to show their loyalty to Rome and then requested that the emperor send them a new governor and garrison.

The emperor could not though. Rome had also been sacked in 410, so when he received the letter from Britannia he was more concerned with reestablishing his authority at home than sending educated men and trained soldiers off to some far-away province. As tradition says, he told the *civitates*, or cities, of Britain to look to their own defense.[4] From that point on, the Britons were on their own.

To sum up, Britain was unique in the post–Roman period for several reasons. There was no Roman-based government because the natives had overthrown Constantine's officials in anticipation of Rome sending its own. When the empire failed to send officials, the Romano-British were left with only local governments—villages, towns, and cities.

There was no way of reestablishing an island-wide government, either. The aristocrats had been leaving for decades, which meant that no one had the money to get the government restarted. Nor could the military enforce a government or even elect its own leader; Constantine had taken all but skeleton crews from the border areas. All that might seem hard to believe, but apart from a single native source writing decades beyond living memory there is not a shred of evidence that any government beyond the *civitates* survived 410.[5]

In 410, the Britons did control most of the island but had no standing military, no island-wide government and, because of decades without the aristocracy contributing resources for roads and official hospices, there were limited communications. Worse, the Germanic tribes were still raiding the southern and eastern coasts, the Irish were attacking from Argyll down to Cornwall, and the Picts were crossing into British territory at will. It was only a matter of time before the British had new masters.

7

Picts, Irish and the Germanic Raiders

When Roman troops left Britain for the last time, they not only abandoned the Romano-Britons of England and parts of Wales, but left them to contest the island with three other culture groups. There were the Picts, a group of Celtic tribes that had either migrated to Britain before the Britons and had survived the Briton and Roman invasion or Briton tribes that had managed to stay independent during the Roman occupation and were now ravaging the northern Britons. The Irish had been driven from Britain during the Briton invasion but with Rome's weaker presence during the fourth century they had been terrorizing the western coast. The third group was the Germanic peoples. They had come to Britain as Roman *foederati* protecting the southern and eastern coast of England centering around the port city of London in return for food and supplies. There is no record of a barbarian revolt during Late Roman Britain, so in 410 they were probably still protecting the English Channel from raiders.

The Picts

The Picts occupied the northernmost section of Britain, the Highlands. Then as today, the terrain was difficult to pass through and infertile. Historically, these factors kept the region's population low and its people more isolated than in the rest of the island; during the first century before the Common Era when comparable areas were occupied by two or three kingdoms in lower Britain, Ptolemy had listed twelve tribes in the Highlands. They also meant that the Romans were less interested in conquering the region.

It was probably only the fact that the Picts raided northern Britain incessantly that led to a campaign of conquest in the first century of the Common

Era. The Picts responded by banding together into a loose confederacy and harrying the legions as they traveled. When the Picts finally gave battle at Mons Graupius they employed their chariots and exploited Rome's lack of experience; the result was a victory. For their part, the Romans retreated to a line between the Firth of Clyde and the Firth of Forth, built Antonine's Wall, and hid behind it or the later and more southern Hadrian's Wall for the rest of their occupation.

Recently Professor Charles-Edwards has suggested that the Picts maintained their confederacy for the rest of the Roman occupation.[1] In the face of such a powerful enemy, it makes sense that the Picts had retained their loose confederation. Though it began as a defensive alliance, it developed during the centuries of Roman occupation. As Roman defenses grew weaker their relationship allowed them to take advantage of the rich targets that were no longer being protected. Large-scale Pictish attacks are mentioned in the fourth and even fifth century. They were also able to coordinate their raids with the Irish and Germanic peoples in 367 and 383.

From 383 on, and maybe earlier, the Romans would steadily give ground in the North as they tried to find a balance between the amount of soldiers they could field and the amount of territory those soldiers could hold. To help themselves they may have set up buffer states in modern Lothian and Strathclyde; native kingdoms that could insulate the empire from intermittent raiding. Neither of them could have stopped a full invasion, but their presence meant that large numbers Roman soldiers did not need to maintain the northern frontier any more so that they could be stationed in other areas of Britannia.

There were no more major raids though. Even though the fledgling kingdoms could not have presented the experienced Picts with any great challenge, the lowlands of Scotland would remain British. The fact that the Picts did not attempt to invade and occupy suggests one of two possibilities. First, that the Picts preferred their poor soil and harsh winters over the more bountiful southern areas. The second option is more likely, and more in line with Professor Charles-Edwards theory; that the Pictish confederacy was based solely on mutual protection from the Romans. Once the threat of invasion was gone there was no reason to maintain it.

The native sources seem to agree. As has been seen *The Pictish Chronicle*, written in the tenth century, says there were originally seven kingdoms. Jackson's study of the Pictish stones has suggested that the Picts might have used those most famous remnants of the culture as markers and the symbols on them may have represented clans.[2] If his findings are accurate, and stone markings do represent borders for the medieval kingdoms consistent with those found in the *Pictish Chronicle*, they confirm there were at least seven distinct kingdoms during the Early Medieval period. Similarly, the Irish

Annals name several Pictish kings in the historical period who do not match the names on the king-lists, again suggesting there must have been more than one kingdom there.

Why did the Picts harry the province for centuries and then not invade when Rome left. We can only take a guess here, but a reasonable theory would be that invasions are normally the result of overpopulation and the Highlands have always been sparsely settled. There is no way of knowing exactly when the Pictish confederacy broke up, but it is a safe bet that it lost cohesion as Britannia became less of a threat. By the time the Picts would have been able to invade and permanently occupy any part of Roman Britain their alliance had probably disintegrated. Seven kingdoms, with seven different leaders each working toward seven different goals, would have had a difficult time effectively invading what had been Roman Britain. More likely, now that their common enemy was gone they returned to old squabbles between themselves over land, resources, and other traditional gripes between kingdoms.

If that is the case, then why is there no evidence of fighting among the Picts during the late fourth and early fifth century? Simply because neither the Picts, the Britons, nor the Irish would keep accurate records until the late sixth century. Even if the Picts had kept records earlier, they would likely have edited them in or by the ninth century to eliminate any suggestion of infighting. As we have seen, The King-List in the *Pictish Chronicle* is single-minded in giving a roll of kings from a single kingdom. Battles between Pictish kings, like multiple lineages, would have disturbed that illusion.

Pictish Succession

In 1978, Dr. Molly Miller accomplished an intensive study of the Pictish royal family which demonstrated how the Picts selected their kings through matrilinear succession.[3] Work since then has demonstrated the Picts' Celtic cultural roots and therefore their succession through an extended cousinhood.[4] Still, they seem to have relied on matrilinear succession more often than not.[5]

Their greater willingness to inherit through women might have been an advantage while they were a confederacy fighting the Romans; it would have allowed the males from several families to be the leading king, which would have reduced friction between them. That tradition might have continued long after Rome was gone. It would have made for complicated politics, though. There are several instances where one brother was a Pictish king and another was king of his father's kingdom. Below we will meet two likely sons of Maelgwn, Run the most powerful British king of his day and his brother Bridei, the first historical Pictish king and a powerful figure in his own right.

The Irish

Since at least the time of Conn Cétchathach, or Conn of the Hundred Battles, in the second century, Ireland had been divided between four kingdoms who fought with and against each other in typical heroic age warfare.[6] During the last decades of the Roman period, though, they were finally united under a string of high-kings. Traditionally it was believed that Crimthann mac Fidaig and Niall Noígíallach, respectively, had led the Irish in the great raids of 367 and 383. Thanks to the work of several Irish scholars, we now know that it was probably Muiredach Tírech and his father Fiacha Sroiptine who were high-kings during that period.[7]

Crimthann and Niall were then high-kings in the fifth century, at the very end of the Roman occupation and at a time when Rome had abandoned the western coast of Britain. It is important to note here that legend credits Niall Noígíallach with making several raids onto the continent (rect. Scotland) before his death on campaign.

We also know that several Irish groups settled in Britain during the fifth century. Crimthann mac Fidaig built Dind Traduí or Dinn Traduí, probably a site in Cornwall.[8] If it was, Crimthann may have hoped to take advantage of the tin trade coming out of nearby Tintagel by stealing from the mines, raiding trading vessels, or possibly even mining the tin himself.

In other areas of Britain, Eochaid Allmuir of the Déisi settled a group of people in Dyfed during the fifth century. Through intermarriage and conquest, his family would establish itself and eventually grow into the dynasty ruling Dyfed. An Irishman named Brychan traditionally settled Brycheiniog. In time the monarchy there would develop a stable and long-lived kingdom. Anglesey would be settled by a fourth group of Irishmen. The *Historia Brittonum* claims that Einion Yrth's dynasty established the kingdom of Gwynedd by driving those colonists back to Ireland.[9]

Argyll was also settled by Irishmen, but the entire region was probably not ruled by one Irish prince from the start.[10] The overall impression of the *Vita Columba* is that no chieftain ruled the entire area when Columba landed, and that Comgall and Gabran, brothers in the official Dal Riata genealogy, did not have a common father. The difficulties of navigation would have made the entire area a good hiding place for ships and small groups of warriors but poor for settlers hoping to maintain contact with Ireland. As the author will demonstrate below, Columba himself brought the various factions together under one king around 575.

The Irish and the Picts, though of similar culture, responded to the Roman withdrawal in very different ways—while the Picts lost interest in raiding the south after a few decades and never attempted to conquer any Briton areas the Irish continued to raid and eventually settled large parts of the western coast. This is because the Picts had been brought together by the common threat of Rome; they had only united to retain their independence. Once Rome was gone the confederacy broke up and they likely returned to their interkingdom squabbles.

The Irish, on the other hand, were never exposed to Roman legions. They were not united because of Rome, nor was the high-king's power based on Rome's presence. Because of that, Ireland remained united long after Rome had left Britain and its warriors and princes found an outlet for raiding and conquest mainly in Britain.

The Germanic Tribes

There were actually two groups of Germanic tribes involved with Britain in 410. The first were mercenaries of the Romano-Britons, *foederati*. They would remain loyal to their employers for several decades. These *foederati* had been hired to combat their cousins, the second group.

These other Germanic people had been raiding the English Channel for decades. The Romans had not been able to stop them because of their ship, the *karvi* or longship. Each *karvi* could hold between fifteen and forty warriors, making them small and maneuverable enough to elude Roman warships while giving them the numbers to overwhelm merchant ships. The Romans, practical as always, had hired Germanic boatmen to guard the shipping lanes because they understood that only people who had been raised with *karvi* would have the expertise to combat them.

During the last years of Roman Britain, these pirates were able to live off of their raids. After 410 though, when Rome officially severed contact with Britain, all commerce to and from the continent would have diminished substantially, leaving them with fewer and less rewarding targets. It only makes sense that they began attacking the English coast. With the regular army gone and the British people without an island-wide government, the only group stopping them would have been their cousins the *foederati*. We cannot be sure if the *foederati* did, though. As we learned in our overview of the source material, the English Channel was safe enough for a bishop to travel across in 429 and communications to the continent were regular until 441, but our only source for this phenomenon, the *Vita Germani*, suggests that the British were left to fend for themselves on land.

As the fifth century progressed, the Germanic raiders probably also tried to overwhelm the local populations. But no piece of evidence, not even the most biased piece of Anglo-Saxon propaganda, suggests they managed that until well after 441. It was at that time that the settlement of eastern England began.[11]

410 Through the Early Sixth Century

8

The Romano-Britons

The year 410 heralded the end of that era because it shocked Honorius and all Romans into the realization that the barbarian tribes did not consider Rome inviolable—it was just another city. Accepting that fact it was clear that the legions had become overextended leaving the capital vulnerable. Honorius realized that if his empire was going to survive, Rome had to be protected. That meant that his legions had to be reassigned so that Rome and all roads to it were protected. With his new set of priorities the protection of an isolated and troublesome island would have been relatively insignificant.

That is not to say that he had given up on Britain, or any of the less important or more troublesome provinces. Honorius had been raised a Roman and therefore knew that Rome had existed for a thousand years. He also knew that Rome had been sacked before—by the Celtic chieftain Brennus. He also knew the rest of the story; that his city always rebounded to become stronger than ever. Honorius probably believed that this event was no different, that in a few years Rome would be more stable than ever and then he could send out legions and governors to reacquire Britain and the other provinces of the empire.

He was wrong. The Western Roman Empire would limp back to health after 410, but only because the Germanic tribes respected the empire and allowed it to recover. It would also outlast Attila the Hun in the 440s and 450s, but only because of his death. It would not survive another sacking, though. When the Ostrogoths took the city in 476, they occupied it, and the Western Roman Empire was over.

Britannia was gone long before then. When the Romano-Britons had removed the governor and presumably his bureaucracy to make it simpler for Rome to reassimilate them, they had left themselves without any government beyond the local and the *civitates*; they had made themselves militarily vulnerable. Worse, when Rome did not send a representative there was no one in the province who was legally justified to. In the short term, all that could exist was what Constantine had not changed—the local and the *civitates* governments.

Britain in 441, with black representing the British people, dark gray the Germanic peoples and light gray the Irish settlers.

The problem was not limited to the government, though, that had just been the last evidence of Roman rule. As has been seen in the chapters above, raiding intensified from 367 on. After that date, all land within easy reach of the sea or rivers were targets for Irish or Germanic attacks and the entire northern frontier was victimized by Pictish raids. After 367, Britannia lost the security of a traditional Roman province.

Constantine was only the last man elected emperor in Britannia, several people had come before him. When each would-be ruler had returned to the continent to claim their crown they had stripped Britannia of as many soldiers as it could spare. At first, it made no difference. When the usurper died, Rome had simply sent enough soldiers with the next governor to replenish the garrison. After 367, though, soldiers were more difficult to come by. Each emperor coming out of Britannia permanently reduced the number of soldiers there. Obviously the reduced numbers made further attacks inevitable and further reduced security as a result. However, they also meant less Roman currency coming into the province as pay.

The increased attacks by the Germanic peoples meant that fewer luxury items like wine, olive oil, and other exotic goods came to Britain. Some of the wealthy left the island for the continent, leaving their property to be managed by the hired help; both changes had reduced the Roman-ness of the province.

Those who remained, as we have seen, stopped contributing to public works. For Britannia, both decisions crippled society. The wealthy had traditionally maintained the bathhouses, circuses, and temples. Without them these and other government buildings fell apart. Roads were not repaired and the way stations had to be abandoned. These alterations to life in Britannia would only have made administering the province more difficult in the late fourth and early fifth centuries, but once island-wide rule was dissolved the wealthy's lack of government involvement would have made regaining control of the province that much harder.

Tax money, mainly from the wealthy, had funded *grammatici* and *rhetori* as they educated future government employees. Without it, or a high enough demand to privately educate the wealthy's children, many teachers left for the continent throughout the fourth and early fifth century. As their numbers dwindled, so would the number of educated people on the island. The Britain of 410 already had too few people trained for work in the government.

Christianity was having difficulties as well, both from the inside and the out. During the late fourth century Pelagius, a native of Britain, had taught the doctrine of Free Will. He had been opposed by St. Augustine and several other leading churchmen who believed in "Predestination," however, and by 411 "Pelagianism" was officially condemned throughout the empire. Continued work by Augustine led to Pelagianism being declared heretical in 418.

Forced out of the empire, many believers escaped to Britain where they formed an influential segment of the population. As late as 429, St. Germanus came to the island to stamp out a large group of Pelagians who were probably centered around London.[1]

Although Christianity had been the state religion for over a century by 410 it appears that not all Romano-Britons were Christians. Several rural pagan temples were refurbished at the beginning of the fifth century, suggesting a rejuvenation of the pre–Roman religion, possibly a response to the decaying Roman Empire and the attacks from multiple groups.

The author has provided strong evidence for the existence of several fertility groups during this period as well. Samson's episode with a *theomacha* is one example.[2] Numerous non-motifal connections between Arthur and powerful witches provide another.[3] The Arthurian corpus is rich with references to the British religion from the earliest literature to the tales of Malory in its Holy Grail scenes and its many Bran and Belatucudros name-forms.[4]

Even as the government, structures, education, and religion of Roman rule crumbled, though, many Britons did retain a sense of being Roman. It shows up as late as Gildas, whose immaculate Latin represents an excellent education,[5] and whose story about Ætius shows a continuing respect for Rome.[6] He was not alone, either. The only other contemporary Briton writer is Patrick and his Latin is also good compared to his continental contemporaries. Holy men were not the only people who spoke Latin; it was common enough into the 430s that St. Germanus had no trouble being understood on his second visit to Britain.[7]

It is also obvious in the Roman coins from the late fourth and early fifth centuries. Everything that has been recovered suggests they were used for decades after 410. The Briton economy would be bartering for centuries, so their continued use suggests that the Roman economy continued for as long as the roads were in good enough condition for merchants to travel on them.

Even the village level government probably remained Roman. It has been seen that the Britons overthrew Constantine's government, but that can only have been the governor and his bureaucracy; everything below the provincial level would have remained intact. We have also seen that the wealthy either left the island or simply stopped participating in government at the end of the fourth century, but that need not have ended the tradition that the most prosperous persons in the community acted as the local board of elders. We do know that medieval villages had a council of the wealthiest people. They may not have paid for all public buildings during the medieval period, but following the rule of Occam's Razor it only makes good sense that a simplified form of the local Roman government persisted in the villages and towns of what had been Roman Britain throughout the Middle Ages.

As likely as it is that some sense of Roman-ness continued for the Briton,

8. The Romano-Britons

it was not practical to remain Roman during the fifth century. We have seen above that during the late Roman period the Irish had been raiding the western coastline and establishing a number of kingdoms there. The Picts, though not invading, were still raiding from the north. The same might have been true of the British kingdoms in Strathclyde and Lothian. There were also the free Germanic raiders based along the western coast of Europe; they had been taking advantage of easy coastal targets for decades by 410.

Britain had been victimized by all these groups, but somewhat protected by Roman legions. Once Britain was no longer an official Roman province the Romano-Britons lost that. To survive, they had to find a new way to defend themselves. Since they no longer had a provincial government, that new way would have been on a much smaller scale.

In their new order they would also have help, the *foederati*. Cousins to the Germanic raiders, Rome's mercenaries had protected Britain's coasts effectively during the last decades of the Roman occupation. Some *foederati* were also stationed along Hadrian's Wall and had worked well there over the years, too. Even when the legions had left permanently, evidence shows that the *foederati* uniformly protected their assigned areas admirably—as we will see, the Britons only called for Roman aid again between 433 and 441.[8]

The *foederati* were only mercenaries though. Because of the declining situation in Late Roman Britain they had never Romanized into Latin-speaking citizens of the empire. Instead, they had retained their original Germanic heritage. As a result they did not consider themselves part of the empire and were paid in food, supplies, and gold.

Like many of the Germanic tribes, the *foederati* in Britain were generally respectful of Rome's culture and loyal to its citizens. However, they were also practical. They were not farmers and had not been given farmland to work, nor did they have the tools or the training to work the land. They were fighters, and they needed the food provided by their employers.

That need was the glue in their relationship with the empire. In 407 Constantine left and all aid from Rome withered with him. In 410 the citizens dismantled his provincial government and no Roman governor ever returned to Britain with a new bureaucracy. Without officials to manage the processing of food, supplies, and gold, naturally the unaffected areas of Britain stopped making contributions. It was left to the local towns and villages to make up the difference.

The greater responsibilities put an extra strain on the nearby settlements; they simply could not produce enough surplus to support the *foederati*. It was inevitable that their payments became inconsistent, and only a matter of time before the *foederati* reserves ran low. At that point revolt was inevitable.

According to the *Gallic Chronicles*, the mercenaries reached that breaking point in 441. In that year the adjusted chronicles record that all of Britain was overwhelmed by Germanic tribesmen then. Archaeology has never confirmed that, though. What fits the evidence is that, half-starved and angry, the *foederati* sacked all the coastal areas for the food, supplies, and money they had been promised. Naturally, with all continental harbors plundered, it would have seemed to anyone in Gaul that the barbarians had overrun the entire island.

Returning to their settlements, the former *foederati* would have approached the villages they had been hired to protect with a new attitude—the realization that they had the real power and their employers were only shadows of the Romans they had once made a bargain with. They forced the Romano-Britons into submission at the point of spearheads and battle-axes; overnight transforming from hired thugs to local chieftains. And, with no concern about maintaining contact with Rome, they had no reason to patrol the English Channel. They focused their energies instead on keeping their villages under control and making certain they produced enough food to support them while keeping the neighboring tribes were kept in check.

The *foederati* revolt would have left the English Channel unprotected and given the raiders free rein over all shipping there. It would also give the Germanic tribesman safe passage to Britain. This would have two lasting effects on the continent. The first was the Hunnish invasion under the leadership of Attila between 434 and 453. The Huns would cut a swathe through the Roman Empire and displace dozens of Germanic tribes into migration outside of their area of influence. Many of them would travel to Britain where they would put pressure on the tribes already settled there and overrun more of the Romano-Briton areas in their search for land.

The second change would be Rome itself. In 476, Romulus Augustus would formally abdicate, effectively ending the Roman Empire in the West. Trade must have diminished after the 410 separation, and again after the 441 revolt; but when Rome ceased to exist as a political entity there would have been no need for trade into Britain and raiding would have become obsolete overnight.

The Romano-Britons could not stop the migrations or the cessation of trade. It is reasonable that some local militias had formed in the decades since 410, but no standing military and nothing to compare with the professional warriors their opponents could field. That is why they were so easily conquered when the *foederati* revolted. Migrations from the continent could have started right after that, too quickly to recover from the initial attacks and too extensive for any substantial counterattacks. As a result, the new groups of Saxons came further inland than the former *foederati* had raided, settling up the Thames river valley to Roman Londinium and well into the mainland.

Despite being severed from Rome, the Romano-Britons still considered themselves Roman and they responded accordingly. Somewhere between 433 and 454, someone wrote a letter to a Roman general named Ætius. Whenever that happened, Ætius never responded. As he spent the majority of his career putting down revolts and fighting with Attila he probably could not have left the continent.

The Britons probably did not know much about his movements. All they could have been certain of was that he was Rome's greatest general and therefore their most likely savior. When he failed to respond and did not send legions to help them, the Romano-Britons must have realized they were on their own; the Romans would not help them. If they were going to survive they would need to do it themselves.

The Britons probably responded in several different ways. In some areas a charismatic leader might have organized several villages together in order to defend their homes. In others, a few wealthy landowners might have taken advantage of the situation to buy a group of strongmen as his personal bodyguard. Adventurous young men might have joined the Germanic or Irish raiding parties all throughout the first half of the fifth century. If they had returned home after 441, these experienced fighters could have created their own war-bands in response to the new threat. Still other villages might have been far enough from the coast to avoid being conquered and isolated enough to avoid being raided. They might have avoided any local leadership throughout the fifth century only to be conquered by foreigners or absorbed by native kings later.

The path each region took is really not important. The end result everywhere was the same—the return of British kingship. When Rome abandoned the Britons and there was no longer a regional bureaucracy the Germanic, Irish, and Pictish raiding parties began to overwhelm the Britons. They responded with the first seeds of kingships. Local kingships meant that all villages were force to contribute equally to feeding and supplying the king's warriors; that helped to avoid the problems that caused the *foederati* insurrection. It also meant that the king and his warriors could immediately respond to any attack made on one of the settlements under his protection.

Along with kingship came the rejuvenation of the bardic class in Britain. Professor Koch has suggested that outlying areas like Gododdin, modern Lothian, might have had active bards from the early fifth century.[9] Whether or not this is true, it looks like the first generation of remembered bards and the earliest bards who were active in Late Roman Britain dated to the last decades of the fifth century.[10] As will be seen, they would be fundamental to the mystical aspects of Celtic kingship and useful as professional praisers and entertainers for the new class of warriors.

9

The Germanic *Foederati* in the Fifth Century

Beginning in the fourth century the Roman Empire had been settling Saxon tribes along the southern and eastern coastline to keep the shipping lanes in the English Channel open and stop other Germanic tribes from pirating. In exchange for food, supplies, and their own land within the empire they functioned as Rome's navy there. The *foederati* installations worked well, too. The warriors were diligent in their patrols, with each new tribe reinforcing the system.

The Romans had hired the Saxons because they were the best seamen of the time. That is not why the arrangement worked so well though. For the Saxons, the attraction was not the easy food and supplies or the fighting. The big appeal was the empire itself. Decades ago, people thought that the Germanic tribes had overrun and destroyed the Roman Empire. The truth is that the empire collapsed internally.[1]

Some tribes, like Attila's Huns, did despise everything Roman. Not most of them though. Most tribes held the Roman Empire in awe and served it till the end. Many of its best and most loyal generals, Stilicho and Aetius among them, were of Germanic descent. For the Saxons who settled on the British coast, being a *foederati* was more than income. It was a chance to live within the empire. They realized that they would never become Roman themselves but they could hope that their children might.

However, the sequence of events that would lead to the end of Rome was already in motion when the first *foederati* settled in Britain. As we have seen, Saxon raiding did affect trade and the attacks by Picts, Germanic tribesmen, and Irish—both individually and together—did make living conditions less appealing. The fourth century would see many of the richest Romans moving back to the continent. When they left, the public structures they were responsible for stopped being maintained. With them went a level of *romanitas* as well. The arrival of Saxon *foederati* also coincided with the first generals being elected as emperor. Each time a new man was declared emperor he took as many Roman troops as he could in order to go to the continent and pursue his claim.

What that meant for the *foederati* and their families was that they saw less of what was Roman, what impressed them. They saw fewer regular soldiers and were supervised less because there fewer around. When they traveled they did it on roads that were no longer pristine, and when they arrived they saw public structures that were slowly falling apart.

No contemporaries mentioned the *foederati* during the coups of 383 and 406–7. They probably stayed at their posts patrolling the English Channel and keeping a look out for raiding parties in the best Roman tradition as their Roman and more civilized employees selected new emperors, installed new governments, stole garrison troops, and left for the continent. It seems ironic that even as every successful Roman general was ripping the empire apart while he tried to become the next emperor, the outsiders were doing what they could to protect the empire's borders.

Their devotion to duty did not matter in the end though. The barbarian attacks came again around 410. The Roman citizens still overthrew Constantine's government and invited Honorius to send a new bureaucracy. Honorius still told the *civitates* of Rome that they were on their own, leaving local villages to keep the *foederati* supplied with food, clothing, and tools.

At first the events of 410 would have had little effect on the Saxons. Their employers still spoke Latin, were a part of Roman culture, and acted Roman. Local villages probably could not support the *foederati*, but the Roman Empire would have set up storehouses to store surplus grain and other supplies in case of a drought. The locals could have used them and replenished as they could while they waited for the Roman Empire to return in force and reestablish order.

However, the Roman Empire never did come back. It struggled along for six more decades, but never had the strength to bring send soldiers and another governor to Britain. The surplus *foederati* materials were exhausted within a few years. Local villages and *civitates* may have been able to work something out for a few years after that, but it was nothing permanent. By 441, they would have been tapped.[2] It was not, as Gildas would have us believe, the incompetence of a single man that allowed the Germanic peoples to invade Britain. Nor was Bede correct, that the brilliant manipulations of another man created the opportunity.

Britain fell to the Germanic tribes because the British people made a series of intelligent decisions based on an incomplete knowledge of their situation. They also had no foreknowledge of how their decisions would play out. Their only serious mistake was their inability to find a way out of the situation they had put themselves in.

10

The Irish in the Fifth Century

At the western edge of inhabited Europe, Ireland was in a unique position: all of its trade and any information from the continent had to first go through Britain. Throughout Ireland's history that had caused no real hardship—the Britons and the Irish were distant cousins after all. They had traded, raided, and swapped stories and myths with each other.

However, during the Roman occupation the Irish perspective of Britain had changed. Trade had still occurred, but Irish raiding parties had no chance against a single Roman ship. Roman legionnaires moved too efficiently and fought too intelligently to make good targets, and Roman cities were always well guarded.

The Picts had enjoyed similar relations with the Britons during the pre-Roman period, but unlike Pictland, the Irish had never been threatened with invasion. This meant that the Irish were never forced to band together into a loose confederation so that they could remain independent. Instead, the lesser threat implied by Rome stimulated a slow and stable centralization of Irish power into four major kingdoms—Ulster, Connaught, Leinster, and Munster. These kingdoms would remain stable and intact throughout the medieval period.[1]

As the author mentioned above, when the security of Britannia began to weaken during the fourth century the Irish, Germanic tribes, and Picts united to make attacks on it. The dramatic change from difficult to easy and profitable target might have been all the incentive the Irish needed to elect or fight among themselves for the position of over-king. Muiredach Tírech and his father Fiacha Sroiptine are the most likely rulers during the raids of 367 and 383. Legend and tradition say very little about what they actually did, though. Nor do they give us much about Eochaid Mugmedon and Crimthann mac Fidaig, who followed them.

We can guess at their power, though. They might have had the respect of every king in Ireland. They might have even collected tribute from all the kingdoms sporadically. However, high-kings could not have actually ruled all the Irish kingdoms in any sense we would understand. Instead, it is probably better to see the position as more of first among kings than the political equivalent of an emperor, if it even existed.[2] The simple fact that Patrick had non–Irish colleagues in Ireland demonstrates that political fact.[3]

Niall, son of Eochaid Mugmedon and known to history by his epithet "of the Nine Hostages," followed Crimthann. Active in the second quarter of the fifth century,[4] Niall was probably the most powerful Irish king of the post–Roman period. Legend says he made raids into Gaul, but that is impossible; Gaul was still a part of the Roman Empire at that time and there is no mention of him on the continent. Other historical evidence indicates that he attacked Pictland.[5]

Niall was not the only Irishman leading raids into Britain during the fifth century. In fact, as we will see below, Irish raids and occupations occurred all over the western coast of the island during the fifth century. These were each led by different people coming from different kingdoms with no clear strategy, making it clear there was no true over-king controlling the attacks.

There seems to have been a single mindset to most of the attacks though; they were not initially interested in conquest and settlement from the outset. If they had been, the entire western seaboard south of Hadrian's Wall would have been open to them as the British kingdoms would not develop kingdoms for decades after 410.

More likely, the attacks were initially for prestige and money. The author mentioned above that succession worked through ithagenic inheritance; all male descendants of a previous king were eligible for the kingship up to three generations.[6] Within that group of candidates, kings were chosen based on popularity, war-band size, wealth, and success in battle. Given that set of priorities, the Britain of the late fourth century and the early fifth century would have been a bonanza, the easiest way for a prince to gain a battle reputation and earn enough wealth to become an attractive candidate.

Soon there were raiding camps in Britain; bases from which to launch a series of attacks and collect their loot before the voyage home. Dind Traduí in Cornwall may have been one of them; it was close enough to Tintagel that it could have raided the tin, oil, and wine going to and from it. Likely the Dyfed and Gwynedd kingdoms started off as convenient places to stage attacks on Roman trading vessels heading up the western coast of Britain. Brycheiniog originated as an inland Irish kingdom. The *Vita Columba* suggests that Dal Riata, in modern Argyll, began as a pirate haven for several clans or clanless groups.[7]

Niall was succeeded at about mid-century by his son Lóegaire.[8] Tradition has it that he was the high-king that Patrick converted, so it only makes sense that we know more about his activities than those of any predecessors.

Strangely, the records of Lóegaire's era contain not a single raid into Britain. This suggests two possibilities; either Ireland became an easier place to gain a reputation or Britain became a more difficult target in his time. Lóegaire's several known insular battles on the one hand and the rise of kingships (see below) on the other suggests that both options might be accurate appraisals of the situation.

Lóegaire probably died about a decade later. From that time, his brothers appear in several battle references. The picture their notices create is of Niall's clan fighting to retain its position as the most powerful family in Ireland. The annals say Coirpre the son of Niall succeeded Lóegaire, but was followed by Aillil Molt of the Uí Fiachrach only a few years later. The outsider high-king is connected with many battles against Niall's grandsons according to the Irish annals before finally dying at Faughan Hill over two decades later.

The details of the Irish struggles are beyond the purview of this book. What is important here is that during the last half of the fifth century Ireland went from politically stable to unstable. For Irish princes, that would have meant that their home had plenty of opportunities to win the fame and warriors necessary to become a king and Britain was no longer necessary. The Cornish site was abandoned before 500 and Anglesey was conquered from the Irish by the Gwynedd dynasty around then as well.[9] Presumably the reason that a fledgling king was able to do so was because the Irish were no longer committed to keeping it.

The dynasties in Dyfed and Brycheiniog managed to remain on the island permanently. Our limited records indicate that by 500 they had both intermarried with native dynasties at that point and assimilated to the British culture before the sixth century. That possibility will be explored more fully below.

The cause and effect of the Irish in Britain is only speculation of course, we don't have any personal memoirs or even enough official records to really know what was happening in the British Isles, let alone why. What the theory above does have going for it is that it meets with the facts as they are currently understood. In the latter half of the fifth century the Irish were fighting amongst themselves and by about 500 the Irish had lost enough interest in their British holdings for them to be abandoned or easily conquered. Apart from a branch of the Connaught family migrating to Dal Riata in the mid-sixth century,[10] Britain would be relatively safe from the Irish for the rest of the early Middle Ages.

Dal Riata itself would be a different story. As a scattered grouping of islands, peninsulas, and shallows the region was a perfect home for pirates because it was a difficult area to navigate. Throughout the fifth and sixth centuries, Dal Riatan raiders probably attacked Pictish, Irish, and British targets without any serious reprisal. Dal Riata's geography simply made an invasion too hazardous. Even the Pictish kings, intent as they had been on attacking all areas to the south during the fifth century, seem to have left the neighboring region of Dal Riata alone.

On the other hand, the very same geography that made Dal Riata a difficult target and therefore an excellent base for pirates would also make it a problematic region to bring under one king. It would take nearly another century and a strong-willed Irish abbot to manage that feat. Until then, Dal Riata's pirates would remain an economic thorn but a political nonentity in Britain.

11

The Picts

Among academics and laypeople alike, the Picts had long been considered a separate ethnic group from the British peoples. Their unique language and general separation from the British during most of the fifth and sixth centuries were the basis for that argument. However, beginning with the realization that the Pictish language was similar to British,[1] that stance has changed. The current belief is that the only original difference between the northern Britons and the Picts was that the Picts remained independent of the Romans throughout the Roman occupation, while the Britons did not[2]; as late as Tacitus the northerners of Britain were still known as simply Britons.

Nevertheless, the Picts were separated from the other Britons for centuries, developing enough differences to warrant their own chapter here. Pictland, or Pictavia, was essentially the Scottish Highlands, consisted of seven kingdoms according to the ninth-century *Pictish Chronicle*—Cat, Fidach, Ce, Circind, Fotla, Fortriu, and Fib. As we have seen in the study of *The Pictish Chronicle*, we know almost nothing about most of their rulers during the fifth and first half of the sixth centuries—probably around ninety people in all. Instead, all we have is a single list of kings said to rule all the Picts, dated accurately from around 563 with the reign of Brude/Bridei.

The other kings did exist though, we can be sure of that. In 1988, Anthony Jackson offered an interesting theory based on the Pictish Stones that dot the Highlands. The Pictish Stones are a regional curiosity; large boulders with symbols carved in them that no one has ever managed to translate or explain. Jackson offered a simple suggestion; what if each dynasty had claimed one symbol and what if marriages were celebrated with the carving of a symbol stone that featured each dynasty's symbol. Looking over all the Pictish stones with two symbols he found seven that were paired consistently, and if they were put on a map they outlined the borders for the seven traditional Pictish kingdoms.

We do also have outside evidence of other Pictish kings in the pre–Bridei period. One local legend, *Culhwch ac Olwen*, and Caradoc's *Vita Gildae* all claim that Hueil son of Caw was a Pict who raided Arthur.[3] The *Vita Cadoci* says that the saint raised the chieftain Caw from the dead, and that Caw had originally lived beyond the mountain Bannauc.[4]

The above is more than enough to show that the Picts of the time were not a single united kingdom, but give us no idea of whether they cooperated with each other or were rivals. In fact, since we only have specific evidence of one other Pictish dynasty, it is impossible to know much at all about the internal politics of the Picts or the development of kingship during the period.

Instead we have only a few scattered clues. As late as the fifth century, Tacitus spoke of the northernmost part of the island being occupied by a confederacy of several tribes. From local legends and *The Pictish Chronicle* it seems safe to accept there were at least two active dynasties. Jackson's theory would confirm the existence of five more.

There are also indirect pieces of evidence. From the stories of Caw and Hueil to the suggestions within *Y Gododdin*,[5] the Picts continued to raid the Briton kingdoms well into the sixth century, but they never attempted to invade or conquer those areas.

Dal Riata also provides a fascinating insight into Pictish politics. Somehow, small groups of Irish pirates managed to infiltrate and maintain control over the traditionally Pictish area from at least the fifth century. This only makes sense if there was no united Pictish power strong enough to evict them initially; the Irish pirates had forced the original inhabitants out of Dal Riata or subjugated them and had been too strong to be forced out themselves. By the time of Bridei they would have been well established.

Finally, there is the example of Bridei, or Brude, the details of whose reign will be examined below. For now it is only important to note that he was considered the major king of Pictland during his own lifetime. He was the only Pictish king worthy of a visit by Columba. We can be certain he was no leader of a confederation, either. There is no mention of a confederacy, and the sixth century had no threat to match the Romans.

Reasonably, the fact of multiple kings in the late fifth century and one dominant Pictish king by the late sixth century suggests that there was some serious warfare among the Pictish tribes during the interval. There may have been raids to the South—for prestige, for wealth, or maybe just out of tradition—but the wars were fought in Pictland.

The Picts of the post–Roman period appear to have broken up their confederacy almost as soon as the Romans were no longer a threat; which makes sense if the current theory is true and they had only come together against the Romans. Likely former allies for centuries did not immediately turn against each other, but they did take up old rivalries eventually. Within a century there was a dominant king of Pictland. His career will be the focus of an entire chapter below.

12

The Rise of British Kingships

By approaching the four different culture groups separately, it becomes clear what likely happened during the fifth century, even without more source materials. To sum up, the Romano-British were probably given a new governor and bureaucracy by Constantine before he left for the continent. When Britain was attacked again around 410, they deposed the governor and his bureaucracy in anticipation of Honorius sending a new one, along with a bureaucracy more closely aligned with Rome. The problem was that 410 was a catastrophic year for Rome: the city was sacked. And Honorius, realizing that without Rome the empire would not survive, turned down their request.[1]

That decision, intelligent as it was for the empire, left the Romano-British without a provincial or even a regional government, without the means to generate a new one, and with a minimal amount of soldiers protecting her borders and coasts—as the Irish, Picts, and Germanic peoples raided them from all sides. Fortunately, they could do without for the time being. The Picts were not interested in conquest, only raiding. The *foederati* were able to turn away most if not all of their Germanic cousin's attempts to settle along the eastern coast. The Irish did establish bases along the western coast, but only so that the princes who led them could gain money and battle experience to help their chances of being elected as the next chieftain back home.

As the fifth century wore on, the Picts became more interested in Highlands politics than the plunder to be had in the south. On the death of Niall at mid-century, the most powerful Irish dynasties began competing amongst themselves for primacy. The change in politics meant that princes had more opportunities at home to enhance their reputations. They probably lost interest and stopped sending resources to Britain shortly thereafter.

The evidence suggests that the *foederati* maintained their posts for several decades after the end of Roman Britain. However, their willingness to protect the shipping lanes and British villages had always hinged upon two key points; a steady supply of food and supplies and their respect for Rome. The problem was that as of 410 Britain had lost official contact with Rome.

12. The Rise of British Kingships

Its citizens still spoke Latin and were culturally Roman, but they were no longer a part of the Roman Empire. The *foederati* must have become aware of this as they saw no more ships carrying grains and coins after Constantine left in 407. They would have also seen fewer and fewer Roman soldiers as the fifth century continued, and those soldiers would have been less and less awe-inspiring as their discipline inevitably declined without pay or any other connection to Rome.

The Romano-Britons no longer had a provincial government, either, which meant there was no islandwide authority to control the collection of food and supplies for the *foederati* and leaving the surrounding villages to provide all the necessary provisions. Those settlements, asked to contribute several times what they had been overnight, would have buckled. Reserves might have compensated the difference, but they cannot have lasted for long.

The final blow must have come in 441. By then it would have been clear to the *foederati* that the Romans were not returning and that the local villages would never provide them with enough food, supplies, and coinage to live comfortably. So they "revolted," or more accurately they resigned as *foederati*.

We have reports from both Gallic Chronicles on the continent and Gildas in Britain and they give us basically the same information about what happened next. All three agree that the Germanic peoples overran Britain and cut off all communications with the continent.[2] After that the continental sources are silent. Gildas alone tells his audience that some Britons resisted and eventually forced the Germanic people out of some regions.[3]

But these were events that had occurred decades before Gildas and were not specific; it would only make sense that they would be exaggerated with time. Archeology tells a different story. It shows a steady migration and subjugation by Germanic clans beginning on the eastern and southern coasts, not a wave of conquest our sources indicate. There is also no clear sign of kingship. At least one prominent archeologist has interpreted the evidence as one or two clans imposing themselves onto several British villages.[4] This would suggest that the *foederati* rebelled, divided into groups of one large or two small clans, and each absorbed enough villages near their original posts to comfortably support themselves. More of England would slowly come under Germanic control as additional clans migrated to Britain in search of land over the next few decades.[5]

Both Charles-Edwards and Bassett have argued that a grand army first conquered the region to open it up to these smaller groups, but the argument falls apart once the context of post–Roman Britain is remembered. The Britons were not organized beyond the local level and had been dependent on the *foederati* to protect them until very recently; the Germanic tribes would have had no need for a grand army to conquer the Britons.

For visual purposes Charles-Edwards has suggested a comparison to

Clovis' conquest of Frankia,[6] but that is flawed too. The conquest of Gaul was managed by one charismatic leader. In Britain, a sophomoric examination of the sources shows several leaders at any one time between 450 and 500, and more critical examinations have demonstrated that all of them have been either transported from another time, invented, or telescoped to the fifth century by extending a royal lineage. Unlike in Frankia, no leader emerged, no single kingdom developed, there is no real evidence of a large army except for the *Gallic Chronicles*, and they cannot be trusted quite that far.

Several Germanic histories tell us what happened after the revolt, but as we have seen they were written well outside of living history for this period and for nationalistic reasons; they are unreliable. Archeology tells us that the local clans had no interest in any political gains once they had enough farmers and craftsmen to serve them. Instead they turned to raiding. During the slow but warm periods of the year, young males attacked nearby clans to steal livestock—mainly cattle and pigs. With the stakes being nothing more than a few cows and personal recognition, the forays were probably not fatal as a rule. However, as Arnold has pointed out, raids would have been a useful activity for helping the males of a clan to safely vent their aggression.

Meanwhile, the British of the mid-century had Irish and barbarians living next to them who might attack their villages at any time and steal whatever valuables they had—cattle, jewelry, even women. It's very possible that some young Britons might have envied their attackers and set off to join their warbands. When they had gained some experience they might have made useful war leaders among their own people.

If there were any wealthy Romano-Britons left after 441, they might have used their money to form a personal bodyguard. In other villages a great hunter or a charismatic speaker might have attracted enough people to participate in the defense of their homes. It is even possible that a British leader might have formed a war-band of Germanic warriors; but that prospect will be explored below.

Once villages accepted that they needed "professional" protection an arrangement would have naturally followed. In exchange for safety, each settlement would provide enough food and supplies to help support the local *teulu* or war-band. The arrangement was similar to the one the Romans had held with the *foederati* except for one important detail; in the new arrangement, British kingships were supported by only the villages they protected, while the *foederati* had been supplied by the entire province. It was a necessity of the times, but would inevitably force the lower classes to contribute a large share of their income to the Briton kings and lead to a distinct separation of the classes.[7] But, that is a different subject entirely.

The British system was more reliable, more immediate, and gave the

12. The Rise of British Kingships

British villages a guaranteed protector; if the villages were not protected then the warriors would stop getting the silver, good, and supplies they survived on.

So, when did British kingships emerge? That would have depended on the means by which they formed. While a wealthy man collecting a private bodyguard might have declared himself a king within months of the 441 revolt, war-bands formed from raiding veterans might have taken twenty or more years to develop. It is safe to say only that all kingships that would form had already been founded by roughly 500, by which time the Britons' sense of *Romanitas* had largely disappeared, bards had been reintroduced among the southern Britons, and Badon had been fought.[8]

13

Heroic Age Politico-Economic Dynamics

In 1912, Hector Chadwick dubbed the period between Alaric's sack of Rome and the Cadwallon's campaign of 632 the "British Heroic Age."[1] He then compared it and the Anglo-Saxon Heroic Age to the Greek Heroic Age. When a scholar studies the literature of both insular cultures of the time it is hard to deny that many of their values and attitudes are identical to those found in the *Iliad* and other Greek literature from the same era.

However, an heroic age is more than simply a consistent philosophy about life and death, it is a complete political and economic system. At the center of the heroic age is the king. It is his personality and personal charisma that bonds the warriors together in the first place. His reputation and the confidence that he brings inspires villages to pay tribute. His successes in battle and the loot he acquires on raids are what attract new warriors to him and allow for his fame to expand and his band of warriors to grow from a handful of warriors to dozens.

The cult of a specific individual is what allows for kingship to develop initially, but a king who rules solely by the force of his personality can only survive for so long. In the modern world many leaders have had personal charisma, but many have not. Leaders are able to lead because of two key elements—tradition and the moral authority to rule.

The British chieftains that emerged after Roman rule had neither a tradition nor a moral authority over the people. They had authority over villages only because they had an army and the villages needed protection. They controlled their army because they had the money pay them and the warriors' respect. When any element in that chain faltered, their ability to rule disintegrated.

Which is why bards among the Britons, Irish, and Picts and *skops* among the Germanic tribes were an invaluable element of society for kingship— they gave the illusion of moral authority and tradition to the early kingships.

We have no direct knowledge of what both groups were taught as part of their educations but they were probably similar. They were probably taught all of the essential myths and legends of their people as well as hundreds of lesser stories. They probably also picked up as many current events as they could—battles, raids, generous and stingy kings, silver-tongued and ugly warriors, anything that might prove useful in the king's hall. We can be confident that both groups were also taught how to create extemporaneous poetry quickly using hundreds of motifs and pneumonic devices. They were shown techniques that helped them adjust to different audiences, time limits, and even values.

Any person who completed their formal education would have had all the tools to become an excellent entertainer. He, or she, could tell myths and legends in many different ways, keeping the old stories fresh by stressing different themes and perspectives. They could create new stories and poems to praise their patrons as events occurred.[2]

We have to keep in mind, though, that the bard and the *skop* were much more than just entertainers. Their ability to innovate gave them an almost mystical reputation among their people—what they said was the truth and the power of their words made what they predicted inevitable.[3] The education also made them natural historians; ancient peoples who kept no written records made little or no distinction between mythology, legend, and history.

In the late fifth century among the Britons and the mid-sixth century among the Germanic peoples, their significance was magnified. Both culture groups had not needed kings for at least three generations and were only just beginning to reintroduce them. In that context, the historians infused the new group of chieftains with a respectable lineage several generations deep. This was possible because of the relatively short life span of the average person at the time,[4] and the fact that any history beyond the lifetime of the oldest member of society was extremely flexible.[5]

Asked to construct a lineage for his king, a bard would begin with the information that was widely known—probably all of the current king's accomplishments and his father's name. Beyond that, a bard was free to insert famous local kings into his king's genealogy. This gave the king's warriors and the villages under his protection a sense of consistency by reinforcing the belief that their leader was not only an excellent war-leader but that he came from a long and rich tradition of legendary ancestors.

Bards and *skops* were also responsible for creating the illusion of a kingship's sanctity. Family history was part of that role because it demonstrated a king's right to rule. However, the office of king itself was sacred. The two cultures did this in different ways, but the common denominators were that the clan from which kings were chosen had divine favor and the man chosen as king was believed to be the most favored.[6] Secondly, part of the inauguration ritual included marriage to the land. Among the British the land was symbolized by an old hag who transformed into a beautiful young woman when married to the right king.[7] For the English the king married a deity, Freyja, and so there was no transformation.[8]

Among the Celts legend had it that the wife, and the land she symbolized, would remain youthful and beautiful for as long as the king ruled well. Knowing that, a peasant only needed to look at his own fields to be reassured his king had divine grace.

Marriage to the land made for an effective image. However, daily reminders like praise poems were also useful because they could approach the same subjects from different angles and served many different purposes: To reinforce the king's stature as a generous and successful leader, to point out the unique talents of his men, to support the bond between a king and his warriors.

Warriors were an essential part of the equation. While a king's personality might attract warriors and win tribute it was the warriors' willingness to stand beside their leader and often die in battle that made kingship successful. Achilles was once offered the choice of living a long life and being forgotten when his children died or dying young but enjoying eternal fame; he made the same choice as every other heroic age warrior. Their numbers made it possible for the king to defend villages from raiders and eventually to make their own raids. The warriors' presence helped to enforce the agreement between king and villages for food and supplies. Without them, the king had nothing.

These villages, and the villagers who populated them, were the foundation of every kingdom. Each year they produced the grains, honey, *bragawt*, livestock, labor, and smiths that kept the king, his warriors, and his servants fed, sheltered, and armed. Without their support British kingship could not exist. The mutual need of all four groups—king, bards, warriors, and villages—is what made the system work.

One other element was absolutely necessary for British kingship to survive—an enemy. The original reason for kingships was the raiding and settling of the Germanic tribes and Irish princes. Both groups were real threats in the middle and late fifth century. But, as has been seen, the Irish had lost interest in Britain by 500 and evidence will be produced that Germanic tribes had stopped migrating into Britain by then. Both groups probably still conducted raids into the sixth century, but by then they had likely settled into a pattern of stealing livestock and defending their own cattle from other villages.

As has been seen, the British chieftains also took part in raiding British as well as Irish, Germanic, and probably Pictish targets. Raiding helped a king develop a reputation as a battle leader and a man who was able to take booty. What is normally overlooked is that the act of raiding also served the raided kingdom. If foreign kings could be beaten off it would enhance the defender's reputation, but whether he was successful or not, raiding parties could be portrayed as the new enemy; without the king to defend the peasants those raiding parties would have attacked the villages themselves.

Every element in the heroic age system was necessary. The king's charisma and leadership ability bonded the warriors to him and made the villages believe he could protect them. Bards lived on kings' largesse but provided them with a genealogy of famous local kings and tapped the divine nature of their position while using their skills to entertain. The warriors were attracted to kings because of their abilities and their wealth. In return for the wealthy lifestyle the kings gave their warriors, the king's men followed them into battle, putting their lords' lives before their own.

All three groups were fed, clothed, and paid by the villages. In return for a small portion of their annual crops, as well as some livestock and labor, they had a king who was sworn to protect them. That protection might not have been as secure as it had been under the Romans but it gave them more safety than they had enjoyed since the Romans, while demanding fewer resources than raiders took.

Despite the interdependence of the different groups the system was still fragile. It might have been based on ancient traditions, but it was new. Bards were invaluable in making the political shifts an accepted part of British culture. But changing attitudes took time. That may have been one of the reasons for the witch hunts of around 500.[9]

14

The Early Kings

In earlier chapters, the military, political, and economic situation that forced the creation of British kingships were explored. In the last chapter the author laid out the new economic and social reality, demonstrating the delicate balance between kings, bards, warriors, and peasants in every kingdom. Together, they should have provided a solid foundation for understanding the context of British kingdoms in the late fifth century.

But the above essays have only given us a broad look at how the kingdoms came into existence and functioned. We know little more about specific kingdoms, and much of that information is based on outdated information. Most of our knowledge comes from Gildas and his perceptions of British history up until the battle of Badon. But as we have seen in Chapter 3, Gildas could not have known what was happening much before the rise of Ambrosius.

His statements about a single person, his tyrant, ruling post–Roman Britain were based on the assumption that the *foederati* came to Britain after Rome had left and during that hazy period before he was born; he needed a vehicle to explain how the Germanic people had come to be settled on the island and why they had attacked and his *superbus tyrannus* served that purpose. If he had known the *foederati* were already on the island by 410 he would have had no need to include his tyrant. And if Gildas had omitted him then *Historia Brittonum*, Bede, *The Anglo-Saxon Chronicle*, and all later histories that based their fifth-century history on him would have had no reason to add him.

Gildas is clearly not a reliable guide for early British kingships. We do know the names of several kings who were active during the fifth and early sixth centuries and even a few about whom we know more than their names and their patronymics. Those few—British, Irish, Pictish, and Germanic—will be examined in the following pages to see if they might throw more light on the nature of early kingships in Britain. They will be listed by region and culture first and only then by chronology. With any luck the essay below will

14. The Early Kings

help to provide a better perspective on how kingship developed in post-Roman Britain.

Y Hen Ogled

The Pictish kings and many of the northern British lived in regions that had been under little or no Roman rule. It seems reasonable that many of the kings from this area already had a working kingship tradition by the late fifth century.

Cunedda is traditionally credited with establishing the kingdom of Gwynedd after a migration from Gododdin.[1] As his son Einion has traditionally been generally dated to about 500 (see below), Cunedda has been placed in the last third of the fifth century.

Between Molly Miller's genealogical work and John Koch's examination of *Marwnad Cunedda*, there is little doubt now that Cunedda probably never left the north.[2] That the poem does not mention his ancestors suggests that the bardic tradition may not have been fully developed at the time of his death. If so it would push Cunedda's floruit back to the range of 410 to 470.[3]

Meirchion is best known as the grandfather of Urien and Llywarch. In fact, that is all that is known about him—no battles or place-names are connected to him anywhere in British literature. The period does not have too many sources, so that fact would not normally seem too unusual but Urien had the most famous bard of the period on his payroll. And as the court bard it would have been Taliesin's duty to record every praiseworthy act of his patron and his patron's ancestry.

It would have also been his obligation to extend Urien's family history back artificially with locally famous kings when Urien's ancestors were no longer remembered. With such short lifespans it is possible that Urien never knew his grandfather (mathematically there is a 50/50 chance he knew his father as an adult), so that Meirchion might have been unrelated chieftain from the same area who was attached to Urien's family tree to make it more prestigious.

The same argument could be made about Meirchion's "sons," Cynfarch and Elidyr, but the triads do mention that Llywarch son of Elidyr was one of the chieftains who never reclaimed their inheritance, which indicates his father held lands and lost them. If Cynfarch was a king it is extremely unlikely that he ruled a different area than his brother, so that Cynfarch would have ruled the same kingdom first. Following that line of reasoning, Urien gained his kingdom by conquering it from whoever had taken it from his uncle.

Meirchion and his sons point out the uncertainty of kingship during the period. Urien, one of the most famous kings of this era, may not have been the son of a king and there is no way of knowing who his historical grandfather actually was.

According to both versions of the *Vita Kentigerni*, Lleudun was a king of Dun Pelder, a hill-fort in Medieval Lleuddinyawn and modern Lothian. Lleudun does not appear in any genealogies or king-lists, but as we've seen these *vitae* are some of our oldest sources. Both report that he was Kentigern's (born 483x519) grandfather and Cynan Colledawc's (465x521) father.[4] That would put Lleudun's floruit anywhere from the middle of the fifth to the early part of the sixth century, which meshes well with what we already know about other rulers of Lleuddinyawn; outside of the *vitae* Ymellyrn is the next known chieftain of the region and he was active in the early to mid-sixth century.

The *vitae* also tell us something about the geography of Lleudun's kingdom. He is only associated with sites located within a few miles of Dun Pelder. When he is pursuing his daughter and grandson he stops as soon as they cross the Firth of Forth. Lleudun disappears from the story after that. Both these details suggest that Lleudun ruled over a fairly small area.

In Arthurian stories there is a Loth of Lothian who is Arthur's brother-in-law. Lleudun was probably the inspiration for his character. Arthur lived during the late-fifth and early-sixth century, so it is even possible that the two were contemporaries.

Arthur was already a popular figure in British lore before 1136, but it is because of Geoffrey of Monmouth and his translators that he became the most popular figure of the period. By the end of the Middle Ages, regions throughout the island and people from as far away as Cornwall and the Highlands were connected to him in legends and folk tales. His legend spread in time too; mythological figures and people living as late as the twelfth century were eventually connected to him.

We know a great deal less about the historical Arthur. Most of his early stories involve raiding or defending against raids. Hueil's attack has been mentioned above. *The Welsh Triads* say he attempted a raid on Drystan son of Tallwch.[5] The *Vita Cadoci* claims Arthur helped Gwynllyw in the abduction of Gwladys daughter of Brychan,[6] though the *Life of Saint Gwynllyw* is clear that the marriage was peaceful and Arthur was not present.

Where he lived has been debated as well. Local legends focus on Wales, but that was where the last independent British kingdoms were. As the author has shown, the most credible evidence is to be found in other areas. Personal name data is useful; Pelles, Pellinore, Pellam, and several other names are forms of Belatacudros, who was a British god closely connected to Hadrian's Wall.[7] Of the other warriors associated with Arthur in the earliest materials, most of those that have any geographical connections are linked to Cumbria and Galloway.[8] Once their bias is accounted for, several native sources mention

14. The Early Kings

Carlisle or something that might be a confused form of Carlisle.[9] The romances, too, seem to point to Carlisle.[10]

Carlisle might just have been the legionary fortress of Luguvalium,[11] which would have given Arthur a pre-existing base along with a connection to Rome.[12] We do know that Carlisle was inhabited during the late sixth century and that at that point its Roman structures were still visible.

How much power did Arthur have? Medieval legends have him conquering much of Europe. The earliest literature makes him a simple raider and assigns him a handful of men. What has been seen above suggests many active kings in the late fifth century, each controlling small areas of land. It is reasonable to think of Arthur being one of them.

Ceredig, the next northern king under study here, was never put in an extant saint's life. What we know of him comes from two sources. In the genealogies he is given the title *gwledig*, which means at least dynastic founder,[13] but has been interpreted as "emperor." Strathclyde was located above Hadrian's Wall, and as we have seen the Romans abandoned that area decades before they lost control of Britain. In the Late Roman period, it was common for the Romans to create buffer states between themselves and any potential threat to Rome. It has often been suggested they did so in northern Britain too. If they did, which would have been useful in protecting the northern borders against the Picts, it is very likely that the region would have went through the process of several competing chieftainships into a united kingdom as early as the mid-fifth century. As the first king of the region *gwledig* would have been a legitimate title.

The second source is Patrick's *Epistola*, where he is called *Coroticus*. E.A. Thompson suggested that Patrick could have been speaking to an Irish king because the context of the letter is that Ceredig had remained near to Patrick,[14] and because Patrick was able to excommunicate him.[15] However, Ceredig could have remained in the area days later if he had set up a camp and was conducting several village raids. As Dumville once pointed out, we have no idea what the politics of the fifth century were. We have no idea about the religious politics either. Patrick might have had the authority to excommunicate any ruler acting in his area of influence. He might not have had the authority and might have done it anyway. That would explain the writing of his *Confessio*.

A second possibility is the Ceredig who was the eponymous ruler of Ceredigion. Now that Ceredig has been dissociated from the Gwynedd lineage,[16] there are only dates that can be associated with members of the dynasty—a Ceredig's death in 616 and his descendant's obit in 807. Allowing for a three-year window on either side of both dates we are given Ceredig's birth year in the mid- to late-sixth century.[17] Even if Ceredig's obit is thrown out, it is only possible that this Ceredig was Patrick's nemesis if Ceredigion managed 35-year generations, Ceredig was a young man, and Patrick very near his death at the time of the *Epistola*. All these conditions are feasible but unlikely, especially when we keep in mind that Patrick's area of activity was northeast Ireland, which was easiest to access from Stathclyde.

As Charles-Edwards recently pointed out, the way Patrick addresses Coroticus only makes sense if his kingdom had a consistent history as a Roman client.[18] Strathclyde would have from the second century, Ireland could not have and Ceredigion could only have been a client kingdom sporadically over the last century or so of Roman occupation.

This means that Patrick, an ecclesiastic with little or no political knowledge, probably just got it wrong when he called Ceredig a chieftain. Actually, his assumption speaks more to his own background. If he assumed that Ceredig was a simple chieftain who ruled a hall and nearby villages, then that might have been the norm in the area where he completed his training. The evidence suggests that this area was transitioning into kingships during his early adulthood.

Cynfelyn has the same problem as Cynfarch above, the actions of his son Clydno Eiddin, and even grandson Cynon, are known but we have nothing on Cynfelyn himself. So, starting with what we know, the *Black Book of Chirk* gives Clydno the epithet Eidyn. As Eidyn was Late Medieval Welsh for modern Edinburgh, it is reasonable to assume that Edinburgh was his central location. And, as the body of Welsh literature suggests no British conquest of Edinburgh, it is reasonable to assume that if Cynfelyn was a chieftain he probably ruled from there too.

Cynfelyn's grandson Cynon participated at Catraeth in the late sixth century, while Clydno was active a few years later during Run son of Maelgwn's reign, placing Cynfelyn's floruit in the early part of the sixth century.

Cynfelyn and his "son" and "grandson" are interesting because we already know that Dunpelder, a second hill-fort in Lothian, was also occupied during the early sixth century. Lleudun, of Dunpelder, may have been Cynfelyn's contemporary.

Coel should also be mentioned in any kings of the Old North list. The genealogies say he fathered several dynasties, but work by Dr. Miller showed that to be chronologically unlikely if not impossible.[19] She proposed instead the same sort of bardic intervention we have come across already; Coel was a popular early British hero whose name was added to several dynasties to enhance their traditions.

We can be certain that Coel was a famous king in his time and that his name was remembered. However, since no credible historical source mentions him that could give us any idea when he lived we have no idea if he was active in 410 or 510.

We cannot even know where he was active. Our only clues are in the genealogies themselves and oral tradition. Tradition is easy; it says that the Kyle area in what was Pictland is named after him and that he was buried in

Coylton, what would become Strathclyde but was not near the capital of Dumbarton.[20] Of course one of oral tradition's big flaws is that it is passed down by word of mouth, in this case for millennia.

The family trees give more difficult results because in them he is the ancestor of kings from Reged (Cumbria), Edinburgh, somewhere in the Pennines Mountains, Elmet, and around Arthuret. The logical conclusion is that Coel controlled all these regions but as we have seen the theme during the early Middle Ages was of small kingdoms absorbing one another, not of large kingdoms breaking up. More frustrating, none of his "descendants" are located anywhere near either Kyle or Coylton. If there is any useable data here it is the association of Coel with Kyle, suggesting that Coel was actually a Pict.

The Anglo-Saxon Shore

As has been seen, Germanic chieftains were being settled along the southern and eastern shore of Britain as *foederati* during the fourth century. A careful examination of known early chieftains should reveal something about the nature and development of their kingship tradition.

The first named chieftains to appear are Fraomar and Ansehis. According to Ammianus Marcellinus the first was sent to Britain in 372 with the title of Tribune.[21] The *Ravenna Cosmography* tells us Ansehis came to Britain as a *foederati* at about the same time. Linguistic and folkloric studies have connected Ansehis with the legendary section of Kent's royal genealogy.[22] More will be said about him below.

Neither Ammianus nor the cosmography provide us with any further information and no other source names either chieftain, leaving us with nothing specific about either man's career. However, the fact that they are mentioned does tell us something about Britannia as a whole. In the middle of the fourth century, the most important Germanic chieftains were two simple tribal leaders who were totally insignificant to the rest of the empire.

The next leader in the records is Soemil, a Northumbrian figure who only appears in the *Historia Brittonum*. There it is claimed that he separated Deira from Bernicia,[23] suggesting he was the first king of the region. The comment is made in the genealogies, where he is listed as the five-generation ancestor of Edwin,[24] placing his birth-range in the second quarter of the fifth century and suggesting he was active at just about the time of the 441 Germanic revolt. But as has been seen, neither the archeology nor the literature supports a Germanic kingship so early.[25] It is possible that Soemil led a contingent of *foederati*, but not probable. No other region managed to remember the names of their leaders, and Deira had no better recordkeeping than anywhere else.

In fact Northumbria only took an interest in recording history decades after Kent. It seems somewhat more likely that Soemil was active during the Late Roman period, like Ansehis. This scholar, however, taking note of the claim that he separated Deira from Bernicia, would like to suggest that he was one of the first kings in Deira, perhaps the founder of the Deiran dynasty in the middle sixth century.

At first that might seem highly unlikely; our sources for that time frame have proven to be unreliable at best. However, several scholars have also noted that medieval historians had a tendency to gather contemporary or near contemporary local kings and telescope them into a sequence of prehistoric rulers for the surviving dynasty (one of the bard's duties).[26] It seems reasonable that Soemil was a victim of just such manipulation. It will be seen that a British alliance controlled much of Northumbria in the middle sixth century; perhaps Soemil separating Deira from Bernicia was in fact Soemil making his small kingdom free of British rule.

What is really interesting here is that Soemil is credited with leading a rebellion against the British at all. According to all other sources the Kentish heroes Hengest and Horsa led the uprising against the Romano-British and led all the Germanic peoples during the entire struggle. Whatever his dates, Soemil's connection with the separation from Berneich is likely historical, and if he can be safely placed in the range 533x567 he is not called a king. This is very informative about the political situation at the time.

The Britons

Dr. Miller once suggested that a Padarn Peisrud, "red tunic," traveled south from Gododdin into Gwynedd (northwestern Wales) at some time between Maximus departure in 383 and the last Romano-British emperor elections in 406–407.[27] However, she never was able to provide evidence of that happening. What we do know about Padarn is that he is unknown outside of Gwynedd and that red tunic was a well-known badge of office in the Late Roman army. That suggests that Padarn was from the area originally. He may or may not have been a Roman officer, or Roman official, or wealthy Roman who transitioned into a chieftain during the early fifth century. He could just as easily been a Romano-Briton who used "Peisrud" to connect himself to the stability and credibility of the Roman past in the late fifth century. We may never know which possibility is historical fact.[28]

Up until around 1970, Einion Yrth was believed to be just another member of Maelgwn's dynasty—the man who initiated the conquest of Môn, which turned out to be the last region of medieval Gwynedd to be conquered.[29]

Things have changed a lot since then. The discovery of Aberffraw, the medieval capital of Gwynedd, on Môn demonstrated that Gwynedd was centered on the island.[30] Dr. Miller's work showed that the dynasty may have begun with the conquest of the island around 500[31]; the conquest was not just another addition to the kingdom. More recently, Professor Koch has eliminated Einion Yrth's "father" Cunedda from the Gwynedd lineage leaving Einion as the founder.[32] We now know that when he came to power he controlled only part of an island off the coast of Gwynedd and that at the time of his death around 500 Môn was not entirely in his possession.

Ambrosius is a unique character in British history. He is not connected to any specific dynasty or region in the early materials and yet he is the only British figure of the fifth century mentioned by Gildas in his *De Excidio Britanniae*.[33] Gildas places him after the Germanic attack of 441 and before (and possibly including) the Battle of Badon. Badon has now been securely placed in the range 478x491,[34] meaning that the British ecclesiastic Ambrosius' floruit was somewhere between 441 and 491.

Gildas is vague on where Ambrosius was active. His only real clue is that *De Excidio Britanniae* focuses on people in modern Wales and Cornwall and Ambrosius seems to be the holy man's ideal of a lay-hero.

The *Historia Brittonum* would connect Ambrosius with two sites. The more memorable is Arfon in Gwynedd, where his presence would bring about Vortigern's downfall. However, the author has already demonstrated that Vortigern's character developed in that history to suit Dyfed's tenth-century political needs.[35] The second notice is the Battle of Wallop,[36] against Guitolin. It has generally been placed near Nether Wallop in Hampshire.

Wallop is a stroke of luck because it has no clear motivation, yet tells us where Ambrosius was active directly through the battle site, and indirectly through Ambrosius' connection to Guitolin, a member of the same pedigree as Gwrtheyrn and Gloiu. The latter name is important here because it is the eponym for Gloucester[37]; he and his brothers Bonus, Paul, and Mauron are even named as the city's builders. It would seem that Ambrosius was active near Gloucester/Wallop.

As outlined above, kingships in the South only formed as a result of the Germanic rebellion and the raiding and invasions that followed. It has also been suggested that the first generation of kings would have had little or no tradition to rely on for continuing a royal line. At first glance at least, it looks like Ambrosius was a victim of that developing convention; either his entire family was gone before he died or his bards had not yet re-established the basic tenets of Celtic kingship and his personal credentials by that time.

Guitolin, participant at Wallop and son of Gloiu, also gives us some useful information because he is not connected to a region or a kingdom, like the figures from other dynasties,[38] instead he is linked with a single city. That suggests he ruled a very small area. It also suggests that, as he was Ambrosius' rival, either they rose to prominence at roughly the same time or that Ambrosius was never more than a locally important leader. Chronologically, Ambrosius was active between 448 and 491,[39] and intersected with Guitolin's career at some point making the Gloucester chieftain a figure of the late fifth century as well. As we have seen above, his kingdom was centered on Gloucester.

Cadell first appears in the *Historia Brittonum*, where he is the central figure in Powys' foundation story.[40] Dr. Miller's work with the genealogies has demonstrated that he was active in the first decades of the sixth century,[41] while Professor Koch has suggested Powys might not have been a unified kingdom until the 700s based on linguistic evidence and an historical confusion over the ruling dynasty.[42] The consequences of these realizations are that Cadell may or may not have been the first ruler of his dynasty, but he was definitely only a chieftain with control over a limited number of villages.

Cadell's name is also interesting; it derives from a shortened form of Roman Catellinius—Catell. The personal name Cadell would be used throughout the Middle Ages, but this is the first time it was used in Britain after Rome left. Its presence suggests a continuing respect for Roman culture and possibly a lingering sense of *Romanitas* among the native population.

Gwynllyw is known from the *Vita Cadoci* and the *Vita Gundleus* as the father of Cadoc and the husband of Gwladys. These connections place his floruit in the early sixth century, a calculation confirmed through less direct calculations.[43]

Both *vitae* also claim that Gwynllyw and his six brothers inherited a portion of their father's kingdom, with Gwynllyw acting as overlord for the group. That sounds a lot like the traditional Gwynedd origin legend. As we have seen above, Cunedda was not part of the Gwynedd dynastic family and his "sons" were actually kings of separate kingdoms who were only connected to the ruling family when the royal dynasty tried to solidify its control by making all of the conquered kingdoms a part of the foundation legend. Probably, the similarity means the same thing here as it did for Gwynedd; Gwynllyw's brothers were not chieftains with their own kingdoms and Gwynllyw probably only controlled a small kingdom himself.

The Picts

Like Ceredig, Caw was also from the north. The *Vita Cadoci* has Caw saying he was from a place "beyond Bannawc,"[44] which probably means Pictland. One of Caw's sons was Gildas, while a second son Hueil raided Arthur,[45] putting Caw's birth-year at roughly the middle of the fifth century.[46]

In the *Vita Cadoci*, Caw also says that he spent his life raiding. In the context of a saint's life the commentary makes sense; it would not do for a chieftain to boast about how wide an area he controlled or how many battles he had been in. However, the information is there for the taking anyway.

If Caw was a Pict, then the region he controlled had never been under Roman control. That probably also means that Caw was a king and not the simple raider he is called. If he was, then Caw was one independent Pictish ruler from the later fifth century.

Caw's son Hueil is also placed "beyond Bannawc" in Caradoc's *Vita Gildae*. According to the story he came south as a raider into Arthur's kingdom, making him a contemporary and therefore active somewhere in the two decades on either side of 500.

Drystan son of Tallwch is found in *The Welsh Triads*,[47] *Culhwch ac Olwen*,[48] and an obscure poem in *The Black Book of Carmarthen*.[49] *The Welsh Triads* is the only source that says anything about him though. Triad 26 names him as the only chieftain Arthur ever failed to steal from.

Drystan's short entry gives us two facts to work with. The first is his name and the name of his father. Drystan is a form of Drust. Drust is found all over Britain but most of the time in Pictland. Tallwch is the Welsh version of Pictish Talorcan and is only found in Pictland. More than likely that means that Drystan, too, was Pictish.

The second is the fact that Drystan was a chieftain whom other chieftains tried to raid. Among the Briton and Germanic kingdoms cattle raiding disappeared as soon as larger kingdoms developed and stabilized enough to form empires and make alliances[50]; it just was not practical. If the fifth and sixth century Pictish kingdoms were stable and of a comparable size, they should have stopped cattle raiding as well. That cattle raiding continued in Drystan's time suggests one of two things. Either Drystan lived in a different period than Arthur or the Pictish kingdoms were still not very large or stable in the late fifth and early sixth centuries. But we know that Drystan was active in Arthur's time, he is mentioned with Arthur in the earliest stratum of the triads, meaning Drystan must have lived during the British Heroic Age (late fifth century until about 650).

Medrawt, or Modred, is another northern figure associated with Arthur early on; he appears in the *Annales Cambriae* as well as in three separate triads. The annals record that both men fought at Camlann. And, since warriors are generally ignored there it is safe to assume that Medrawt was a king. His association with Arthur suggests that, like him, he was active between the late fifth and the early sixth century.

Now whether the two were friends or foes is hard to determine; the sources are ambiguous. The worst is *Annales Cambriae*, which says only that they fought at Camlann. The entry could easily be interpreted as the two men fought against each other, but the more natural reading is that they fought on the same side.

The triads are of no help either. Triad 58 says that two of the great ravages of Britain were when Medrawt went to Arthur's court and ate everything and when Arthur returned the favor. Those do not seem like the acts of allies, but then again a king would not normally play host to his enemy either.

Irish Kingdoms

Eochaid Allmuir is only listed in one Dyfed genealogy, the *Expulsion of the Déisi*.[51] Normally, that would make him highly suspect as an historical figure. In this case, however, it is the more believable genealogy; it is the oldest and the only one that does not claim the family was descended from Emperor Maximus' daughter Anna. Maximus, we will remember, was the general who had left for the continent in 383 to claim the emperor's crown in Rome. In 383 Britannia had been relatively stable, still reasonably capable of keeping its enemies at bay. The reasoning for adding Maximus to the lineage is simple, though; he would have given the family prestige because of his heritage. Just as obvious is the reason Eochaid was eliminated; he was the original Irish settler of a dynasty that would claim to be of British origin during the later Middle Ages.

Tradition says that he settled in Britain during the late third century, but a closer examination of the genealogy by Dr. Miller has demonstrated he was active in the early fifth century.[52] Miller's conclusions make better sense with what we know of Roman Britain, too, it included Dyfed until well into the fourth century.

Tradition has it that the Irish were eventually forced out of Dyfed. The *Historia Brittonum* claims Cunedda and his sons accomplished it,[53] and elsewhere Urien and his sons were given credit. However, some detective work by Dr. Miller long ago showed that Clydwyn, who was active in the middle of the fifth century, was the local hero.[54] Instead of beating the Irish back though, Clydwyn's daughter Gwledyr married Aed Brosc, son of Eochaid. It seems that the two dynasties intermarried.

What does that mean for a study of British history? First of all, it shows that there were at least two kingdoms in mid-fifth century Dyfed. Secondly, it suggests that though the Irish dynasty continued thought the fifth century it hid or buried its Irish origins in favor of its native ancestors.

Aed Brosc, son of Corath and grandson of Eochaid Allmuir, was active in the last third of the fifth century. All we know about him comes from the *Vita Carantoci*, which says that he invaded Ceredigion during Carantoc's youth. That little tidbit is valuable information though. Ceredigion and Dyfed have a natural border in the Teifi River; there would have been no reason to invade Ceredigion until Aed was in control of Dyfed. And if he was, then we have a good idea of when Dyfed was first brought under one king.

Taken in conjunction with his father and grandfather a little more can be learned about Dyfed's development in particular and the maturation of kingdoms in general during the fifth century. His grandfather had settled in Dyfed early in the century but only controlled a portion of what would become medieval Dyfed. His father successfully expanded the kingdom, eventually marrying a local princess in order to assimilate a second kingdom. Either Corath or Aed Brosc (son or grandson) managed to conquer the entire area, and only then did Aed attempt a foreign invasion. Within two generations and under ideal conditions, petty chieftainships could have grown into the recognizable kingdoms of the Middle Ages.

Domangart son of Nisse was an independent Irish chieftain or pirate who controlled Kintyre in Dal Riata during the years around 500.[55] Domangart was not the ruler of Dal Riata, but one of many chieftain/pirates operating from the region.[56] Domangart's son Comgall probably only controlled Kintyre too. As has been seen, the shallow waters and innumerable islands in Dal Riata would have made it an ideal spot for that kind of activity.

Several *vitae* tell us about the legendary first ruler of Brycheiniog, Brychan. They also say he was the son of Anlach and the grandson of Coronac (possibly Cormac), an Irish king, which by Celtic law would have made him a prince. British genealogies claim he was the father of dozens of sons and daughters, which makes it hard to believe any of them were his children. Only Rhain Dremrud and Glwadys were connected to the same area and are mentioned independently of him. Using them as reference points Brychan would be a figure of the late fifth century; but those are uncertain points of reference. What we can be sure of is that the Irish had been mainly driven out of Britain by 500. It is safe to assume that Brychan had established the kingdom by then and either he or a successor had assimilated it into British culture. From the *Vita Cadoci* we also know that the capital of Brycheiniog was Talgarth.

Conclusions

Separating the earliest kings by culture and then ordering them by chronology has shown us several useful aspects of post–Roman kingship. The earliest kings came from the non–Roman areas of Britain, areas that had kings before the Romans left like the Picts, or that may have been developing them in the Late Roman era like Strathclyde and Lothian. These were followed by the Irish colonists who were already settling the western coast in the early fifth century. The Britons themselves established chieftainships during the late-fifth century, likely as a response to the Irish settlements in the West and Germanic expansion from the East. Germanic kingships, as we will see below began in the middle of the sixth century.

The above study has been useful from the perspective of size as well. Most of the British and Irish chieftains discussed above have left no evidence of their kingdom's size. Those who did, though, seem to have ruled over very small areas. For instance, Coel is remembered as a great king in Welsh history, but only the territory of Kintyre is named after him. The early kingdom of Gwynedd began as one of at least two kingdoms on Anglesey and only managed to conquer the whole island around 500. Together, all the above evidence suggests that the earliest kingdoms were very small—maybe a hall and all the villages within sight at first.

The exception to this rule seems to have been the kingdoms that were already in existence or developing before Rome left—the Picts and the north British regions. Regardless of size, though, all the kingdoms of early post-Roman Britain seem to have been more interested in simple raids than conquests. In the context of the heroic age and as a political tool this makes perfect sense. Raiding made for good stories and praise poetry, which could be used to spread a king's reputation. It was also not decisive; if a king failed to make a successful raid he had not lost a battle. He probably had not lost any men. On the other hand, a king who was regularly the victim of raids and had a hard time making them himself would lose his reputation and the confidence of his villages.

The size of the original petty kingdoms would grow in time. Poor raiding, a chieftain's death without heirs, or even the rare loss in a battle would weaken many kingships enough to be absorbed by their more competitive neighbors. Other kingdoms would grow through military successes, good harvests, and access to natural resources, assimilating those regions that were less fortunate along the way. Wise rulers would add individual villages to their kingdoms at opportune times. By as early as 520, the surviving kingdoms all over Britain were already developing into the sizes they would become during the medieval period.

Power does not equate to fame, however. While Urien's rise to control all of Reged is an extant historical record, his accomplishments are the result of Taliesin's work. Not all widespread conquerors had the good fortune of having Taliesin on their payroll. The man who consolidated all of Kent remains obscured by time, as are the historical activities of Æthelberht before 597, the Pictish and Germanic leaders of 367, and most of the wealthy kings of Tintagel during the late fifth and early sixth centuries.

Gwrtheyrn was likely the most powerful person in southern England during most of his floruit in the middle of the sixth century, and yet many modern scholars still place him in the wrong century. Further, he was blamed for the Anglo-Saxons presence in England because of a misunderstanding of *De Excidio Britanniae*'s manuscript history and a misinterpretation about one of his more obscure titles. This confusion was undoubtedly helped along by the fortune of Gwrtheyrn's name among his descendants. The political motivations of Kent made use of both strokes of luck to give themselves validation for their land and their presence in Britain. Gwrtheyrn was not a victim, however; he courted his own disaster. If he had hired a bard of Taliesin's caliber, the ravages of time and the machinations of the Germanic kingdoms would have had no effect on how his activities came down to us.[57] From *Historia Brittonum* on he would have been known as one of the most powerful and crafty kings of British history instead of as the fool who lost Britain for the Britons.

15

The Germanic-Controlled Territories

As has been seen in the previous chapter, the early post–Roman kingships were much smaller than they would be in the later Middle Ages. The Pictish confederacy fractured within a few decades of Rome's withdrawal and its former members apparently fell to infighting and simple raids. The Irish set up colonies around the same time. The Germanic raiders continued to attack settlements and shipping. The Britons and Germanic *foederati* maintained their Roman existence for as long as they could.

The raid of 441—the event that caused continental communications to temporarily shut down, and that Gildas writing decades later remembered as cataclysm—changed the political landscape of Britain. Once the *foederati* had attacked their employers and taken whatever food and supplies they could, it was impossible to return to their former arrangement. They had taken matters into their own hands and in the process changed their relationship from employees of a culture they respected to masters over the local villages.

As has been suggested above, once the provincial Roman government had broken down only the villages that were directly protected by the *foederati*, their neighbors, would have had any reason to continue giving them food and supplies.

Reasonably, and following Professor Arnold's evidence, the Germanic groups divided themselves into clans and assumed control over as many nearby villages as they needed to support themselves.[1] A family, occasionally two, took a leadership position in each village so that they could directly ensure that they were given what they needed; the beginnings of Manorialism.

Keeping the shipping lanes clear had been a Roman concern, but the Empire was no longer involved with the island. And, as everything the Germanic groups needed was now locally produced, they would have had little

15. The Germanic-Controlled Territories

reason to continue guarding the English Channel. They would have had little reason to maintain any contact with the continent.

Their only concern was in protecting their new possessions, the villages full of farmers and craftsmen who provided everything they needed. And the only groups that threatened them were the Germanic tribes who hadn't been *foederati* and were still roaming the English Channel pirating and raiding as opportunity arose.

The changed situation put the raiders at a disadvantage against their cousins. They would have had greater numbers—at least fifteen against a handful of defenders, but the former *foederati* only had to protect one place and they would have known the terrain better than the attackers. The raiders would also have had few supplies, little food, and no safe base from which to conduct raids.

Those adventurous war parties that traveled further west, though, eventually came across British villages that were not occupied by their cousins. They would have been easy targets, and eventually easy conquests that provided them and their families with enough tribute to live comfortably.

Britain must have seemed like an attractive place for migration during the mid-fifth century. On the continent, the various tribes were scrambling to get away from Attila and his Huns as they pillaged and killed Germanic and Roman alike. He died in 453, but we know that the migration of peoples and the uncertainty of life in general continued until the final collapse of the Western Roman Empire and the subsequent occupation of its territories. It was only then, in the last years of the fifth century that the continent would stabilize and Germanic migrations into Britain would finally stop.

Life in Britain seems to have been different once the tribes were settled; there is no sign of serious warfare in the early Germanic-occupied villages. This led Professor Arnold to suggest a matriarchal society might have existed. Considering the suddenness of the proposed change, though, that seems a little unlikely.

A middle ground is more probable. We know that cattle raiding was prevalent. There is also no evidence of starvation among these villages but a continuing presence of weapons and armor in the gravesites. Leadership may have been informal, with cattle raiding used as an acceptable way of bleeding off unwanted male aggression in the family. In imagining a fifth-century cattle raid, we should picture a very brutal form of American football or rugby. Deaths and severe injuries must have occurred but could not have been the norm.

Whether the Germanic rulers operated in a matriarchal government, a monarchy, or an oligarchy is unknown; their *skops* or the bards of their culture have left none of their work from this period and the archeology is ambiguous. We cannot deduce anything from the lack of evidence either. The *skop*'s work might not have survived for over a hundred years in an oral environment, it might not have been recorded by the first Christian monks because it was pagan, or maybe *skops* did not exist without kings and the Germanic tribes had none. Fortunately, how they ruled themselves is not all that important in this era.

What is important is that the Germanic peoples ruled themselves; they controlled and protected nearby British villages in return for food and supplies. It is also important to understand that each family was at a disadvantage—strategically, economically, and numerically—against the British kingdoms at this stage of their development.

Toward the end of the fifth century, Germanic wanderers would have run into British kingdoms, effectively ending the migration period.

16

Growing Pains of British Kingship

British kingship seems to have been a reaction to Germanic migration and settlement—the timing is right and the motivation makes sense. The historical fact is that the British had developed primitive kingships by the end of the century. If they had not, they might have all been speaking Anglo-Saxon in another hundred years.

There was much more to Celtic kingship than just military leadership and living in a hall. A king not only had to be a good warrior and leader, he had to come from a long line of strong kings, which is why lineages often consisted of famous heroes of the area, along with actual ancestors of a dynasty. The Irish law texts say he had to make consistently correct judgments in legal matters for his people. He could never turn his back in battle.[1] He could not lie or tolerate bardic satire.[2] His body could have no blemishes.

Kings had to be all these things because of their connections to the supernatural. A Celtic king did not just rule his kingdom; during his inauguration he literally married the land in the form of a woman,[3] and legend had it that for the rest of his reign she would reflect his rule by her appearance. He married a young and beautiful woman because he had demonstrated to his clan and the people that he was the best candidate for the position. As long as he behaved like a king she would remain youthful and attractive, but if he ever lost his kingly virtue she would become an old hag until he was replaced with a worthy king.

This connection to the land as symbolized by a woman gave the king an authority beyond the question of normal humans, putting their kingship and by extension their clan as far superior beings in the eyes of peasants. When Celtic kingship developed, though, it had taken time to germinate. Bards had gradually added people and stories, of actual ancestors and adopted ones, to each kingdom's official history along the way. The mystical elements probably developed after dynasties were long established. As Vansina has demonstrated, anything beyond living memory can be easily changed and rechanged as local politics and events occur.[4]

The Britons of the post-Roman era did not have the luxury of time as they reestablished their original culture, though. The Germanic tribes began migrating onto and controlling villages from around 441. The result was that the British kingships that did emerge did not have the solid foundations necessary. It would not have mattered how good their bards were at creating impressive genealogies and personal histories for their first generation kings or reinvigorating the mystique behind kingship. The simple fact was that in the late fifth century people still remembered a time without kings.

And because kingship was such a new establishment for the Romano-Britons, fifth-century kingships would have been based almost solely on the personal chemistry between the chieftain and his men. When he died, or even when he lost too many battles, that chemistry could dissolve and any person who was able to generate a new bond might succeed him. A son, brother, or cousin might have succeeded him but that was only one of several possibilities. A nearby king might absorb the *teulu* or a former champion might assert himself. It may never be possible to list all the petty chieftainships that arose in the late fifth century, or the ways in which most of them disappeared from history.

On the other hand, the fact that none of the early kingships were stable is probably one of the main reasons why the early British kingdoms grew so quickly; without a strong tradition there would have been no kingdom identity among villages and therefore no resistance to changing kings. The unique situation of the fifth century would have allowed a ruler to simply absorb a chieftainless *teulu* just as easily as a victorious king could absorb his dead enemy's villages.

17

The New Economic System

As we have seen, the Roman Empire's administration had been exemplary—a stable bureaucracy that possessed an intelligent set of checks and balances which adjusted over time and changing circumstances. Far-sighted lawmakers had adapted the government so that it could integrate new provinces and cultures. By 400, every local government from Britain to India had a variation of the Roman model.

Through foreign and domestic wars, its income had also been stable. Taxes had been individually assessed based on personal holdings and then collected in the form of coins. Tradition had made the wealthy elite responsible for local administration, as well as local project funding—forums, baths, public buildings, and roads had all been a part of their normal responsibility.

At the provincial level, money had been used to pay for the hospices along the highways that were used by official travelers as well as craftsmen, artists, and traders. Reserves were left alone in case of emergency. The empire paid the military and the officials who had been publically educated, but the senators came from wealthy families and had been given nothing for their public service by tradition.

Then Constantine had displaced the Roman governor and his bureaucracy and installed his own. When the Romano-British citizens revolted and overthrew Constantine's government, the provincial government collapsed. Severing the connection with Rome meant no more income, no military support, and only limited contact with the empire. Dismantling the provincial government meant no local military or political order.

The local governments had remained intact and functioning through all that. However, throughout the last half-century of Roman rule the wealthy had been either immigrating to the continent or their country villas in Britannia where they had stopped performing public service. By 410, most of them were no longer contributing their resources to the villages and towns.

The departure of the wealthy from public life was just as catastrophic as the loss of provincial government. The wealthy had maintained local buildings and roads throughout Britain. Without them, all of these things fell into disrepair. Their business relations had kept them connected to other settlements and to the greater empire. Without them, villages were suddenly isolated.

As we have seen, the core of Roman civilization was education. Teaching a single language and mythology united the upper class in a common culture that spanned across the empire while educating the most talented among the poor at the public's expense and then pushing them toward government positions had ensured a high level of competency at all levels of government. It had also made government employees unusually loyal to Rome.

However, the *grammatici* and the *rhetorici* that had done the teaching had been funded by the education of the rich, so without them the teachers would have had no patrons in Britain. Probably, some of them remained behind and found work where they could (Gildas' education is proof of that), but those who insisted on their traditional income were forced to leave for the continent.

Along with the political changes came economic adaptations. Coins had been coming to Britain for centuries as pay to government officials and soldiers. They had then spent their money on the island and dispersed the new money. But as of 410 Britain was no longer part of the empire and received no more shipments of coin.

Judging by the wear of later Roman coins, money was used for a long time after the last shipments—we think it was still in circulation until maybe 430 or 440. They were used until no one could read them any more. After that, the Britons drifted into a bartering system as it was practiced among the Irish and had been among the pre-Roman British—with a female slave, a milk-producing cow, and an ounce of silver as equal standards of exchange.[1] Bartering meant that trade would be more limited from that point on; artwork, specialists, and weapons were still easily transportable, but cattle were the most convenient unit of exchange and they were more difficult.

For centuries Britannia had been protected by the Roman military, but the military had been paid by Roman coins and those were no longer free flowing after about 407, which means that whatever official military forces Constantine had left behind had probably dispersed long before 420.

During the last few decades of Roman Britain, the *foederati* had been protecting the eastern and southern coast from pirating and raids. They had been paid by food and supplies as well as coins, and probably by more and more trade items after 407. As we have seen, even these protectors would eventually revolt and conquer the very lands they had been protecting. That would leave the Britons on their own to protect themselves with homemade spears, bows designed and used for hunting, and any sharp household objects they could find.

The new economic system was local in the extreme—with a bartering system in place, it had to be. It also ensured that the social, military, and even political aspects of post–Roman Britain were also local. Public buildings and roads crumbled from lack of maintenance. Local governments went from a well-educated bureaucracy to an informal group of town elders. The effect was as significant to them as the sudden loss of internet would be to us in the modern world.

18

Arthur

The author has elsewhere given a point-by-point rebuttal of Professor Dumville's and Professor Padel's papers arguing Arthur's non-existence.[1] They can be summed up as follows: The sources for the period are not impossible to make use of, they just require a strong understanding of the materials used in their creation, and of the biases of all the authors involved, a lot of research into what has been discovered, and a strict adherence to those findings.

Of course Arthur is not mentioned much, and of course where he is mentioned he is often connected to the supernatural—he lived in an heroic age period where oral literature dominated. As anyone who studies oral literature can tell you, stories in an oral-tradition society change, much like the message in a game of telephone. Even two generations can make a huge difference. Urien was remembered in oral literature too, but since he lived just a little later his legend did not grow as much as Arthur's.

Arthur bears no reasonable comparison to Fion macCumhail—none! Not by his activities, the linguistics, or his introduction into the historical sources. Despite the contrary claims, the earliest sources—*Y Gododdin* and the *Northern Memorandum* as found in the *Historia Brittonum* and *Annales Cambriae*—all name Arthur in an historical context.[2] Adjusting for the known biases, all the historical and even literary sources are consistent in where and when they place Arthur. He lived right around 500 in the Carlisle/Old Carlisle region.

To this the question: "If he is a northern historical figure why is he not listed in the 'Men of the North' genealogy?" Simply put, the genealogy was a political tool; it deepened the alliance of British kings by giving them a common ancestor. By that time, neither Arthur nor his descendants were active so there was no reason to insert him.

Speaking of historical sources, the *Historia Brittonum* says that Arthur was present at twelve battles, while *Annales Cambriae* confirms his presence at Badon and adds Camlann. Both sources took their Arthurian information from the *Northern Memorandum*, whose information might extend back to the late sixth century with Rhun son of Urien, even if the writing in its present form only goes back to around 750.³ All this has made those thirteen battles a hot topic for Arthurian enthusiasts hoping to prove Arthur's existence.⁴ No theory has ever gained much traction though. It may not even be possible to place all the battles in one area. Battle lists are notorious for being composites of participants and regions. The Arthurian battles have two problems on top of that. The *Historia Brittonum* battles are twelve in number and are located at nine sites; both numbers were symbolically important for the Celts. There are also indications of rhyme in the list that suggests the author found it in a poem that included the battles of several kings.⁵

To make a comparison, pretend for a moment that we live in a society with a tradition of oral history. Now accept that MacArthur and Rommel were the two best generals of World War II. In a battle list drawn up a hundred years from now we might find that they had fought each other on D-Day, at the Battle of the Bulge, El Alamein, Midway, and the Philippines, despite the fact that neither man was at several of those battles and that they never met on the battlefield. With that in mind, the only battles with any historical value are Camlann and possibly Badon.⁶

When did Arthur live? By mid-century, every known British king is consistently placed in one kingdom and most of them are associated with contemporaries. Arthur is connected with no one site and his associations are with kings and saints from all over Britain. Some scholars have believed this makes him less historical, but as has been seen in the pages above the fifth century was a period of transition between Roman and British cultures. The first British bards we know of were active no earlier than about 470, so naturally the first generation or so of rulers they spoke of would be a little shrouded in legend. For these reasons and several more, Arthur was probably active somewhere between roughly 480 and 520.⁷

Where did he live? Old Carlisle seems the most likely guess. It would explain his predilection with things Roman in *Historia Brittonum* and would fit roughly in the center of the geographical area from which Arthurian figures seem to come from. Oddly enough, when the author listed all the sites associated with Arthur's hall in the literature and history and eliminated every entry that was used for a clear literary, political, or personal reason, Carlisle was far and away the most commonly named location.⁸ We also know that Old Carlisle was a consistently occupied city during the period in question.⁹

Old Carlisle may also have been the command quarters for Hadrian's Wall. In an era when the Roman Empire was tearing itself apart that may not mean anything. However, according to the archeological record the years around 500 were when several former Hadrian's Wall forts were reoccupied. That is stranger because Roman forts throughout the rest of the island were vacant.

What it has suggested to Professor Dark, Koch, and the author is that some powerful force (a single king or alliance) might have controlled the entire area and initiated the reoccupation.[10] If that force was Arthur, it would help to explain why he was remembered more vividly than any other king of the period; it would have made him the leading person on the island in a very real way.

Politically, he would have taken tribute from more people than any other person on the island.[11] Holding an entire east-west stretch of land might have allowed him to limit communications between the North and the South. Actually, he might have been able to limit the movement of traders, bards, and craftsman to and from the North. Hadrian's Wall would have also given him a psychological edge. Old Carlisle had been a Roman fort, and Hadrian's Wall a Roman system of fortresses. Reoccupying them would have helped him claim a little more of Rome's lingering mystique.

A reoccupation of Hadrian's Wall could also have served a military purpose. During the Roman occupation, it had served as a blockade against the Picts, a bulwark against the constant attacks on the British people. In the hands of a Briton, Hadrian's Wall might have been used to give the British people a sense of unity. In previous centuries it has been argued that they could have come together against the Germanic peoples who had already settled a good portion of eastern England, but it could equally have served against the Picts or the Irish.

Which raises another question: who were Arthur's enemies? According to Gildas, the Battle of Mount Badon was fought between British and Germanic tribes, and the principles may have been exactly that. We cannot believe that the lines were that simple, though. As has been seen above, several Irish dynasties would eventually intermarry with local kingships in Wales. It has long been noted that Cerdic, traditional founder of the Wessex dynasty, has a British name.[12] The court-list in *Culhwch ac Olwen* contains several Anglo-Saxon figures who were roughly contemporary with Arthur.[13] As we shall see below, the most famous poem of the period, *Y Gododdin*, is about two mostly British armies fighting each other, both with several Anglo-Saxons. The Mercian king Penda was allied with British Gwynedd for most of his career. Arthur may very well have fought against the Irish, Picts, and Anglo-Saxons during his kingship. Just as likely, Arthur may have had an Irishman, a Pict, and an Anglo-Saxon in his personal war-band.

With that in mind, it is not really important what culture his enemies were a part of. Nor does it matter what language his neighbors spoke; he would have been just as willing to make raids on Anglo-Saxons, Picts, and Irish just as he would have on Britons. He would have been just as likely to ally with another culture group, too. We must always keep in mind that Arthur did not live in an environment where fighting was based on national

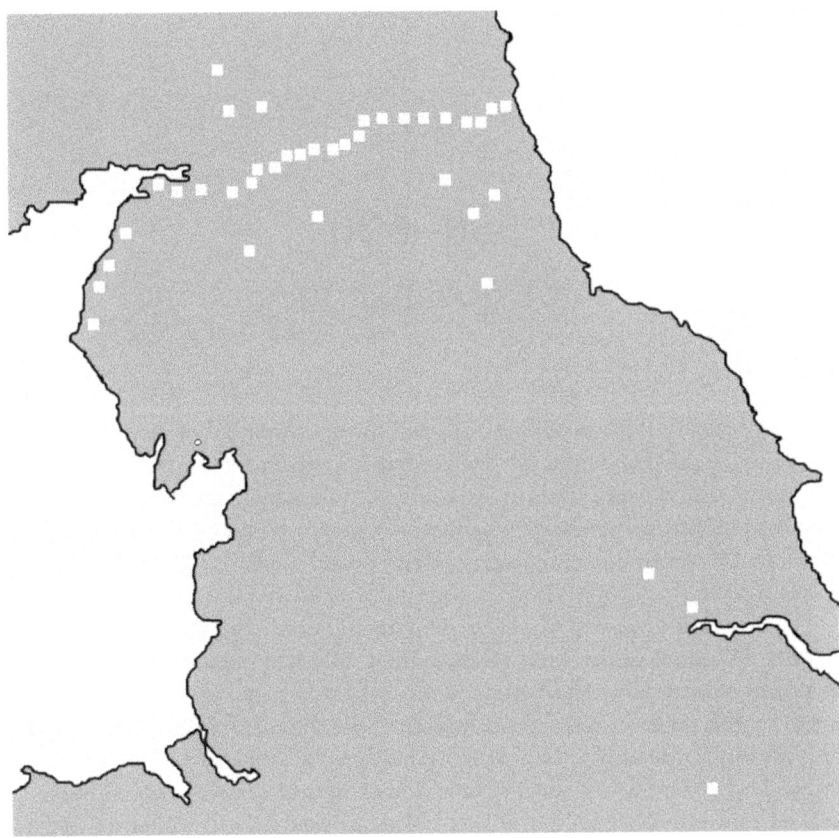

Roman fort revival around 500.

identity.[14] None of the kings from this period—Urien, Maelgwn, Rhun, Gwrtheyrn, or the mysterious king of Gododdin did. There was no need in Arthur's time, because the Germanic people were not a threat. Arthur spent his career working to enhance his fame, wealth, and the number of warriors in his war band.

19

530–600
An Expanding View

After the initial rise of kingships and the development of more powerful kingdoms in the first half of the sixth century, it was inevitable that the British kingdoms would begin to think on a larger scale; a small kingdom is only be concerned about its immediate neighbors because he is only likely to be attacked by them. However, once it has expanded beyond a handful of villages larger issues come into play—trade, alliances, and control of waterways for instance.

The first indications of a larger playing field centered around Gwynedd, the one kingdom of the early sixth century that had been able to maintain its power consistently; it had retained the same ruling dynasty through several kings as well. At some time in the middle of the sixth century, one of its more famous kings, Maelgwn, died. Hoping to tap into some of Gwynedd's reputation and power, a Gwrwst Priodor (kingdom unknown) made an unsuccessful raid into Gwynedd and was killed. In retaliation an alliance of five northern kings—Rhydderch, Clydno Eidyn, Mordaf, Nudd Hael, and Elidyr Mwynfar representing Strathclyde, a Gododdin kingdom, and three unspecified kingdoms invaded Gwynedd. They were beaten back by Rhun, who then collected his own army and marched north.

The campaigns themselves are of little note. As far as we know no kingdoms were conquered and no territories were won or lost because of them. What is interesting is that Rhun's Gwynedd was matched by an alliance of kings. This was probably the first British alliance since the Picts.

The next example of the Britons' expanding awareness is found in the *Historia Brittonum*, which claims that Urien was the head of a powerful alliance in northern Britain that included Rhydderch, Morgant of Gododdin, and Gwallog of Elmet. It was interested in more than revenge, too. The Taliesin poems and the *Historia Brittonum* say it fought against the Germanic peoples, and *Historia Brittonum* even says they beat the invaders back to Lindesfarne before the coalition broke up.

The poem *Y Gododdin* makes a similar claim; a confederacy against the Germanic peoples. This alliance was led by Gododdin and included kings from Cornwall in the south to Pictland in the North as well as Elmet, at least one Germanic chieftain, and the Gododdin king himself. This joint army was solely interested in beating back the Germanic peoples. It met with them at the battle of Catraeth but was annihilated.

Both the Urien and the Gododdin alliance in isolation are two more examples of just the sort of wider political awareness that was mentioned at the beginning of this chapter. However, recent scholarship has suggested that they may not have come together against just the Germanic peoples. As Professor John T. Koch pointed out, one of the Taliesin poems claims that Urien won a major battle at Catterick (the most widely accepted site for the Battle of Catraeth).

There is more to the theory than that of course. As we have seen above, Rhydderch had already been involved in an alliance against another British king. The Taliesin poems are very clear that Urien spent the early part of his career fighting Britons. Koch has noted evidence in *Y Gododdin* that the chief enemy might not have been Germanic—that the Germanic warriors who were involved were serving a British king.[1]

Added to the above evidence are the parallel members of each alliance. The Morgan who was Urien's ally may well have been a king in Gododdin ruling from Din Peledyr. The leader of the Gododdin alliance hailed from Din Eidyn. Gwallog son of Lleenog was the ruler of Elmet, but *Y Gododdin* names a Madawg Elmet in the Gododdin alliance.[2] From what we know of epithets (Maelgwn Gwynedd and Urien Reged), he was probably a part of the Elmet ruling family and therefore Gwallog's rival. Catraeth was a clash of major British kingdoms. It was not fought simply for prestige or the theft of cattle; the participants seem to have had multiple reasons for participating.

This alliance represents another advance in British politics. It would have been impossible in an era where kings only ruled the area that could be seen from their hall and was impractical until the British kings had built larger kingdoms.

The last major alliances under discussion here show up at the Battle of Arfderydd. According to the *Annales Cambriae*, it was fought in 573. Though the *Welsh Triads* confirm the battle did happen, we have seen above that this event was probably not recorded within living memory the date might not be too accurate. Tapping various earlier sources we learn that Dunawd, Cadrod, Cynfelyn, Dingad, Dreon, Rhydderch, Peredur, Gwrgi, and Gwenddoleu (all northern rulers apart from Dingad and Dreon of "Powys") were present and an alliance of Rhydderch, Dunawd, Cynfelyn, Peredur, and Gwrgi opposed Gwenddoleu. This, again, is two opposing alliances dominated by Britons.

Which brings us to Gwrtheyrn. As far as historical interactions and genealogy are concerned, he was a king of the early to middle sixth century.[3] Given the developing size of kingdoms during the period and the suggestive name of the Gwrtheyrnion region in modern southern Powys, Gwrtheyrnion might have been Gwrtheyrn's original kingdom. The other possibility is that he was active in roughly the modern country of Gloucester, where his official ancestor Gloiu had once been the eponymous ruler of Gloucester.

Most scholars have seen the *Kentish Source* as found in Bede and *The Anglo-Saxon Chronicle* as using Vortigern in order to legitimize the presence of the Germanic people in Britain.[4] This goes without saying; without him Kent had no legitimate reason for migrating and no legal acquisition of Kent. But how powerful was the historical Gwrtheyrn? Maybe, just maybe, he was southern counterpart to one of the northern alliances. No other southern king seems to have interested later historians as much.

The above has mentioned several northern British alliances, a powerful Gwynedd king, and a possible over-king in southern England all of whom were expanding their kingdoms, but nothing about Cornwall and Devon. We can guess that the same sort of thing was happening there. We even have a little evidence; scattered information in the *vitae* and local legends tell us that a Theodoric and Cunomorus were powerful kings. There are no "historical" sources, though, and there is too little of the oral traditions to make any real sense out of beyond a rough chronology.[5] Other regions that were already conquered by 650, like western England, may well have had over-kings as well that we know nothing about.

The expanded geography of kingdoms also meant exposure to larger rivals and the inception of more pitched battles. In the author's *Hengest, Gwrtheyrn, and the Chronology of Post-Roman Britain* it was proposed that the events of Rhun's campaign north, the Battle of Arfderydd, and the Battle of Catraeth occurred in that order. Though there is no way of knowing the politics or even exactly who the participants were in the latter two events, two conclusions can be drawn. First, that they can all be safely placed in the last two-thirds of the sixth century. Second, that they are the first events that affected a large region of Britain. As such they deserve a little closer scrutiny.

20

Rhun Son of Maelgwn

In the previous chapter the raid on Rhun son of Maelgwn's kingdom, and his retaliation, was mentioned. The author has previously placed that invasion in the thirty year range of 543–572, because of the participants, their other activities, and the people they were related to.[1] So how does that fit into the development of British kingdoms in the sixth century? We have already seen the overall picture: kingdoms were getting bigger and their kings were thinking bigger.

But there is more to it than that. Admittedly, we do not know where all the raiding kings were from, but we do know that a ruler in Strathclyde and another from Lothian came down to northwestern Wales; we know that at least two kings passed through several kingdoms or took very long boat rides to get to Gwynedd.[2] We also know that Rhun responded with his own campaign north.

In the era of Arthur, only decades earlier, kings had made their names by raiding nearby kingdoms and stealing cattle. Their reputations had depended on their ability to steal others' livestock and to protect their own. Leaving their kingdoms alone for the days it took to make a raid on a nearby kingdom would have been risky—perhaps downright suicidal. That is, until Rhun's era.

So what changed between the last decades of the fifth century and the middle of the sixth century that made these raids possible? To begin with, it seems likely that the British kingdoms had reached or were reaching their natural limits, given the circumstances. This does not mean that the kingdoms had all expanded until their borders were major rivers or mountains. In some cases that was doubtless true; for instance, Gwynedd and Stratclyde had the Irish Sea on their west. In this case, though, economics and military practicalities were also involved; think of a kingdom as being only as large as each ruler could protect and keep under their control given the conditions of the time—horse transportation, limited communications and mobility.

Just as important were the traditions of kingship and tribute-giving.

Kings may have needed to keep personal connections with every village under their protection. That meant a limit to how many settlements they could keep.

The time they were living through was even more important. As we have seen, communications had broken down at the end of Roman Britain and were only slowly mending. The rise of kingdoms was helping villages to become more interconnected, but it would have been a slow process. Even in the later Middle Ages travel was limited.

But why wouldn't a king demand tribute from villages he had no intentions of protecting? For a ruthless modern warlord that might be a good short-term solution, but among the Celts that sort of fraud would not have been in their best interests. As has been seen, to collect tribute would be to claim the area as a part of the kingdom, and if a king was unable to protect his lands he was an ineffective ruler. Among the Celts through the Early Medieval period, an ineffective king could, by tradition and Celtic law, be replaced.

So, what could kings do in the middle sixth century when they realized they could not expand their kingdoms any further but wanted more power? They could get involved with alliances. In the example of Rhun, an alliance served to help each king punish the more powerful sovereign Rhun. An alliance might have provided a deterrent against an otherwise more powerful king. An alliance might enable a king to pass through other kingdoms on his way down to, say, Gwynedd without fear of his own kingdom being attacked. An alliance might also provide trade options and connections to other kingdoms. In short, alliances would have expanded each kingdom's awareness on the island as they became familiar with their allies' connections.

The second lesson to take away from the episode between Rhun and the northern allies is the strength of Gwynedd. Five allies made a raid on Gwynedd but Rhun alone took his warriors on campaign up North. The results of that campaign are unimportant.[3] What is essential to understand is that the kingdom was strong enough that Rhun believed he had a reasonable chance of taking retribution on all of the allies and returning home alive. Somehow, the geography of Gwynedd was such that it could support more warriors, or was better organized, or had a better fighting reputation than all five of the northern kingdoms put together.

Professor Charles-Edwards has proposed the intriguing suggestion that the Gwynedd of about 500 may have formed some sort of alliance with the newly powerful Irish Feni in order to gain a reprieve from Irish raids. It is even possible that the Gwynedd dynasty might have been Irish[4]; if it was that might explain the extraordinary lengths to which the dynasty went to portray itself as a native dynasty whose first act was to push the Irish out of Gwynedd.[5] It might also explain the bogus claim that it was descended from Romans and a Gododdin chidftain.⁶ Practically speaking, the alliance might have given Gwynedd a distinct advantage for many decades. It might have been the reason behind Rhun's overconfidence in his army.

The raid on Rhun's kingdom and his retaliatory campaign up North are two unique events in Early Medieval British history. Studying them gives the historian a snapshot of what the middle sixth century looked like by providing us with many clues about the state of development among the British kingdoms.

As discussed in the introduction, most historians still believe post-Roman Britain was based on the divisions Rome had imposed, which had in turn been based on pre-Roman tribes. What we see here is that this was not always the case. Britain was fractured in 410. Only a century and a half later were its kings capable of thinking and operating much beyond their own borders. Even the northern kingdoms, which had been freed of Rome soonest and allowed to develop the longest, were not immune.

21

Battle of Arfderyð

Through the entire fifth and sixth century, very few battles are listed in the *Annales Cambriae*. There are of course the "Arthurian" battles of Badon and Camlann, but even if we can believe that they took place there is no way to corroborate that they happened in 516/7 and 537/8, respectively; they could be dated wrong by decades.[1] The first event we can be confident of is the Battle of Arfderydd. It is listed at 573 in the *Annales Cambriae*, along with the notice that Gwenddoleu died there. Even that late, we cannot trust it completely though, three decades later it misdates the Battle of Chester by at least a decade.

The annals also fail us in not giving any real context for the battle. As we will see below Peredur and Gwrgi were present at the battle and died in an unknown battle in 580. Another participant was Dunawt son of Pabo and the annals give his death at 595, but in both instances we are given nothing else, no useful information. To gain a better understanding of what was happening in the sixth-century North, we must explore the smattering of information to be found in several less traditional sources.[2]

Vita Kentigerni

The *Life of Kentigern* only mentions Arfderydd in passing. In one of the later episodes we are told that a half-insane man who had been living in the woods for twenty years was once in the service of Gwenddoleu as a bard. When his king was killed at Arfderydd, this Myrddin lost his mind and ran into the woods. Basically, all this source does is confirm everything in the annal and add the name of a bard. Myrddin might be interesting in his own right (as the literary forefather of the more famous Merlin) but is not much help here.[3]

Trioedd Ynys Prydein

The battle is mentioned in four different places here. None of the triads give a clear picture of the battle itself, but overall they do tell us that Gwenddoleu was on one side and Cynfelyn, Dunawt Fawr, Peredur, and Gwrgi were on the other.[4] Dreon, Dunawt Fawr, and Dinogad are also connected to the battle but their alliances are not given.[5]

The battle is listed in another triad as one of the three futile battles of Welsh legend.[6] However, it is one of the last and least trustworthy sections of the triads.[7] We have already seen with *Y Gododdin* and the *Historia Brittonum* materials that Gwynedd had been interested in developing a sense of unity against the English kingdoms during the ninth century. Could the entry have been influenced by that nationalistic movement? Possibly. One way or the other, though, it does not help us to understand the sixth century any better.

What can we take away from this battle? It was mentioned in several sources early on, which made it impossible for the Gwynedd editors to alter the fact that British kings had fought against British kings. Otherwise it might have suffered the same fate as Catraeth and confused British historians even more.

Dr. Miller did a wonderful job of piecing together a reasonable scheme, but in the end she had to admit that there was no way of being certain about who was on whose side and why.[8] As quickly as things may have changed in the period, the author is not even certain that sort of information would be all that useful even if it were possible.

We can be certain of several broader items, though. For one, we can now add Arfderyö to the short list of battles we know much about in the sixth century—along with Catraeth. Arfderydd seems to be an accepted spot for the battle, too, because the connection is made for us in the *Vita Kentigerni*. We also know that both battles were fought primarily between British kings.

Second, there are the distances involved, which we can see by the participants. Traditionally Gwrgi and Peredur have always been connected with York; in the Welsh Arthurian stories Peredur's father is Efrawc, which is derived from the Latin word for York, *Eburacum*, called *Ebrauc* in the *Historia Brittonum* list of *civitates*.[9]

The connection of Peredur and Gwrgi to late sixth-century York had made no sense up until the last couple of decades because York had been within the borders of Deira, and Deira was traditionally founded decades before Arfderydd or the deaths of Peredur and Gwrgi. However, now that we understand Germanic kingships were only forming in the mid-sixth century and that the British kingdoms were still dominant into the late sixth century, the association makes a little more sense; York had not yet been absorbed into Deira during the brothers' lifetimes. We will see below when and how York ended as a kingdom, but for now this piece of information is mainly useful as a clue about politics in the last third of the century.

Dunawt Fawr has been tentatively connected with modern Dent, also in Yorkshire, because of an allusion in Eddius' *Vita Wilfridi* to *regio Dunotinga* which was given to the church of Ripon in 675.[10] It is tentative because Dunawt was not an uncommon name.[11] However, Dunawt spent his career allied with Gwallog and fighting Owain and Pasgen the sons of Urien,[12] and all three of them were from the same area.

The other names—Gwenddoleu, Dreon, and Dinogad—are people we can only guess generally about. Hector Chadwick and William Skene placed Gwenddoleu's hall a few miles north of Arthuret.[13] Dreon is as yet unidentified, while Dinogad might have been the son of Cynan Garwyn somewhere in Powys.[14]

Even a Dinogad from northeastern Wales makes sense with what we have already learned about the late sixth century. Politics had already advanced well beyond cattle stealing and alliances went beyond standing together against a common enemy.

22

Urien's Alliance and *Y Gododdin*

In chapter 63 of the *Historia Brittonum*, we are introduced to Urien and his exploits in one brief entry.

> Hussa reigned seven years. Against him fought four kings, Urien, and Ryderethen, and Guallauc, and Morcant. Theodoric fought bravely, together with his sons, against that Urien. But at that time sometimes the enemy and sometimes our countrymen were defeated, and he shut them up three days and three nights in the island of Metcaut; and whilst he was on an expedition he was murdered, at the instance [sic] of Morcant, out of envy, because he possessed so much superiority over all the kings in military science.

The author has elsewhere examined what we know about Urien's final campaign and concluded that it happened during the middle third of the sixth century.[1] However, a simpler approach works just as well. As has been seen, the earliest kingships were local in the extreme, with chieftains taking tribute from villages within sight of their own halls and not much further. It was only in the second third of the sixth century that regional British kingships developed. The history of Northumbria is fairly well laid out from 593, when Æthelfrith took the Bernician throne. Within twelve years he had conquered Deira and the other kingdoms of Northumbria, making it unlikely that any alliance of British kings had made him pay tribute. In 605 he threatened Chester, which tells us that there were no northern British kings strong enough to face him.[2] As we will see in the pages below, Northumbria was too strong after that to be seriously threatened for several decades.[3]

But what about the four British kings? The *Historia Brittonum* does not say they were allied, nor does it state outright that Urien was even the most powerful king of the group. It is fairly clear that he meant Urien was the most powerful king and the leader. Urien is named first, Urien bottles up the Germanic army, and Urien's death ends the campaign. One gets the sense that Urien had the same role as Agamemnon in the *Iliad*.

But then we remember the nature of the source, *Historia Brittonum*, a compendium history written in the ninth century to strengthen the legitimacy of the new Gwynedd dynasty, which claimed to be descended from Urien. It was in the author's best interests to represent Urien as the leader of kings because it demonstrated how powerful the dynasty's most famous ancestor had been. His assassination was a stroke of genius; it led to the dissolution of the alliance and a resurgence of the Bernicians.

We must not forget a second theme in the book: when the Rhodri Mawr was having it written he was trying to unite the British kingdoms under his leadership to beat back the English. Urien was supposed to represent him and serve as a lesson; when the British united they were invincible, and when they started bickering amongst themselves the English kings could easily defeat them—as the *Historia Brittonum* demonstrated with the rise of Æthelfrith after Urien was killed. The above examination leaves us only with a confederacy involving four kings whose known members—Urien, Ryderethen (Rhydderch), and Guallauc (Gwallog)—ruled in the North, and Morcant was likely from Gododdin which was also in the North.

Y Gododdin

As has been seen, *Y Gododdin* is a eulogy to a group of warriors who went on a campaign against the Deirans to their south and died at the Battle of Catraeth. At this point, Catraeth is fairly well established as modern Catterick in what would be medieval Northumbria, which means that the participants listed in *Y Gododdin* were attacking the same rough area as Urien and his alliance had.

For the same reasons listed for the Urien alliance, the thinking has gone that the battle was fought after the first third of the sixth century but before 605 by which time Bernicia had conquered Deira and the other kingdoms of Northumbria and was too powerful for the British kings to attack. As far as a sequence of events, most scholars have argued that the Urien alliance was first because it was able to drive the Germanic peoples nearly off the island. At some point after Urien's demise the Gododdin chieftain gathered a confederacy around himself and attacked Deira.

Catraeth

Recently, Professor John T. Koch of Cambridge presented a more efficient theory. As we have seen, *Y Gododdin* had existed in two forms, but both were eventually written down in Gwynedd during the same period that saw the collection of the same materials which were used in *Historia Brittonum*. Koch's study and reconstruction of the *Y Gododdin* poem showed the same Gwynedd interests were in the poem—to extol the virtues of British unity and portray the English as the enemy.[4] He noticed several details in his reconstruction that indicated the enemy's identity had been kept intentionally vague; the Deirans had been at the battle but they might have had British allies.

Going back over the historical Taliesin poems (which he had also done some work on),[5] Koch noted that Catraeth was one of the settlements over which Urien ruled.[6] In itself that was nothing unusual; it made sense that a powerful ruler would have claimed lands well beyond his central territories. However, all of a ruler's claimed territories would not be listed in praise poems, only his significant holdings. And what would make a settlement more important than if a decisive battle had been won near it?[7]

The theory Koch laid out amounted to this; Urien and his allies—from Strathclyde, Elmet, and probably Lothian—were either allied with the Germanic peoples in the area or ruled over them. The Gododdin king, seeking a balance of power in the North, collected a large group of like-minded kings and Anglo-Saxon leaders,[8] and marched against Urien and the other kings around the Catraeth region. The campaign was a disaster, but the bravery of the men involved lived on in the poem *Y Gododdin*. Later Gwynedd, capitalizing on the extant literature from both sides, used the Urien alliance's success to support their hopes for a united British people and the Gododdin's failure as an epitaph for the brave warriors who had fallen against the Germanic invaders.

Historically of course that did not happen, nor did the *Historia Brittonum*'s account that Urien and the other kings beat back the Northumbrian kings in a cultural war. All we can really be certain of is that Urien's coalition won the battle of Catraeth, controlled a large part of Northumbria as a result, and that at least some of their opponents were Germanic. When Urien's alliance broke up that control fizzled. It would be the last time the Britons would have the upper hand against the Germanic peoples for decades.

23

Gwrtheyrn

Four chapters ago Gwrtheyrn was briefly mentioned as an example of evolving British kingship during the sixth century. Eleven chapters before that, his development as a literary character was examined as a part of the *Kentish Source*'s development. To understand his career better, it will be simplest to focus on his progression as a character in British history and then critically examine that against what we have already learned.

Gwrtheyrn first appears in Gildas as *superbus tyrannus*—"Overking."[1] There he is credited with inviting the first Germanic tribes over to Britain. In the Late Roman tradition, he settled them in the troubled areas of the island and promised to feed and house them in return for their services as mercenaries against the Picts and their fellow Germanic tribesmen.

This story is all wrong, though. As we have seen, there is no evidence that a single king controlled Britain during the fifth century. In fact, from the breakdown of Roman provincial government to the settlements of the Irish, the known activities of the fifth century kings, and the sixth century alliances demonstrates a consistent trend of emerging and developing kingships beginning in the late fifth century. As we will see, these kingdoms continued to increase in size and complexity until they became the medieval kingdoms that would remain in place for most of the Middle Ages.

We have also seen that the Romans had been bringing Germanic tribes as *foederati* to Britain from the fourth century; they were already on the island when Gildas had his *superbus tyrannus* inviting them in the fifth century. Realizing that, we can see why Gildas had to include an over-king in his history; he needed one to explain why the Germanic peoples were on the island.[2]

Knowing what we know now we can empathize with Gildas. He saw the Romans as the instruments of God's forgiveness and because of that could not imagine them ever making the mistake of bringing the Germanic peoples to the island. What made more sense to him was that a Briton king had been at fault, someone who must have ruled Britain so that he had the necessary power.³ That was why he placed the introduction of the *foederati* after Aetius,⁴ that and a probably weak oral memory of the time between Aetius and Badon.

Following him was Bede, a man who was no fool by his exquisite Latin and careful scholarship. He was locked into the story though. By the time he wrote two hundred years later, Gildas was already remembered as a great scholar and his history as the history of post–Roman Britain.

Even if he had been willing to challenge Gildas, his ecclesiastical superiors had given him the *Kentish Source* as the official history and it confirmed everything Gildas had written. Bede really had no other choice but to write the story he had in front of him. We know he expanded the Gildasian history, probably using the *Kentish Source*, adding the names of the two Germanic chieftains, Hengest and Horsa, and along with a brief biography. Because we know that he was so strongly Northumbrian, it was probably he who had added a snippet about two additional chieftains who fought in the north but were related to Hengest. His contribution to the history strengthened Northumbria's claim to power in his century by connecting the kingdom's earliest leaders with the famous the man who had outwitted the British overking and legally been given possession of Kent.⁵

When the *Historia Brittonum* was originally written during the ninth century, most of that story was probably ignored. After all, it was written in Powys by the son-in-law of the Powysian king, and Rhodri had the history written to help him unite the British kingdoms under his kingdom's leadership.

It was rewritten in the tenth century, though, and the purpose of the Dyfed revision was to undermine Powys' authority by attacking one of its most revered kings. At the time, Hywel Dda ruled the kingdom and he was firmly allied with Æthelstan, so Hywel probably had access to the *Kentish Source* through him. He made use of it, for the first time blending the British memory of Gwrtheyrn's power and dynastic importance with Vortigern's control of Britain, flaws, and chronology through the suggestion of their name similarity—Vortigern was the Latin form of Welsh Gwrtheyrn.

In this new version of history, Gwrtheyrn had emerged as the leader of all Britain after 410 but was still being attacked by the Picts and Germanic peoples. Hoping for a solution he took counsel with his nobles and decided to invite Anglo-Saxon mercenaries onto the island to help him. These *foederati* performed their jobs well, but then their leaders fooled him into allowing more and more warriors from the continent. They fooled him again when they introduced him to a Germanic woman who seduced him. He insisted on marrying her, and Hengest insisted on Kent as a dowry. That was when he had lost control.

His son Vortimer (properly Gwrthefyr, if the information had come from a Briton source) now emerged to beat the Anglo-Saxons nearly back to the eastern coast, but he was killed in the fighting. At that point, old Gwrtheyrn returned to the story. He was captured when all of his nobles were killed and ransomed for more territory. When the ransom was agreed upon, he spent his remaining days hidden inside a fortress, only to be burned alive when two dragons emerged from its foundations.

Alfred, or whoever commissioned *The Anglo-Saxon Chronicle*, happily made use of the story about the cunning Germanic chieftains and the fool they had stolen Britain from. Besides cutting back the story to fit into a chronicle form, the editor(s) only made two changes to the tale. The first was that Gwrtheyrn's son was never mentioned because the English probably had no memory of one. The second was that they reversed the order of the battles so that it looked like the Anglo-Saxons were conquering territory instead of losing it.

Without doubt what we know about Gwrtheyrn comes mainly from Gildas and the mistaken association between his *superbus tyrannus* and the historical Gwrtheyrn. Sorting through the information gaps, personal, religious, and political motivations, there is very little else to be learned about Gwrtheyrn—but there is something of value.

First of all there are the names. The interchangeability of roles between the *superbus tyrannus*, Vortigern, and Gwrtheyrn have been widely accepted as showing the two characters and one historical figure were considered the same people in the historical tradition. The *Historia Brittonum* also names an Outigern as roughly contemporary to Maelgwn, Ida, and the five bards and implies that all eight men were important in their time—the bards for their abilities and the kings for their successes; Koch has even suggested that the here implies that the first named poet, Talhaearn, was attached to Outigern. Yet we know nothing whatsoever about this king otherwise.[6] In *Hengest, Gwrtheyrn, and the Chronology of Post-Roman Britain*, the author proposed a simple scribal error; dyslexia might have switched Votigern to Outigern, and Votigern is a close form of Vortigern.[7]

Finally there is Gwrthefyr son of Gwrtheyrn. His name translates as "great prince" while the name of his "father" translates as "over-king"; similar but not identical. He also only appears in *Historia Brittonum*, and only so that he can fight Hengest in four battles—Thanet, the Darenth river, Epsford, and near a great stone. Bede says there was fighting between Vortigern and Hengest, but names no battles making it possible that he had simply eliminated British victories from his history.

The Anglo-Saxon Chronicle also says the battles were fought between Vortigern and Hengest but names them; Ægelesþrep (Aylesford), Crecganford (Crayford), Wippedesfleot (near Ebbsfleet), and a fourth unknown site.[8] *Historia Brittonum* names them too; Thanet, the Darenth river, Epsford, and near a great stone.[9]

None of the seven sites match which means that the information was probably not taken from the same source. However, Epsford is probably Aylesford, and all seven sites are usually located in Kent. That at least suggests that both the British and the English had a memory of a series of four battles fought by Hengest. The fact that Gwrthefyr shows up nowhere else but replaces Gwrtheyrn for them suggests that Gwrthefyr is yet another doublet, a seam in the blending.

As aspects of Gwrtheyrn's career that were apparently uninfluenced by the Gildas/*Kentish Source* tradition Outigern and Gwrthefyr might just allow us to see something historical about the Gwrtheyrn; he was a king recognized as Maelgwn's equal who fought several battles in or at least near Kent.

That is really not much. However, there are two other details to consider which will throw some light on the mysterious Gwrtheyrn; we know almost nothing about Iurminric the father of Æthelberht and the northern British kings seem to have dominated the Anglo-Saxons of Northumbria during the same time frame. Let me explain.

It has not really bothered anyone that we know nothing about Iurminric, and that strikes this scholar as odd. Consider, Æthelberht allowed the Christian mission into his kingdom in 597, along with its ability to write and the potential power that gave the king. A fifty-five year old man at that time could easily be expected to remember back to 557. Æthelberht may have married his Frankish wife (who brought her priest) around 580,[10] meaning that oral memory might have gone back to 540–530 if a fifty-five year old at the time had remembered any events back when he or she was five. On the other hand, Iurminric was born in the range 523x560.[11] No matter how you work the numbers, he spent his entire adult career within the limits of oral memory, yet the only two details we have about him are that his name is Frankish—implying a relationship with the Franks back another generation—and that he was the father of Æthelberht. This is very odd.

Next piece of information: the northern British kings. As we have seen, there were at least five different alliances over the last half of the sixth century, at least two of which took tribute from Germanic-held territories. This was a period of British revival and expanding political awareness because the British had already developed kingship and with it access to a stronger political organization along with more warriors under one king. The only southern king we have seen was active during this period outside of Wales and Cornwall is Gwrtheyrn.

Take those unrelated facts and add that to a question about the Hengest battles against Vortigern/Gwrthefyr. We know they could not have been remembered if they had taken place in the fifth century; that and neither Hengest, Vortigern, nor Gwrthefyr would have been around to fight them. So why were they remembered in both traditions? What would have been the point of remembering them before they were made a part of the *Kentish Source* and attached to the *Historia Brittonum*?

To answer that, we return to the fact that Iurminric would have been active during the middle of the sixth century, roughly the same era as Gwrtheyrn himself. Gwrtheyrn, as we have seen, was remembered in the north for being a powerful king. In the north, the powerful men of his era controlled land all the way to the eastern coast. Is it too much of a stretch to suggest that Gwrtheyrn might have as well?[12]

It would make sense. the *Kentish Source* was focused on showing the legitimacy of Kent's rule by demonstrating that its early kings had been smarter and better warriors than their British counterparts. Its writer(s) had not made up the initial landing and the outwitting of Vortigern, so why would they have started making things up with the battles? It seems more likely, at least to the author, that those battles would have been taken from oral memory, and oral memory would only have extended back to the middle sixth century, suggesting that Iurminric might have been the man fighting the battles against Gwrtheyrn.

Why was Iurminric not connected to them? As they are used in Bede and *The Anglo-Saxon Chronicle*, they are battles of conquest on an island that the Germanic people had just come to. However, if Iurminric was fighting them they would have been battles for independence. Independence might have a certain attraction, but it would also mean that at some point the royal house of Kent had willingly submitted to British authority and that would have gone against the basic purpose of the *Kentish Source*.

So, instead of deleting the battles altogether, they did what all good medieval historians seem to have done: they repurposed and redated them. The decision demonstrated Hengest's superior leadership and eliminated the potentially embarrassing fact that as late as the middle sixth century Kent had been paying tribute to the Britons. When in the tenth century Dyfed eliminated the pro-Gwrtheyrn version of the *Historia Brittonum* and rewrote British history it was an unhoped-for stroke of luck for Kent.

Of course even if the above theory is right there is no way to know who won what battle, or even the campaign. Probably our safest source for that is *The Anglo-Saxon Chronicle* because of its writer's habit of explicitly saying when the English won and being vague when they did not. It states that Hengest and his son Æsc won Ægelsþrep (probably Aylesford) and another battle and implies that they won at Crecganford (probably Crayford), while it is mute on the victor at Wippedesfleot.

Who was Gwrtheyrn? He was a powerful king who lived at the climax and the twilight of British power. It seems reasonable that Gwrtheyrn claimed some sort of tribute over many of the Germanic clans in the south. The author's appraisal would be that there was a revolt late in his career. Maybe it was led by Iurminric but Ælle, Bede's first *Bretwalda*, is a more likely possibility; it would explain his place in Bede's list and fit in well with the chronology of events that has been worked out above.

More probable still would be that several leaders emerged among them Ælle, Ceawlin, and Iurminric.[13] In that scheme the former two could have been contemporary *Bretwaldas*, bringing dozens of villages under one ruler in imitation of the early British kings.

As for Gwrtheyrn's end, we can learn nothing certain from the British sources. The Germanic historians never claimed that he was defeated and killed in battle, which suggests that the fighting was indecisive during his lifetime but not long after the Germanic peoples in the south claimed their independence.

In *The Anglo-Saxon Chronicle*, Vortigern is not mentioned after the first battle. It is possible that he lost it and died, and whoever followed him could do no better. Again, we may never know.

24

530–580
The Setting for the Rise of Germanic Kingships

One alliance against Rhun, two at Arfderydd, two at Catraeth—and the only Germanic chieftains that actually do anything up until the last decade or the sixth century are the ally of Gododdin, the two Northumbrians that Urien and his allies fought against, and the Ælle whose people the future pope Gregory came across. Part of the reason the names of the Germanic leaders are so rare is because the Germanic people themselves were not literate throughout the middle part of the sixth century.

Another reason is propaganda; we should know more about Iurminric than we do, but because the people of Kent needed a clear history of superiority over the British his activities did not measure up. Northumbria put all of its known chieftains into a single king-list, but we know now that several of the people on that list were contemporary rulers.

Finally, until the last century or so of this period, the Germanic people did not have real kings. At the beginning of the century they operated in clans, and during the time of the British alliances during the middle sixth century they transitioned into local kingships themselves.

There is archeological evidence of this transition; high-status sites only emerge around mid-century and become fewer and wealthier as they approach the end of the century,[1] telling us in the physical record the same thing we can guess from the historical record.

The question is how did the Germanic kingships go from nonexistence before around 550, to relative obscurity, and then regional and island-wide dominance by the early seventh century? In the distant past it was assumed that the *Historia Brittonum, Historia Ecclesiastica, The Anglo-Saxon Chronicle,* and *De Excidio Britanniae* were not only consistent with each other but provided an accurate account of the Germanic kingships; they had begun with

Hengest receiving Kent and the landings of the future kings of Wessex, Sussex, and so on. In that model, there was no great transition apart from the dynasties finishing up the conquest of their respective kingdoms from the British at around that time.

More recently, Professor Arnold and others have proposed that the unstable nature of early kingship and the need for each dynasty to prove its worth would have resulted in conflict and the rapid assimilation of chieftainships into progressively larger and more powerful kingdoms.[2] This sounds very much like the model the author has suggested for British kingships. There is one significant difference, though. We know that kingships in the Romanized areas began around 470 or so, when the first known bards appear. By perhaps 530 (60 years later), powerful regional kingships like Rhun and Gwrtheyrn had emerged. Even through the early kingship of Urien, though, bards still spoke of cattle raiding and no British leader from this period ever assimilated as much land as Kent or Northumbria into a single kingdom. On the other hand we hear of no dateable and historical Germanic leaders until no earlier than 550, and already by 600 or earlier (50 years) we see the first full size kingdoms.

What is more interesting is that, though we know from the physical evidence that there was cattle raiding among the early Germanic kingdoms there are no *skop* poems that speak of them. Though there are a couple figures we could equate with the vague British *gwledig* of the past like Dewrarth and Coel in Soemil and maybe Ida, the Germanic people in Britain never generated an heroic cycle like Arthur, Conchobar of Ireland, or Hrolf Kraki in Denmark. We could guess that by the time the Germanic people had the ability to record they were no longer living in an heroic culture, but it is hard to believe that no memory of the recent past would have been preserved somewhere.

So, with a long history of kingship on the continent, the Germanic people took around eight decades longer than the Romanized Britons to develop kingship, but once they did they took less time to build larger and stronger kingdoms. How could the Germanic people have formed stable political units so smoothly, and just in time to take advantage of the failing British strength?

It has been hypothesized above that Gwrtheyrn controlled Kent at the peak of his power. The *Historia Brittonum* claims that Urien had conquered much of Northumbria during his ascendancy but likely Morcant and Gwallog, who ruled kingdoms adjacent to Northumbria, had territories in the region too. For *Y Gododdin* to be so interested in Deira,[3] at least some the kingdoms involved must have taken tribute from villages in the area as well.

It has also been shown that the taxation system collapsed throughout Britain when the Roman government was decapitated at the provincial level. When they developed, the local British kingships used a new kind of taxation system, one where villages as a whole were responsible for collecting a predetermined amount of food and goods and passing it along to the local king.

As local kingships were absorbed by the more successful dynasties, the villages continued to give their taxes to the original dynasty or to a man installed by the new king, who then passed it along to his king. The system was not equally fair to all villagers or villages, but it did mean that the time an over-king spent collecting tribute did not grow too much as his kingdom expanded.

That worked well when British kings were adding British territories to their kingdoms. However, if the archeology has not mislead us and the Anglo-Saxons of the early to middle sixth century had no kings or kingdoms, it would have made taking tribute from them time consuming. As each village had its own ruling clan, every settlement in an area would need to be passed through. An over-king like Urien might theoretically spend the entire summer collecting tribute from a large enough territory.

It seems to this author that the simplest way to overcome that problem would have been to appoint an Anglo-Saxon to do the job. A local man, or better yet an Anglo-Saxon from the king's war-band, would be ideal. Either would be aware of the culture and know the language; both attributes would help to avoid many problems involved in ruling a different culture. And as with all the king's tributaries, this hypothetical tax collector would be allowed to erect a hall and gather his own band of warriors to enforce collection of the tribute and protect the territory.

Under the powerful kings who dominated the middle of the sixth century, these hypothetical puppet tax collectors would have been very useful, saving the British kings time and effort and delivering money, livestock, and supplies. However, the last of the dominant British kings faded in the last third of the sixth century.

As British power declined, their former tax collectors would have been in a perfect position to assume independent authority themselves; they had been collecting tribute already and had a group of warriors at their command. The author has no direct evidence for this suggestion, only the fact that it fits the evidence and the curious detail that Northumbria, Wessex, Sussex, and Kent, the same regions that were most likely controlled by British over-kings during the middle or late sixth century, were the first regions to develop regional kingships.

Once the Germanic kingdoms had emerged as regional powerhouses the British days were numbered. England, then as now, is far more fertile in the south and east than in the north and west, and much more fertile than either Wales or Scotland. Greater fertility meant they could grow more food with less labor. Greater amounts of food meant the Germanic kingdoms could support a larger population. A larger population in turn guaranteed more warriors for the battlefield. Once the Germanic people had the chance to take full advantage of their numbers, the British people would find it impossible to match the English armies.

25

550–575
Columban Dal Riata

When St. Columba arrived in Scotland as part of his penance for his part in the Battle of Cuil Dremne (563), legend says that King Conall of Dal Riata granted him the island of Iona for use as a monastery. He soon had a local *scriptorium*, writing center, so that from that time on historical events were recorded in Dal Riata.

Before 563, there would have been only oral memory. We only have one historical source for that period, the *Senchus Fer n'Alban*. It was written in around 660, a century after Columba arrived, and for the express purpose of generating nationalistic sentiment against Northumbria. The work gives a clear genealogical descent from Conall and Gabrán back to their common paternal grandfather Domangart.

The only other Dal Riatan source for the period is Columba's biography, written in about 697 and based on Iona's historical records and whatever oral legends were to be had. Considering how much longer a monk could live than a layman, there might have been quite a few stories floating around. Anyway, the *Vita Columba* gave Conall and Gabrán's parentage, but never named their common grandfather.

You might say the writer, Adamnan, simply had no interest in family trees, but Adamnan was a relative of Columba and a descendant of kings. It might be argued that Columba somehow did not know, but to be ignorant of a host kingdom's royal family would have been unthinkable. We must at least consider that Gabrán and Conall did not have a common grandfather.

That suggestion demands a second look at the book, and perusing the *Vita Columba* we see that Columba never seems to go to any hall, castle, or even hill-fort while in Dal Riata. It was not that Adamnan opposed speaking of royals, either. If his royal heritage is not enough to prove he had no compunctions about them, he does go into detail about Columba's visit to Brude's fortress in Pictland.[1]

Another omission is also important. Although the "official" history makes it clear that both Loairn and Óengusa of Cenéls Loairn and Óengusa were active around this time, neither one of them is mentioned. Conall and Gabrán are, and so are several members of the official family that are not in the official history, peasants, thieves, and monks; just not cenéls Loairn and Óengusa.

Many of the people Columba talks to in Dal Riata do not even seem to be noble. Actually, paging through the book the word pirate comes to mind. For instance, Erc is blatantly addressed as "the Robber."[2] There is also a chapter about Johan, son of Conall, son of Comgall, in which he is clearly described as a bandit with his own group of men.[3]

All of the above suggests that the family tree was altered in the *Senchus*. More than that, it puts into question whether or not there was even a royal Dal Riata dynasty at all when Columba arrived.[4]

Stronger evidence of that last thought can be found in what little we know of the Convention at Druim Cett (574). Now there is a consensus that the High-King of Ireland, Áed mac Ainmuirech, conceded that Scottish Dal Riata would pay no tribute and provide no warriors. In return, Dal Riata promised that its fleet would be at his command.[5]

In the past, those believing that Scottish Dal Riata was originally part of Irish Dal Riata believed that this compromise gave Scottish Dal Riata its first taste of freedom from Ireland. Looked at from Áed's perspective, though, the compromise is all wrong. He would have had no reason to give up tribute and fighting men. On the contrary, considering the weakened state of his dynasty and the fact that his predecessors had needed to fight throughout their reigns, he would have had every reason to believe he needed more military strength.

Instead of Druim Cett signaling the beginning of Scottish independence, we should think of it more as an acceptance of dependence. In return for making their veteran crews available to the high king, the Irish pirates in Britain were accepted as a nominal kingdom under the high-king and as such they were protected from all the kingdoms they had stolen from.

So if there was no royal family in the Dal Riata of 563 and for years afterwards what was there? We will be wisest to start with what we know; that is not in the *Senchus* but the *Vita Columba*. There are, in fact, at least three distinct clans to be found there—the families represented by Domnall, Gabrán, and Conall. There are possibly others. Erc "the Robber" is a likely clan leader. Colgu was an important person in Ireland, so his presence in Dal Riata raises the possibility that a lesser line may have migrated there.

Why should we think of the Dal Riatans as pirates, or at least raiders whose leaders came from royal families? As mentioned above, during the fifth century the western coast of Britain was invaded by the Irish, who used bases in Britain to stage attacks further inland. What we know about them is that the Irish who held the land and managed to build a kingdom were related to Irish royalty, but we have no way of knowing if they were in every case the only group that settled in an area or just the most successful one. It is only because of the *Vita Columba* that we know there were several clans in Dal Riata.

Dal Riata's geography made for a good pirate base, and in some ways was the best British base. The region has many islands with shifting beaches. Sea depths can change. An area like that would have been navigable for someone who lived there but hazardous for anyone hoping to attack in heavy ships. It would thus have been more practical to attack in smaller ships, *currachs*. The problem with that was that a *currach* could only carry a few men and as soon as it came into a narrow strait it would have been vulnerable to ambush by land or sea.

Because it was so easy to hide or defend, it would have been difficult to unite the area as well; a raiding party could evade any chieftain trying to unite the raiding crews almost indefinitely.

Not that there would have been any general need for unity during the fifth and sixth centuries. Each raiding group was mobile and could function independently. Irish and British targets were available on the sea and land, and there was no real threat to any group at the time and no potential threat in the foreseeable future.

Yet, with all these factors against unification, within about a dozen years of Columba landing Dal Riata was unquestionably united under a single king—Áedán. That timing, coupled with the strength of Columba's overpowering personality, tells us that the Irish saint was probably the cause, but why?

The most obvious reason is stability. Columba had left an island where dominance was contested by a few kingdoms, but within each region there was general unity. Dal Riata had none of that. As an intelligent man raised in a dynastic household, Columba would have been aware of the political and economic advantages, and awareness of the Picts' and Strathclyde's power would have given him an imminent reason to force Dal Riata together. The Battle of Teloch or Delgu (574), at which Dúnchad, son of Conall, and many other Dal Riatan leaders died, would have served as a good warning for the Dal Riata chieftains—no one could conquer Dal Riata, but none of the bands were safe, either.

So many different factions would have opposed him—how would he administer to them all equally? One leader of Dal Riata would have eliminated that issue.

Once the wheels were in motion, Columba thought he could influence them; he hoped to make Eoganán, son of Gabrán, the king,[6] though no specific reason is given. (The author brings this up because interfering in political affairs is what had gotten the Irish saint exiled in the first place.) Columba eventually allowed the election to take place naturally and duly crowned Áedán, Eoganán's brother, as king.

The Dal Riata after Druim Cett took on a new persona, an extroverted one. Though we are uncertain about dates, it is known that Áedán raided Orkney, fought at the Island of Man, battled the Miathi of the Upper Forth, warred against the Picts, and plundered the capital of Strathclyde—Alt Clut or modern Dumbarton. We also know that he fought multiple battles against the Northumbrians leading up to his signal defeat against Æthelfrith at Degsastan. The moment Dal Riata was joined into one kingdom it became an island wide power and Áedán was clearly not shy about testing the extents of that power. He was so active, and his exploits so influential, that he is one of the few non-Welsh figures remembered in the Welsh Triads.[7]

26

The Decline of the British Kingdoms

Most of the British histories the author has read focus on the Anglo-Saxon kingdoms between Rhun's campaign, and the alliances of Urien and the Gododdin on one end and Cadwallon on the other, ignoring the British people completely. Historians do this because we know little about the British people during this time—not much more than the names of several kings, really.

Several people have offered their theories. Hamerow argued that the Germanic peoples' local and extended kin-groups gave them a distinct advantage over the British social structure.[1] However, we are not exactly certain how those kin-groups functioned but judging by existing kingship customs and the extant law codes of the period they seem to have been similar to the Celts. In both cases, an extended cousinhood protected each clan member among the freemen. It could be argued that the English tradition was closer to the modern system of justice with its concept of crimes against the state, but that would not have given the English any obvious advantages in warfare.

In studying the period, Professor Higham realized the unusual weight Badon had on both British and Germanic histories,[2] and suggested that it might have been important independent of Gildas. He suggested that after the battle some sort of a compromise was worked out between both sides that in the short term forced the Anglo-Saxons to pause in their advance into British territories, but in the end allowed them to develop whatever political structure or military strength they needed to conquer Britain.[3]

The problem with that theory is that it requires some unlikely assumptions. The first is that the battle had islandwide importance. Gildas' interests and knowledge were fairly local within his lifetime; he focuses on modern Wales and Cornwall with the kings for instance. It is at least feasible that the Battle of Badon was only locally important too. The knowledge we have gained about political development supports that possibility; we have learned that the British kingdoms were only just forming in the late fifth century and regional alliances were still decades off, while the Germanic people of the late fifth century were still organized into clans controlling individual villages.[4] While it might have been possible for several British chiefs to band together, bringing hundreds of villages under a confederation, unless they were being invaded themselves, would have been a impractical.

The fact that the Germanic people were still organized into local clans also means that there would have been no way to work out a compromise after the battle, either. It would have been difficult to make dozens of British chieftains agree on terms, but negotiating with hundreds of Germanic clans would have been impossible unless they had been virtually annihilated—and Gildas makes no claims about that.

Consider the logistics: A mounted war-band might travel thirty or forty miles in a day. At that speed, and allowing at least one full day for a battle, it is possible that most Germanic and British war-bands would be able to get to and from the battle in only three days. However, for those three days the entire kingdom would be vulnerable to attack.[5]

Gildas claimed that Badon was the major battle of a generation, and if it was the absolute victory he claims it makes sense why English historians never delved into the details. But, if the battle was followed by a compromise that eventually allowed the Germanic people to dominate the island, the English reaction should have been different. One would think that the eventual benefactors would have remembered it with pride as another instance when they had outwitted the British (like Hengest) and as a more important event than the regional accomplishments of Cerdic, Ceawlin, or Ælle. The fact that they did neither probably means that Badon was a major defeat for them. As that seems more likely, we need to look elsewhere for an explanation about why the British kingdoms decline after the mid-sixth century.

The behavior of the British kingdoms after Urien and Rhun seems like the state of ancient Greece after the Persian and Peloponnesian Wars, or the aftermath of a wild New Year's Eve Party—maybe both comparisons are valid. By the end of the sixth century, the British had been in a state of perpetual raiding and warring for over a hundred years, with battles growing larger and more intense as kingdoms grew and allied together in an attempt to control ever larger portions of the island. On the other hand, we hear almost nothing of the Germanic peoples for decades after roughly 500. While the British were involved in larger and larger battles, the Germanic people were still just raiding. Is it possible that British manpower had been sapped? Battles would deplete the warrior ranks, while invasions would have meant the loss of farmers, without whom there was no food.

At the same time, England has the best farmland on the island.[6] While the British lost warriors and peasants to internecine warfare from the late

26. The Decline of the British Kingdoms

fifth to the late sixth century and survived on lesser farmland, the Anglo-Saxons lost little or nothing and had better crops to grow their population on.

Of course, battles alone did not reduce the British from the dominant power on the island to victims in just a century. It must have strained them, but not so much that they might not have reconquered Britain. There were other issues. Dr. Andrew Breeze has pointed out to me some major volcanic activity in 535-6 which caused major climatic changes throughout the world.[7] This would have affected crops and livestock.

At mid-century, Justinian's Plague hit Britain,[8] and that must have put the Britons over the edge. Some scholars have suggested that the British were hit harder and the resulting deaths weakened the British enough that they never recovered.[9] That theory seems unlikely on its own though. For one thing, scholars have shown that the Germanic peoples traded both with the continent and the British peoples, demonstrating more than enough contact with bubonic plague regions to have infected their entire population.[10]

But, if the undermanned British kingdoms had been stretched by nearly a century of war before the plague hit and the Anglo-Saxons had thrived in the meantime, the disease could have hit both groups equally but affected the British much more.

The plague was just the anima though. In organizing the Germanic areas to make tribute-taking more efficient during the early and middle sixth century, the British had inadvertently created the political structure for the Germanic kingdoms—leader, hall, warriors, and villages giving tribute. Once the British people no longer had the strength to control them because of the pandemic,[11] the Germanic tax collectors would have simply stopped paying tribute.

So, why do the British kingdoms have an interlude from history after Urien and Rhun of Gwynedd? They were recovering, and the Germanic peoples were too focused on developing from local chieftainships to kingdoms. That focus would allow for the rise of the first Germanic over-kings like Ælle, Ceawlin, Æthelberht, and Æthelfrith while giving the British kingdoms time to replenish their numbers.

Rise of the Germanic Kingships: Late Sixth Century to 664

27

Germanic Kingship

Primitive Anglo-Saxon chieftainships developed during the middle of the sixth century, possibly emerging because of a structure the powerful British kings installed there. Once present, they conducted their survival of the fittest contest through battles, marriages, and religion, the seven luckiest and strongest dynasties forming into the Heptarchy in a matter of decades.

How they transitioned from newly created kingdoms into a sort of political statement has been studied extensively. Traditionally, historians have tried a biographical approach, going from major leader to major leader in chronological order and with a minimum of background as they survey the period on their way to later periods.[1] Occasionally, scholars have studied the major kingdoms separately; this has usually been accomplished with regional experts writing on their topics in collaboration.[2] More recently, books have been written on entire kingdoms or centered around one source.[3] All of these approaches have had their benefits for better understanding the period. However, none of them helps a lay reader to see the big picture about the English kingdoms from their origins to their maturity in the seventh century.

In this section the author will take a slightly different approach. After discussing the rise of the Germanic kingdoms, we will use a staggered chronology in our study of the rest of the period—roughly 575 through 654. It will begin with the Picts up through the reign of Bridei son of Maelchon in the 580s. The next major leader was Áedán of Dal Riata, so we will explore the history of his kingdom from the death of Columba until Áedán's demise. In this chapter we will go from leader to leader, examining the origins of each kingdom from the point where we left off up to a natural stopping point, the Synod of Whitby in 664. At that point we will survey what we know of the lesser kingdoms, integrating that information into our overall history. It is hoped that the approach as outlined will better help to make each kingdom's development and their interactions with each other more understandable than has been possible before.

Before we begin, though, it is best to explore and appreciate the nature of Germanic kingship. In many ways, post–Roman Celtic kingship was similar.

Celtic kingship assumed a powerful connection between a king and the land he ruled which was symbolized in his marriage to the land in the form of his wife. Germanic kingship did as well.[4] The Celtic king was also the highest judge, whose rulings as well as his courage in battle ensured the land remained fertile. The same was true with the Germanic king.

It has been seen in chapter 16 that the British king was at the center of the new politico-economic system. He led the warriors and through them protected the villages, which allowed for economic and political stability throughout his kingdom. He hired bards, whose function was threefold; to entertain the king and his warriors through praise poetry which reinforced the relationship between the two groups, to remind the villages of the king's importance to their well-being, to generate a royal genealogy that gave the king famous and respected progenitors, and to associate the king with a supernatural relationship to the land along with his superhuman wisdom and battle luck.

The warriors were his personal comrades, who lived in his hall and promised to fight and die in return for his hospitality. Without them there was no protection of the villages and the villages had no reason to pay the tribute that brought the king and his warriors the wealth to buy spears, shields, swords, and armor. At the foundation of the system were the villages, who provided the king with silver to give away and purchase armaments with, livestock, food, and labor to keep his buildings intact.

The Germanic king was part of a similar arrangement, with the *skop* instead of a bard as the educated poet among his people. However, the Germanic king had one additional mechanism that gave him an even greater control over his people than the British kings enjoyed—decent from a king.

Whereas the British rulers tapped the most ancient traditions for their power and their bards padded that mystique with more tangible heroes of the past, they and the people they ruled were influenced by Christianity, which only accepted God, and him remote. Germanic gods were much more hands-on. Their myths involved battles against the *Jotuns* to protect mankind, and their royal genealogies were often founded by Woden or Deor, better known as Odin and Thor. This connection not only gave the Germanic kings a claim to semi-divinity themselves, but also to the divine *mana*.[5]

Now Celtic kings were believed to have a connection with the divine too, which was why a kingdom traditionally chose each ruler (even though in reality the entire clan chose a successor which was then ratified by priests), but descent from a god made the Germanic connection more powerful. And because they practiced this form of kingship during their conversion to

27. Germanic Kingship

Christianity, it and specifically the concept of *mana* remained an important characteristic of Germanic kingship well beyond the seventh century.

What was *mana*, roughly translated as divine luck? It was not lucky like we would understand it, having great timing, always getting good cards, winning the lottery, etc. A ruler with powerful *mana* was successful in battles, led a fertile kingdom, made just decisions, and was loved by his warriors.[6] It was believed that the gods themselves were looking out for him and everything he possessed.

Mana was passed along in bloodlines, just like the modern world sees traits like strength, speed, and mathematical abilities as genetically influenced traits. And, as athletic and intellectual abilities are passed along in varying degrees, so it was with *mana*.[7]

Because *mana* was such a valuable commodity in a king, it was important for any potential ruler to prove that he possessed the quality in abundance. For that reason it was common for princes, any descendent of a king from three generations back, to form their own war-bands and go raiding to prove themselves.

The royal *mana* largely kept the nobles and warriors from questioning the royal family's right to rule. However, it did not always keep royals safe from their own relatives. When a king died it was not uncommon for princes to fight for the right of succession if it was not clear who the "luckiest" man was. Even during a king's reign, he was not above his relatives trying to usurp his throne under the right circumstances; as we have seen in the story of the *Northern Memorandum* and will see in the next chapter, a debatable policy could bring on a revolt while a major defeat meant almost certain death. There are even several Norse stories and Roman references to kings being sacrificed to Woden/Odin when their kingdom suffered several seasons of bad harvests.[8]

28

The Southumbrian Theater

History is full of "what-ifs." For instance, Bede names Æthelberht of Kent as a *Bretwalda*, over-king. However, Bede received most of his early information from the *Kentish Source*. Kent had the earliest history simply because Æthelberht was converted first among the Germanic kings. He probably was not assigned the first Anglo-Saxon bishop because he was the most powerful king in Britain, though. The continent would have had no clear knowledge of who was powerful and who was not, after all. It only had contact with Kent, and that contact was the reason why Kent received the first missionary.

So what would have happened if some other kingdom had been in contact with the continent? Some other kingdom would have received Augustine and given Bede his source material for the early history of Britain. It would not have changed one thing though; Æthelberht's place on the list of *Bretwaldas*. In addition to Æthelberht, Bede also tells us that both Ælle of Sussex and Ceawlin of Wessex preceded Æthelberht as over-kings,[1] but never names any other Kentish king there—not even Hengest. The *Kentish Source* was all about highlighting Kent and minimizing the accomplishments of other kingdoms if it mentioned them at all, so the fact that the list includes rulers from other kingdoms gives it some credibility in this instance.

Of course it does bring into focus another question; now that we know Germanic kingship did not even emerge until the mid-sixth century, how did Sussex, Wessex, and Kent go from the dozens if not hundreds of clan-controlled villages to three powerful kingdoms in a matter of decades?

We have already seen evidence that Gwrtheyrn might have taken tribute from much of southern England. Ruling over so large an area would have been a logistical nightmare for a relatively new kingship; his war-band could not hope to protect such a large area from raiders and he could not hope to personally tour through his entire "empire" collecting tribute from every village.

So he likely assigned men their own regions outside of the kingdom he had inherited with the responsibilities of collecting tribute and protecting the villages. These vassals were probably Germanic (the better to communicate with and understand their wards)[2] and most likely began their careers with Gwrtheyrn.[3] They would have been expected to form their own warbands in order to carry out their duties.

Whatever precautions Gwrtheyrn did take, they were not enough. We cannot know whether the villages united under a group of leaders or they simply stopped paying tribute for whatever reason. It is also possible that Gwrtheyrn died and, as happened in the north, the next generation was unable to maintain the same control over them. All we can be certain of is that the regions south of the Thames probably revolted and managed to assert their independence at some time during the middle or late sixth century.

We know very little about what happened next, either. It is possible that Ælle led a revolt and afterwards slid into a position of over-kingship over the region only to be followed on his death by Ceawlin and eventually Æthelberht.[4] Perhaps several regional leaders emerged during the revolt—Ælle, Ceawlin, and possibly Iurminric of Kent—and they were remembered as consecutive leaders instead of contemporaries as we have seen occurring in many genealogies.

It is also possible that Gwrtheyrn died peacefully.[5] If that is what happened, then his former Germanic tributaries might have simply taken advantage of the power vacuum that followed. Short of finding another source or his gravesite, we may never know how the transition occurred.

This hypothesis might seem like too much guesswork, but the evidence does seem to hang together around the theory. It also has the advantage of being more believable than the historical record as it stands. To begin with, everything we know about Ælle apart from his title of *Bretwalda* are elements of the typical Anglo-Saxon foundation legend as found in *The Anglo-Saxon Chronicle*—as happens with Wessex and Kent, he lands with a son or sons and fights three battles. This is followed by a notice that he founded his dynasty five or six years after the landing.[6] There is nothing else about the kingdom until many decades later, suggesting that whoever wrote those entries actually knew nothing about Sussex apart from a few names but wanted to include the kingdom in the history.

Ceawlin fairs no better. He appears with a full lineage in *The Anglo-Saxon Chronicle* and the *West Saxon Genealogical Regnal List*, but we already know that both sources are useless as far as the fifth and early sixth centuries are concerned because the register of names there is an integration of at least three different dynasties into a single dynastic list,[7] meaning that the untrustworthy source was further altered later on.

The many battles in the area as listed in *The Anglo-Saxon Chronicle* may have occurred historically, but they are too early to be trusted in that context.

If they are actually historical, they fit in just as well with the revolt scenario offered above; in that case *The Anglo-Saxon Chronicle* gives us the names of chieftains and battles of the revolt. Alternatively, they might have been later battles as well, fought between Germanic chieftains.

We cannot even put too much faith in the succession information of the mid-sixth century. Ceawlin is listed as ruling from 560–592, which is possible if not probable. We know Æthelberht's reign of 56 years is highly improbable even though this is the most likely reign-length to be accurate in the sixth century.[8] More likely 56 was his age when he died, and even that stretches probability for this period. If we cannot even put our faith in reign durations, there is no way of confirming exactly when or even how long Ceawlin ruled. That realization also means that the battles he is connected to—Beranburh (556), Wibbandun (568), Dyrham (577), Feþanleag (584), and Adam's Grave (592)—may or may not have been fought by him,[9] and probably have not been dated accurately either.[10]

Though knowing more about *The Anglo-Saxon Chronicle* means we can believe little about either Sussex and Wessex's history, we can know something about early Kent and guess a great deal more. Kent not only made the best use of trade with the continent to have a steady influx of Frankish goods from the sixth century on,[11] they were also connected to the Franks politically. It has already been noted above that Æthelberht's father was named Eormenric, an unpopular name among the Anglo-Saxons but a common Frankish one in the form of Iurminric. As he was born in the range 523x560, we must assume that Eormenric's father, or at least someone from the same generation, was the first to initiate official diplomacy with the Franks at about that time.[12] As no other southern Germanic kingdom was in contact with the Franks, the most likely time for that to have occurred would have been after Kent had made itself independent, so after mid-century rather than before.

Kent's ties with Frankia were consistent for decades, too. Æthelberht, born between 561 and 578, would marry a Frankish princess before he began his reign over Kent at some time before 593.[13] By the time Kent became the dominant kingdom in the south, it had already built up the most intimate ties with the most powerful local kingdom on the continent.

Æthelberht exploited his position in two ways beyond the collection of tribute. First, he used his power to pressure lesser kings into accepting Christianity. This change of religion would have bonded any chieftain to him by isolating him from those kings who were still pagan. Accepting Christianity would also have weakened their position; as we have seen the basis of Germanic was in its connection to the living land and descent from their gods.

Secondly, he called for the codification of laws. As has been discussed above, the codification might have been done at Augustine's request or to imitate some of the more famous continental kings, but that does not mean it did not have uses for Æthelberht. Every kingdom under his control would have been expected to follow his law code. The clever part about the code was that the laws were mostly based on common traditions; the freemen complied with Æthelberht without changing any aspect of their own laws.

The evidence, when looked at on a broad scale, seems reasonable. How else could the Germanic kingdoms have emerged so quickly out of the shadows of their British neighbors without a push from their former overlords? How were they able to develop large kingdoms unless they had already been organized?

However, it is only in studying individual kingdoms that we can really see their development, and only in studying them as a whole that one can understand the dynamics. In this *The Anglo-Saxon Chronicle* is our best tool; even though the date it gives are provably inaccurate, it has been shown that the events it mentions are based on traditional materials. Unfortunately, *The Anglo-Saxon Chronicle* focuses on the kingdom of Wessex first. Southern England and the rest of the Germanic peoples are relatively insignificant, which means that as we examine it for clues we will find more information about it than any other region, even when we factor in the information in *Historia Brittonum* and *Historia Ecclesiastica*.

So what about the "prehistoric" kings south of the Thames? We should begin with Hengest, the first Germanic king mentioned and the earliest king by all accounts. Bede speaks of him arriving in Britain between 449 and 456,[14] but as we have seen there is no archeological evidence that Germanic settlement in Britain started so late. We have also seen the Germanic people did not begin to write down their histories until the very end of the sixth century, at the earliest. That would mean well over a century between the end of Hengest's career and the first written word; too much of an interval to trust any information about him.

Hengest is also mentioned in one other source, a story embedded in *Beowulf*.[15] There, Hengest is a great warrior who happens to survive his king in a battle, losing all his honor in the process. By ancient and well known custom he had to leave the kingdom.[16] If a *skop* had helped develop the *Kentish Source*, that detail might have made him the perfect legendary hero to found the Kentish dynasty.

In all English and Welsh sources his brother and partner is Horsa, who is not a traditional hero. Horsa is pure invention. His name means "stallion," while Hengest's means "pack-horse," making him a doublet of Hengest,[17] much like Remus was a doublet to his more famous brother Romulus.[18]

According to Bede Hengest's son was Orric, surnamed Oisc.[19] From him the Kentish dynasty was named the Oiscingas. That is no misprint; Bede tells us that Kent's dynasty is named after Orric's nickname. That is a red flag that information has been lost (probably fused from two characters). The fact that Bede himself refers to him exclusively as Oisc after his introduction is another.

Orric is only mentioned by Bede who, as we have already seen, was forced by academic integrity to follow the materials he had at hand—namely the *Kentish Source*. However, he was not above adding to it—especially when it benefited his beloved Northumbria. He places this Orric in a northern campaign before lending his surname to Kent's dynasty, which probably means that our venerable author has here added a Northumbrian hero and his accomplishments to a predominantly Kentish history.[20]

Oisc is a little different. That the Kentish dynasty called itself after him is some evidence that he was historical and the founder of the lineage.[21] In *The Anglo-Saxon Chronicle* Hengest's son is named Æsc, possibly a simple regional variation.[22]

With that understood, a short lesson in the history of the name is in order. Oisc is the modernized form of Old English *Oski*, which comes from Old Germanic *Anski*. The word means "semi-divine." As a personal name it is *Anschis*.[23] In the transmission of manuscripts the corruption of "c" to "e" was common, giving *Ansehis* as a possible variant. *Ansehis* we have already met; he mentioned in the *Ravenna Cosmography* as a *foederati* arriving in Britain during the late fourth century. If they are the same person, which seems at least plausible, then Oisc was simply a famous chieftain from the past who was injected into the Kentish lineage to give it more prestige.

The kingdom of Kent itself has been argued over as well; several scholars have considered it was originally two kingdoms. The argument is that eastern Kent had essentially Jutish and Frankish culture whereas western Kent was more connected with Saxon culture. They have also cited several instances of joint ruling to support their claim.[24]

An alternate explanation is that Kent was originally composed of hundreds of clans—the eastern being Jutish and trading with the Franks and the western being Saxon. Eventually these clans united into several kingdoms—Northumbria had at least four. And like Northumbria, the dynasties of two survived into the historical period, producing several instances of joint ruling until one dynasty finally outlasted the other.

The next characters mentioned are from Sussex, and we know next to nothing about the region after Ælle other than Bede's statement that he was a *Bretwalda* and *The Anglo-Saxon Chronicle*'s placement of him in the early sixth century. Given that kingdoms did not even appear until mid-century, though, it seems more likely that he was active later rather than sooner. Sussex history is limited because in Ælle's time there was no Christianity, and his Christian descendants, if they had enjoyed the same kind of power he did, neglected to remember any more of him.

Wessex was luckier; we have so much information about its earliest figures that some of it conflicts. First there is Cerdic and Cynric, his son in the official Wessex genealogy. They either arrive in the late fifth or early sixth century (depending on the source), which means that their entire careers were beyond the 75-year threshold of living memory and the dates cannot be trusted. The battles they are connected with in *The Anglo-Saxon Chronicles*, though, might have been remembered accurately. They can all be placed in the same region of what would become Wessex. It seems likely they were members of a Wessex dynasty.

The genealogies also say that Ceawlin was the son or grandson of Cerdic and brother or son of Cynric (again, depending on the source) and call him the founder of the Wessex dynasty. This is probably a later fusion of dynasties, though. Cynric and Ceawlin were active in entirely different areas of Wessex. Maybe Cerdic was another rebel whose dynasty was later absorbed by Ceawlin's descendants.

The author's research has also shown that Cutha represents a third Wessex dynasty. He was active during the mid-sixth century and he and Ceawlin fought together against Æthelberht at Wibbandun,[25] and then against the Britons at Fethanleag.[26]

In the entry for 501, *The Anglo-Saxon Chronicle* says that Port landed in Britain with his sons Bieda and Mægla. Port is clearly the eponymous founder of Portsmouth. Neither of his sons appear again, suggesting that they were ancient kings around Portsmouth who were never attached to one of the surviving dynasties.

Stuf and Wihtgara are granted the Isle of Wight after their kinsman Cynric conquers it 534, according to *The Anglo-Saxon Chronicle*. Wihtgara is an eponym for Wight; Cynric's "gift" to the pair was a tenth-century claim to Wessex ownership.[27] Earlier Kent had made its own claim when it had made Wihtgara a part of its official genealogy.

Stuf, on the other hand, might have been an historical Saxon chieftain. He was not Cynric's relative though; Stuf does not sound like a Wessex name. More likely he was the historical conqueror of Wight and the Wessex dynasty paired him with Wihtgara and called him their kin to strengthen their claim to the island. Stuf is never mentioned again, nor are any of his descendants. His kingdom was probably swallowed up by Kent early on.

Finally, there is Middlesex and Essex. We know nothing about either region until they are associated with Kent. This is probably because there are no indications that the regions were controlled by a British king who would have given them the basic structure to form a kingdom in the middle sixth century. The first ruler we hear of is Sledd of Essex, who married Æthelbert's sister Ricula. We know nothing more about him.

Sledd's son was Sæberht, whom we first hear about in 604 when he

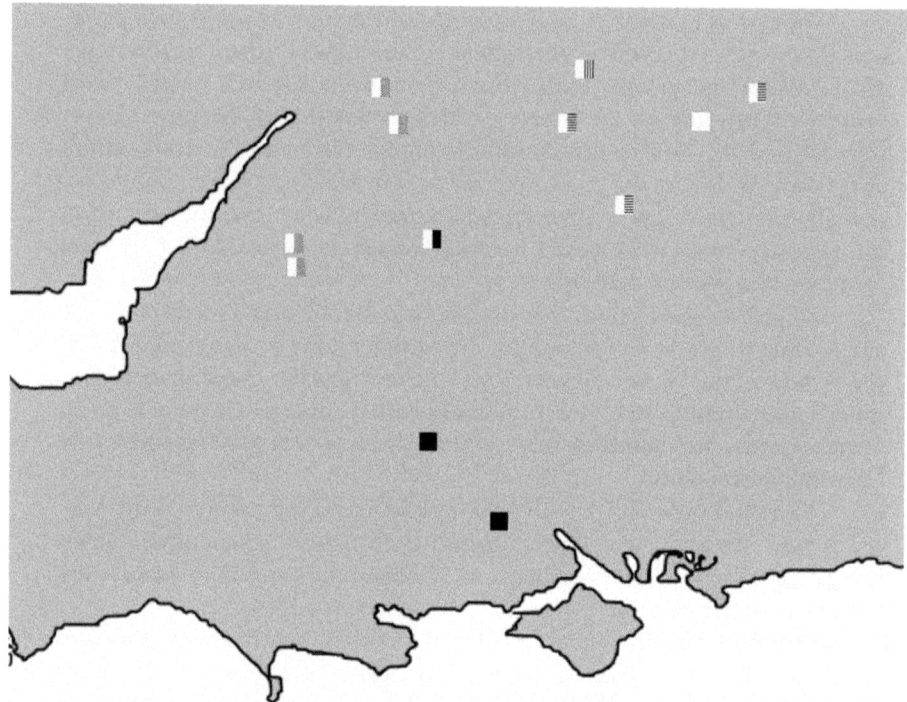

Areas of activity for early Wessex kings: Cynric=Black; Cuthwine=Checkered; Ceawlin=White; Cutha=Vertical Stripes; Cuthwulf=Horizontal Stripes

converted to Christianity under Æthelberht's patronage in 604. Sæberht's sons remained pagan, though, so when he died in 616 Essex had no Christian patron and no one to record its history. Middlesex had no memorable kings. We know almost nothing about it until the territory was added to the kingdom of Essex.

29

The Northumbrian Theater

In the South, it seems at least feasible that Gwrtheyrn's ascendancy created the infrastructure that helped form the first Germanic kingdoms, otherwise there is the unlikely coincidence of Gwrtheyrn/Vortigern's floruit, Vortigern/Vortimer-Hengest's battles in Kent (no matter which way the campaign went, Hengest was at some point defending his own kingdom instead of being on the offensive), and the sudden emergence of several Southumbrian overlordships within (at the most) a couple decades after archeology says the first kingships formed.

In the North, we have a very different type of evidence for the same situation. The traditional belief had been that the ill-fated Gododdin expedition had fought at Catraeth in around 600, when Northumbria already had fully formed kingdoms and was approaching unification. As has been seen above, more recently the date for that battle has shifted from around 600 to perhaps 570 or even 540. Just as important, Gododdin's opponents in the battle have been reimagined not as Germanic kings but British chieftains—Urien, Gwallog, Morgan, and Rhydderch. Both sides apparently had Germanic allies or tributaries fighting alongside them.

This change of dating and focus is in perfect agreement with the archeology, the Taliesin poems, and *Historia Brittonum*; Urien does fight two Germanic chieftains in the history, but he fights them only in Northumbria and never as threats to his kingdom. In the poems, no Germanic chieftain is mentioned by name against Urien at all. Fflamddwyn, the nickname of a "Bernician" chieftain,[1] does appear in a poem fighting against Owain, but that battle could have been as much as a generation after Catraeth; plenty of time for the Germanic clans to have developed into substantial kingdoms especially now that we know how quickly they grew in size and strength.

In fact, the Taliesin poems can be used to support the new dating and reinforce our new views on the political situation. In the eighth Taliesin poem, "Gweith Gwen Ystrat," line 9, Urien is named as the Lord of Catraeth. This piece of evidence was used by Professor Koch to show Catraeth's political and military importance to both Urien and the Gododdin expedition.[2]

Catraeth, generally agreed upon as modern Catterick Bridge,[3] was well within Northumbria once it was united in 604/5 by Æthelfrith. If the battle was fought after that or even when Bernicia was an established kingdom (by 593 at the latest), one would imagine Bernicia and/or Æthelfrith would figure prominently in the battle poems; they do not. The fact that Catraeth is in what would be Northumbria by 605 but was in Urien's possession and was fought over by two predominantly Briton confederacies is strong evidence that there were no developed Germanic kingdoms at the time of the battle, which in turn forces us to the conclusion that Catraeth was fought long before 593.

Alright, so we know that Urien and Gododdin's confederacies were active long before 593, and also that the Germanics of the time were not a significant military presence. Even better, we are fairly certain there was no cultural/racial hatred in the era. *Historia Brittonum* tells us that Urien's last campaign was intended to drive the Germanic people into the sea. But if there were no Germanic kingdoms that would not have been a major task, and if the Britons did not hate the Germanics for being Germanic there would have been no desire to. So what was the purpose of the campaign? Was he forcing more Germanic clans to pay tribute? Fighting the Gododdin confederacy? Koch has argued eloquently that the Urien and Gododdin confederacies were at war, but are the two mutually exclusive?

Even if there were no significant Germanic kingdoms around the time of the Battle of Catraeth, the archeological record does show that power and wealth was beginning to centralize among the northern Germanic villages. Why?

Again, what fits the evidence best is that the region was already organized by the dominant British kings to make tribute taking and defense from other British chieftains easier and more local. Briton-directed organization would also explain the clear presence of Germanic warriors at Catraeth without the clear evidence of Germanic chieftains leading Germanic warriors there.

What happened next? In the South, Bede handed the modern historian a string of three consecutive over-kings, which date-guessing has shown bridged the gap between British suzerainty and the rise of Germanic kingdoms. Because his northern sources had no Northumbrian equivalent to the *Kentish Source*, he could offer no such favors for his beloved Northumbria. Instead, all he had was simple oral history from the moment writing was possible.

Without Bede's help, we are left with the raw materials in the *Historia Brittonum* and its attached genealogies. The former says that Ida was a figure of the mid-sixth century and that his eleven sons—Glappa, Adda, Æthelric, Theodric, Frithuwald, and Hussa among them, ruled immediately after him. Date-guessing using the primary sources has proven that this official scenario is highly improbable.[4] It seems more likely that several of the people named above were the rulers of other Northumbrian kingdoms; they were probably plucked from their historical positions and inserted into Bernicia's royal family.

There is some evidence for this hypothesis. The conflicting information to be had from our sources is one piece and the unsatisfactory results of date-guessing are another. Others are less obvious; none of the "brothers" were active in the same place. Theodric is mentioned in *Historia Brittonum* only at Lindesfarne where he was besieged by Urien and his allies.[5] According to the *Welsh Triads*, Adda fought against the York kings Peredur and Gwrgi at Caer Greu.[6] We also know that Hussa fought against Rheged, Elmet, Strathclyde, and probably a Gododdin kingdom, which suggests he was from a northwestern Bernician kingdom—but this is the weakest of the three connections.

The above clues do not give us a conclusive argument, but they do suggest a theory that agrees with archeology, that there were multiple kingships in pre–Æthelfrith Northumbria. It also has the advantage of not conflicting with itself or the sources as we understand them.

The established history has neither. Northumbria did not have its first monastery, and the *scriptoria* that came with it, until probably 635. If historical writing started immediately (and Aidan was renowned for traveling ceaselessly so this is a "big if") and had access to someone who was the maximum of fifty-five, then he would have had access to living memory back no further than 585 under the best of circumstances. More likely he would have had access to accurate memories only back to 595. Even if we assume that Paulinus started writing Northumbrian history when he accompanied Æthelburg up to Northumbria in about 625 (when he established churches, not monasteries), living memory for him would have extended no further back than about 575, and probably 585. There is no conceivable way that there could have been any historical memories regarding a 547 Ida, and probably little or no living memory about Glappa, Adda, Æthelric, Theodric, Frithuwald, and Hussa. The only thing that would have been accessible at that time would have been heroic poems and whatever *skop*-derived genealogies were in existence.

And even if all the above calculations are wrong, our received history of sixth-century Northumbria clearly conflicts with contemporary British poetry and any attempt at date-guessing. It also does not explain the clear association of at least two kings with specific areas within Northumbria.

Actually, when put like that the scenario bears a little comparison to another dynasty we have already met, Wessex. There at least three dynasties were smashed together to give the impression of a single and united kingdom from its first day of existence by giving several key individuals a genealogy that connected them to a common founder—Cerdic.

In Northumbria, it looks like the process was simpler, or less developed, as all of the suspicious persons were made the sons of Ida. The solution not only bonded the history of Bernicia's kingdoms into a history where Bernicia had always been united, it push Bernicia's foundation date further back in time and made the dynasty seem older and more respectable than it actually was.

So when did all the chieftains in the official king-list live? In the South, the genealogies of Wessex have previously been worked out with rough birth-years for most individuals. Not so with Bernicia. However, knowing that Theodric and Hussa were contemporary to Urien and that Hussa's son was active in 603, the author has previously date guessed several early members of the official Bernician family:

Ida: 497x550	Adda, "son of Ida": 515x585
Æthelric, son of Ida: 535x568	Hussa, "son of Ida": 530x570
Theodric, son of Ida: 515x585	Hering, son of Hussa: 548x588

It makes sense that both Æthelric and Theodric would be the sons of Ida. Ida is the legendary founder of the line and he is connected to Bamburgh Castle. In the *Historia Brittonum* Theodric was laid siege to at Lindesfarne, which is a nearby island. Æthelric is also reasonable as Ida's son because it was his son Æthelfrith who first united Bernicia and Deira and had the power to create the official (oral) history at a time when there must have been survivors from the various kingdoms he had conquered. It would have made no sense to choose another father in place of his own when his father's name would have been well known. And as the official genealogy has Ida as his grandfather and the conflicting chieftains as his uncles, it would have made no sense to choose another grandfather, either.

Hussa, on the other hand, is clearly not a son of Ida. The king lists specifically say that Theodric ruled first. *Historia Brittonum*, on the other hand, tells us that Hussa fought Urien and that Urien died while laying siege to Theodric; clearly a chronological gaff in the re-sewing of Bernician history.

Frithuwald likewise causes problems as a son of Ida. In the official king-list he is placed between Theodric and Hussa, but in the *Historia Brittonum* he is still alive when Augustine arrives in Britain at 597.[7] It is also clear, in Bede and elsewhere, that all the sons of Ida were dead by 593, when Æthelfrith, from the third generation, began his reign. If Frithuwald was a son of Ida, he could not have been alive in 597. We already know that the king-list has been tampered with, and the *Historia Brittonum* (and *Northern*

Memoranda writer) would have had no foreseeable reason to make the synchronization; Frithuwald was not the son of Ida.

Previously, the author had listed Adda as a son of Ida. On further consideration, however, Adda was probably not in the same dynasty. He is not necessary for the genealogy, nor is there any geographical consistency between himself and either Ida, Theodric, or Æthelric. On the contrary, Adda is only noted for battling the York-oriented brothers Peredur and Gwrgi at Caer Greu.[8] His interests were either around York or in an area near to it.

Almost nothing is known of the last brother Glappa, only that he is listed as Ida's first successor. It is possible that Glappa was an historical son of Ida, but considering the tendencies shown above, it is more likely he was not. It may well be that the reason he immediately succeeds Ida in the official genealogy is that Glappa was the most powerful rival in the bardic records. In that case, his place as Ida's first-born would have been meant as a nod to Glappa's surviving family.

So, what do we know about Deira before Æthelfrith conquered it?[9] Soemil has already been discussed; he seems to make the most sense as the person who separated Deira from British-controlled Bernicia in the middle sixth century; he was a northern counterpart to the Sussex Ælle, Wessex Ceawlin, and possibly Kentish Iurminric.

The next person we know anything about is Ælle, but what we do know is conflicted. *The Anglo-Saxon Chronicle* says that he came to the throne in 560 and reigned for thirty years. However, it also says he succeeded Ida—of Bernicia! 560 and his reign length are both unbelievable; there is also no way there could have been written records in Northumbria before 575?

Bede relays a continental memory, that Gregory saw some of Ælle's people as slaves before he became pope. As this comes directly from a contemporary continental source it is credible. It also means, as Miller noted, that Ælle was active between when he returned from Constantinople in 585/6 and 590.[10] That is not much, but it does give us one small range of dates in which he know someone was king in Deira.

How long was Soemil active if he was a rebel figure of the mid-sixth century? There is no way to tell. When did Ælle come to power? Again, we cannot know. Is it possible that one succeeded the other? Yes, but not in any way probable. If Soemil was remembered for separating Deira from Bernicia, he would have been famous enough for any intelligent *skop* to insert into his king's pedigree. So it is very possible that the two were not even related to each other.

Looking forward, we are told that Æthelric succeeded to the kingdom when Ælle died in 588.[11] The inconsistency between the date and the supposed thirty-reign of Ælle (560 + 30 = 590) is a reminder that we cannot trust this date either. Nor does the entry give us a relationship between Ælle and

Æthelric either. Were they brothers? Father and son? Competitors from different dynasties?[12] That, too, we do not know and have no way of learning.

In the South, Gwrtheyrn's reign created the organization for several late-sixth century kingships in Sussex, Wessex, and Kent. By about 600 these had coalesced into at least four distinct kingdoms. Above the Humber river, it would seem that the alliance of Urien, Rhydderch, Morcant, and Gwallog aided in the creation of several kingdoms in Bernicia and at least two in Deira. By the historical period these had merged into two, and were well on their way to forming the single kingdom of Northumbria by 604. It would be the continuing struggle between the houses of Deira and Bernicia that would engage Northumbria for most of the rest of the period in question, with several kingdoms only becoming involved long enough to shift the advantage from one house to the other for a few years at a time.

30

Between the Thames and the Humber

Between the major kingdoms of the South and Northumbria in the North were literally dozens of small chieftainships. The area, eventually becoming Middle Anglia, Mercia, and East Anglia, did not develop powerful kingdoms before 600 and would only produce one family of any significance to English history that was important for more than a decade or so. It is important to ask "why?" It is more important to understand the history of these kingdoms so that we can understand what the area between the two great rivers lacked or had too much of in comparison to Northumbria and the South.

The most prominent kingdom of the region was Mercia. In some ways it is better understood than the kingdoms discussed above; the historical record gives us a single and consistent line of rulers from the early seventh century onward and the genealogical record gives us an unbroken line back to Icel, the founder of the Iclingas dynasty that ruled Mercia. It is not better understood, though, it is just more consistent because Mercia did not leave us any official history and the historians of the period only mentioned Mercia when it affected the other kingdoms.

As with the other kingdoms, there is no historical record that many of the earliest members of the dynasty even existed. For instance Icel seems to be in the place-names, but there is no evidence Icel's son Cnebba, or his son Cynewald. There is not even evidence for Cynewald's son Creoda; the only reason his death is normally placed at 593 is because *The Anglo-Saxon Chronicle* records the death of a *Crida* in that year and it has been assumed that the two were one person. However, we know now that Crida was probably from Wessex and was confused with the Mercian character by later medieval historians.[1] Pybba, a few years later, is the first Mercian we can be sure of; both *The Anglo-Saxon Chronicle* and *Historia Brittonum* name him as the father of Penda. Unfortunately, that is all we can know about him.

Like Mercia, East Anglia also has a straightforward progression of kings from its foundation into the historical era without a discrepancy. Beginning with Wehha and followed by Wuffa and Tytila the kingdom appears to begin in the middle of the sixth century.

When we look a little closer, though, the early history falls apart. Wehha and Wuffa are not mentioned anywhere except in the official genealogy. It has been suggested that Wehha could be a diminutive form of Wihstan,[2] the father of Wiglaf and connected to the Swedish dynasty of Scylfings in *Beowulf*.[3] If East Anglian Wehha and the Scylfing Wihstan were the same person, then Wehha was probably a continental legendary figure added to the pedigree, like Hengest.

The second ruler, Wuffa, was the eponym for the Wuffingas dynasty. But Wuffingas means "descendants of the wolf," which makes Wuffa sound more like a totemic symbol than an historical symbol. If so, the name Wuffa might have been invented in the Christian period to explain the embarrassing or forgotten pagan symbolism.[4]

Whether or not Wuffa comes from Wihstan and Wuffa was invented to explain the Wuffingas name makes no difference in an historical study of post–Roman Britain though. The fact is that neither person is mentioned in our historical sources. We cannot prove that either person existed, let alone if they were members of the East Anglian dynasty.

Tytila is the third official East Anglian ruler, and though none of the histories mention anything he did either, they do tell us he had two sons, Rædwald and Eni, and they lived well into the historical era. Most scholars have placed his obit at least into the seventh century, while Professor Lapidge has suggested a date as late as 616.[5]

Along with the East Anglia and Mercia, many kingdoms are known to have existed in what was known as Middle Anglia. We know about them from a variety of sources, Bede and a few English *vitae* mention several kings. We learn the most about Middle Anglia, though, through the *Tribal Hidage*. Estimates have varied, but Professor Higham believes there may have been sixteen independent tribes active in the area as late as the early seventh century.[6] In some ways, these small and obscure kingdoms are the most interesting feature of the area between the powerhouse of the North and the southern kingdoms.

Archeology has shown us that small Germanic kingships were originally scattered throughout England in the middle of the sixth century, and the histories of Wessex, Deira, Kent, and Bernicia have provided us with some evidence of localized kingdoms early in their respective histories. But in both cases we only have clues that they existed; a reign-length or two that makes no sense with the other available data, a kingdom mentioned within what we thought was a larger kingdom, or two different areas of activity for a single lineage.

30. Between the Thames and the Humber

Middle Anglia is filled with these kingdoms, only they existed well into the historical era. That fact has allowed us to get a little more information about them, which is potentially useful in understanding more about primitive kingships throughout Britain. Here, though, we will ask ourselves why? Why did Middle Anglia not develop into a single regional kingdom when every other Germanic region did? And relevant to that question is, why do Mercia and East Anglia emerge later than the other major kingdoms.

The most obvious reason, in this scholar's opinion, is that Mercia, East Anglia, and Middle Anglia were never under the control of a British overking who would have organized the areas to make it easier to collect tribute. We have seen some evidence that it was this organization that eventually led to the development of Germanic chieftainships and the rapid development of regional kingships. Without that initial foundation East Anglia and Mercia took longer to forge into single kingdoms than their counterparts and Middle Anglia never did.

What little we know about the sixth-century tells us that the Britons had the upper hand and were not driven by any racial hatred against the Germanic people; which means they had no reason to drive them off the island but instead to make use of them. Organizing them to make tribute taking easier and more efficient was the best way to do this. Unfortunately for the Britons, by organizing the Germanic peoples they gave their vassals the means to not only win their independence but to forge their own kingdoms, kingdoms that would rival and overwhelm the Britons in a matter of decades.

The area that would be Mercia, East Anglia, and Middle Anglia, though, had no overlords during the sixth century (from what we can tell). Because of that they were never organized and had to forge their kingdoms beginning at a much more local level. They developed slowly. From what we can tell, the former two had only just become kingdoms when the other regions had assimilated into their medieval sizes, while the Middle Anglian kingdoms were probably behind that.

The end result for the Mercians and East Anglians was that they became major players in English politics later than their counterparts, which in Mercia's case only meant that it took longer to become the dominant power in Britain. Only Middle Anglia really suffered. It would eventually be absorbed by the Mercians.

31

An Interwoven History
600–664

Unfortunately, Pictish history before Brude son of Maelchon in the last third of the sixth century must remain guesswork. No Pictish king before him is mentioned in any primary source, nor do any Pictish kings appear in the annals, *Historia Brittonum*, or Bede. In a very real sense Pictish history starts with him, which makes an understanding of Brude's background fundamental to understanding the Picts.

We should probably start with his parentage. Depending on the source, he is the son of Melcho/Maelchon/Maelchú/Meilochon. Several linguists have commented on the linguistic similarity of those names with Maelgwn, the Gwynedd king.[1] Professor Morris was also kind enough to add historical evidence.[2]

(1) The name of Maelgwn is rare.
(2) The Picts would not have elected the son of an obscure person as their king.
(3) Maelgwn was married to Digwc, who is called an Irish Pict.

That and the linguistic resemblance make for a fairly sound argument, but Morris could also have added that Maelgwn was not just "not obscure," he was one of the most powerful British kings of his era. If the Picts were willing to infuse non–Pictish blood into their royal lineages, he would have been the best option of the time. And we already know the Picts were willing. As Miller demonstrated, powerful men outside of Pictland fathered them— Nectu son of Gwyddno of Strathclyde and Talorcen son of Eanfrith of Northumbria are just two of many examples.

Brude's career is more complicated. If we accept that we have no reliable sources before the late sixth century and that those during Brude's lifetime do not give accurate dates, we are left with the following events of Brude's reign:

554x558	Begins his rule (*Pictish Chronicle*)
558x560	The flight of someone before him (*Annals of Ulster, Annals of Tigernach*) Tigernach says the Scots fled.
563+	At least two visits from Columba to Inverness where we learn he was lord over the Orkneys (*Vita Columbae*)
584; 581/590	Bridei dies (Annals of Innisfallen, Ulster, and Clonmacnoise; *Annals of Tigernach*)

Admittedly this is not much information, but it is something. He fought against (possibly) the Scots. There is a record that Aedan attacked the Orkneys in 580/1, but no mention anywhere that Brude was attacked. He was visited by Columba, possibly to convert him and/or as a diplomat for Dal Riata who only came to see him and the Scots whom he lived among. He reigned for roughly 30 years.

The above tells us that Brude controlled a large area of western Pictland. If he did defeat the Scots early in his reign, it might have given Columba leverage for uniting the Dal Riatans. His victory might also explain why Columba considered it so important to keep on friendly terms with him; even united early Dal Riata was no match for him.

However strong Brude might have been among his people, though, we do know that he did not rule the entire Highlands. The *Annals of Clonmacnoise* clearly say that Galam and Kenneth, both kings of the Picts, died in 580, at least four years before Brude. Maban the son of Cian from *Y Gododdin* was probably not a common warrior, either.[3] All three men would have been Brude's contemporaries.

After Brude, Pictish history gets difficult for the next few decades. For instance Galam Cennalath is recorded as dying in 580 according to the *Annals of Ulster* and the *Annals of Tigernach*. According to some versions of the *Pictish Chronicle* he ruled jointly with Brude for one year.

The *Pictish Chronicle* says that Brude was followed by Gartnait, whose relationship to Aedan has been suggested and rejected.[4] More recently his very existence has been called into question.[5]

Nechtan descendent of Uerb followed him. *The Pictish Chronicle* records that he reigned for 20 or 21 years. He has been connected with a Nechtan son of Canu who died in 621 according to the *Annals of Ulster*. It has also been suggested that he is the Neithon who ruled from Alt Clut.[6] He may have been both people. It is possible he was neither. Cinioch, called the son of Luctren in the Irish Annals, succeeded him and died in 629 (*Annals of Tigernach* and *Annals of Clonmacnoise*), 631 (*Annals of Ulster*), 633 (*Annals of Innisfallen*). According to the *Pictish Chronicle*, he reigned for 14 or 19 years.

Cinioch was followed by Garnait II son of Fioth or Uuid (linguistic variants of the same name) who reigned for four years according to the *Pictish*

Chronicle and died in 635 according to the *Annals of Ulster*. His brother Bridei son of Uuid reigned for five years according to the *Pictish Chronicle*. He died in 637 according to the *Annals of Tigernach* and 641 in the *Annals of Ulster*. His brother Talorc son of Uuid followed him, reigning for twelve years in the *Pictish Chronicle* and dying in 653 in both the *Annals of Ulster* and the *Annals of Tigernach*.

Talorc was followed by Talorcan son of Eanfrith, himself a son of the Æthelfrith who had united Northumbria and whose uncles and first cousins would also rule there. Eanfrith and his brothers had been forced into exile in Dal Riata when Rædwald had killed their father at the Battle of the Idle River in 616. It only makes sense that the brothers would have pursued diplomacy to strengthen their position for a return to Northumbria, and marriage to a Pictish princess would have been ideal if they were looking for a powerful alliance. That his son was made king years later could have helped strengthen that alliance, or it is possible that Oswiu used his widespread influence (as we will see he was the most powerful man in Britain at about the time Talorcan was made king) to install him. That would explain why Bede claimed that most of the Picts were Oswiu's tributes.[7] We also know that he defeated and killed Dúnchad son of Conaing from Dal Riata in 654.

With Talorcan, the only other well-documented Pictish king, we are also certain he did not rule all the Picts. According to the *Annals of Clonmacnoise*, King Lochyne son of Finnie was active in 642 and both Moyle Keith son of Scanalt and Eochie Jarlaly were ruling in 662.

What does any of this tell us? That the Picts had more than one kingdom until at least 664? That the Picts were secretive about themselves? Both true. What little they did leave us says that they did not mind intermarrying with British and Anglo-Saxon kings. We are certain that Talorcan was the grandson of Æthelfrith. The connection between Bridei and his father Maelgwn seems reasonable. Nechtan may have been descended from a Strathclyde prince, may have even ruled Strathclyde.

Áedán Son of Gabran

When Áedán had been born sometime after 550, Dal Riata had been filled with independent camps that had probably raided the Picts, Irish, and British indiscriminately. None of the groups had ever been safe, but the region was so difficult to navigate that its inhabitants must have felt insulated anyway. Columba's will and diplomacy along with the Battle of Teloch or Delgu changed that. It was around 574 that Dal Riata united under one king. Through Columba again, the kingdom accepted Irish lordship and promised its ships in return for the protection of the Irish king.

With Irish patronage and a fresh unity, Áedán must have felt like the most powerful king on the island; he was definitely the ruler with the most political momentum by looking outward. Though we cannot know everything he did during his nearly thirty year rule, we do know of several of his activities. He raided Orkney in around 580. He conquered the Isle of Man around 583. He fought a battle in Circinn, Pictland, in or after 599 (we do not know against which king though). In about 590 he fought and won the Battle of Leithreid or Leithrig, maybe somewhere near the upper Forth against the Maeatae.[8] At some point he lost his son Domangart in battle against the Bernicians.[9]

There are suggestions of more fighting. The *Prophecy of Berchán* says that he fought thirteen consecutive years against the Picts. A Welsh triad claims that Áedán's raid on Alt Clut, capital of Strathclyde, was one of the three unrestrained plunderings of Britain. The poem *Peiryan Vaban* speaks of a battle between Áedán and Rhydderch of Strathclyde.

His main concern must have been Bernicia though. In 603 Áedán hosted the Irish high-king and his warriors and allied himself with Hering, the disenfranchised prince of an absorbed Northumbrian kingdom to attack Æthelfrith at Degsastan. The battle was catastrophic for him; it probably ended his kingship by shattering his reputation as a war-leader. It was a blow for Dal Riata as a whole; the kingdom would be inactive for many years and the Irish would never threaten Northumbria again. And of course, by crushing Dal Riata Æthelfrith opened up all northern Britain to his influence.

Kent Through the Reign of Æthelberht

The earliest known ruler of Kent was probably Iurminric/Eormenric, the father of Æthelberht. We have no direct evidence for this assumption, but the fact that his son married a Frankish princess, Bertha, at a time when the Franks were emerging as a continental powerhouse is strong evidence that Kent was independent of the British by Eormenric's time and that he was a king there.[10]

Besides Eormenric's independence from the British and his diplomatic connections with the Franks, we also know that trade with the continent increased in the middle to late sixth century.[11] That tells us that Kent was a wealthy kingdom. And as Kent was England's main contact with the continent, it is reasonable to assume that Kent was the supplier of continental goods to the Anglo-Saxons. That would have provided the kingdom with the best kind of prestige over the Anglo-Saxon kingdoms; the kind that could not be overturned in battle or the death of a king.

This is probably a good time to mention one more curiosity about Kent.

In 568, *The Anglo-Saxon Chronicle* says that Æthelberht lost a battle against Ceawlin and Cutha. It has elsewhere been shown that the battle could not have involved Æthelberht on various grounds.[12]

So who did fight Ceawlin and Cutha? There really is no way to tell. What is interesting, though, is that Kent lost, which means there would have been no reason to put it in the *Kentish Source*. Wessex would have had a reason to remember, though, and as we have seen *The Anglo-Saxon Chronicle* was written in Wessex. Could the battle notice have been an historical memory that was used by the chronicle? Maybe. We have seen evidence that the Battle of Dyrham notice (577) has accurately recorded names whose linguistic structures are within a century of the battle, maybe closer.

On the other hand, the notice names Æthelberht specifically, and that must be wrong as things stand. If the battle did occur there are really only three possibilities. First, that the date was accurate and as no one living remembered who the king of Kent had been at that time and Æthelberht was the only royal they knew of from the sixth century they guessed it was him. Second, that Æthelberht did fight in the battle and the date was a guess. Third, that the date and Æthelberht's presence were both guesses. Either way, we can be fairly certain that at some point during Ceawlin and Cutha's careers (557–616) a king of Kent fought and lost a battle against them. That is not much help here, but we might find a use for it later on.

The great Æthelberht is the next ruler we know about, but we know very little about him. Bede says that he accepted the first papal dignitaries and himself converted to Christianity, giving a plot of land in Canterbury to his first bishop, Augustine.[13] He also patronized the conversion of Essex where his maternal nephew Sæberht ruled.[14] None of this explains why Bede named him as the third *Bretwalda*, nor would that battle against Wessex, but as a *Bretwalda* he probably took tribute from all the English kingdoms south of the Thames and several between the Thames and the Humber River.

It has been assumed, based on what we know about later *Bretwaldas*, that Æthelberht must have fought some decisive battle and because of that he gained a strong enough reputation as a warrior king to make all the kingdoms of southern England want him as their protector. The author must admit to having accepted that reasoning without question in the past as well. After studying the period in depth, though, that assumption has one serious flaw. What battle? *The Anglo-Saxon Chronicle* gives us several important battles that Ælle and Ceawlin won before Æthelberht and that Æthelfrith and Rædwald won after him, but apart from that 568 notice (which he lost), there is not a single recorded battle for Æthelberht.

It has been mentioned that the archeological evidence suggests a strong and consistent trade with Frankia throughout the sixth century that included wares, art, and weaponry. The personal name evidence of Eormenric, and

Æthelberht's marriage to a Frankish princess tells us that Kent had longstanding diplomatic ties with some of the most powerful kings on the continent. It would have given Kent and especially its kings a great deal of prestige.

So what if Æthelberht was not powerful because of his battle reputation, but because of his ties to the continent and the wealth and access to weapons and armor that relationship gave him? The suggestion would explain the relative dearth of Kentish battles in the later sixth and early seventh century. It would also explain why Kent never fell to the status of Essex and yet avoided fighting any major battles after 600.

Æthelfrith

Æthelfrith is the first Northumbrian king we know anything about. His father according to the official genealogies, Æthelric, was probably his real father. His five official "uncles," though, are another story. As the author has demonstrated, there is strong evidence that they were contemporary rulers of kingdoms in various parts of Northumbria,[15] who were later integrated into one family for the sake of Northumbrian political unity. It was only because Deira remained independent and rebellious well into the historical era that its late sixth century rulers were not added to his family, too.

We know even less about his early career, but there are three things we can be certain of. First, that his twenty-four year reign ended in 616 or 617 and therefore that he became king in 592 or 593.[16] Second, that he ruled all of Northumbria for the last twelve years of his reign.

Third, that the Urien confederacy fought against several kings from different Northumbrian kingdoms.[17] That might seem a little off-topic, but the Britons were active in the range 574x620,[18] and more likely 574x604, and Northumbrians were their vassals or tributaries during that period.[19] That means that Æthelfrith probably spent most of his first dozen years as king of Bernicia conquering several kingdoms as well as Deira.

Whatever he did, it must have been quick and decisive. Even before he had conquered all of Northumbria in 604,[20] Áedán gathered a force together that included at least one exiled Northumbrian prince and the High-King of Ireland and fought him at the Battle of Degsastan. Æthelfrith won, leaving him the most prestigious war-leader in the north and possibly a tribute-taker there.[21]

Within the next two years Æthelfrith absorbed the last kingdoms of Northumbria. At that point his career becomes a little more visible. He married the last Deiran king's daughter, Acha, either before (in which case it may have led to his assumption of the Deiran throne) or after (in which case he would have been legitimizing his new position) he conquered Deira,[22] and at some point after 604/5 he forced the Deiran heir Edwin into exile.

The Welsh campaign was between 613 and 616.[23] Traditionally scholars assumed his attack was part of a larger strategy to divide the Britons of the North from Wales, but this is not supported by the evidence. As Stenton pointed out, Bede never mentions a strategy.[24] Koch has noted that that there is little or no evidence of pagan Germanic settlement in the area.[25] It also does not make sense with what we know of Æthelfrith. He did absorb Northumbria into a single kingdom but never did the same with Dal Riata. It is very likely that Northumbria was as large a kingdom as could be managed at the time. So if he was not trying to expand his kingdom, he was probably either defending it (as he may have been against Dal Riata) or winning more prestige and tribute for his kingdom (as he probably had after Degsastan).

During his campaign Æthelfrith first massacred the monks of Bangor-Is-Coed. Bede tells us this was divine retribution, but Ziegler has suggested it was to dishearten the Britons before he fought them.[26] When he did fight a Briton alliance under Selyf and Cetula (probably Cadwal), he defeated them decisively at Chester. Again, there is no mention that he took advantage of the situation in any way. It makes sense that he would have taken tribute from the Welsh kingdoms too.

In 616 or 617 he learned that Edwin of Deira, now an adult and a threat, was hiding with Rædwald in the kingdom of East Anglia. He demanded that Rædwald give him up. Rædwald agreed. However, when Æthelfrith came to claim him, legend says that Rædwald's wife convinced him to fight instead. In the Battle of Idle that resulted Æthelfrith was killed and his army defeated. Edwin took the Northumbrian throne and Rædwald became the most powerful man in northern England.

East Anglia Up Through Rædwald

Like Æthelfrith, Rædwald is the first member of his dynasty of whom we know anything. His son's name was Sigeberht, which is a name otherwise only found in Kent.[27] It has been suggested that he married into the Essex royal house and that put him in contact with Kent. The traditional view is just as probable, that Æthelberht's prestige brought East Anglia under Kent's influence. This had happened by around 604, when he accepted Christianity and his lord served as a witness.[28]

Regardless of his reasons for accepting Christianity, Rædwald was never able to convince his people to convert—not even his queen. He remained Christian but as a compromise he kept a Christian and a pagan altar in the royal temple.

Probably in 616 but possibly earlier, the exile Edwin asked for sanctuary from Æthelfrith. Rædwald gave it and allowed the Northumbrian prince to live among his household. When Æthelfrith found out where Edwin was hiding he demanded that the prince be returned to Northumbria. After a third envoy had come promising great wealth and threatening war, Rædwald agreed to hand Edwin over. It was only when his wife convinced him he was being a coward that he decided to fight instead.[29] He won the resulting Battle of Idle in either 616 or 617.

Æthelberht had already died in February of 616, so after the battle Rædwald would have been considered the most respected war-leader in the south and as he had killed the most respected war-leader in the north he was the most feared man on the island. That is probably why Bede called him a *Bretwalda*.

He was not just the most powerful man in Britain though. Æthelberht died in 616 and his nephew Sæberht King of Essex died in the same year. Both men were succeeded by pagans who drove out the Christian missionaries. That left Rædwald the only major Christian Germanic king in England until Eadbald of Kent converted. As such, he was the only contact with Rome and any kingdoms aligned with Roman Christianity. It is probably no coincidence that during this period Gipeswic, modern Ipswich, developed into an important trading center along the North Sea.[30]

It is widely believed that the famous and extremely wealthy burial at Sutton Hoo, known simply as Mound 1, was built for Rædwald. Several points of evidence have been raised over the years,[31] while the editors Judith McClure and Roger Collins have noted that the actual evidence of Rædwald is almost nonexistent.[32] Alternative persons have also been suggested—another East Anglian king, a prestigious foreign visitor,[33] or even a wealthy man.[34] This scholar would suggest a simple compromise; as with his temples in life Rædwald may have chosen to divide his faith in death; he arranged for a traditional burial at Sutton Hoo but had himself buried in a normal Christian grave elsewhere.

Edwin

Edwin the son of Ælle was born a prince of the Deiran kingdom. So, when Æthelfrith was declared king of all Northumbria, including Deira, in 604, it was only a matter of time before he was forced to go into exile.

Where and when he went are less certain. Later historians say that he spent his childhood with Cadfan son of Iago, but that is unlikely because it served the clear literary purpose of drawing biblical parallels between him and his "foster brother" Cadwallon, who would kill him in 633. Bede tells us he spent time in Mercia under the protection of Cearl where he married the princess Cwœnburg; we do know he was there by the 610s.[35]

We have no idea when he left, either. We do know that in 616/7 he was in East Anglia and under the protection of Rædwald, who at first buckled under the threat of invasion from Æthelfrith but eventually (thanks to his pagan wife) chose to give battle and killed Æthelfrith. We also know he installed Edwin as king of Northumbria and probably forced Æthelfrith's sons into exile.

Whether because of the debt Edwin owed Rædwald or because of the very real prestige Rædwald had earned at the Battle of Idle River, Edwin paid homage to Rædwald during the latter's lifetime. That did not mean Edwin was not a powerful and active lord in his own right, though. In 616 he evicted Cerdic from Elmet and assimilated the region into his kingdom. A now-lost poem detailed Fiachnae macBáetáin's campaign against Dún Guaire (likely Bamborough) during the early 620s,[36] and the *Annals of Ulster* and the *Annals of Tigernach* recorded the siege and possible capture of Bamburgh in 623 and 624, respectively.

Around 625, Rædwald died and Edwin became a little more aggressive. It was around that time that he asserted himself as the overlord of the English kingdoms by offering protection to some of the lesser Germanic chieftains. He absorbed Elmet into his kingdom in 626.[37] He also conquered the minor territory of Lindsey and managed to collect tribute from the Isle of Man, Mercia, and Anglesey.

Diplomatically he married Æthelburg, the daughter of Æthelberht and the sister of Eadbald. The price of that marriage was conversion to Christianity, which he initially accepted but then hesitated to follow through on.

On Easter of 626, Cwichelm of Wessex sent an assassin to kill Edwin, but failed. Edwin responded by having his daughter baptized and promising to convert if his retaliatory campaign was a success. It apparently was; in 627 he and his entire war-band became Christians.[38]

According to the *Annales Cambriae*, in 629 Cadwallon of Gwynedd attempted to free his kingdom from tribute but failed. He either went into exile or paid homage to Edwin.[39] It was only when Cadwallon rebelled again, this time in alliance with Penda of Mercia, that Edwin was defeated and killed at the Battle of Hatfield in 632/3. When he fell, the prestige of being the most successful war-leader on the island fell to the senior partner in the alliance, Cadwallon.

Gwynedd and the Briton Kingdoms

In the decades between the fall of Urien in the North and Rhun's campaign from Gwynedd at the end of the sixth century, and the victory of Cadwallon and Penda in 632/3, we know very little about what happened among the Britons. It amounts to a loss at the Battle of Dyrham, as recorded in *The Anglo-Saxon Chronicle* for 577, an alliance between Strathclyde and Dal Riata according to the saint's lives of Columba and Kentigern, Ceredig of Ceredigion invading someplace in Dyfed, Selyf losing the Battle of Chester between 613 and 616 according to the *Annales Cambriae*, Bede,[40] and the *Annals of Inisfallen*, Cerdic of Elmet poisoning the Northumbrian prince Hereric and later having his kingdom absorbed into Northumbria, and Edinburgh being sieged in 638 according to the *Annales Cambriae*. And of course we have the genealogies. Few of these events have any context. Small wonder that little ink has been spilled on these decades.

What can we make from this? The author has suggested a combination of factors weakened the British in the mid-sixth century, but whatever was the cause seems to have been devastating. It is safe to assume that the British kingdoms all had internal conflicts or conflicts between themselves during this period, but no strong leader emerged to dominate or even unite the Britons at this time. In other words, the reason history records nothing interesting among the British for about fifty years is probably because nothing interesting happened during that time.

Cadwallon would change that. Either the son of King Cadfan of Gwynedd as the genealogies claim,[41] or of Guitcun from northern Britain,[42] he was the charismatic and strong-willed leader the Britons needed. He was not undefeated though. When Edwin attacked Puffin Island in 629, Welsh traditions say that he defeated Cadwallon. The *Welsh Triads* say he escaped to Ireland after that. Ireland is where he turned his career around. He forged an alliance with the pagan Penda and several Briton kingdoms. When he was ready he returned to Britain and led his confederacy against Edwin. In 632 or 633, he attacked Edwin at Hatfield Chase, killing him and routing his army.

Bede tells us that Cadwallon spent the next year or so trying to kill every last Anglo-Saxon.[43] We know that is not true though; he was loyal to his alliance with Penda and did not attack any other English kingdom. In fact his actions might have been admired by the English. As Professor Koch has pointed out, Cædwalla of Wessex was born in the next generation, possibly out of respect for Cadwallon's accomplishments.[44]

Within Northumbria, Edwin's successor Eanfrith tried to sue for peace but was killed. Eanfrith's successor, Oswald, gave battle. Though he was outnumbered and his opponent had the psychological advantage being the veterans who had already beaten him, Cadwallon won the Battle of Heavenfield and killed Edwin in the process.[45]

Oswald

In 616, at the Battle of Idle, Rædwald had defeated and killed Æthelfrith, forcing his sons Eanfrith, Oswald, and Oswiu into exile in Dal Riata.[46] When

Edwin was killed, the brothers saw an opportunity to reclaim their birthright and came back to Northumbria. Eanfrith approached Cadwallon, probably offering tribute in return for instatement as the king of Northumbria, but was killed. Oswald fought against Cadwallon instead, probably with help from Dal Riata, and won.

It was not just a victory though. The night before the Battle of Heavenfield Oswald received a vision from Columba that told him Christianity would win him the battle. Telling his followers what had happened, he convinced them to be baptized as soon as they had won the battle. Perhaps the Christian fervor Oswald had engendered in his warriors brought him victory.

Heavenfield not only won him Northumbria, but gave him the reputation of being the greatest war leader on the island. Adomnán, writing decades later, said that he was emperor of all Britain and Bede says he ruled every kingdom in Britain.[47] The only hint of discord comes from the *Annals of Tigernach*, which says that several Anglo-Saxons banded against him in 637; Penda was probably one of the rebel leaders. Nothing came of it though.[48] Dr. Stancliffe has suggested that this must have been only one of several rebellions that he put down his career; they have been forgotten because they did not last long.[49]

Instead, Oswald focused on spreading Christianity. He requested that Iona send someone to spread the faith and Aidan responded. There are many stories about Oswald's personal charity but maybe the most illustrative is that, as Aidan did not know English and Oswald had learned Irish as an exile, he served as Aidan's translator while the bishop was teaching.[50] He died in the Battle of Maserfelth, generally located at Oswestry in 642, leaving the field to Penda.

Mercia

We know almost nothing about the origins of Mercia, despite the fact that it dominated Britain for over a century. This is because Mercians never did write their own history like Kent, Northumbria, or Wessex, and no one ever bothered to add them to their own, as happened with Sussex and Essex. However, we do know it probably developed late, with settlers coming from the east.[51]

What we know from credible historical sources up until the first mention of Penda in 626 amounts to this; at some time after 604 Edwin came there as a refugee. The king, Cearl,[52] gave the refugee his daughter Cwœnburg in marriage.[53] Genealogies tell us that he was preceded by Creoda and Creoda's son Pybba. We are only told that Cearl was Creoda's kinsman.

It has been suggested that Pybba and Cearl were dynastic rivals.[54] It is also possible that the two clans controlled two different territories in what would become Mercia,[55] like Deira and Bernicia in Northumbria. Higham has suggested that the Battle of Chester may have destroyed the power of Cearl's clan.[56] Alternatively Penda or one of his family might have done the job. By the time Penda emerges as the Mercian king all traces of Cearl are gone.

We have no idea when the greatest of the seventh-century Mercian kings began his kingship; not because of a lack of testimony, though, more because we have too much and it all conflicts with each other. *The Anglo-Saxon Chronicle* says he came to the throne in 626. Bede says he died in 655 having ruled 22 years,[57] possibly from Edwin's defeat in 633. The *Historia Brittonum* gives him a reign of ten years,[58] but that makes no sense at all.

What we do know is that he was active in 628 when he fought Cynegils and Cwichelm according to *The Anglo-Saxon Chronicle*. Sources agree that he allied with Cadwallon to help defeat Penda at the Battle of Hatfield Chase, but was not with him at Heavenfield.

After that his career gets fuzzy again. It has been suggested that his brother Eowa may have ruled during Oswald's kingship.[59] In any event, he still commanded his own war-band and made use of it. At some point he killed Edwin's son Eadfrith, a dynastic rival of Oswald,[60] but also a potential thorn to himself if he had decided to take revenge for the deaths of his father (Edwin) and grandfather (Cearl).[61] Somewhere between 635 and 641 he defeated King Ecgric and former king Sigebert of East Anglia.[62]

We cannot even be sure he was the king during Oswald's reign. Bede did say that his fortunes were mixed during his 22 years in power,[63] and both the *Historia Brittonum* and *Annales Cambriae* say that Eowa was a king of Mercia in the years before Maserfelth. Considering the history of joint kingships it is very possible that both men were ruling during this period.[64] It has also been suggested that his brother may have been installed by Oswald as a puppet during his reign.[65] Because of this we are not certain of the Battle of Maserfelth's background, either. All we know is that Penda won, Oswald and Penda's brother Eowa were killed, and he was probably aided by one or more Welsh kings.

Maserfelth left Penda as the most prestigious war-leader on the island and dominant in the north; for a few years Northumbria fractured back to a Deiran (Oswine) and a Bernician (Oswiu) king. He eventually installed his son Peada as King of Middle Anglia. He also had influence in the south; the West Saxon king Cenwealh married his sister.

That did not mean he was not tested, though. Penda spent most of the rest of his life trying to maintain what he had won. In 645 Cenwealh abandoned Penda's sister and took another woman as his wife. Penda had him exiled. In 654 he killed Anna, the East Anglian king who had given refuge to Cenwealh. It seems likely he installed Anna's brother Æthelhere as a puppet king of East Anglia.[66]

Penda also had a complicated relationship with Northumbria. He waged several campaigns against Oswiu, but in 653 Peada married Alhflæd daughter of Oswiu and Oswiu's son Alhfrith married Cyneburh Penda's daughter. What is really confusing is that Peada's marriage was only accepted when Peada and Penda agreed that Peada would accept Christianity as a condition to the union.

Maybe Penda had not worried about the religion and only realized too late what an effect it was having in Middle Anglia.[67] Maybe Oswiu was attempting to reunite Northumbria and Penda went in to stop him.[68] Whatever the reason, Penda invaded Northumbria again in 655.

He came in force, too: 30 war-bands, including Cadafael of Gwynedd, Æthelhere of East Anglia, and Æthelwald the brother of Oswine, whom Oswiu had murdered. Numbers did not help, though. When he met Oswiu at the Battle of Winwæd/Hatfield Chase he died and his army fled in defeat.

Oswiu

Like his brother Oswald, Oswiu had spent most of his childhood exiled in Dal Riata. He had also converted to Christianity and married the Reged princess Rieinmellth while there or shortly after his return; his son Alhfrith was born of their union. Returning to Northumbria on Cadwallon's death along with his brother, he had maintained his own war-band and married the Ulster princess Fín. In about 650 she gave birth to Aldfrith according to the author's date-guessing.[69] Oswiu ascended the Northumbrian throne after his brother fell at Maserfelth.

He inherited Northumbria, but only because Penda allowed it. Even that was a challenge; Deira was rebellious during the first few years of his reign.[70] Still, he managed to remain an irritant for Penda; Mercian armies went into Northumbria several times between 642 and 655. They never broke Oswiu's power, either; in 653 Penda's son and daughter married Oswiu's daughter and son. Penda even made conversion a condition of Peada's marriage.

The dual marriage did not end the animosity between Oswiu and Penda, though, and when Penda rode into Northumbria in 655 it was with an overwhelming force. It met the Northumbrian army at Winwæd/Hatfield Chase. It was a total success for Oswiu. Penda and his East Anglian ally Æthelhere fell. The Deiran king Œthelwald had not taken part in the fighting at all and probably lost his right to rule because of it; he disappears from the historical record. That left Oswiu the absolute master of Northumbria and the most dominant king in Britain.

He responded by exercising that power. He installed his son Alhfrith as king of Deira. Æthelhere's brother was elected King of East Anglia, possibly with the help of Oswiu and his ally Eorcenberht King of Kent. Cenwealh of Wessex may have returned from his exile in this period, making him a natural ally if not a tributary. Peada, the son of Penda but a docile ally since his conversion, was installed as the king of Mercia. In the north, Oswiu's nephew Talorcan son of Eanfrith was made a king of the Picts within a few years of 655 and had defeated Dal Riata in 654.

The extent of his power did not last, though. Oswiu probably campaigned in Wales during the late 650s to bring Penda's former allies under control,[71] and while he was away his empire fell apart. The Essex king Sigeberht was murdered and replaced with his brother Swithhelm. Swithhelm was probably subject to East Anglia during his rule.[72]

In 656 Peada was poisoned. Oswiu replaced him with several non-royal governors, but the Mercians would not accept them. They had soon driven out Oswiu's puppet government and replaced it with Wulfhere,[73] the supposed son of Penda. Wulfhere would recognize Oswiu's lordship and accepted Oswiu's kinsman Trumhere as his bishop,[74] but would spend the rest of his career gaining power in southern England.[75]

In 664 his own son Alhfrith would revolt from his stronghold of Deira and would use his descent from Urien and the *Northern Memoranda* to generate support. The Synod of Whitby, also in 664, is probably the most famous action of Oswiu's reign. In it, the Irish practice of Christianity was overturned by the Roman practice. Oswiu's power and influence, weakened as it was, would eventually change over every English church.

British Kingdoms

Banded together against Northumbria, the British kings under Cadafael had remained allied to Penda after Cadwallon's death. Throughout his campaigns they remained at his side and enjoyed a renaissance of political power; contemporary poetry tells us they won large amounts of loot during their campaigns with him.[76] When Penda fell Peada replaced him and was loyal to Northumbria. Wulfhere, his eventual successor, was never able to renew the alliance and Oswiu was taking their tribute within a few years.

East Anglia

Edwin's benefactor Rædwald probably died around 625 and Edwin helped his son Eorpwald to the East Anglian throne after he had converted to

Christianity. Edwin probably hoped he had a loyal ally. Eorpwald was assassinated a few years later by a pagan nobleman named Ricberht assassinated him. Ricberht may have ruled for about three years.[77] Around 630, Ricberht was killed and succeeded by Eorpwald's brother Sigeberht and his kinsman Ecgric.[78]

Sigeberht had returned from his exile in Gaul where he had been converted to Christianity. As the senior partner in the takeover, he ruled the kingdom, working with Edwin to spread Christianity and establishing a bishopric under the Burgundian Felix. Sigeberht also established a school for learning Latin on the Frankish model. The kingdom restored and stable, he retired to a monastery after a few years.

Ecgric succeeded him. He may have been pagan. He was killed, along with Sigeberht, when Penda invaded East Anglia in the aftermath of Heavenfield.

Ecgric was succeeded at some point before 645 by his kinsman Anna, the son of Eni and a paternal nephew of Rædwald. Anna was a devout Christian whose children—a son and his daughters—were all canonized. Anna himself converted Cenwealh of Wessex during the latter's exile in East Anglia starting between 645 and 648 and lasting three years.[79]

Anna was also a competent war-leader and politician who resisted Penda throughout his career. He attempted to extend his own influence into Middle Anglia.[80] He probably provided military support to Cenwealh when he returned to his kingdom from Penda's exile in the range 648x651. He married one daughter, Seaxburh, to Eorcenberht King of the Kent,[81] and another daughter Æthelthryth in around 651 to Tondberht, a prince of the South Gyrwe who lived along his western borders.[82] Æthelthryth would later marry the future Northumbrian king Ecgfrith.[83]

Anna's intrigues forced Penda to drive him into exile in 651. He returned in 654,[84] when Penda invaded the kingdom. *The Anglo-Saxon Chronicle* simply says that Anna was killed but it is a safe assumption that Penda killed him. His brother Æthelhere succeeded to the throne. Æthelhere was a loyal vassal to Penda until he was killed the next year at the Battle of Winwæd. He was followed by a third brother, Æthelwold, who was an independent ruler until he died in 664.

Kent

After the death of Æthelberht in 616, his son Eadbald succeeded him. Eadbald spent at least a year on the throne as a pagan, which probably hurt his connection with Frankia, and when he did convert the face of Britain had changed. Rædwald had defeated Æthelfrith and become the most feared and respected warrior king. As a Christian he would have inherited communications with the continent, and as an intelligent ruler he had used his new position to generate trade with East Anglia.

Eadbald was relatively inactive over the next few years, but he did manage to retain some of Kent's old power. In 625 he married his sister Æthelburg to Edwin, the new or soon-to-be new over-king of England, and sent her along with her priest Paul to convert Northumbria. And when Edwin died she escaped to Kent but sent her sons on to Frankia so that they could not be used for her brother's political games.

Eadbald's son Eorcenberht succeeded him in 640 and continued the same policy of diplomatic maneuverings. He married Seaxburh the daughter of Anna in an era when Penda dominated the English kingdoms. He died in 664.

Dal Riata

After Áedán's death, Dal Riata was quiet under his son Eochaid Buide's rule. He co-ruled with Connad Cerr, possibly his son or the son of Conall from an opposing dynasty. Connad died fighting in Ireland in 629, and Eochaid died later in the same year.

Eochaid's son Domnall Brecc followed him, and during his reign Dal Riata became more active in international politics. Domnall had already fought at the Battle of Cend Delgten, Ireland, in 622. During his reign he ended the Dal Riata alliance with the Northern Uí Néill which Columba and Áedán had started and sided with the Dál nAraidi. The result was major losses at the battles of Mag Rath and Sailtír (637). Closer to home he lost two battles against the Picts (635 and 638). He died at the Battle of Strathcarron in 642 fighting against the Strathclyde forces under Eugein I, the same year as Oswald fell at the Battle of Maserfelth.

Ferchar son of Connad Cerr succeeded him, and he resumed Dal Riata's old alliance with the Northern Uí Néill. He was followed in 650 by Dúnchad and Conall Crandomna. We know nothing about their reign other than that Dúnchad died in about 654 and Conall about 660.

Wessex

Northumbria was united in 604/5. Æthelberht was the ruler of a united Kent in 597 when Augustine came to Britain. He may have been king in 593. With other kingdoms one individual emerges as the first known leader without any hard dates. Penda in Mercia, Sæberht in Essex, and Rædwald in East

Anglia were kings long before they appeared in 633, 604, and 616—they may not have been the first either.

We have no such luck with Wessex; there is no certain time or person we can point to and say "This is when Wessex was a single kingdom." The historical record has been so muddled with the fusion of at least three dynasties that it may never be possible to know exactly when, or with whom, Wessex finally united. In many cases we cannot even be certain if there were one or two contemporary kings of the same name active in different Wessex kingdoms.[85]

What do we know? That Ceawlin was remembered as an Hwicce and an over-king. Cuthwulf was a contemporary king. Ceawlin won the battle of Deorham but later lost the Battle of Woden's Barrow. After that his son and heir Cuthwine went into exile. We also know that Ceol son of Cutha is assigned the next place in the Wessex king list but probably was not from the same family.[86]

In fact the rest of Wessex history is a frustrating jumble of persons. Ceol was succeeded by his brother Ceolwulf who is said to have fought against the English, Britons, Picts, and Scots, but whose only recorded battle was against the South Saxons.

Cynegils, probably the son of Cuthwine and grandson of Ceawlin, is the next king listed. He fought at Beandun with his son (?) Cwichelm[87] and against the Welsh in 614. In 626 Cwichelm orchestrated the assassination attempt on Edwin, possibly without his father's knowledge. In around 626 someone from Wessex also invaded Essex and killed Seaxred and his brothers. Cynegils and Cwichelm are placed at the Battle of Cirencester in 628 where they fought against Penda and apparently lost. Cwichelm was baptized in 635 as one of the conditions of "alliance" with Oswald and against Penda. It was probably more of an overlord/tributary relationship though, as Oswald dominated the Germanic kingdoms in 635 and Penda may not have been a king at that time.

Cynegils was succeeded by Cenwealh, who is connected to no battles and whose reign extends beyond the scope of this book. Between 645 and 648 he was forced into exile in East Anglia where he converted to Christianity. Probably with Anna's help he returned three years later. It was some time after that when he divided his kingdom into two bishoprics, centering on Dorchester and Winchester.

Essex

Essex never had a powerful king equal or greater in standing than its contemporaries. It survived as an independent kingdom through the period though. The first verifiable king was Sæberht, son of Sledd, who was the nephew of Æthelberht through his sister Ricula. He accepted the bishop Mellitus and with him Christianity in 604.[88] He died in 616, the same year as his uncle.

He was followed by three brothers, Seaxred, Sæward, and an unknown. They renounced Christianity and banished Mellitus. Nothing more is known of their rule until Cwichelm of Wessex invaded in 626, killing all three brothers.

What happened over the next few decades was not recorded by any credible sources, but eventually Sigeberht the Good inherited the throne in about 653. Yorke thinks he might have been the son of Sæward.[89] He converted to Christianity on one of Oswiu's estates and then returned to Essex to evangelize his people with the help of Cedd. Sigeberht was murdered in 660 or 661 by two brothers who were his kinsmen.[90] Succeeding to the throne, his brother Swithhelm was converted in 662 by Æthelwald of East Anglia. He died in 664.

Sussex

The kingdom of Sussex is the least known of the major kingdoms. After Ælle, it is not mentioned again until Wessex invaded and its king, Æthelwealh, managed to create an alliance with Mercia. The result was continued independence and Wulfhere's patronage of his baptism. As an ally Wulfhere gave him Wight, the Meon valley, and marriage to Eabe a princess of the Hwicce,[91] suggesting that even though the kingdom had not been mentioned for over a hundred years it had remained a significant dominion in England.

What can we take from a survey of the English states' in the years leading up to the Synod of Whitby? Hopefully, by tracing each kingdom, the interweaving dynasties, battles, and religious work of the period are a little more clear.

And we can see that, for whatever reason, whenever Northumbria was not fighting a civil war it had a natural advantage over the other kingdoms. That is not to say that Northumbria was always dominant, just that it took something extraordinary for another kingdom to have the ascendancy over her. Rædwald was allowed a position of superiority over Edwin out of respect for what he had done, but Edwin slipped into the *Bretwalda* position without a battle once he was gone. Cadwallon needed an alliance with many British kingdoms as well as Penda to defeat Edwin. Penda had the same advantage. Even then it was not always enough. Æthelfrith fought an alliance of Dal Riata and Irish forces, while Edwin was a threat to his throne, and was still the dominant figure in the North for over a decade. Oswiu and Oswald were both dominant figures when they ruled both Bernicia and Deira.

Northumbrian dominance would of course fade by the end of the century. Mercia would become and remain the most powerful kingdom in Britain until the Danish invasions of the ninth century. However, Northumbria had the strongest armies and the most charismatic leaders in the period.

Finally, we can see that Kent's kings fought battles and remained a serious political force throughout the period, but they were not relevant because of their armies. Diplomatic ties to Frankia and the papacy helped, but so did several intelligent marriages and its position with Roman Christianity. Just as important, after the rise of Northumbria, Kent never challenged the power of a dominant kingdom. Instead they allied with them, making the risk of battle (to take a guess) not worth the pay off of Kent's total capitulation. As we will see, once Northumbria accepted Roman Christianity, Kent's advantage in that dynamic would dissolve.

RELIGION IN POST-ROMAN BRITAIN

32

The Age of Saints

In modern parlance, a saint is any person who has achieved a high level of holiness in their religion. In the Catholic Church a saint must also achieve two posthumous miracles and have someone petition the Vatican.

Things did not work quite that way in medieval times, and especially not among the Celts. As we have seen in our study of the native materials, saints were declared by their monasteries and saints' lives were written and rewritten for religious, economic, and even political reasons. Why has the century or so between the late fifth century and the late sixth century been called the "Age of Saints"? Because dozens of these uncanonized saints were active during the period. Holy men of the period were connected with the political development and eventual stabilization of the Celtic kingdoms.

Traditional thinking is that this period was marked by the conversion of the remaining pagans on the British Isles. As we will see in the next chapter, that is not entirely true. There were many conversions during the period though. In 431, Prosper tells us that a Palladius was sent to Ireland to convert the Irish people. Professor Dumville has shown us that Patrick returned to Ireland after that.[1] We have also learned that the remnants of Palladius' mission may have helped him or have continued evangelizing the rest of the island[2]; there is no way to know for certain how many converts were already in Ireland when Patrick arrived.

In Pictland, one of the most common names associated with early church sites is Uinniau. As the "U" could be pronounced as a "V," the inspiration for these place-names may have been Finian. Professors Dumville and Clancy have both suggested that this hypothetical Uinniau/Finian may also have been Columba's mentor,[3] the man who traditionally suggested he be exiled to Scotland. If so, Finian of Clonard evangelized throughout the Highlands early in his life, from the second quarter of the sixth century until some time before 563.

Dal Riata had its own unique holy man, Columba. Exiled from his native Ireland in 563 for blessing one army over another at the Battle of Cuil Dremne,

Columba may have converted whatever pagan Irishmen there were in the area and may have contributed to converting Brude of the Picts and his people through his visits to Inverness. We know he founded a monastery at Iona and several churches in the Hebrides.

It was in the political arena that he made the most immediate impact though. Columba's biographer never tells us he attempted to convert the Picts when he met with Brude so it is at least possible his trips there were diplomatic. As we have seen, within a dozen years of Columba's landing Dal Riata was united under its first king and allied with the most powerful Irish dynasty. We are also told he visited Kentigern,[4] and assured King Rhydderch of Strathclyde that there would be peace with Dal Riata.[5]

In the South we hear less about diplomacy, but St. Cadoc was actually a king for a short while.[6] There is no way of knowing exactly what Garmon did, but he was clearly involved with the politics of one or two Powysian kingdoms.[7] Gildas' *De Excidio Britanniae* could be seen as an attempt to broker peace and stability among the Briton kingdoms.

The "saints" of the period were not just evangelists and diplomats, though. When the devastating Justinian Plague hit the British Isles in about 547, many Britons migrated to the continent. Strangely, the names most closely associated with the mass migration at the time are not kings or nobles but ecclesiastics—Samson, Gildas, Leonorus, Brioc, Paul Aurelian, and Kentigern. This is because kingdoms or even regions were not migrating, families were.

Holy men were also probably responsible for organizing, controlling, and at times paying for the ships that brought Britons to the continent. In a very real way, they were the leaders of these migrants, shepherding their flocks to safety, working with local landowners as well as the Frankish kings to provide them with a place to settle in a way the secular Briton leaders would not have been able to do.[8]

Christianity also helped to rebuild the social structure of the Briton people by serving as educators. By 400 many of the Roman-appointed teachers of the *Trivium* and *Quadrivium* had migrated back to the continent. There would have been no government funding after 407. We have seen that Latin was still spoken up until 429 and possibly into the 440s. Patrick tells us he was educated in basic Latin before he was kidnapped and decided to become a priest. Decades later Gildas clearly had a full traditional Roman education. Education was not limited to people who would become ecclesiastics, either. Columba was nearly an adult when he decided to forego the chance to be high-king in favor of a religious career. Gildas attacks Maelgwn with such venom in *De Excidio Britanniae* that is has been suggested that Maelgwn was fully trained as a priest before he decided rejoin the political scene and murder his own relatives so he could be the king.

32. The Age of Saints

Along with educating the next generation of priests, ecclesiastics took on the responsibility of collecting and preserving libraries during the fifth century. It was necessary; while some Roman citizens had large collections of manuscripts in 410 (or 476 on the continent),[9] they did not have the means to protect their treasures nor would they live forever.

Monasteries would not have been better protected but they were out of the way and normally too poor to attack. As institutions they could also survive for centuries, making them more stable places. They were also connected to one another; not just all monasteries founded by the same person but all monasteries were connected. This meant that books could be lent to one another, read and copied, and then returned. Most of the classic works, from Homer up to Ovid, have been found in manuscripts all over Europe. And because a manuscript could be copied an infinite amount of times, the destruction of one or several sites was not a catastrophe.

There was really only one weakness in the system. Monks only requested books that they wanted to read while they were copying. So, whatever subjects or authors were less interesting to them were copied less often and had a smaller chance of surviving the raids, Norse and Muslim pillaging, and chance fires or other natural disasters of the Middle Ages. We know by the references of surviving books that dozens of authors and hundreds of books have been lost to us because they were not as popular or as lucky as the books that are extant. It is likely we lost many more authors and books that we know nothing about.

There is no way to tell how many manuscripts, or even how many monasteries, Britain had in 410. We know that they produced and reproduced a massive quantity of books, though. The continuing changes in script are evidence enough of that.[10] So are legends about Columba stealing a manuscript and copying it overnight, or having copied hundreds of manuscripts in his lifetime. Illtud is said to have had an even larger library, as did Gildas. Bede, writing decades after the end of this era, may have had access to the largest library of them all.[11]

33

Religion as a Political Tool

Among the Britons, Christianity had been introduced by the Romans and spread as a means of Romanization. The Germanic peoples were first introduced to the religion in 597, and though the mission had been sent by Rome, the religion was spread by kings. Because of that, Christianity was used as a form of political manipulation during the last few decades under study here.

Because Rome had introduced Christianity to the world, the religion came to represent a symbolic link to the Roman Empire. For the Britons that connection was a comfort—a remembrance of a time long past when they had been a part of something much larger and more secure than anything they would enjoy again.

For the Germanic peoples, Christianity was a way of becoming a part of the Roman Empire, of bringing some of Rome's prestige to themselves. In some ways, Christianity was their way of sharing in the Roman experience much like being a *foederati* had been their ancestors' and cousins' way.

As important as being Roman was, though, Christianity also represented a diplomatic door too, a secret handshake that allowed kingdoms to trade with the continent and be directly connected to some of the most powerful people in Europe—the pope and Frankish king among them. It also opened up doors of marriage and alliance to kingdoms on the continent, many of whom had much greater technology, wealth, and power than anything to be found in Britain at the time.

Kent had been fortunate in its relations with the continent. Archeology and what we have learned of Iruminric's parents tell us that the kingdom had maintained a regular and friendly contact with the Franks since at least the early sixth century, possibly before the Franks had converted to Christianity. In other words, Kent had been grandfathered into relations with the continent.

Kent had never enjoyed relations with Rome, but Æthelberht enjoyed good fortune there too. At some point between 585 and 590, the future pope

Gregory saw pagan slaves from Britain. In 590, he became pope. He took advantage of the Frankia-Kent relationship and sent a personal invitation to accept Christianity in 596. No political fool, Æthelberht accepted and welcomed a bishop the next year.

Æthelberht probably never regretted that decision—it helped him and his kingdom in too many ways. For one, it improved his status among the Germanic kingdoms. Before 596, Æthelberht had been a descendant of the king of the gods, but one of many descendants who were also kings. He had been a part of the old religion of his fathers, but a religion that was not connected to Rome. As the first Christian king among the Germanic people in Britain, he was unique; and as the only king with a Roman representative, he had an exclusive and prized connection to Rome.

Christianity also unlocked trade routes with other Christian kings. That meant more than just access to exotic foods and goods though; trade meant access to a wider reservoir of knowledge and occasionally technology.

Accepting Christianity also gave Kent access to the written word. Æthelberht probably would not have cared that he could read (once he had learned how to read) Homer and Ovid, but the power of the written word must have struck him, and the ability to create documents would have fascinated him. As we have seen above, the *Kentish Source* was likely written during his reign. It was probably the single most important document Kent ever created because it established prehistorical Germanic history as beginning with Kent's leader, Hengest, who had earned the "freedom" of all Germanic peoples through his heroism and cunning.

As the sole holder of that connection to Rome, Æthelberht could also control who received Christianity and how. By patronizing the conversion of tributary kings to Christianity he became their link to the new religion and strengthened his hold on them. At the same time, by breaking away from their old religion those kings were cutting ties with the Germanic religion that had traditionally given them the descent from gods and the concept of *mana* that had kept them securely in power. By renouncing Woden, Deor, and the other gods a chieftain undermined his own right to rule, weakened his hold on the kingdom, and made himself more dependent on Kent.

We have seen that Kent, Essex, and East Anglia both reverted back to paganism after the death of their first known Christian king. It is reasonable to assume this happened among the lesser kingdoms as well. In the North, Mercia would resist conversion till midway through the seventh century. Undoubtedly, faith in the old religion played some part (in Kent at first for instance), but it is also reasonable that politics were a factor as well; some of the royals from these kingdoms realized how much Christianity benefited Kent. In Mercia, the kings realized the power Kent was gaining from the religion.

Once introduced, though, the spread of Christianity was inevitable and paganism a political liability. Mercia would find itself politically alone because of its pagan stance. Penda did eventually manage to ally with the Welsh, but only because the Northumbrians had burned the monastery at Bangor-on-Dee.

When Kent and Essex went apostate, Rædwald's kingdom took advantage of its unique relationship with the continent by building modern Ipswich and attracting a healthy trade with the continent. Rædwald's successor Ricberht was a pagan, and he probably lost most of the trade East Anglia had enjoyed. He was killed by Sigeberht and the pagan Ecgric, both of whom understood the advantages of a Christian kingdom. Ecgric may have been a life-long pagan,[1] but never interfered with the spread of Christianity in his kingdom.

Nor did Edwin. He probably accepted Christianity when he lived among the Irish, but as an English king he had other concerns. He married Eadbald's sister Æthelburg in order to tap Kent's connections with the continent but did not dare have his brother-in-law oversee his baptism; that would have placed him and possibly his kingdom permanently in a position inferior to Kent. Instead, it seems reasonable that he had Rhun of Reged sponsor him.[2]

After Edwin was killed, Oswald eventually took the throne. He had also lived among the Dal Riatans during his exile, he had also been baptized there, and he also recognized the potential complications of accepting Kent's patronage of Northumbrian Christianity. So, instead of attempting the balancing act Edwin had managed, he bypassed Kent altogether. He contacted Iona, a politically neutral monastery, and requested that it send someone to teach his people Christianity. Aedan was the second choice, but he managed to convert much of Northumbria without any interference from Kent.

Oswald's brother Oswiu would do one better. He used religion as a weapon against Penda, making baptism one of the terms for Peada's marriage to his daughter Alhflæd. This was followed by the introduction of four priests into Middle Anglia, who spread Christianity and threatened to weaken Penda's hold on Mercia itself. The success of the Christian movement might have been one of the reasons Penda attacked Oswiu in 655.

Once he had established his own political and military authority, Oswiu undermined Kent's religious and diplomatic advantage. In 664 he called together the leading Iona and Roman scholars for a meeting to decide which form of Christianity would be followed in Northumbria from that day forward—Celtic or Roman. Wilfrid won the day for Rome. By bringing together legitimate representatives from both sides he made Northumbria the leading English proponent of Christianity.

While there is no denying the longevity and strength of Christianity in

33. Religion as a Political Tool

Britain, its political usefulness for the most powerful kingdoms in sixth- and seventh-century England is also beyond question. What seems on the surface to be differences in faith and worship were, on further investigation, calculated and politically motivated decisions by kings and the members of royal families.

34

Native Religions

Pelagianism arose in the late fourth century, when a possibly Briton monk named Pelagius, widely regarded as a pillar of Christianity, came to Rome and began teaching a slightly different take on the religion: He believed that God's grace allowed a person to do good works, but that it was a person's choice whether or not they did them. He also believed that others would know whether a person would go to heaven or hell by their works.

Pelagius and his followers were opposed by Augustine, mainly. Augustine believed in Predestination, the idea that God had already decided whether or not a person would go to heaven by giving them his Grace.

This conflict between "Pelagianism" and "Predestination" was the cause of major concern in Christianity by the early fifth century. After heated debates, Pelagianism was accepted as part of Christianity at the Council of Diospolis in 415. That did not end the issue, though, and because of Augustine's influence it was condemned as heresy in 418 at the Council of Carthage.

Pelagianism was important in post–Roman Britain because many of the authors we have met during the course of this book—Constantius, the *Gallic Chronicles* authors, Prosper of Aquitaine, and Gildas—all had a strong bias against Pelagianism. For some, their anti–Pelagian sentiments were their main reason for writing.

Even more significant was how long it survived, and how influential it was. Pelagianism was still a major factor in fifth-century Britain for several reasons. The events between 406 and 411 effectively and permanently separated Britain from the Roman Empire, leaving the island free to ignore the heresy decree. The English Channel was also a factor, especially with the Anglo-Saxon piracy going on there. Finally, if Pelagius was a Briton his home was probably where the strongest concentration of Pelagianism was.

Pelagianism was the reason Germanus came to the island in 429. If he did return between 437 and 448, it may have been to put the heresy down again.

Druids

In a post-Roman history of the British Isles, the druids only appear as opponents for the saints; they ply their magic against the holy men and inevitably lose. They always seem to be present as the king's wise man/sorcerer/seers. We have seen one as Brude's counsel, who tried to block Columba from seeing him. Druids were also present to help Vortigern build his castle.

Unfortunately, the druids themselves did not write (like the Pelagians above) and did not become the center of a body of literature (like the fertility worshippers below), so we are left with mainly the *vita*-writers along with the Greeks and Romans as their witnesses and our earlier sources are no better than the *vitae*. Both the Greeks and the Romans were known to project what they saw as barbaric onto foreign peoples and then use that projection to confirm their cultural superiority.[1]

That means that there are obvious instances where we cannot believe them, like when they claim the druids practiced sacrifices.[2] It is also a warning to be careful; an unknown author may have projected a detail onto the druids and then been repeated by several later scholars making it seem like the same custom was reported independently when it was not.

That said we know that part of their education was spent memorizing large numbers of verses. We can believe that since several seemingly independent ancient authors made the claim, nothing of druidic practices has survived through their writing, and accusing a culture of oral learning was not necessarily an insult.

All sources seem to agree that druids were central to Celtic society, but what they did is a little less clear. They were, depending on the author, the diplomats, philosophers, scientists, priests, and/or lawgivers of Celtic society.[3] In native pre-Christian legends they were generally portrayed as sorcerers capable of casting spells and divining the future.

We know even less about their philosophy. They believed the mistletoe grown on the oak was extremely important. They were aware of the Greek alphabet but wrote nothing down. Finally they believed in reincarnation. No person yet has figured out how those three aspects were related.

History tells us that the Romans suppressed them, actively attacking the druids as a group on Môn and believing they had wiped out the entire cult. We do not know why the Romans attacked, though. Several emperors were involved so we can speculate that it was a problem with the group and not individuals.

There are a number of theories. If druids were priests then they were probably attacked because they had refused to worship the emperor. However, as priests they would have directed the Celtic people to do the same thing and the Britons were never suppressed. In fact, the Gallic druids were never attacked by Julius Caesar during his years of campaigning there.

There are plenty of other possibilities. Druids were routinely linked to prophecy; it is feasible that the British group predicted Rome's downfall? As diplomats they may have attempted to unite the Celtic tribes against Rome? As lawgivers and cultural preservers they may have taken issue with the Romanization of Britain? We may never know the reason or reasons why the Romans attacked them. Which is too bad, it might have given us some great insights into who they were and what they believed in.[4]

Belatacudros/Cernunnos Worship

At least one other religious group survived into the post–Roman period, this one centered around the Celtic god Belatacudros and/or Cernunnos. Belatacudros was connected to the sun and farming, while Cernunnos was associated with animals.[5] The few archeological representations that have survived are of Cernunnos. In these he has horns,[6] a symbol of male fertility.

Belatacudros is almost absent from the historical written record, but in his shortened form of Beli/Pelles/Pellinore he is a regular of Arthurian and especially grail literature, and Belatacudros worship was at the center of the grail phenomenon.[7]

The grail itself was a *corn*, the root word for cornucopia,[8] which is a logical symbol for an agrarian fertility god and also the Holy Grail as a giver of food, healing, and even life. Agriculture and the cycle of birth, death, and rebirth were normally intertwined in the ancient world—in the cults of Adonis, Osiris, and several other male figures around the Mediterranean from earliest historic and maybe even prehistoric times.[9]

The platter and the cauldron are also cornucopic symbols. The former is listed in the treasures of Britain as a limitless producer of food while the tales about Bran the Blessed name a cauldron as the restorer of life.[10] A cauldron can also be found in "Preiddeu Annwn" and *Peredur*,[11] where it seems to have a religious importance. Eventually the platter, horn, and cauldron's qualities would be brought to the continent where they would become the basis for all the Holy Grail literature.

In Britain, the cauldron was connected with magic and women and in every instance the cauldron was either captured or destroyed and the women are killed. The theme of killing witches recurs in *Pa Gur?*, *Culhwch ac Olwen*, and the *Vita Samsoni*.[12]

Why bring these associations up? So that the reader can see that Belatacudros/Cernunnos worship was the basis for the grail legend. Historically, these pagan cults were destroyed wherever they were found. In Britain this "crusade" is usually associated with Arthur or Peredur, so conceivably one or the other started the movement.

Before the reader cringes at the thought of the noble Arthur being involved in something so unseemly, take a step back for a moment. Around 400 St. Martin would lead a movement on the continent to destroy all pagan temples and attack all pagan worshippers. The slaughter of groups is well recorded there. From 1100 almost until the end of the Middle Ages, millions of knights and peasants would march into the Holy Land and treat Muslims and Jews alike as pagans. Closer to home, the Inquisition and a plethora of witch hunts would attack any women with independent thoughts because Christian dogma of the time said that Eve had been the guilty one in the Garden of Eden, that she had been seduced. That was the environment Arthur and Peredur lived in. As crusaders and destroyers of pagan cults they would have been considered heroes to their contemporaries.

By the time grail literature began in the twelfth century, the historical fact of the Belatacudros' cult destruction had been forgotten and whatever stories there were about Peredur made no sense. Even if they could have been reconstructed they would not have appealed to Philip of Flander's concepts of nobility and Christianity.[13] In history's place Chrétien de Troyes invented a new hero based on an idealized version of his patron Philip of Flanders. Philip had been to Jerusalem once, like Peredur was once at the Grail Castle. And like the hero, Phillip hoped one day to return and correct his former mistakes.[14]

35

The Dark Ages

Britannia in 367 was not the province it had once been but it was still Roman Britain. There were *grammatici* and *rhetorici* teaching the wealthy and intelligent. The wealthy would grow up to administer the government as they had for generations, using their business connections to help the villages and contributing their own funds for public buildings. The intelligent would loyally serve the Roman Empire for their entire careers.

Roman highways were well maintained with stations every few miles for repairs, supplies, horses, and spending the night. Every village was responsible for them because they allowed the military to come to their defense quickly, merchants to move safely, and messengers to travel without difficulty throughout the province, as they could throughout the empire.

Those three groups represented the lifeblood of the Roman Empire—the military, the economy, and the government. Soldiers patrolled the borders, with legions of the late empire rushing efficiently from province to province so that they could beat back threats like Attila the Hun. Merchants allowed wares to go from one end of the empire to the other, allowing the Britons to enjoy olive oil and wine and the Romans to make use of Briton iron and tin. They also spread news and ideas while reminding the Roman Empire's many provinces that they were all part of one massive and powerful government. Messengers relayed information and instructions from throughout the empire.

Germanic *foederati* had been introduced to the island, but they were present only to defend Rome's shipping lanes. All evidence is that these mercenaries were deeply respectful of Roman culture, happy to embrace Roman culture and language in exchange for service. For their part, the Romans were careful to station the *foederati* well away from Roman villages and other *foederati* groups where they could only help the Empire.

The year 367 marked the end of true stability in Britain, though. A succession of major raids on Britain was followed by a series of Roman generals coming in, reestablishing borders, their election as emperors, and their departure for the continent with their own soldiers and as many Britannia-stationed soldiers as the province could spare. Meanwhile, living conditions in Britannia grew worse as raiding continued. The wealthy migrated to the continent where things were still more stable. When they left, so did most of the funding for the public buildings and the connections to maintain highways. Reduced funding caused fewer merchants to travel. Fewer travelers meant that settlements became more isolated as trade and news spread more slowly and less consistently across the island. As the island shifted from rebel to loyal and back again during the decades between 367 and 410 its government workers must have found it difficult to remain faithful to their responsibilities.

In 407, the last emperor wannabe, Constantine, departed from Britain, his government left in place. Within the next few years, Britannia was attacked again. Giving up on Constantine, the citizens overthrew the government and requested that Rome send its own governor and enough legions to reestablish order. But Honorius could not manage their request, leaving Britannia leaderless, isolated, and under attack from all sides.

The former province struggled on for a few years. Without the Romans, the Picts turned inward and the Irish settled along the western coast. Travel would have become more and more difficult as brigands stationed themselves along the major highways. Pelagianism erupted at least once. The villages along the southern and eastern coast still had *foederati* and gave them whatever food and supplies they could, but without a provincial government the supplies only came locally. Eventually the villagers were unable to satisfy the Germanic mercenaries, and in 441 the former soldiers-for-hire responded in one largescale and devastating raid that must have extended many miles inland.

That event changed everything: the mystique of Rome was demolished. Overnight the local Romano-Briton employers transformed into slaves and their Germanic employees into owners. Village elders no longer ran the local governments; one or two Germanic clans replaced them. Just as devastating, after 441 the *foederati* stopped being *foederati*, which meant that no one was protecting the shipping lanes or preventing other Germanic groups from migrating into Britain.

The Briton villages further inland (raided but not immediately under Germanic control) had been insulated by the coastal areas so they had never developed a military. They had never developed regional governments, which meant they were disorganized. The raid of 441 left them paralyzed or at least unable to react. When fresh migrants came to Britain these settlements were easily captured and ruled over by Germanic clans.

The migrations might have continued for decades but eventually Briton leaders emerged, Ambrosius was the most famous but there must have been several; local communications were all that could be managed considering how fragmented the Britons were by this time. Each leader would have made arrangements for food and supplies in return for a group of warriors able to rush to a village's defense at a moment's notice. In time that simple arrangement would develop into primitive and fragile chieftainships. Through attrition, cattle raiding, fame bought by bards, and time they developed into fewer, larger, and more stable kingships.

These kingships did not begin stable, though. Without generations of tradition, they amounted to the loyalty a king could generate among his warriors. As the kingdoms grew, it also meant the loyalty they could engender in vassals that no longer lived in their hall. Kingdoms could only grow so fast, and stability could only come so quickly. Still, by the middle of the sixth century many medieval kingdoms—Gwynedd, Dyfed, and Strathclyde among them, had increased to their full medieval size.

Christianity also helped the political and social order by establishing schools of learning and a tenuous link back to Rome with Latin, libraries, and of course the Roman religion. In times of plague and famine priests and monks guided the population, allowing kingdoms to remain structured. Christianity may have been the anima for the witch hunts.

By the mid-sixth century, most of the Briton kingdoms were too established to fall apart because of poor kings or an unlucky battle, so the most powerful formed alliances and extended themselves into Germanic territories to take advantage of their resources and wealth. They organized their new pagan territories for easy tribute-taking and may have called on them for warriors to fight in their rivalries.

Those decisions were the seeds of their destruction. The Britons' farmland was less fertile than English farmland, which meant that it could support a smaller population per square mile. The Britons pushed those limitations for decades with raiding followed by full-scale warfare in the middle of the sixth century.

Meanwhile, the Germanic people had consolidated their villages from 441 on. Unable to raid and pillage Briton villages by the end of the fifth century they had resorted to cattle raiding each other—simply one village stealing cattle from another. Casualties had been common, but deaths rare and damage to farmlands and the peasants farming them negligent.

In 536 there was heavy volcanic activity in the Americas that effected temperature, air, and crops. It must have lessened harvest numbers all over the world, but the Britons were more affected because they had already been making the most of what they had. In 547 the Justinian Plague hit Britain, followed by several lesser plagues over the next few decades.

The years of bad crops and plague impacted the Germanic-held territories, but must have devastated the Britons by the late sixth century. The next generation of Briton rulers probably had fewer warriors and was definitely less interested in regional politics; the Germanic people took advantage. By open revolts or simply by not paying tribute, the already organized regions took their independence and organized themselves into primitive kingships.

Beginning at a more developed point than the Britons had, it took the Germanic chieftainships less time to develop into larger kingdoms. By c. 600 Kent was unified while Northumbria and Essex, at least, were well on their way.

Christianity was introduced to the Germanic peoples at about this moment. No doubt the Britons had tried somewhere along the line to convert their pagan neighbors but they had not gotten very far. Coming from Rome the new religion was much better received. Kent welcomed it first, allowing a Christian center to be set up at Canterbury. Kent also influenced Essex and probably many of its satellite kingdoms into accepting the new religion too. Through marriage and manipulation, Kent would keep spreading the faith through the rest of the period. Through Christianity and the connection to the continent it represented, Kent would maintain its influence over the Germanic kingdoms.

Penda understood the power Christianity had and remained pagan his entire career to avoid weakening his position. His successes against the Northumbrians gave him political power independent of Kent, but his decision to allow his son to convert was a mistake. It weakened his kingship and his hold on his son.

The Northumbrian kings understood the power and influence Kent enjoyed because of its connections to the continent and its conversions. They also grasped the political and social importance of Christianity so they responded by accepting the religion from 616 on, but cautiously. In 633 they would bypass Kent altogether by inviting an Iona monk to convert them. Eventually, Oswiu would hold a synod between Irish and Roman holies and decide once and for all which was the better version of Christianity. And since he decided, he weakened Kent's position in the process.

At some point while all this was happening Kent wrote, or more accurately developed, a history of the Germanic people in Britain. It began with the information to be found in Gildas' *De Excidio Britanniae* about a great tyrant and *foederati* but the writer or writers went further. They translated his *superbus tyrannus* into English Vortigern, which was the name of a recent Briton overlord. They pulled a name from their own legends to act as the *foederati* leader, Hengest. Then they developed the story, drawing Vortigern as a character strong enough to lead the Britons through the horrors of the fifth century but not intelligent enough to keep Hengest at bay.

They portrayed their hero as resourceful and cunning. Then they created a link between him and Eormenric, their first remembered king. The lineage went through another legendary leader, Æsc/Ansehis.

Hengest's ancestors still included Woden, but he was not the founder of their line because Woden was no longer considered a god. Æthelberht, or whichever king authorized this history, would have understood that by accepting that fact he was undermining what had always been a Germanic king's greatest claims to kingship, mandate from the gods and the concept of *mana*. However, by presenting Hengest as a more worthy ruler than Vortigern he probably hoped to compensate for that loss; he did. And by convincing the other Germanic kingdoms to accept Christianity he made Kent the most prestigious kingdom on the island.

Meanwhile, without the same origin legend the other Germanic kingdoms weakened their position by converting. The result was infighting and occasional rebellion; exactly the kind of environment Kent would have wanted to maintain order and consolidate its power.

The (nearly) three hundred years between the Great Raid and the Synod of Whitby saw massive, and for the Britons cataclysmic, changes. They began the period as a semi-rebellious but valuable province in the greatest empire in existence. A hundred years later they were the most powerful kingdoms on the island. By 664 the Britons were silent at best, absorbed into the Germanic kingdoms at worst, and all Britons were fighting for their survival as an independent people.

The Pictish confederacy broke apart after the Roman departure. What little we know about them says that they fought among themselves until the end of the period, with the kings around Loch Ness becoming the most powerful among them by the end of the sixth century. They might have remained independent until Kenneth MacAlpin of Dal Riata united them in 843.

The Irish began the period as tourists; camping and raiding villages along the western coast. Many of them returned to Ireland by 500 but a few, like those in Dyfed and Dal Riata, would remain and establish enduring kingdoms of their own.

Finally came the Germanic tribes. In 410 we know they were loyal *foederati*. All evidence shows that they remained loyal for some time afterwards. Over the next two centuries necessity, good fortune, and circumstances brought them to a dominant position over the island. It was a status they would retain consistently, through many different kings and shifting alliances, up until the Danish invasion over two hundred years later.

Appendix
The Vortigern Figure

In the pages above, the Vortigern character has been separated from the historical Gwrtheyrn as much as possible. However, as Gwrtheyrn has been so consistently connected to Vortigern, it is probably a good idea here to explain exactly why they are distinct. So, having explored the historical Gwrtheyrn we will here chronicle the development of the literary Vortigern

Gildas wrote *De Excidio Britanniae* in the range 521x535. In it, he never mentioned either Gwrtheyrn or Vortigern. What he did say was that a certain *superbus tyrannus*, great tyrant, ruled all of Britain and invited Anglo-Saxons to the island as his mercenaries. They did their jobs, but eventually brought more of their kinsmen to the island and revolted.

So to backtrack, Gildas was born in 477x491, meaning that under the best of circumstances he might have remembered hearing something first-hand back to 402 but more likely that in the social and political upheaval of the fifth century there was no one as old as 80 when he was five. The first year he could reasonably be expected to remember back to is 427, and as we have seen the earliest accurate information he gives could date back no further than 433. In other words, Gildas could have had no idea about when and under what context the *foederati* originally came to Britain.

What did Gildas know? From the language he wrote with and the ruins around him he knew that Rome had once governed Britain. From the continent he knew that former Roman provinces often developed a native rule. He also knew that Rome had hired Germanic mercenaries as *foederati*.

He also had a theme for his historical prelude; that the Britons were God's chosen. Like the Israelites his people made mistakes and bad leaders misled them, but the Romans were God's protective hand and the Anglo-Saxons his punishment. He could hardly make the Romans introduce the *foederati* and still maintain that the Romans were protectors. So he did not. Instead, Gildas introduced a native *superbus tyrannus* to rationalize the limited history he knew of the middle fifth century. Apparently it was a reasonable one to his contemporaries; his letter survived and he was known throughout the Middle Ages as *sapiens* or wise.

Bede is the first person to actually mention Vortigern by name. As we have seen, though, he relied almost exclusively on the *Kentish Source* for early post–Roman history and it is a safe bet that its author(s) were aware of Gildas. So probably his source named Vortigern as a translation of Gildas' *superbus tyrannus*.

The Dyfed may originally have carried over the bare bones of Gildas' history but would not add anything else; Powys was an ally in 829. A second tradition, unaffected by Gildas, made its way to Gwynedd in the form of Outigern, a powerful king of the mid-sixth century who was contemporary to Talhaearn. More may have been said about him, where he lived, what battles he fought in, etc., but we have no idea what that might have been because the entire history was edited under Hywel Dda's direction in the tenth century.

Hywel Dda, as we have seen, ruled nearly all of Wales during his career except for Morgannwg and Gwent and when he had the *Historia Brittonum* rewritten he was busy subverting Powys. Powys was struggling for credibility; Cyngen had the Pillar of Eliseg erected sometime before his death in 855 and in it he claimed Gwrtheyrn as an ancestor. Hywel Dda wanted to exploit that weakness. Through his relationship with Athelstan he may have had access to the *Kentish Source* directly, but more likely he started with Bede.

In the Dyfed version there is Vortigern and the invitation of Hengest and Horsa, but instead of Hengest simply manipulating him for more men and eventually revolting, several new elements are added. Hengest introduces Vortigern to his daughter Ronnwen, whom the old man lusts over so much that he gives Hengest Kent in exchange for her. Hengest then uses his position as father-in-law to relegate Vortigern into a weaker position before finally revolting, or rather responding to his social inferior's superior political status.

A second element is Vortipor, likely another historical remembrance of Gwrtheyrn. He appears and fights four battles against the Germanic warriors before dying just on the cusp of victory. The story then returns to Vortigern, who hides away in his castle where he has a son by his daughter, is denounced by a young boy, and is excommunicated by St. Germanus before finally expiring.

The last source to add anything significant to the Vortigern character was the *Anglo-Saxon Chronicle*. Its editors took the story as found in *Historia Ecclesiastica* and added in the Welsh version of the battles as found in *Historia Brittonum*. The compilers probably knew nothing about Vortipor so they did not mention him. The details of Vortigern's career were not important either, as Wessex was not concerned about establishing its right to rule over the Britons.

In short, Vortigern started out as a rationalization of British history during the fifth century that made sense with what Gildas knew and fit into his goals. From there, Kent's political interests explored the character as a strong leader who was not intelligent enough to keep control of the Germanic warriors. *Historia Brittonum* would ignore this development at first, but during its tenth-century editing Vortigern's character and actions were fully developed, describing him as a weak, corrupt, and blasphemous fool who had no right to wear a crown. His presence in the *Anglo-Saxon Chronicle* with some of his new actions confirms that the English had accepted the new development as well.

Chronology: 367–664

325x450	Deisi invade Dyfed
367	Coordinated raid by Pictish, Irish, and Germanic tribes
368	Theodosius sent to Britain
372	Ansehis and Fraomar come to Britain as *foederati*
378	Ammianus Marcellinus writes his history
383	Coordinated raid by Pictish, Irish, and Germanic tribes; Maximus sent to Britain
387	Battle of Adrianople
388	Maximus killed
400+	Irish groups begin settling in portions of Cornwall, southern Wales, and Anglesey
406	Roman soldiers elect a series of emperors
407	Constantine leaves for the continent
410	Honorian Rescript
c. 410	*Rufinus' Chronicle*
411	Constantine killed
415	Pelagianism declared acceptable at the Council of Diospolis
418	Pelagianism declared a heresy at the Council of Carthage
429	Germanus combats Pelagianism in Britain
430x440	Coins pass out of use
431	Palladius to Ireland
433x441	Letter to Aetius
437	Possible year of Germanus' second visit
441	*Foederati* revolt; possible year of Germanus' second visit
443x473	Patrick made a bishop
453	Attila the Hun dies
448	Possible year of Germanus' second visit
448x461	Ambrosius' career begins
449x456	Bede says the Germanic invasion began in this range
451	Battle of Chalons-sur-Marne
456	Aetius killed
c. 470	First bards and Briton kings
476	Rome sacked by Ostrogoths

478x491	Badon fought
480x520	Arthur's floruit
480x490	Constantius writes the *Vita Germani*
491x518	Zosimus' *Historia Nova*
500+	Irish settlements in Cornwall, Dyfed, and Anglesey abandoned
521x535	*De Excidio Britanniae*
530	Regional Briton kingships
536	Heavy volcanic activity in the Americas
543x572	Rhun's Campaign
547	Justinian Plague hits Britain
550+	Irish annals begin
c. 551	Procopius' *Wars of Justinian*
563	Columba founds Iona monastery
573	Gregory consecrated bishop of Tours
573x579	Battle of Arfderydd, Myrddin goes mad
574	Convention of Druim Cett
576x593	Battle of Catraeth
577x583	Peredur and Gwrgi die
580x593	Æthelberht marries Bertha
590	St. Gregory made pope
592/3	Æthelfrith inherits Bernicia
597	Augustine arrives in Kent
597x616	The *Kentish Source* probably and the *Code of Æthelberht* definitely written
600s	*Vita Samsoni* written
603	Battle of Degsastan
604	Sæberht converted
611/2	Rieinmellth marries Oswiu
613	*Isidore's Chronicle* ends
615/6	Battle of Chester
616/7	Battle of Idle River, Æthelberht dies
616x626	*Tribal Hidage*
625x650	*Northern Memoranda* first written
626	Elmet absorbed into Northumbria
632/3	Battle of Hatfield
633	Battle of Heavenfield
635	Aedan is given the bishopric of Northumbria
642	Battle of Maser
644	Battle of Cogfry
645x648	Cenwealh exiled from Wessex
648x651	Cenwealh returns to Wessex
650x660	*Senchus Fer n' Alban* written
651	Anna exiled from East Anglia
654	Penda kills Anna
655	Battle of Winwæd/Hatfield Chase
656	Peada is poisoned

664	Synod of Whitby
664x671	Second draft of *Northern Memoranda*
676x685	*Code of Hlothere and Eadric* written
688x694	*Laws of Ine* written
c. 695	*Code of Wihtred* written
697	Adomnan writes *Vita Columba*
699x705	Anonymous *Vita Cuthberti* written
709x714	Stephanus' *Vita Wilfridi*
731	*Historia Ecclesiastica* written
757x800	*Vita Kentigerni* written
795	Contemporary records begin at St. David's
829	*Historia Brittonum*
833x899	*Canu Heledd* composed
840	St. Garmon/Germanus inserted into the Cadell story
843	Kenneth MacAlpin unites the Picts and Scots
855+	Pillar of Eliseg finished
891	*Anglo-Saxon Chronicle* probably written
913	*Chronicle of Ireland* compiled
942x950	*Laws of Hywel Dda*
971x995	*Pictish Chronicles* written
1066	Battle of Hastings
c. 1100	*Culhwch ac Olwen* first written down
1107	Urban made bishop of Glamorgan
1120	Urban's involvement in property disputes with St. David's and Hereford begins
1120x1134	*Llandaff Charters* altered
Early 1200s	*Trioedd Ynys Prydein* first written down
1136	Geoffrey of Monmouth writes *Historia Regum Britanniae*

Glossary

Armaria: Latin; a bookcase of citrus wood inlaid with ivory in which the scrolls of a library were displayed.
Bard: Celtic; A person educated in British history, mythology, and legend (considered to be one category) and taught how to rhyme, tell stories, and use motifs for effect, their intricate verse was considered to have a magical quality. A bard's prophecy was considered to be particularly accurate.
Bragawt: British; Honey wine.
Bretwalda: Germanic; A king who had proven that he could protect his kingdom and who attracted tributaries who wanted to be under his protection.
Britannia: Latin; The Roman province in Britain, constituting all of England, Wales and beyond Antonine's Wall at its greatest height but probably shrinking to England apart from the north by 410.
Cauponae: Latin; an inn on the public Roman road, for use by anyone. All prices were standardized throughout the empire.
Ceorl: Germanic; a freeman.
Civitas: Latin; the social body of Roman citizens as a public entity, e.g., a village, city, or even province.
Comes: Latin; a formal rank deriving from Alexander the Great's "Companions." It was a mark of confidence without having any specific military or political responsibilities.
Comes Britanniarum: Latin: literally "Count of the Britains." The Comes Britanniarum was a title for generals who had reestablished order in Britannia.
Comitatus: Germanic; a king's war band, those who lived in his hall or nearby.
Corn: British; a horn as in cornucopia.
Currach: Irish; a skin-covered boat used to carry a small number of people across inland lakes and occasionally the sea.
Eorl: Germanic; a nobleman who was given land by his king generally in return for the promise of tribute and arms.
Foederati: Latin; the warriors of a tribe who have promised to work for the Roman Empire in exchange for short-term food, supplies, and lodging and eventual acceptance as Roman citizens.
Gwledig: British; significant ruler, e.g., dynastic founder or widely respected king.

Glossary

Y Hen Ogled: British; The Old North, referring to the British kingdoms north of modern Wales, e.g., Reged, Gododdin, Strat Clut, and several other vague or unnamed kingdoms.

Hide: Germanic; roughly 120 acres, or enough land to support one household.

Iudice: Latin; judge, or another name for king in Early Medieval Britain.

Karvi: Germanic; a longship capable of holding fifteen and forty warriors with all of their equipment.

Mana: Germanic; divine luck in battle, a fertile kingdom, just decisions, and with warriors.

Mansione: A full-service government hotel, which could be found every twenty-five to thirty kilometers.

Mutatione: A station every fifteen to twenty kilometers where a traveler could hire a wheelwright, cartwright, or veterinarian.

Quadrivium: Latin; the secondary education of the upper class and the most intelligent from the lower classes. It consisted of arithmetic, geometry, music, and astronomy—the essentials for the higher learning of philosophy or theology.

Romanitas: Latin; an identity with being Roman; i.e., common values, customs, morality, and way of life.

Sapiens: Latin; wise.

Scriptorium: Latin; a room in medieval monasteries devoted to writing, copying, and designing manuscripts. Practically speaking, a monk who wanted to write (Columba or Bede for instance) would use their own cubicle.

Skop: Germanic; A person educated in British history, mythology, and legend (considered to be one category) and taught how to rhyme, tell stories, and use motifs for effect, their intricate verse was considered to have a magical quality.

Superbus Tyrannus: Latin; over-king.

Testudo: Latin; turtle. A legionary formation used in sieges. The front and top of the soldiers are covered with their shields.

Teulu: British; a family. Used by the post–Roman Britons to encompass a king's war-band who were fed, sheltered, entertained, and armed at the king's expense until they proved themselves in battle. At that time they were given land of their own.

Theomacha: Latin; a witch. The word was used to describe practitioners of fertility religions which worshipped a mother goddess and not Christianity.

Torah: Hebrew; the first five books of the *Bible* which were traditionally composed by Moses. They are *Genesis*, *Exodus*, *Leviticus*, *Numbers*, and *Deuteronomy*.

Trivium: Latin; the core education of the upper class and the most intelligent from the lower classes. It consisted of grammar, logic, and rhetoric—learning the mechanics of language, the mechanics of thought, and the transmission of language and thought to others.

Vita: Latin; a saint's life. Originally they gave a reasonably accurate summary of a saint's accomplishments but as time went on certain motifs and supernatural "miracles" became commonplace. By the eleventh century, saints' lives were being used by monasteries to give them added sanctity and entitle them to more land.

Guide to Period Sources

***Actus Silvestri*:** Written by Victorius of Aquitaine who wrote the official Paschal (Easter) Tables. Not much is known about him apart from the fact that he lived in Aquitaine, France and was a contemporary to Prosper of Aquitaine (c. 390-c.455). *Actus Silvestri* is about the life and works of Pope Sylvester.

***The Anglo-Saxon Chronicle*:** Originally compiled by someone sympathetic to Alfred, in Wessex, during Alfred's reign (871–899, likely 891 or later), the history was designed to unify the surviving free English under Alfred's banner against the Danes who had conquered most of England.

***Annales Cambriae*:** Written by a series of monks who were opposed to Urien's dynasty between 795 and 954, most likely in the range 829x904, the annals were probably written at St. David's. They took information from *Isidore's Chronicle*, the *Northern Memorandum*, and the Irish annals.

***Annals of Clonmacnoise*:** Written by a series of monks beginning in 740, the annals also added information from the *Chronicle of Ireland*. There was no political purpose to the entries, only an interest in their immediate world, i.e., obits of abbots, local and national kings, and major battles.

***Annals of Innisfallen*:** Based on the *Chronicle of Ireland*, Innisfallen only added locally important entries after 913 for the era studied here.

***Annals of Ulster*:** Based on the *Chronicle of Ireland*, Ulster only added locally important entries after 913 for the era studied here.

Anonymous *Vita Gildae*: Written by a monk of Rhuys during the ninth century.

***Canu Heledd*:** Written in the last two thirds of the ninth century by an anonymous poet, the cycle describes a fictional conquest of a kingdom within Wales, though the family names and other details seem to be accurate.

Caradoc's *Vita Gildae*: Written by Caradoc of Llancarfan in the early twelfth century, it was designed to strengthen Glastonbury's place as monastery by bringing famous historical figures there—in particular Arthur.

***Chronicle of Ireland*:** Composed at some time in the eighth century from annals taken from Bangor (c. 600), Iona (c. 680), and Lismore (c. 700), which were kept in County Louth or eastern Meath until 913. At that point, the monastery at Innisfallen, a second Ulster monastery, and Clonmacnoise each took a copy and started their own annals from which most of our early annal information comes from.

The Code of Æthelberht: Composed during the height of Æthelberht's power, 596–616, the code was a compilation of oral laws designed mainly as a means of solidifying his hold on his kingdom and those under his protection. It focused on standardizing payments for personal and property injuries but also dealt with trade.

The Code of Æthelstan: There was no one Code, *per se*. Athelstan wrote or had several written throughout his reign (924–939), dealing with everything from theft to clerical issues. They may have been written by Wulfhelm his bishop or directly supervised by Athelstan himself.

The Code of Hlothere and Eadric: Finished between 676 and 685 by lawyers under the Kentish kings' direction, the laws focus on injuries and property damage but detail proper legal procedures for accusations and land purchases in London.

Code of Wihtred: Created around 695 for Wihtred of Kent, it focused on church law.

Columbanus' Epistoli: A series of letters written to the pope around 600. In them, Columbanus treated the pope like a less experienced equal. The letters had the long term effect of bringing the Celtic practice of Christianity to the papal attention.

Culhwch ac Olwen: An adventure romance first written down around 1100 by someone with a bard's education and specialized knowledge about Christianity.

De Excidio Britanniae: Written by Gildas in 482 or the range 521x535, probably in the southern regions still controlled by the Britons. Gildas wrote in order to call the Britons back to their former morality.

Eddius Stephanus' Vita Wilfridi: Written between 709 and 719 by an unknown author, the saint's life has more firsthand information than Bede's version but is heavily biased towards its subject, which Stephanus idolized.

Epistola ad Hilarium: A letter written by Victorius of Aquitaine in the last half of the fifth century.

Epitoma Chronicon: Written by Prosper of Aquitaine in 455, it was his version of world history with a focus on the Pelagian controversy.

Expulsion of the Déisi: An anonymous document written in the eighth century. It was written in an area of Ireland where the *Déisi*. Its purpose was to give the *Déisi*, historically vassals, a royal lineage and background.

Gallic Chronicle of 452: A simple annal written in Gallia Narbonensis that continues the history begun by Eusebius and maintained by his son Jerome up through 378. It ends in 452 and was possibly written by Faustus of Riez.

Gallic Chronicle of 511: A simple annal written in Gallia Narbonensis that continues the history begun by Eusebius and maintained by his son Jerome up through 378. It ends in 511.

Gregory's Dialogi: A collection of four books written by Pope Gregory that chronicles the miracles, signs, wonders, and healings of holy men from sixth-century Italy. The second book is a *vita* for Saint Benedict of Nursia.

Y Gododdin: Composed in the sixth century to commemorate an alliance and ultimate defeat at Catraeth, this group of elegies was brought to Strathclyde for a time before migrating to Gwynedd. There one version was written down in the seventh century while the other remained in an oral environment till the ninth. Both show clear signs of having been tampered with by Gwynedd as it attempted to united the Britons against English.

Historia Brittonum: Anonymously written in 829 Gwynedd for Merfyn Frych whose purpose was to unite the Briton kingdoms against the English. It was edited in tenth-century Dyfed under Hywel Dda with the intent of undermining the credibility of Powys' royal family. The history was based on *Northern Memorandum*, the *Kentish Source*, and several local and islandwide legends and myths.

Historia Ecclesiastica: Composed by Bede in 731 at his Northumbrian monastery, it was biased first towards Bernicia, then Roman Catholicism, and finally against the Britons. His sources were Gildas, the *Kentish Source*, and the historical records of several monastic communities.

Historia Franconum: Written by Gregory of Tours, the history is more of a personal diary of the events he was a part of or learned about from some of the most influential people of the sixth century. Gregory had his biases, especially against the Bretons, but he never sat down and wrote a themed history. That makes him a useful witness to sixth century events in Frankia.

Historia Nova: Written by Zosimus of the Byzantine Empire around 500. He mentions Britain at the opening of the fifth century and uses Olympiodorus, exclusively for all his information there.

Historia Regum Britanniae: Written by Geoffrey of Monmouth in the years up to 1136, it used elements of *De Excidio Britanniae*, *Historia Ecclesiastica*, *Historia Brittonum*, Welsh genealogies, and at least one unknown source. Geoffrey's bias was in winning the support of a patron, and so he loosely based his Arthurian campaigns on contemporary events and people.

Isidore's Chronicle: Also known as the *Chronica Maiora* of Isidore of Seville, was written in in 615 and was intended as a universal history.

The *Kentish Source*: A history derived from Gildas but heavily influenced by Kent's aim of showing that it was the first and most legitimate kingdom in Britain. It was probably written between 597 and 616, but could have been written anywhere between 580 and 731. It was likely altered as Kent's priorities changed.

The *Laws of Hywel Dda*: Composed under Hywel Dda's direction probably between 942 and 950 but at any time in the range 920–950, they were designed to help standardize law and centralize authority. As such they are a fair representation of Welsh society.

***Laws of Ine*:** Designed to strengthen Ine's control over warriors, it also reveals the growing strength of the church. It was written between 688 and 694 in Wessex.

***Llandaff Charters*:** Originally local charters, they were heavily edited between 1115 and 1134 and under Urban's direction for the purpose of extending Glamorgan's bishopric into St. David's and Hereford.

***Llywarch Hen Cycle*:** A group of poems dating to the ninth century in which Llywarch is an old man sending his sons out to die in protection of the kingdom. It is probably contemporary to the fall of Powys.

***Marwnad Cunedda*:** A death song for Cunedda, it is possibly contemporary (c. 410x470).

***Marwnad Cynddylan*:** A eulogy for Cynddylan from c. 655. It is important as a firsthand account of Briton relations with Penda.

***Northern Memorandum*:** A history first written down by a monk from one of Rhun's monasteries between 625 and 650. It was added to and altered for political reasons when Alhfrith attempted to take the throne between 664 and 671 and used his descent from Urien to attract high-ranking Britons. It was updated around 685 with the Battle of Nechtanesmere. The Anglo-Saxon genealogies were added at this time.

Patrick's Epistoli: Written by Patrick to a chieftain named Ceredig and to a Briton council of his peers, respectively, at some point late in his life but before 493, they are possibly the only firsthand accounts of life in fifth-century Britain.

Peiryan Vaban: A prophecy poem found in a fifteenth century manuscript. Myrddin is credited as the author but the language is centuries later.

"Pen Urien": This cycle of poems is culturally dateable to the sixth century but linguistically is late eighth to ninth century. Each are told from Llywarch Hen's perspective but were created by bards.

The Pictish Chronicle: Written between 971 and 995 by Gaelic-speaking monks. It was written in three parts; the origins of the Picts, a Pictish king-list, and a chronicle of the kings of Pictland. Its living history horizon is 662x668 and entries much before 600 were added between 712 and 726.

Pillar of Eliseg: Erected by Cyngen son of Cadell in the years before 855 in honor of his great-grandfather Elisedd. It claimed his dynasty's decent from Gwrtheyrn.

Procopius: Writing at or after 551 in the Byzantine Empire, he relied on hearsay for any information he knew about Britain in his *Wars of Justinian*.

Prophecy of Berchán: A long historical poem of two parts written in the twelfth century or later. Designed as a prophecy poem, the first part is in the voice of an Irish abbot named Berchán and tells about his monastery through the reigns of nineteen kings. The second part is in the voice of Patrick's lifetime and gives Scottish history of his death, the careers of Columba and Áedán, and from Kenneth to Domnall Bán (843–1097).

Ravenna Cosmography: Written in the seventh century by an anonymous Ravenna cleric, it combines information from the fifth century with outdated and invented data.

Senchus Fer n' Alban: Written during the reign of Conall Crandomna (650–660), it is an official history of Dal Riata which fuses several different houses into one extended Dal Riata national history.

Taliesin's Poems: A group of praise poems originally composed by Taliesin in the sixth century.

Tribal Hidage: A tribute list, believed to date from Edwin's time (616–633), it names major kingdoms as well as dozens of minor ones along with their size.

Trawsganu Cynan Garwyn: A praise poem to a sixth-century Powysian chieftain, updated until the tenth century.

Vita Cadoci: A life of "Saint" Cadoc written by Lifris of Llancarfan in 1086 in order to enhance Llancarfan's standing and keep it from being dissolved.

Vita Carantoci: An anonymous life of "Saint" Carantoc written around 1100. It legitimized Carhampton's existence as monastery.

Vita Ceolfrith: Written by a monk of Wearmouth or Jarrow who accompanied Ceolfrith in or soon after 716.

Vita Columba: Composed in 697 by Adomnán, it was based on an earlier work by Cumméne Find. The life is generally accurate apart from miracles and the author's habit of sidestepping anything that was embarrassing for his distant relative, the subject.

Vita Cuthberti: Written by a single Lindisfarne monk between 699 and 705.

Vita Germani: Written by Constantius probably between 480 and 490 but definitely before 494. It is generally free of the fanciful but is vague about Britain.

Vita Kentigerni: Two extant lives originating from an original written between 744 and 756. It was written by a monk who favored Roman Christianity; its sole purpose was to make Kentigern one of its proponents.

Vita Samsoni: A saint's life probably written in the seventh century and possibly by the saint's great-nephew. It is generally free of the fantastic elements of later *vitae*.

Vita Sancti Antonii: Written in about 360 by Athanasius of Alexandria, it depicts Anthony the Great's life as a desert monastic and his supernatural temptations.

Vita Sancti Martini: Written around 400 by Sulpicius Severus, a wealthy heir who gave up his wealth to follow Martin.

Welsh Triads: Mnemonic devices used by bards to associate characters of history, legend, and mythology with certain qualities. Forty-six are useful, they are all to be found in manuscripts of the thirteenth century but were probably first written down in the early twelfth century.

Chapter Notes

Foreword

1. Dumville, "'Nennius' and the *Historia Brittonum*," *SC* 11 (Cardiff, 1976), 78–95.
2. Chadwick, "Early Culture and Learning in North Wales," *Studies in the Early British Church*, ed. Nora K. Chadwick (Cambridge, 1958), 29–36; Dumville, "*Historia Brittonum*: An Insular History from the Carolingian Age"; *Historiographie im frühen Mittelalter*, eds. A. Scharer and G. Scheibelreiter (Munich, 1994), 411; Higham, *King Arthur: Mythmaking and History* (New York, 2002), 130.
3. Kirby, "Bede and Northumbrian Chronology," *EHR* 78 (London, 1963), 514–527; "Bede's Native Sources for the *Historia Ecclesiastica*," *BJRL* 48 (London, 1965–1966), 341–371; "Problems of early West Saxon history," *EHR* 80 (London, 1965), 10–29; "Vortigern," *BBCS* 23 (Cardiff, 1970), 37–59;, "Northumbria in the Time of Bede," *St. Wilfrid at Hexham*, trans. and ed. David Kirby (Newcastle-upon-Tyne, 1974), 2–4.
4. Dumville, "Sub-Roman Britain: history and legend," *History* 62 (London, 1977a), 173–192.
5. *The Gododdin of Aneirin*, trans. and ed. John T. Koch (Cardiff, 1997); *Cunedda, Cynan, Cadwallon, Cynddylan: Four Welsh Poems and Britain 383–655*, trans. and ed. John T. Koch (Cardiff, 2013).
6. *Legendary Poems from the Book of Taliesin*, trans. and ed. Marged Haycock (Cardiff, 2007); *Early Welsh Saga Poetry*, trans. and ed. Jenny Rowland (Cambridge, 1990).
7. Arnold, *An Archaeology of the Early Anglo-Saxon Kingdoms* (London, 1988); Stephen Bassett (ed.), *The Origins of the Anglo-Saxon Kingdoms* (Leicester, 1989); eds. Leslie Abrams and James P. Carley, *The Archaeology and History of Glastonbury Abbey. Essays in Honour of the Ninetieth Birthday of C.A. Ralegh Radford* (Woodbridge, 1991); Higham, *Rome, Britain and the Anglo-Saxons* (London, 1992b); Dark, *Civitas to Kingdom: British Political Continuity 300–800* (Leicester, 1994); Higham, *An English Empire* (Manchester, 1995); Higham, *King Arthur: Mythmaking and History* (New York, 2002); ed. Scott DeGregorio, *Innovation and Tradition in the Writings of the Venerable Bede* (Morgantown, 2006).
8. Weston, *The Legend of Sir Gawain* (London, 1897); *The Quest of the Holy Grail* (London, 1913); *From Ritual to Romance* (London, 1920); Nutt, *Studies on the Legend of the Holy Grail* (London, 1888).
9. *Celtic Myth and Arthurian Romance* (New York, 1927); *Arthurian Tradition and Chrétien* (New York, 1949); *Wales and the Arthurian Legend* (Cardiff, 1956); *The Grail: From Celtic Myth to Christian Symbol* (Cardiff, 1963).
10. Bromwich, "First Transmission from England to France," *The Arthur of the Welsh*, eds. Rachel Bromwich, Brynley F. Roberts, and Alfred O.H. Jarman (Cardiff, 1991), 273–298; Bullock-Davies, *Professional Interpreters and the Matter of Britain* (Cardiff, 1966).
11. Nothing is to be gained by listing individuals or their works. The fact that a physics professor has written as an equal to experts in this field is telling enough about its integrity.
12. Charles-Edwards, "The Date of the Four Branches of the Mabinogi," *THSC* (London, 1971), 263–98; Laurie, *Two Studies in Chrétien de Troyes* (Geneva, 1972); eds.

Danielle Buschinger and Michael Zink, *Lancelot-Lanzelet: Hier et Aujourdhui* (Reineke, 1995); eds. W.H. Jackson and Sylvia A. Ranawake, *The Tristan of the Germans* (Cardiff, 2000); eds. Karen Pratt and Glynn Burgess, *The Arthur of the French: The Arthurian Legend in Medieval French and Occitan Literature* (Cardiff, 2006).

13. *Trioedd Ynys Prydein: The Welsh Triads*, trans. and ed. trans. Rachel Bromwich (Cardiff, rev. 1978); Brouland, "Peredur ab Efrawg," *Perceval-Parzival; Hier et Aujourdhui*, eds. Danielle Buschinger and Wolfgang Spiewok (Reineke, 1994), 59–70; Bugge, "Fertility myth and female sovereignty in the weddynge of Sir Gawen and Dame Ragnell," *CR* 39.2 (University Park, 2004), 198–218.

14. Goetinck, *Peredur: A Study of Welsh Tradition in the Grail Legends* (Cardiff, 1975); Busby, *Gauvain in Old French Literature* (Amsterdam, 1980); Gowans, *Cei and the Arthurian Legend* (Cambridge, 1988).

15. Johnson, *Origins of Arthurian Romances* (McFarland, 2012); *Evidence of Arthur* (McFarland, 2014); *Hengest, Gwrtheyrn, and the Chronology of Post-Roman Britain* (McFarland, 2014).

Introduction

1. The real Britain was quickly forgotten. This is the period when Belisarius would offer it in trade for Sicily; Procopius, *De Bello Gallico*, trans. Henry B. Dewing (London, rep. 1971), 2.6.

2. This is an argument that will be developed in the next few chapters. As will be seen, there is simply no practical evidence that Britain ever had a single ruler after 410.

3. The tin of Cornwall was a necessary and rare resource in the making of weaponry, but trade between Cornwall and the continent continued long after the fall of the Western Roman Empire in 476.

4. The second visit is still debated but does seem feasible; as will be seen the author was credible with his British information, if sparse. The seminal work for the life from the perspective of British history is still Professor Thompson's *St. Germanus of Auxerre and the end of Roman Britain* (Woodbridge, 1984).

5. Prosper of Aquitaine, *Prosper of Aquitaine. Prosperi Aquitani opera*, trans. Charles T. Huegelmeyer (Washington, 1962), 429.

6. *Chronica Minora I*, ed. Theodor Mommsen (Berlin, 1886), 515–660; Miller, "The Last British Engry in the Gallic Chronicles," *Brit* 9 (Stroud, 1978b), 315–318; Jones and Casey, "The Gallic Chronicle Restored: A Chronology for the Anglo-Saxon Invasions and the End of Roman Britain," *Brit* (Stroud, 1978), Burgess, "The Dark Ages Return to Fifth-Century Britain: The Restored Gallic Chronicles Exploded," *Brit* 21 (Stroud, 1990), 185–95.

7. *The Gododdin of Aneirin*, trans. and ed. John T. Koch (Cardiff, 1997), cx–cxxvii.

8. Johnson, *Hengest, Gwrtheyrn, and the Chronology of Post-Roman Britain* (McFarland, 2014), 79–81.

9. Charles-Edwards has written some interesting thoughts about post-Roman British culture. See the bibliography.

10. As has been mentioned above the Gwynedd dynasty may well have come from Ireland or at the very least was closely allied and possibly intermarried with an Irish royal family. Tradition has it that Dalriada, Dyfed, and Brychieniog were also ruled by Irish families even though they were treated like native dynasties in the historical period.

11. The symbol stones are simple phallic monuments with several Pictish symbols on them. There are dozens of unique symbols. Anthony Jackson has suggested that each might have symbolized a royal family emblem; A. Jackson, *The Symbol Stones of Scotland* (Orkneys, 1984).

12. The literary piece *Culhwch ac Olwen* is a perfect example of the phenomenon. The story was clearly an example of Joseph Campbell's, "Six Go Around the World" archetype hero tale in the beginning, but Arthur's influence has changed the entire narrative of the story. Campbell, *The Hero with a Thousand Faces* (Princteon, 1949).

13. *Trioedd Ynys Prydein: The Welsh Triads*, trans. and ed. Rachel Bromwich (Cardiff, rev. 1978), lxxx–lxxxiii.

Chapter 1

1. Adamnan, *Life of Saint Columba, Founder of Hy (Iona)*, trans. and ed. William Reeves (Llanerch, rep. 1988), 1.1, 1.10, 2.33, 2.35, 2.42.

2. Vansina, *Oral Tradition as History* (Madison, 1985).

3. Charles-Edwards, *Wales and the Britons 350–1064* (Oxford, 2013); *The Law of Hywel Dda*, trans. and ed. Dafydd Jenkins (Llandysul, 1986); Binchy, *Early Irish and Welsh Kinship* (Oxford, 1993) and "Celtic and Anglo-Saxon Kingship," (Oxford, 1970).

4. Lloyd Laing and his wife produced several educational works in the 1970s and 1980s.

5. We can only hope that Professor Koch will offer some sort of an overview of the development of Welsh literature in the next few years.

6. *The Welsh Life of David*, ed. D. Simon Evans (Cardiff, 1988); *Lives of the Welsh Saints*, trans. G.H. Doble, ed. D. Simon Evans (Cardiff, 2015).

Chapter 2

1. I will explore the lesser government positions in Chapter 6. For now it is only important to understand that they were not personally connected to the governor or the emperor.

2. A modern example might serve well here. In the United States, the, "Peace" symbol is the index and middle finger pointed in a "V" with the palm or the knuckles facing a person. In Britain and Commonwealth nations, "Peace" is strictly where the palm is facing the person being communicated with. The reverse, with the knuckle facing them, is an expletive. Taken within a U.S. context, an insult could be interpreted as just the opposite.

3. Cameron, *Claudian: Poetry and Propaganda at the Court of Honorius* (Oxford, 1970).

4. Though a layman he defended Augustine's position in *De vocatione omnium gentium* and responded to the opposition of his day, going so far as to work through Pope Leo I.

5. Jones and Casey, "The Gallic Chronicle Restored: A Chronology for the Anglo-Saxon Invasions and the End of Roman Britain," *Brit* 19 (Stroud, 1978), 367.

6. Miller ("The last British entry in the 'Gallic Chronicles,'" *Brit* 9 (Stroud, 1978b), 315–318) believed the original text had been heavily edited while Burgess ("The Dark Ages Return to Fifth-Century Britain: The 'Restored' Gallic Chronicle Exploded," *Brit* 21 (Stroud, 1990), 185–195) questioned the inconsistent dating.

7. Wood, "Continuity or Calamity: The Constraints of Literary Models," ed. John Drinkwater, *Fifth-Century Gaul: A Crisis of Identity* (Cambridge, 2002), 14.

8. Modern scholarship has generally leaned toward believing the corrected date is 441. *Chronica Minora I* (Berlin, 1886), 515–660, ed. Theodor Mommsen; Miller, "The last British entry in the 'Gallic Chronicles,'" *Brit* 9 (Stroud, 1978b), 315–318; Jones and Casey, "The Gallic Chronicle Restored: A Chronology for the Anglo-Saxon Invasions and the End of Roman Britain," *Brit* 19 (Stroud, 1978), 367–398; Burgess, "The Dark Ages Return to Fifth-Century Britain: The 'Restored' Gallic Chronicle Exploded," *Brit* 21 (Stroud, 1990), 185–195.

9. For instance, he uses Eunapius up to 404 and Olympiodorus from 407, leaving 405 and 406 absent in his history.

10. Mendelssohn, *Zosimi comitiset exadvocati fisci historia nova* (Lipsiae, rep. 1963).

11. Levison, "Bischof of Germanus of Auxerre und die Quellen zu seiner Geschichte," Neus Archiv der Gesellschaft für ältere deutsche Geschichtskunde 29 (1903–4), 112; Bardy, *Saint Germain d'Auxerre et Son Temps* (Auxerre, 1950), 96–97; Thompson, *St. Germanus of Auxerre and the end of Roman Britain* (Woodbridge, 1984), 26.

12. Bardy, *Saint Germain d'Auxerre et Son Temps* (Auxerre, 1950), 107; Thompson, *St Germanus of Auxerre and the end of Roman Britain* (Woodbridge, 1984), 8–14.

13. Thompson argued passionately and persuasively to that effect in *St Germanus of Auxerre and the end of Roman Britain* (Woodbridge, 1984), 13–14.

14. *St Germanus of Auxerre and the end of Roman Britain* (Woodbridge, 1984); Scharf, "Germanus von Auxerre—Chronologie seiner Vita," Francia 18.1 (Paris, 1991), 11–12. However, it should be remembered that there is no overriding reason why Germanus visited Britain a second time and no external source corroborates Constantius. Contra Barrett, "Saint Germanus and the British Missions," *Brit* 40 (Stroud, 2009), 197–217.

15. Professor Thompson, trained as a classical scholar, occasionally used Procopius in his work on reconstructing fifth-century Britain.

16. 3.2.31.
17. 8.20.6–10.
18. 8.20.4–5; Thompson, "Procopius on Brittia and Britannia" *CQ* 30 (London, 1980), 498–507.
19. Thorpe lists them (Gregory of Tours, *The History of the Franks*, trans. and ed. Lewis Thorpe (New York, 1974), 26), they are mainly enrichments of his religious passages. He did apparently write drafts of Book IV and possibly earlier books which he had used other sources to write about.
20. Thorpe again lists these (32). They are his quarrel with Felix, his argument with Chilperic, and his personal trial at Berny-Rivière for having slandered Queen Fredegund among others.
21. Dalton, *The History of the Franks by Gregory of Tours* (Oxford, 1927), 36.
22. *The Life of Samson of Dol*, trans. Thomas Taylor (Llanerch, rep. 1991), xxxix; Poulin, "Hagiographie et Politique. La Première vie de S. Samson de Dol" Francia 5 ((Paris, 1977), 1–26.
23. Chapter 26 and 27. Duine, "La vie de S. Samson, à propos d'un ouvrage récent," AdB 28 (Paris, 1912–13), 332–56; W. Davies, "Property Rights and Property Claims in Welsh, "Vitae" of the Eleventh Century," *Hagiographie, cultures, et sociétés ive-xiie siécles*, ed. Evelyne Patlagean and Pierre Riché (Paris, 1981), 515; Wright, "Gildas's Geographical Perspective: Some Problems," *Gildas: New Approaches*, eds. David N. Dumville and Michael Lapidge. (Woodbridge, 1984), 199 fn. 25; Sharpe, "Gildas as Father of the Church," *Gildas: New Approaches*, eds. David N. Dumville and Michael Lapidge (Woodbridge, 1984), 193 fn. 25; *La Vie ancienne de saint Samson de Dol*, trans. and ed. Piere Florent (Paris, 1997).
24. Richmond and Crawford, "The British Section of the Ravenna Cosmography," AC 93 (1949), 1.

Chapter 3

1. The theory is based on Gildas' passage about a "superbus tyrannus," proud tyrant, inviting Hengest and Horsa to Britain as mercenaries. Professor Alcock could be considered the first person to seriously question the, "over-king" scenario (Alcock, *Arthur's Britain* (London, 1971)) while Professor Higham effectively buried it (Higham, *Rome, Britain and the Anglo-Saxons* (London, 1992b). But that has not stopped others from continuing to make this nonexistent figure a key character in fifth-century Britain. A more reasonable view was proposed by Campbell, who suggested that more local sub-Roman rulers made use of *foederati* on an individual basis; (Campbell, "The lost centuries: 400–600," *The Anglo-Saxons*, ed. James Campbell (London, 1982), 20–3.
2. Higham, *Rome, Britain and the Anglo-Saxons* (London, 1992b), 52.
3. Jones, *Saints' Lives and Chronicles in Early England* (Cornell, 1947 rep. 1968); *Bedae opera de temporibus*, ed. Charles William Jones; (Cambridge, 1943); Poole, *Chronicles and Annals* (Oxford, 1926).
4. Mohrmann, *The Latin of St. Patrick: Four Lectures* (Dublin, 1961).
5. Dumville once suggested that the letter was an open one, not to be handed directly to Coroticus. This seems likely given the contents of the letter, but has no bearing on the evaluation given above. (Dumville, "Coroticus," *St Patrick: A.D. 493–1993*, ed. David N. Dumville (Woodbridge, 1993), 107.
6. The author's date-guessing results gave the broad range of 413–443 for Patrick's year of birth and Dumville has already established that his obit was 493, suggesting Patrick might have lived in all three periods.
7. Haycock, *Legendary Poems from the Book of Taliesin*, trans. and ed. Marged Haycock (Cardiff, 2007), 490.
8. Lapidge, "Gildas' Education and the Latin Culture of Sub-Roman Britain," *Gildas: New Approaches*, eds. David N. Dumville and Michael Lapidge (Woodbridge, 1984), 27–50.
9. *Ibid*, 32–5.
10. Wright, "Gildas' prose style and its origins," *Gildas: New Approaches*, eds. Michael Lapidge and David N. Dumville (Woodbridge, 1984), 107–28.
11. Schaffner, "Britain's Iudices," *Gildas: New Approaches*, eds. David N. Dumville and Michael Lapidge (Woodbridge, 1984), 151–155.
12. Johnson, *Evidence of Arthur* (McFarland, 2014), 154–163, 230–45.
13. D. McCarthy and Ó Cróinín, "The 'Lost' Irish 84-year Easter table rediscovered," Peritia 6–7 (Galway, 1987), 227–42.
14. Charles-Edwards has given an invaluable guide for the development of British

writing during the period based on native remains and comparison to the continent, but there are no extant remains of chronicles or annals; Charles-Edwards, *Wales and the Britons 350–1064* (Oxford, 2013), 116–73

15. He figures in *Mabinogion*, "The Dream of Maxen" and as a principal ancestor of Gwent and Powys.

16. An opinion supported by the traditional evidence, which places him in Strathclyde at birth and makes him the son of a known Pictish king named Cau in the *vita* by the monk of Rhuys and the son of Nau of Scotland according to that by Caradoc of Llancarfan; A Monk of Rhuys and Caradoc of Llancarfan. *Two Lives of Gildas*, trans. Hugh Williams (Llanerch, rep. 1990), 12–15 and 84–5. Wade-Evans, "Notes on the Excidium Britanniae: A Contribution towards a Re-Statement of Early Saxo-Welsh History," *CR* 1 (Edinburgh, 1905), 289–95; Wade-Evans, "'The Ruin of Britannia': A Contribution towards a Restatement [sic] of Early Saxo-Welsh History," *CR* 2 (Edinburgh, 1906), 46–58 and 126–35; Thompson, "Gildas and the History of Britain," *Brit* 10 (Stroud, 1979), 203–226; Field, "Gildas and the City of the Legions," HA 1 (1999), Web.

17. Miller, "Relative and absolute publication dates of Gildas' De Excidio in medieval scholarship," *BBCS* 26 (Cardiff, 1976b), 169–174; Sims-Williams, "Gildas and the Anglo-Saxons," *CMCS* 6 (Cambridge, 1983a), 1–30; Dumville, "The Chronology of De Excidio Britanniae, Book I," *Gildas: New Approaches*, eds. David N. Dumville and Michael Lapidge (Woodbridge, 1984b), 61–84; Wright, "Gildas's Geographical Perspective: Some Problems," *Gildas: New Approaches*, eds. David N. Dumville and Michael Lapidge (Woodbridge, 1984), 85–105; Higham, "Gildas, Roman Walls and British Dykes," *CMCS* 22 (Cambridge, 1991), 1–14; Dark, *Civitas to Kingdom: British Political Continuity 300–800* (Leicester, 1994), 258–266.

18. Charles-Edwards, *Wales and the Britons 350–1064* (Oxford, 2013), 51.

19. *Cunedda, Cynan, Cadwallon, Cynddylan: Four Welsh Poems and Britain 383–655*, trans. and ed. John T. Koch (Cardiff, 2013), 120–32.

20. *Ibid*, 144–5.

21. An argument proposed by Koch and Isaac is that Mwynðawg Mwynfawr was not a person's name, leaving the question of the Gododdin lord still open; Koch, "Thoughts on the Ur-Gododðin: Rethinking Aneirin and Mynyðawc Mwynvawr," Language Sciences 15.2 (Amsterdam, 1993), 81–9; Isaac, "Mwynddawg Mwynfawr" *BBCS* 37 (Cardiff, 1990), 111–113.

22. Ifor Williams was the initial proponent but was followed by every major researcher and translator of the poem up until John T. Koch's translation and attempt at a restoration of the work to its original wording. Koch has proposed a date nearer 570, which would mean that the action took place before the rise of the Northumbrian kingdoms of Bernicia and Deira; Aneirin, *Canu Aneirin*, ed. Sir Ifor Williams (Cardiff, 1938), xxviii, xxxi–xxxii; *The Gododdin: The Oldest Scottish Poem*, trans. and ed. Kenneth H. Jackson (Edinburgh, 1969), 8, 11–12; ed. Rachel Bromwich, *The Beginnings of Welsh Poetry: Studies by Sir Ifor Williams* (Cardiff, 2nd ed. 1982), 47–9, 52–3; *Aneirin: Y Gododdin—Britain Oldest Heroic Poem*, trans. and ed. Alfred Owen Hughes Jarman (Llandysul, 1988), xviii–xx, Smyth, *Warlords and Holy Men: Scotland A.D. 80–100* (London, 1984), 20–2; *The Gododdin of Aneirin*, trans. and ed. John T. Koch (Cardiff, 1997), xvi–xxxiv.

23. Koch has suggested this version may have come to Wales between 642 and 655, during the British alliance with Penda; *Cunedda, Cynan, Cadwallon, Cynddylan: Four Welsh Poems and Britain 383–655*, trans. and ed. John T. Koch (Cardiff, 2013), 266.

24. Whitley Stokes' theory has been questioned by some scholars but is now thoroughly disavowed by McCarthy, *The Irish Annals: Their genesis, evolution and history* (Chippenham, 2008), 87–96.

25. *Ibid*, 154–9.

26. Ó Cróinin, *Early Medieval Ireland* (London, 1995), 26.

27. Byrne, "Seventh-century documents," IER 108 (Dublin, 1967), 180.

28. Hughes, *Early Christian Ireland: Introduction to the Sources* (New York, 1972), 121–123.

29. *Ibid*, 118–119.

30. *Ibid*, 141.

31. Grosjean,, "Sur quelques exégetes irlandáis du viie siècle," SE 7 (Sint-Beggaplein, 1955), 67–98.

32. Daniel McCarthy has theorized that they were well established by the middle of the sixth century because the annals recorded plagues, panics, and poor harvests during

roughly the same era as they are recorded throughout the rest of the world. His reasoning is that to keep records during a catastrophe the tradition must already have been established. However, the dates are only roughly accurate, so they might have been recorded after the fact. As the historical horizon for our British documents are the second half of the sixth century (after the catastrophe), it seems most likely that Irish contemporary recording began then too; D. McCarthy, *The Irish Annals: Their genesis, evolution and history* (Chippenham, 2008), 159–62.

33. Wormald, *The First Code of English Law* (Canterbury, 2005), 1 and 17.

34. *Ibid*, 16–17.

35. Oliver, *The Beginnings of English Law* (Toronto, 2002), 16.

36. Wormald, *The First Code of English Law* (Canterbury, 2005), 11–15.

37. Oliver, *The Beginnings of English Law* (Toronto, 2002), 34–41; Wormald, The First Code of English Law (Canterbury, 2005), 13.

38. Wormald, *The First Code of English Law* (Canterbury, 2005), 1–2.

39. Oliver, *The Beginnings of English Law* (Toronto, 2002), 134.

40. *Ibid*, 165.

41. *Ibid*, 173–4.

42. *Ibid*, 166.

43. Kirby, *The Earliest English Kings* (London, 1992), 125–6.

44. *The Laws of The Earliest English Kings*, trans. and ed. Frederick L. Attenborough (Cambridge, 1922), 34; Stenton, *Anglo-Saxon England* (Oxford, 1971), 72–3.

45. Whitelock, *English Historical Documents v.l. c. 500–1042* (London, 1968), 327–37; Kirby, *The Earliest English Kings* (London, 1992), 2;

46. H. Chadwick, *The Origins of the English Nation* (Cambridge, 1907), 161; John, *Orbis Britanniae* (Leicester, 1966), 135–6; Stenton, *Anglo-Saxon England* (Oxford, 1971), 290; Finberg, "Anglo-Saxon England to 1042," *The Agrarian History of England and Wales*, Vol. 1.2 ed. Herbert P.R. Finberg (Cambridge, 1972), 443; Loyn, *The Governance of Anglo-Saxon England, 500–1087* (Stanford, 1984), 32.

47. Abel, *Lordship and Military Obligation in Anglo-Saxon England* (Los Angeles, 1988), 15–25.

48. Miller, "The disputed historical horizon of the Pictish king-lists," *BBCS* 28 (Cardiff, 1978), 1–11.

49. M. Anderson, *Kings and Kingship in Early Scotland* (Edinburgh, 1973), 15.

50. Miller, "The disputed historical horizon of the Pictish king-lists," *BBCS* 28 (Cardiff, 1978d), 33.

51. The early Christian annals began when monks calculated the exact day for Easter each year. It was soon found out that there was a pattern to it, and that the full cycle recurred every 84 years. Many early Christian calculators of Easter took this to mean that 84 was an important number; the Pictish annalist may have altered reign-lengths to maintain the 84-year cycle. If he did, then any reign-length that falls into the pattern is useless for historical dating.

52. Miller, "The disputed historical horizon of the Pictish king-lists," *BBCS* 28 (Cardiff, 1978d), 8–12.

53. Fraser, *From Caledonia to Pictland: Scotland to 795* (Edinburgh, 2009).

54. *Two Lives of Saint Cuthbert: A Life by an Anonymous Monk of Lindisfarne and Bede's Prose Life*, trans. and ed. Bertram Colgrave (Cambridge, 1940), 11.

55. *Ibid*, 13.

56. Stancliffe, "Cuthbert and the Polarity between Pastor and Solitary," *St. Cuthbert, His Cult and His Community to AD 1200*, eds. Gerald Bonner and Clare Stancliffe (Woodbridge, 1989), 24; eds. Anne Williams, Alfred P. Smyth, and David P. Kirby, *A Biographical Dictionary of Dark Age Britain* (London, 1997), 112.

57. Stancliffe, "Cuthbert and the Polarity between Pastor and Solitary," *St. Cuthbert, His Cult and His Community to AD 1200*, eds. Gerald Bonner, David Rollason, and Clare Stancliffe (Woodbridge, 1989), 36–42; Thacker, "Lindesfarne and the Origins of the Cult of St Cuthbert," *St. Cuthbert, His Cult and His Community to AD 1200*, eds. Gerald Bonner, David Rollason, and Clare Stancliffe (Woodbridge, 1989), 103–115.

58. Berschin, "Opus Deliberatum ac Perfectum: Why Did the Venerable Bede Write a Second Prose Life of St Cuthbert?," *St. Cuthbert, His Cult and His Community to AD 1200*, eds. Gerald Bonner, David Rollason, and Clare Stancliffe (Woodbridge, 1989), 98.

59. *Two Lives of Saint Cuthbert: A Life by an Anonymous Monk of Lindisfarne and Bede's Prose Life*, trans. and ed. Bertram Colgrave (Cambridge, 1940), 12.

60. *Ibid*, 12.

61. Wormald, "Bede, the Bretwaldas and the origins of the Gens Anglorum," *Ideal and Reality in Frankish and Anglo-Saxon Society: Studies Presented to J.M. Wallace-Hadrill*, eds. Patrick Wormald, Donald Bullough, and Roger Collins (Oxford, 1983), 114; Dumville, "Essex, Middle Anglia, and the expansion of Mercia in the south-east Midlands," *Origins of the Anglo-Saxon Kingdoms*, ed. Stephen Bassett (Leicester, 1989a), 129.

62. Celtic Christianity was not a different religion, but was more accurately an older version of Christianity. The Irish and Britons dated Easter by a different method and had their monks shave their heads differently. Different practices had been enacted while Britain had been effectively shut off from the continent during the fifth century.

63. *Cunedda, Cynan, Cadwallon, Cynddylan: Four Welsh Poems and Britain 383–655*, trans. and ed. John T. Koch (Cardiff, 2013), 236–41.

64. *Ibid*, 248–50.

65. *Ibid*, 251–4.

66. Bannerman, *Studies in the History of Dalriada* (Edinburgh, 1974), 39.

67. Bede, *A History of the English Church and People*, trans. and ed. Leo Sherley-Price (Baltimore, 1955), 3.6

68. *Ibid*, 1.1.

69. Bannerman, *Studies in the History of Dalriada* (Edinburgh, 1974), 118–132

70. Mulchrone, "Die Abfassungszeit und Überlieferung der Vita Tripartita," ZCP 16 (Berlin, 1926), 411–452; Stokes, *The Saltair na Rann. A Collection of Early Middle Irish Poems* (Oxford, 1883); Strachan, "The Verbal System of the Saltair na Rann," Transactions of the Philological Society 42 (Hoboken, 1895), 1–76.

71. For a complete explanation of the *Vita Kentigerni*'s early dating see *The Gododdin of Aneirin*, ed. and trans. John T. Koch (Cardiff, 1997), lxxvi–lxxix; MacQueen, "A Reply to Professor Jackson," TDGNAHS 3rd series 36 (Dumfries, 1959), 175–83; K. Jackson, "The Sources for the Life of St. Kentigern," *Studies in the Early British Church*, ed. Nora K. Chadwick (Cambridge, 1958), 286–293; MacQueen, "Yvain, Ewen, and Owain ap Urien" TDGNHAS 3rd series 33 (Dumfries, 1956), 107–131; Carney, *Studies in Irish Literature and History* (Dublin, 1950), 79.

72. *The Gododdin of Aneirin*, trans. and ed. John T. Koch (Cardiff, 1997), lxxix.

73. Brooke, *The Church and the Welsh Border in the Central Middle Ages* (Woodbridge, 1986), 16–38.

74. Owen,, "Y Cyfreithiau—(I) Natur y Testanau," *Y Traddodiad Rhyddiaith yn yr Oesau Canol* (Cardiff, 1974), 197–8.

75. Charles-Edwards, *Wales and the Britons 350–1064* (Oxford, 2013), 245–67.

76. *The Llandaff Charters*, ed. Wendy Davies (Aberystwyth, 1979).

77. Johnson, *Hengest, Gwrtheyrn, and the Chronology of Post-Roman Britain* (McFarland, 2014), 86–92.

78. Formerly Eddius Stephanus because of an association between the author and a man named by Bede, "Ædde, also known as Stephen". The connection is no longer considered valid; Goffart, *The Narrators of Barbarian History (A.D. 550–800): Jordanes, Gregory of Tours, Bede, and Paul the Deacon* (Princeton, 1988), 281 fn. 210.

79. Fulk, Cain, and Anderson, *History of Old English Literature* (Malden, 2003), 90.

80. Rowland, *Early Welsh Saga Poetry* (Cardiff, 1990), 120–141.

81. *Ibid*, 141–145.

82. O'Rahilly, "On the Origins of the Names Érainn and Ériu," Ériu 14 (Dublin, 1946), 7–28; MacCana, "Aspects of the Theme of the King and Goddess," EC 6 (Paris, 1955), 356–413.

83. "Hywel Dda," *Celtic Culture: A Historical Encyclopedia*, ed. John T. Koch (Santa Barbara, 2006), 945.

84. Lloyd, *A History of Wales: from the earliest times to the Edwardian conquest* (London, 1911), 337–8.

85. Kirby, "Hywel Dda: Anglophile?," WHR 8 (Cardiff, 1976b), 1–13.

86. Thornton, "Mordaf Hael," *Oxford Dictionary of National Biography* (Oxford, 2015), Web. Other historical asides have often been used by historians including but not limited to several passages about Rhun of Gwynedd, as will be seen below.

87. As will be seen in the essay on *Historia Brittonum*, Hywel Dda was not above propaganda.

88. Rowland, *Early Welsh Saga Poetry* (Cambridge, 1990), 42.

89. *Ibid*, 46–7.

90. *Ibid*, 43.

91. Rowland believes that the beheader had control of the field and took the head as

a trophy, while Ifor Williams believed the act was performed to save the king from disgrace; Rowland, *Early Welsh Saga Poetry* (Cambridge, 1990), 78; I. Williams, "The Poems of Llywarch Hen," *The Beginnings of Welsh Poetry*, ed. Rachel Bromwich (Cardiff, 1972), 143; *Canu Llywarch Hen*, ed. Sir Ifor Williams (Cardiff, 1935), liv.
  92. I. Williams, "Canu Llywarch Hen and the Finn Cycle," *Astudiaethau ar yr Hengerdd*, ed. Rachel Bromwich and R. Brinley Jones (Cardiff, 1978), 234–265.
  93. Rowland, *Early Welsh Saga Poetry* (Cardiff, 1990), 82.
  94. *Ibid*, 87–8
  95. *Culhwch ac Olwen: An edition and study of the oldest Arthurian tale*, eds. Rachel Bromwich and D. Simon Evans (Cardiff, 1992), vxxvii–lxxxi.
  96. Huws, "Llyfr Gwyn Rhydderch," *CMCS* 21 (Cambridge, 1991), 1–37 and Charles-Edwards, "Scribes of the Red Book of Hergest," *NLWJ* 20 (Cardiff, 1980), 246–56; Huws, "Red Book of Hergest," *NLWJ* 22 (Cardiff, 1981), 1, respectively.
  97. *Culhwch ac Olwen: An edition and study of the oldest Arthurian tale*, eds. Rachel Bromwich and D. Simon Evans (Cardiff, 1992), lxxiv–lxxv.
  98. *Trioedd Ynys Prydein: The Welsh Triads*, trans. and ed. Rachel Bromwich (Cardiff, rev. 1978), lxxx–lxxxiii.
  99. *Ibid*, xx–xxi, xxvi.
  100. *Ibid*, cxi–cxv.
  101. Bassett, "In Search of the Origins of the Anglo-Saxon Kingdoms," *The Origins of the Anglo-Saxon Kingdoms*, ed. Steven Bassett (Leicester, 1989), 23; Wood, "Kings, Kingdoms and consent," *Early Medieval Kingship*, eds. Peter H. Sawyer and Ian N. Wood (Leeds, 1977), 18–20; Dumville, "Kingship, genealogies and regnal lists," *Early Medieval Kingship*, eds. Peter H. Sawyer and Ian N. Wood (Leeds, 1977b), 91–92; Yorke, "The Kingdom of the East Saxons," *ASE* 14 (London, 1985), 1–30; Arnold, *An Archaeology of the Early Anglo-Saxon Kingdoms* (New York, 1988), 197–199; *Anglo-Saxon Myths: State and Church*, ed. Nicholas Brooks (London, 2000c), 23.

Chapter 4

  1. Dumville has been perhaps the most potent critic of the *Historia Brittonum*, while the *Kentish Source's* historicity has never really been in doubt. Harrison has provided the best overview of the materials; Dumville, "On the North British Section of the *Historia Brittonum*," *WHR* 8 (Cardiff, 1977c), 345–54; Harrison, *The Framework of Anglo-Saxon England to 900 A.D.* (Cambridge, 1976), 121–123.
  2. It is conceivable and even probable that historians into the sixteenth century had access to the *Northern Memorandum*, but there is no linguistic or orthographic evidence of an early source in any of their works, only the tantalizing information they provide about the period.
  3. Johnson, *Evidence of Arthur* (McFarland, 2014), 154–163, 230–45.
  4. See the appendix, "Vortigern".
  5. Lloyd, *The History of Wales: from the earliest times to the Edwardian conquest* (Cardiff, 1912), 126 fn. 6; H. Chadwick and N. Chadwick, *The Growth of Literature* (Cambridge, 1932), 155; Crawford, "Arthur and his Battles," *Antiq* 9 (Gloucester, 1935), 279; K. Jackson, "The Arthur of History," *Arthurian Literature in the Middle Ages*, ed. Roger S. Loomis (Chicago, 1959), 78; Bromwich, "Concepts of Arthur," *SC* 10/11 (Cardiff, 1976), 169.
  6. Praise poetry focuses praising the patron for his martial abilities and generosity. Most surviving examples give several vague references to battles and raids before speaking about how generous he is to both his men and his bard. None of the extant poems contain enough information in themselves to match what is in *Historia Brittonum*—the alliance, a named enemy, one location, an overall view of a campaign, and an assassination attempt. In fact, all of the surviving Taliesin poems do not give us as much historical information as is found in this *Historia Brittonum* chapter.
  7. Dumville, "On the North British Section of the *Historia Brittonum*," *WHR* 8 (Cardiff, 1977c), 345–354; Hughes, "The Welsh Latin Chronicles: *Annales Cambriae* and Related Texts," *PBA* 59 (London, 1975), 233–258.
  8. Johnson, *Hengest, Gwrtheyrn, and the Chronology of Post-Roman Britain* (McFarland, 2014), 54–8.
  9. We can be fairly confident that Oswiu at one point married Rieinmellth, granddaughter of Rhun and great-granddaughter of Urien himself.

10. Johnson, *Evidence of Arthur* (McFarland, 2014), 154–63. These are extremely generous numbers, but do allow for the maximum feasible life-span of an ecclesiastic during the period.

11. *The Gododdin of Aneirin*, ed. and trans. John T. Koch (Cardiff, 1997), cxxi–cxxiii.

12. As with the *Northern Memorandum*, many later sources claimed access to the *Kentish Source*, but only these three histories demonstrate by their word forms and other evidence that they could have accessed it.

13. Harrison, *The Framework of Anglo-Saxon History* (Cambridge, 1976), 122–3.

14. Johnson, *Hengest, Gwrtheyrn, and the Chronology of Post-Roman Britain* (McFarland, 2014), 77–9.

15. Wheeler, "Gildas' De Excidio Britanniae, Chapter 26," *EHR* 41 (London, 1926), 501–502; Brooks, "The creation and early structure of the kingdom of Kent," *The Origins of the Anglo-Saxon Kingdoms*, ed. Stephen Bassett (Leicester, 1989), 67; Johnson, *Hengest, Gwrtheyrn, and the Chronology of Post-Roman Britain* (McFarland, 2014), 76.

16. Nicholas Brooks clearly favored Æthelberht's reign but allowed for the possibility that the history might have been written in 691–725, the last period of full Kentish independence. He noted that the four battles between Gwrthefyr and Hengest would have helped Kent to claim Essex, Wessex, and maybe even Middlesex territories and suggests that the best time for that to be put in the story was when Mellitus was made bishop of London, in 604 or in the late 660s/early 670s when Ecgberht was installing Eorcenwald at London and establishing the monastery at Chertsey; Brooks, *Anglo-Saxon Myths: Church and State, 400–1066* (New York, 2003), 60, 85–7.

17. Kirby, "Bede and Northumbrian Chronology," *EHR* 78 (London, 1963), 514–527; Kirby, "Bede's Native Sources for the Historia Ecclesiastica," *BJRL* 48 (London, 1965–1966), 341–371; Miller, "Bede's Use of Gildas," *EHR* 90 (London, 1975), 241–261; ed. Scott DeGregorio, *Innovation and Tradition in the Writings of the Venerable Bede* (Morgantown, 2006); G. Brown, *A Companion to Bede* (Woodbridge, 2009).

18. Bede, *A History of the English Church and People*, trans. and ed. Leo Sherley-Price (Baltimore, 1955), preface.

19. J. Turville-Petre, "Hengest and Horsa," *SBVS* 14 (London, 1953–1957), 273–290; de Vries, "Die Ursprungssage der Sachsen," Niedersächen Jahrbuch für Landesgeschichte 31 (Berlin, 1959), 30–32; Olrik, "Epic Laws of Folk Narrative," *International Folkloristics: classic contributions by the founders of folklore*, ed. Alan Dundes (Lanham, 1999), 104.

20. J. Turville-Petre, "Hengest and Horsa," *SBVS* 14 (London, 1953–1957), 287; Sims-Williams, "The settlement of England in Bede and the Chronicle," *ASE* 12 (London, 1983b), 22.

21. Charles-Edwards and others have also been careful to distinguish the historical figure of Gwrtheryn from the *Kentish Source* character of Vortigern. Charles Edwards, *Wales and the Britons: 350–1064* (Oxford, 2013), 53; Brooks, "Canterbury, Rome and the Construction of English Identity," *Early Medieval Rome and the Christian West: essays in honour of Donald A. Bullough*, ed. Julia M.H. Smith. (Boston, 2000a), 245–6; Brooks, *Bede and the English* (Jarrow, 2000b); Brooks, *Anglo-Saxon Myths: State and Church* (London, 2003), 79–89.

22. Bede, *A History of the English Church and People*, trans. and ed. Leo Sherley-Price (Baltimore, 1955), 2.5.

23. J. Turville-Petre, "Hengest and Horsa," *SBVS* 14 (London, 1953–1957), 273–290; de Vries, "Die Ursprungssage der Sachsen," Niedersächen Jahrbuch für Landesgeschichte 31 (Berlin, 1959), 30–32; Olrik, "Epic Laws of Folk Narrative," *International Folkloristics: classic contributions by the founders of folklore*, ed. Alan Dundes (Lanham, 1999), 104.

24. Kirby, "Bede and Northumbrian Chronology," *EHR* 78 (London, 1963), 514–527.

25. Miller, "Bede's Use of Gildas," *EHR* 90 (London, 1975a), 241–261.

26. Bede, *A History of the English Church and People*, trans. and ed. Leo Sherley-Price (Baltimore, 1955), 1.16.

27. Dumville, " 'Nennius' and the Historia Brittonum," *SC* 11 (Cardiff, 1976), 78–95.

28. Chadwick, "Early Culture and Learning in North Wales," *Studies in the Early British Church*, ed. Nora K. Chadwick (Cambridge, 1958), 29–34. As Higham more recently pointed out, this nationalist movement was only possible because of a period of Mercian instability.

29. Johnson, *Hengest, Gwrtheyrn, and the Chronology of Post-Roman Britain* (McFarland, 2014).

30. Professor Charles-Edwards believes that Garmon did not exist because it would deprive Germanus of almost all of his significance in British history. He also denies Garmon on linguistic grounds, citing I. Williams in noting that the failure of lenition (a in place of e) is well documented in K. Jackson, *Language and History in Early Britain* (Edinburgh, 1953), 281; Charles-Edwards, *Wales and the Britons: 350–1064* (Oxford, 2013), 442 fn. 24; I. Williams, *Hen Chwedlau* (Cardiff, 1949), 53.

31. Miller, "The Foundation Legend of Gwynedd in the Latin Texts," *BBCS* 27 (Cardiff, 1978a), 515–532.

32. *The Gododdin of Aneirin*, trans. and ed. John T. Koch (Cardiff, 1997), xxxv–xlii.

33. Phillimore, "The *Annales Cambriae* and Old-Welsh Genealogies from Harleian MS. 3859," *Y Cymmrodor* 8 (Cardiff, 1888), 144.

34. *Ibid*, 144.

35. Hughes, "The Welsh Latin Chronicles: *Annales Cambriae* and Related Texts," *PBA* 59 (London, 1975), 237.

36. Rowland has noted that, while Urien and his allies are entirely absent from the secular records, several of his literary enemies—Gwrgi and Peredur, Dunawt, and Cerdic son of Gwallawg, are present. This has some very interesting implications. However, they are not relevant to the present discussion.

37. Hughes, "The Welsh Latin Chronicles: *Annales Cambriae* and Related Texts," *PBA* 59 (London, 1975), 233–258.

38. Dumville, "*Historia Brittonum*: An Insular History from the Carolingian Age," *Historiographie im frühen Mittelalter*, ed. Anton Scharer and Georg Scheibelreitr (Munich, 1994), 406–34; Charles-Edwards, *Early Irish and Welsh Kinship* (Oxford, 1993), 346–5.

39. J. Davies, *A History of Wales* (New York, 1994), 52 and 72.

40. Hodgkin, *A History of the Anglo-Saxons* (Oxford, 1935); Plummer, *Two of the Saxon Chronicles Parallel*, vol. 2 (London, 1892–1899), civ.

41. Stenton, "The South-Western Element in the Old English Chronicle," *Essays in Medieval History presented to Thomas Frederick Tout*, ed. A.G. Little and Sir Frederick Little (Manchester, 1925), 15–24.

42. There is no evidence that Sussex may have had an origin story before *The Anglo-Saxon Chronicle*, and without the impetus of writing its own history there would have been no reason too. On the other hand it would have been simple enough to ignore the kingdom's creation altogether or give it a foundation later than Wessex without insulting Sussex.

43. *The Anglo-Saxon Chronicle* dates for the early rulers were still earlier than found in the *West Saxon Regnal Table*, however, so in that regard Wessex was still improving its claims. See Dumville, "The West Saxon genaeological regnal list and the chronology of early Wessex," Peritia 4 (Galway, 1985), 21–66.

44. Kirby, "Problems of early West Saxon history," *EHR* 80 (London, 1965), 10–29; Johnson, *Hengest, Gwrtheyrn, and the Chronology of Post-Roman Britain* (McFarland, 2014), 150–2.

45. K. Jackson, *Language and History in Early Britain* (Edinburgh, 1953), 464–466 616–617, and 677; Sims-Williams, "The Settlement of England in Bede and the Chronicle," *ASE* 12 (London, 1983b), 33–34.

46. *The Gododdin of Aneirin*, trans. and ed. John T. Koch (Cardiff, 1997), cx–cxxvii.

Chapter 6

1. Magnus Maximus is one of the few names that Gildas mentions and, as the author has demonstrated, Maximus' activities occurred long before Gildas' historical horizon; Johnson, *Evidence of Arthur* (McFarland, 2014), 159–60.

2. Cleary, *The Ending of Roman Britain* (1989), 134; Reece, "The End of the City in Roman Britain," *The City in Late Antiquity*, ed. John Rich (London, 1992), 136–44, and Reece, "Town and Country: The End of Roman Britain," *WA* 12 (London, 1980), 77–92.

3. Zosimus, *Zosimus: New history*, trans. Ronald T. Ridley (Canberra, 1982), 6.5.2. They rid themselves of Roman administration.

4. It has been argued by some that the historian believed Honorius was addressing the natives in Bruttium, a region in Italy. Birley, *The Roman Government of Britain* (Oxford, 2005), 461–3; Bartholomew, "Fifth-Century Facts," *Brit* 13 (Stroud, 1982), 261–

70. However, no other contemporary historian claimed that Bruttium requested aid.
5. Professors Koch and Thompson agree with that assessment though they come to it by different means; Cunedda, Cynan, Cadwallon, Cynddylan: Four Welsh Poems and Britain 383–655, trans. and ed. John T. Koch (Cardiff, 2013), 81; Thompson, *St. Germanus of Auxerre and the end of Roman Britain* (Woodbridge, 1984), 37.

Chapter 7

1. Charles-Edwards, *Wales and the Britons: 350–1064* (Oxford, 2013), 33–4. As he points out, as late as Tacitus they were considered simply Britons.
2. A. Jackson, *The Symbol Stones of Scotland* (Orkneys, 1984).
3. Miller, "The disputed historical horizon of the Pictish king-lists," *BBCS* 28 (Cardiff, 1978d), 1–34.
4. Byrne, *Irish Kings and High-Kings* (London, 1973), 35, 108, and 287; S. Foster, *Picts, Gaels, and Scots: Early Historic Scotland* (London, 2004), 32–4; Smyth, *Warlords and Holy Men: Scotland AD 80–1000* (Edinburgh, 1984), 67 passim.
5. Miller's work showed conclusively that several kings between the late fifth century and the end of the Pictish kingdoms had inherited their kingdom through their mothers.
6. I will have more to say on this topic in Chapter 15, "Heroic Age Politico-Economic Dynamics".
7. Byrne, *Irish Kings and High-Kings* (Dublin, rev. 2001), chapter 5.
8. Ó Corráin, "Prehistoric and Early Christian Ireland," *The Oxford Illustrated History of Ireland*, ed. Roy Foster (Oxford, 2001), 1–52.
9. Gwynedd's dynasties are a complicated subject the author will explore below.
10. The idea that Dal Riata was not settled by just one group is not a new one. Bannerman seems to have been the first to suggest it (Bannerman, *Studies in the History of Dalriada* (Edinburgh, 1974), 122) while the present author has explained the reasoning and the logical conclusions of that theory more fully in his own work; Johnson, *Hengest, Gwrtheyrn, and the Chronology of Post-Roman Britain* (McFarland, 2014), 132–5.
11. Hines, "Philology, archaeology, and the Adventus Saxonum vel Anglorum," *Britain: 400–600*, eds. Alfred Bammesberger and Alfred Wollmann (Heidelberg, 1990), 17–36; C. Hawkes, "The south-east after the Romans: the Saxon settlement," *The Saxon Shore*, ed. Valerie A. Maxfield (Oxford, 1989), 78–95.

Chapter 8

1. Thompson, *St Germanus of Auxerre and the end of Roman Britain* (Woodbridge, 1984).
2. *The Life of Samson of Dol*, trans. Thomas Taylor (Llanerch, rep. 1991), chapters 26 and 27.
3. Discussed at length in Johnson, *Origins of Arthurian Romances* (McFarland, 2012), 114–120.
4. *Ibid*, 100–2, 194 fn. 56.
5. Lapidge, "Gildas' Education and the Latin Culture of Sub-Roman Britain," *Gildas: New Approaches*, eds. David N. Dumville and Michael Lapidge (Woodbridge, 1984), 27–50.
6. Ward-Perkins has gone so far as to suggest that Gwynedd was the last part of the Roman Empire, though that seems a little extreme to the present author; Ward-Perkins, "Why Did the Anglo-Saxons Not Become More British," *EHR* 115 (Oxford, 2000), 527.
7. Thompson, *St Germanus of Auxerre and the end of Roman Britain* (Woodbridge, 1984).
8. Johnson, *Evidence of Arthur* (McFarland, 2014), 158–60.
9. In his discussion on *Marwnad Cunedda*, which he believes to be contemporary because it does not mention Christians or Germanic warriors; Koch, *Cunedda, Cynan, Cadwallon, Cynddylan: Four Welsh Poems and Britain 383–655* (Cardiff, 2013), 88–9.
10. *Ibid*, 147–51.

Chapter 9

1. Goffart, *Barbarians and Romans 418–584. The Techniques of Accomodation* (Princeton, 1980).
2. Charles-Edwards, *Wales and the Britons: 350–1064* (Oxford, 2013), 44–5. He sees three phases of the Germanic presence

Chapter 10

1. All along the Roman Empire's borders, her simple presence seems to have inspired political turmoil and eventual unity as cultures struggled to present a united front against it in hopes of better resisting conquest. Ireland was simply longer lived in its unity because it was never touched by the Germanic migrations of the fourth and fifth centuries.

2. Byrne argues that the position of highking did not become a political reality until the ninth century; Byrne, *Irish Kings and High-Kings* (Dublin, 2001), 70.

3. Traditionally Patrick was preceded by Palladius in 432 and there is evidence of other bishops in Ireland when he returned. There is also no question that Patrick converted the, "high-king" Lóegaire. If the highking had actually ruled all the Irish kingdoms then any Christian missionary coming to Ireland would have first needed to convince him that Christianity was the superior religion. As that clearly had not happened, Lóegaire at least could not have been the over-king he claimed to be.

4. Byrne, *Irish Kings and High-Kings* (Dublin, 2001), 78–9; Hughes, "The Church in Irish society, 400–800," *A New History of Ireland Vol I: Prehistoric and Early Ireland*, ed. Dáibhí Ó Cróinín (Oxford, 2005), 306–8.

5. Byrne, *Irish Kings and High-Kings* (Dublin, 2001), 76–8; O'Rahilly, *Early Irish History and Mythology* (Dublin, 1946), 220.

6. Charles-Edwards, Early Irish and Welsh Kinship (Oxford, 1993), 211–5.

7. Johnson, *Hengest, Gwrtheyrn, and the Chronology of Post-Roman Britain* (McFarland, 2014), 36–8 and 132–5.

8. Hughes, "The Church in Irish society, 400–800," *A New History of Ireland Vol I: Prehistoric and Early Ireland*, ed. Dáibhí Ó Cróinín (Oxford, 2005), 306–8; Byrne, *The Irish Kings and High-Kings* (Dublin, 2001), 81.

9. It was traditionally believed that Einion Yrth, son of Cunedda, had completed the conquest of Anglesey from the Irish at about this time. Professor Koch's work on Marwnad Cunedda has demonstrated that Cunedda was a figure specifically from Berneich, leaving his traditional son Einion Yrth as the founder of the Gwynedd dynasty as well as the man who forced the Irish out of Anglesey; Isaac, "Cunedag," *BBCS* 38 (Cardiff, 1991), 100–1; *The Gododdin of Aneirin*, trans. and ed. John T. Koch (Cardiff, 1997), cxxi–cxxiii; *Cunedda, Cynan, Cadwallon, Cynddylan: Four Welsh Poems and Britain 383–655*, trans. and ed. John T. Koch (Cardiff, 2013), 72–3.

10. Johnson, *Hengest, Gwrtheyrn, and the Chronology of Post-Roman Britain* (McFarland, 2014), 122–3, 127–8, and 134–5.

Chapter 11

1. Forsyth, *Language in Pictland: The Case Against "Non-Indo-European Pictish"* (Utrecht, 1997); Price, "Pictish," *Languages in Britain and Ireland*. (Oxford, 2000), 127–131; "Place names," *The Oxford Companion to Scottish History*, ed. Michael Lynch (Oxford, 2007); Watson and Taylor, *The History of the Celtic Place-Names of Scotland* (Edinburgh, 2004).

2. Charles-Edwards, *Wales and the Britons: 350–1064* (Oxford, 2013), 33–4.

3. "White Book of Mabinogion," JNLW, 5276D, 334 ff.; *Culhwch ac Olwen: An Edition and Study of the Oldest Arthurian Tale*, trans. and ed. Rachel Bromwich and D. Simon Evans (Cardiff, 1992), ll. 259–60; *Two Lives of Gildas*, trans. Hugh Williams (Llanerch, rep. 1990), 90–5. In addition, several other sources name him as a son of Caw without specifying either was a Pict. See *Trioedd Ynys Prydein: The Welsh Triads*, trans. and ed. Rachel Bromwich (Cardiff, rev. 1978), 408.

4. "Vita Cadoci," *Lives of the British Saints*, ed. Sabine Baring-Gould and John Fischer (Cardiff, 1907–13), ch. 26, "Beyond the mountain Banauc" means Foirtrinn in southern Scotland; *The Gododdin: The Oldest Scottish Poem*, trans. and ed. Kenneth H. Jackson (Edinburgh, 1969), 78–9.

5. Stanzas B^1.13.257, A.22, and A.9 by John T. Koch's organization refers to a Llif son of Cian from Pictland as having participated in the battle of Catraeth, implying that Picts as a whole took part in the Catraeth attack instead of considering them-

selves culturally separate enemies who only make war on each other.

Chapter 12

1. Zosimus, *Zosimus. New history*, trans. Ronald T. Ridley (Canberra, 1982), 6.10.2.
2. *Chronica Minora I* (Berlin, 1886), 515–660, ed. Theodor Mommsen; Miller, "The last British entry in the 'Gallic Chronicles'," *Brit* 9 (Stroud, 1978b), 315–318; Jones and Casey, "The Gallic Chronicle Restored: A Chronology for the Anglo-Saxon Invasions and the End of Roman Britain," *Brit* 19 (Stroud, 1978), 367–398; Burgess, "The Dark Ages Return to Fifth-Century Britain: The 'Restored' Gallic Chronicle Exploded," *Brit* 21 (Stroud, 1990), 185–195.
3. *De Excidio Britanniae*, trans. Michael Winterbottom (Chichester, 1978), 25.1.
4. Arnold, *An Archaeology of the Early Anglo-Saxon Kingdoms* (New York, 1988), 188–210. The limited number of Anglo-Saxon graves and their wealth status are his biggest indicators. He is aware of no high status graves during the course of the fifth century.
5. Charles-Edwards, *Wales and the Britons 350–1064* (Oxford, 2013), 54; Bassett, "In Search of the origins of Anglo-Saxon kingdoms," *The Origins of the Anglo-Saxon Kingdoms*, ed. Stephen Bassett (Leicester, 1989), 23.
6. Charles-Edwards, *Wales and the Britons 350–1064* (Oxford, 2013), 56.
7. The change between the *foederati* relationship and tribute to local chieftains can be seen as the key event in the development of manorialism.
8. Johnson, *Evidence of Arthur* (McFarland, 2014), 143–51 and 154–72.

Chapter 13

1. H. Chadwick, *The Heroic Age* (Cambridge, 1912), 105–9.
2. West, *Indo-European Poetry and Myth* (Oxford, 2007), 30.
3. The bard's power was considered so potent they could predict the manner and time of death. This made a displeased bard one of the most fearsome things in the Celtic world; F. Kelly, *A Guide to Early Irish Law* (Dublin, 1988), 49–51.
4. Wells, *Bones, Bodies and Disease* (London, 1964), 179.
5. Vansina, *Oral Tradition as History* (Madison, 1985).
6. Binchy, "Celtic and Anglo-Saxon Kingship," (Oxford, 1970); Chaney, *The Cult of Kingship in Anglo-Saxon England: The Transition from Paganism to Christianity* (Manchester, 1970), 174–220.
7. Bugge, "Fertility myth and female sovereignty in the weddynge of Sir Gawen and Dame Ragnell," *CR* 39.2 (University Park, 2004), 198–218.
8. Chaney, *The Cult of Kingship in Anglo-Saxon England: The Transition from Paganism to Christianity* (Manchester, 1970), 27; H. Chadwick, *Origins of the English Nation* (Cambridge, 1907), 237–8.
9. Johnson, *Origins of Arthurian Romances* (McFarland, 2012), 100–36 and see below.

Chapter 14

1. "Historia Brittonum," *British History; and the Welsh Annals, History from the Sources 8*, trans. and ed. John Morris (London, 1980), ch. 62.
2. "The Foundation Legend of Gwynedd in the Latin Texts," *BBCS* 27 (Cardiff, 1978a), 515–532; *Cunedda, Cynan, Cadwallon, Cynddylan: Four Welsh Poems and Britain 383–655*, trans. and ed. John T. Koch (Cardiff, 2013), 39–73.
3. Johnson, *Evidence of Arthur* (McFarland, 2014), 147–51.
4. For the date-guessing that gives those birth-ranges see Johnson, *Hengest, Gwrtheyrn, and the Chronology of Post-Roman Britain* (McFarland, 2014).
5. *Trioedd Ynys Prydein: The Welsh Triads*, trans. and ed. Rachel Bromwich (Cardiff, rev. 1978), triad 26.
6. *Vitae Sanctorum Britanniae et Genealogie*, ed. Arthur W. Wade-Evans (Cardiff, 1944), chapter 1.
7. Johnson, *Evidence of Arthur* (McFarland, 2014), 101–4.
8. *Ibid*, 97–104.
9. *Ibid*, 87–96 and 105–115.
10. *Ibid*, 116–25.
11. M. McCarthy, "Thomas, Chadwick, and Post-Roman Britain," *The Early Church in Western Britain and Ireland*, ed. Susan Pierce (Oxford, 1982), 241–256; M. McCarthy,

"A Roman, Anglian and Medieval Site at Black Friar's Street, Carlisle," (Kendall, 1990), 368–372; M. McCarthy, "Carlisle," CA 116 (Friary, 1989), 368–372; Selkirk, CA 101 (Friary Press, 1986), 172–177; Keevil, Shotter, and M. McCarthy, "A Solidus of Valentinian II from Scotch Street, Carlisle," Brit 20 (Stroud, 1989), 254–255; Dark, "A Sub-Roman Defense of Hadrian's Wall," Brit 23 (Stroud, 1992), 112–113.

12. N. Chadwick, *The British Heroic Age* (Cardiff, 1976), 115–118.

13. Dumville, "Coroticus," *Saint Patrick: A.D. 493–1993*, ed. David N. Dumville (Woodbridge, 1993), 114. He points out that the translation need only mean, "ruler," but if so why give it to only a select group of rulers—Ceredig alone in early Strathclyde.

14. Dumville, "Coroticus," *Saint Patrick: 493–1993*, ed. David N. Dumville (Woodbridge, 1993), 109.

15. Thompson, "St. Patrick and Coroticus," JTS 31 (London, 1980), 12–27.

16. Miller, "The Foundation Legend of Gwynedd in the Latin Texts," BBCS 27 (Cardiff, 1978a), 515–532.

17. Johnson, *Hengest, Gwrtheyrn, and the Chronology of Post-Roman Britain* (McFarland, 2014), 188.

18. Charles-Edwards, *Wales and the Britons 350–1064* (Oxford, 2013), 36.

19. Miller, "Historicity and the Pedigrees of the Northcountrymen," BBCS 26 (Cardiff, 1975b), 255–280.

20. *Trioedd Ynys Prydein: The Welsh Triads*, trans. and ed. Rachel Bromwich (Cardiff, rev. 1978), 314.

21. Ammianus Marcellinus, *Res Gestae*, ed. John C. Rolfe (Cambridge, 1971–2), 29.4.

22. J. Turville-Petre, "Hengest and Horsa," SBVS 14 (London, 1953–7), 273–90; de Vries, "Die Ursprungssage der Sachs en," Niedersächen Jarhbuch für Landesgeschichte 31 (Berlin, 1959), 30–32; Olrik, "Epic Laws of Folk Narrative," *International Folkloristics: Classic Contributions by the Founders of Folklore*, ed. Alan Dundes (Lanham, 1999), 104.

23. "*Historia Brittonum*," Nennius: British History and the Welsh Annals, trans. and ed. John Morris (London, 1980), chapter 61.

24. Ibid, chapter 61.

25. Higham reports that the Derwent valley was conquered during the third quarter of the fifth century, but not that a kingship was present there; Higham, *The Kingdom of Northumbria, A.D. 350–1100* (Stroud, 1993), 98.

26. Kirby, "Problems of early West Saxon history," EHR 80 (London, 1965), 10–29; Kirby, "Bede and Northumbrian Chronology," EHR 78 (London, 1963), 514–527; Miller," The Foundation Legend of Gwynedd in the Latin Texts," BBCS 27 (Cardiff, 1978a), 515–532.

27. Miller,"The Foundation Legend of Gwynedd in the Latin Texts," BBCS 27 (Cardiff, 1978a), 515–532.

28. Given the consistency of British kingdoms developing in the late fifth century, this scholar would assume that the latter option is the more likely.

29. "*Historia Brittonum*," British history; and the Welsh Annals, History from the Sources 8, trans. and ed. John Morris (London, 1980), ch. 62.

30. White, "New Light on the Origins of the Kingdom of Gwynedd," *Studies in Old Welsh Poetry: Astudiaethau ar yr Hengerdd*, eds. Rachel Bromwich and R. Brinley Jones (Cardiff, 1978), 350–5.

31. Miller, "The Foundation Legend of Gwynedd in the Latin Texts," BBCS 27 (Cardiff, 1978a), 515–532.

32. *Cunedda, Cynan, Cadwallon, Cynddylan: Four Welsh Poems and Britain 383–655*, trans. and ed. John T. Koch (Cardiff, 2013), 72–3. Koch has shown that *Marwnad Cunedda* predates all other information on Cunedda and the name-form there is incorrect for a person who was remembered orally in Gwynedd; Isaac, "Cunedag," BBCS 38 (Cardiff, 1991), 100–1; *The Gododdin of Aneirin*, trans. and ed. John T. Koch (Cardiff, 1997), cxxi–cxxiii.

33. Gildas, *De Excidio Britanniae*, trans. Michael Winterbottom (Chichester, 1978), 25.3.

34. D. McCarthy and Ó Cróinín, "The 'lost Irish 84-year Easter table rediscovered," Peritia 6–7 (Galway, 1987), 227–42; Johnson, *Evidence of Arthur* (McFarland, 2014), 154–163, 230–45.

35. "*Historia Brittonum*," British history; and the Welsh Annals, History from the Sources 8, trans. and ed. John Morris (London, 1980), chapters 40–42; Johnson, *Hengest, Gwrtheyrn, and the Chronology of Post-Roman Britain* (McFarland, 2014), 86–92.

36. "*Historia Brittonum*," British history; and the Welsh Annals, History from the

Sources 8, trans. and ed. John Morris (London, 1980), ch. 56.

37. *Ibid*, ch. 49.

38. In Gwynedd, all of of Cunedda's sons but Einion Yrth are eponyms for provinces in Gwynedd. One of the Dyfed ancestors is Dimed, eponym of Dyfed itself.

39. Johnson, *Evidence of Arthur* (McFarland, 2014), 161–3.

40. *"Historia Brittonum" British history; and the Welsh Annals, History from the Sources 8*, trans. and ed. John Morris (London, 1980), ch. 47.

41. Miller, "Date-guessing and pedigrees," *SC* 11 (Cardiff, 1976a), 96–109.

42. *Cunedda, Cynan, Cadwallon, Cynddylan: Four Welsh Poems and Britain 383–655*, trans. and ed. John T. Koch. (Cardiff, 2013), 113–117.

43. Johnson, *Hengest, Gwrtheyrn, and the Chronology of Post-Roman Britain* (McFarland, 2015), 157, 158, 166, 171, 178, and 184.

44. *Vita Cadoci*, chapter 26.

45. *Caradoc's Vita Gildae*, chapter 6.5

46. The *vita* has Cadoc raise Caw from the dead, explaining the discrepancy between the fifth-century Caw and the sixth-century Cadoc.

47. *Trioedd Ynys Prydein: The Welsh Triads*, trans. and ed. Rachel Bromwich (Cardiff, rev. 1978), 19, 21, 26, 71, 72, and 73.

48. *Culhwch ac Olwen: An edition and study of the oldest Arthurian tale*, ed. and trans. Rachel Bromwich and D. Simon Evans (Cardiff, 1992), ll. 191–2.

49. "The 'Drystan' Poem," trans. Rachel Bromwich, *SC* 14/15 (Cardiff, 1979–80) 57–8.

50. This was not the case in Ireland, but all of the subkingdoms and sub-subkingdoms there were largely independent.

51. "The Expulsion of the Dessi," trans. and ed. Kuno Meyer, *Y Cymmrodor* 14 (Cardiff, 1901), 101–35.

52. Miller, "Date-guessing and Dyfed," *SC* 13 (Cardiff, 1978b), 33–61.

53. *"Historia Brittonum," British history; and the Welsh Annals, History from the Sources 8*, trans. and ed. John Morris (London, 1980), ch. 14.

54. Miller, "Date-Guessing and Dyfed," *SC* 13 (Cardiff, 1978c), 37–40.

55. *Annals of Clonmacnoise, being Annals of Ireland from the Earliest Period to A.D. 1408, translated into English A.D. 1627 by Conell Mageoghagan*, ed. Denis Murphy (Dublin, 1896); *Annals of Innisfallen* (MS. Rawlinson B.503), ed. and trans. Seán MacAirt (Dublin, 1951); *Annals of Tigernach*, ed. Whitley Stokes RC 16 (Paris, 1895), 374–419; *Annals of Tigernach*, ed. Whitley Stokes, RC 17 (Paris, 1896), 6–33, 119–263, 337–420, 458; *Annals of Tigernach*, ed. Whitley Stokes, RC 18 (Paris, 1897), 9–59, 150–198, 267–303, 390–391; *Annals of Ulster*, ed. Seán Mac Airt and Gearóid Mac Niocaill (Dublin, 1983).

56. Adamnan. *Life of Saint Columba, Founder of Hy (Iona)*, trans. and ed. William Reeves (Llanerch, rep. 1988).

57. Koch has argued that a natural reading of the *Historia Brittonum* makes Talhaearn Outigern's bard (*Cunedda, Cynan, Cadwallon, Cynddylan: Four Welsh Poems and Britain 383-655*, trans. and ed. John T. Koch. (Cardiff, 2013), 27), while the present author has argued that Outigern was in fact Gwrtheyrn remembered in the North (Johnson, *Hengest, Gwrtheyrn, and the Chronology of Post-Roman Britain* (McFarland, 2015), 86–92). If the connections are all valid it might explain why the tenth-century *Historia Brittonum* editor did not or did not want to connect Outigern to his villain.

Chapter 15

1. Arnold, *An Archaeology of the Early Anglo-Saxon Kingdoms* (New York, 1988), 188–210.

Chapter 16

1. *Corpus Iuris Hibernici*, ed. David A. Binchy (Dublin, 1978), 219.17–18.

2. *Ibid*, 15.2–3.

3. O'Rahilly, "On the Origin of the Names Ériu and Ériu," *Ériu* 35 (Dublin, 1946b), 11–13.

4. Vansina, *Oral Tradition as History* (Madison, 1985).

Chapter 17

1. The exact equivalencies seem to have varied by region and time but the basic exchange, the bartering dollar, was the female slave/milking cow/ounce of silver.

Chapter 18

1. Johnson, *Evidence of Arthur* (McFarland, 2014); Dumville, "Sub-Roman Britain: history and legend," History 62 (London, 1977a), 173–192; Padel, "The Nature of Arthur," *CMCS* 27 (Cardiff, Summer 1994), 1–31.

2. Bromwich, "Concepts of Arthur," *SC* 10/11 (Cardiff, 1976), 175–6; Thurneysen, "Zimmer, Nennius vindicatus," *ZDP* 28 (Halle, 1896), 85, 87; Bruce, *The Evolution of Arthurian Romance, from the Beginnings Down to the Year 1300* (Gottingen, 1923), 9. K. Jackson opposed the inclusion of this text in the *Northern History* on the basis of Beulon's request that the Anglo-Saxon genealogies (meaning also the *Northern History* apparently) be omitted from his copy. The task was done to his satisfaction and the Arthuriana information was not included. Therefore, so the reasoning goes, Arthuriana is not a part of the *Northern History* because Beulon knew it was not a part of the *Northern History*. The author believes it more accurate to say that Beulon believed that Arthuriana was a part of the *Northern History*, but his opinion carries no more weight than a modern historian's. It is a good bet that he knew even less about the *Northern Memorandum* or the *Northern History* than we do.

3. *The Gododdin of Aneirin*, ed. and trans. John T. Koch (Cardiff, 1997), cxxiii.

4. The most notable have been Alcock and Jackson. Most recently, Andrew Breeze has located all the battles in the north and placed Arthur in Glasgow; Alcock, *Arthur's Britain* (New York, 1971); K. Jackson, "Once Again Arthur's Battles," MP 43 (Chicago, 1945), 44–57; Breeze, "The Arthurian Battle of Badon and Braydon Forest, Wiltshire," Journal of Literary Onomastics 4.1 (Brockport, 2015), 20–30; Breeze, "The Historical Arthur and Sixth-Century Scotland," *Northern History* 52.2 (Leeds, 2015), 158–81.

5. Lloyd, *The History of Wales* (Cardiff, 1912), 126 fn. 6; H. Chadwick and N. Chadwick, *The Growth of Literature* (Cambridge, 1932), 155; Crawford, "Arthur and his Battles," *Antiq* 9 (Gloucester, 1935), 279; K. Jackson, "The Arthur of History," *Arthurian Literature in the Middle Ages*, ed. Roger S. Loomis (Chicago, 1959), 78; Bromwich, "Concepts," *SC* 10/11 (Cardiff, 1976), 169.

6. The present author had long thought that Badon was an artificially attached battle as well, but Christopher Gidlow has pointed out that few people who have not studied military strategy know about Napoleon's greatest victory at Borodino even though everyone seems to know about his final defeat at Waterloo. It makes sense that Badon is not heavily referenced in Welsh literature. Badon is also the only other Arthurian battle named in *Annales Cambriae*.

7. Professor Koch has suggested that chapter 65 of the *Historia Brittonum* implies Talhaearn was Outigern's bard, that Outigern was contemporary to Ida, and that the other four bards mentioned—Taliesin, Aneirin, Cian, and Bluchbeirdd—were contemporary with Ida, meaning that their relative chronology was three times removed from their placement there (*Cunedda, Cynan, Cadwallon, Cynddylan: Four Welsh Poems and Britain 383–655*, trans. and ed. John T. Koch. (Cardiff, 2013), 27–9). The floruits of these and the other bards of the period are more thoroughly explored in Johnson, *Evidence of Arthur* (McFarland, 2014), 54–61.

8. For a more detailed series of arguments please see Johnson, *Evidence of Arthur* (McFarland, 2014), 87–125.

9. Dark, *From Civitas to Kingdom* (Leicester, 1994), 112.

10. Koch, "Marwnad Cunedda a diwedd y Brydain Rufeinig," *Yr Hen Iaith: Studies in Early Welsh*, ed. Paul Russell (Cardiff, 2003), 176–82; Dark, "A Sub-Roman Defense of Hadrian's Wall?," *Brit* 18 (Stroud, 1992), 111–120; Johnson, *Evidence of Arthur* (McFarland, 2014), 126–32.

11. The Picts may have had a couple of larger kingdoms, but a much less dense population.

12. Myres, *The English Settlements* (Oxford, 1989), 146–7; Koch, "Cerdic," *Celtic Culture: A Historical Encyclopedia*, ed. John T. Koch (Santa Barbara, 2006), 392–3. The name is from British, "Caratacus". It was clearly not a fluke, either. Ceawlin, from an opposing dynasty, also had a British name (Ward-Perkins, "Why did the Anglo-Saxons not become more British?" HER 115 (Oxford, 2000), 513), as did Cædwalla (York, *Kings and Kingdoms of Early Anglo-Saxon England* (London, 1989), 138–9).

13. For a complete list of characters and an explanation of their origins see now *Culhwch ac Olwen: An edition and study of the oldest Arthurian tale*, eds. Rachel Bromwich and D. Simon Evans (Cardiff, 1992).

14. Higham, *An English Empire* (Man-

chester, 1995), 218–240; *The Gododdin of Aneirin*, trans. and ed. John T. Koch (Cardiff, 1997), xxxv-xlii.

Chapter 19

1. *The Gododdin of Aneirin*, trans. and ed. John T. Koch (Cardiff, 1997), xxxv-lvii.
2. B².29, A.68, and B¹.22.
3. Johnson, *Hengest, Gwrtheyrn, and the Chronology of Post-Roman Britain* (McFarland, 2014), 91.
4. Brooks, "The creation and early study of the kingdom of Kent," *The Origins of the Anglo-Saxon Kingdoms*, ed. Stephen Bassett (Leicester, 1989), 55–74; Sims-Williams, "The Settlement of England in Bede and the Chronicle," *ASE* 12 (London, 1983b), 22; Harrison, *The Framework of Anglo-Saxon History to 900 A.D.* (Cambridge, 1976).
5. All that is certain about Theodoric is that his name is Germanic and that he is associated with an unusually large number of British saints. The information about the Cunomorus of southern England is simply that he died in the sixth century. A Cunomorus of Brittany was powerful enough to get Gregory of Tours' interest, but there is no way to be certain that he was active in Britain, let alone if he was powerful there.

Chapter 20

1. Johnson, *Hengest, Gwrtheyrn, and the Chronology of Post-Roman Britain* (McFarland, 2014), 205–6.
2. The *Black Book of Chirk* states that they arrived by sea but fled by land.
3. Legend has it that Rhun died during the campaign. A famous saying is that Rhun's warriors were gone so long that their wives had to sleep with their servants so that they could have children.
4. Charles-Edwards, *Wales and the Britons 350–1064* (Oxford, 2013), 175–180.
5. *Bonedd yr Arwyr*, 29.
6. "Historia Brittonum," *Nennius: British History and the Welsh Annals*, trans. and ed. John Morris (London, 1980), ch. 62.

Chapter 21

1. Over the decades, estimates have put Badon as early as 478 and most scholars have hovered around 500, potentially making the *Annales Cambriae* not up to forty years off.
2. Dr. Molly Miller has written the only serious exploration of the battle; Miller, "The Commanders of Arthuret," *TCWAAS* 75 (Kendall, 1975), 96–117.
3. As Bromwich pointed out, the entry uses the form Merlinus for Myrddin; *Trioedd Ynys Prydein: The Welsh Triads*, trans. and ed. Rachel Bromwich (Cardiff, rev. 1978), 208.
4. *Ibid*, 29, 31W, and 44.
5. *Ibid*, 31W, and 44.
6. *Ibid*, 84. The others being Goddeu and Camlan
7. *Ibid*, xx–xxi, xxvi.
8. Miller, "The Commanders of Arthuret," *TCWAAS* 75 (Kendall, 1975), 96–117.
9. *Trioedd Ynys Prydein: The Welsh Triads*, trans. and ed. Rachel Bromwich (Cardiff, rev. 1978), 489.
10. *Eddius Stephanus: Life of Wilfrid*, trans. James Francis Webb, ed. David Hugh Farmer, The Age of Bede (Harmondsworth, rev. 1983), 126.
11. *Ibid*, 396.
12. *Canu Llywarch Hen*, ed. Sir Ifor Williams (Cardiff, 1960).
13. Skene, *Arthur and the Britons in Wales and Scotland*, ed. Derek Bryce (Lampeter, 1988), 23–5; H. Chadwick, *Early Scotland: The Picts, the Scots, and the Welsh of Southern Scotland* (Cambridge, 1949), 143; H. Chadwick, *The Growth of Literature* (Cambridge, 1932), 109 and 111 fn. 4.
14. "Dinogad," *Oxford Dictionary of National Biography* (Oxford, 2004), Web.

Chapter 22

1. Johnson, *Hengest, Gwrtheyrn, and the Chronology of Post-Roman Britain* (McFarland, 2014), 21–27, 112, 139, 142, 144–5, 154, 162, 168–171, 176–7, and 185.
2. The present author had previously given a range for Urien's confederacy of 574–620. This is still possible given the birth-ranges of the participants, but they could not have been dominant in Northumbria after 605, which means that if Urien's traditional death is the historical one it could not have taken place at or after 605 on Lindesfarne.
3. *The Gododdin of Aneirin*, trans. and

ed. John T. Koch (Cardiff, 1997), xiii–xxvi. This in direct contradiction to the traditional view that argued the years around 600 were the most reasonable range for the Battle of Catraeth (Aneirin, *Canu Aneirin*, ed. Sir Ifor Williams (Cardiff, 1938), xxviii, xxxi-xxii; Bromwich (ed.) *The Beginnings of Welsh Poetry: Studies by Sir Ifor Williams* (Cardiff, 2nd ed. 1982), 47–49, 52–53; *The Gododdin: The Oldest Scottish Poem*, trans. and ed. Kenneth H. Jackson (Edinburgh, 1969), 11–12; Smyth, *Warlords and Holy Men: Scotland A.D. 80–100* (London, 1984), 20–2; *Aneirin: Y Gododdin—Britain Oldest Heroic Poem*, trans. and ed. Alfred O.H. Jarman (Llandysul, 1988), xviii–xx.

4. *The Gododdin of Aneirin*, trans. and ed. John T. Koch (Cardiff, 1997), xiii–xlii.

5. "Book of Taliesin," trans. John T. Koch and John Carey, *The Celtic Heroic Age* (Malden, 1995), 338–42.

6. Taliesin. *Canu Taliesin*, ed. Sir Ifor Williams (Cardiff, 1960), II; *The Gododdin of Aneirin*, trans. and ed. John T. Koch (Cardiff, 1997), xvi.

7. *Cunedda, Cynan, Cadwallon, Cynddylan: Four Welsh Poems and Britain 383–655*, trans. and ed. John T. Koch (Cardiff, 2013), 221–6.

8. *The Gododdin of Aneirin*, trans. and ed. John T. Koch (Cardiff, 1997), xlvii–l.

Chapter 23

1. *De Excidio Britanniae*, trans. Michael Winterbottom (Chichester, 1978), 23.1

2. The author has elsewhere suggested that he may have taken advantage of this gap in his knowledge to blame Arthur for the Germanic presence because of a family feud involving the death of his brother. There is no better evidence for that theory now than there was then, but it would explain his choice of using an over-king to explain the Germanic presence instead of a simple invasion of Britain; Johnson, *Evidence of Arthur* (McFarland, 2012), 42–9.

3. The Late Roman Empire included many powerful men who were able to carve small kingdoms out of the Roman Empire for decades at a time. If Gildas was well read, as recent scholarship has demonstrated, he may have known this and applied that knowledge to what he did not know about fifth-century Britain.

4. It has been pointed out that Aetius was the far extent of his oral knowledge, but that is no guarantee that he had access to an unbroken sequence of events from that famous letter to his present day.

5. Brooks, *Anglo-Saxon Myths: Church and State 400–1066* (New York, 2003), 86.

6. *Cunedda, Cynan, Cadwallon, Cynddylan: Four Welsh Poems and Britain 383–655*, trans. and ed. John T. Koch (Cardiff, 2013), 27.

7. Johnson, *Hengest, Gwrtheyrn, and the Chronology of Post-Roman Britain* (McFarland, 2014), 89; Sims-Williams, "The Settlement of England in Bede and the Chronicle," *ASE* 12 (London, 1983b), 16.

8. *The Anglo-Saxon Chronicle*, trans. George Norman Garmonsway (London, 1953), years 455, 456, 465, and 473.

9. "Historia Brittonum," *Nennius: British History and the Welsh Annals*, trans. and ed. John Morris (London, 1980), chapter 44.

10. Brooks places the marriage between the mid-570s and 581; Brooks, *Anglo-Saxon Myths: Church and State 400–1066* (New York, 2003), 50. Stafford, *Queens, Concubines and Dowagers: The King's Wife in the Early Middle Ages* (Athens, GA, 1983), 35–6, 67–8, 73–4.

11. Johnson, *Hengest, Gwrtheyrn, and the Chronology of Post-Roman Britain* (McFarland, 2014), 222. Brooks places him in the second quarter of the sixth century because his parents must have been influenced by the Franks to have given him that name; Brooks, *Anglo-Saxon Myths: Church and State 400–1066* (New York, 2003), 46–7.

12. Rhun's primary concern seems to have been the north, and legend does say he was gone for a long period of time which would have left a void of power in Wales. Even if he had remained in Gwynedd for the relevant part of his career, Gwrtheyrn's genealogy includes Gloiu, or Gloucester, suggesting that his base was along the Wye River. Their spheres of influence may have never overlapped.

13. It has already been suggested that overlordship probably meant control over less area for the earlier Bretwaldas; Campbell, "The Lost Centuries 400–600," *The Anglo-Saxons*, ed. James Campbell, Eric John, and Patrick Wormald. (London, 1982), 53–4.

Chapter 24

1. Bassett, "In Search of the Origins of the Anglo-Saxon Kingdoms," *The Origins of the Anglo-Saxon Kingdoms*, ed. Steven Bassett (Leicester, 1989), 23; Wood, "Kings, Kingdoms and Consent," *Early Medieval Kingship*, eds. Peter H. Sawyer and Ian N. Wood (Leeds, 1977), 18–20; Dumville, "Kingship, Genealogies and Regnal Lists," *Early Medieval Kingship*, eds. Peter H. Sawyer and Ian N. Wood (Leeds, 1977b), 91–92; Yorke, "The Kingdom of the East Saxons," *ASE* 14 (London, 1985), 1–30; Arnold, *An Archaeology of the Early Anglo-Saxon Kingdoms* (New York, 1988), 197–199.
2. Arnold, *An Archaeology of the Early Anglo-Saxon Kingdoms* (New York, 1988), 211–29; Arnold, "Social Evolution in Post-Roman Western Europe," *European Social Evolution*, ed. John L. Bintliff (Bradford, 1984), 277–94; Scull, "Archaeology, Early Anglo-Saxon Society and the Origins of the Anglo-Saxon Kingdoms," Anglo-Saxon Studies in Archaeology and History 6 (Oxford, 1993), 65–82; Hodges, *Dark Age Economics: The Origins of Towns and Trade A.D. 600–1000* (London, 1982); Arnold, "Stress as a Factor in Social and Economic Change," *Ranking, Resource and Exchange*, eds. A. Collin Renfrew and Stephen Shennan (Cambridge, 1982), 124–31; Arnold, "Wealth and Social Structure: A Matter of Life and Death," *Anglo-Saxon Cemeteries 1979*, ed. Philip A. Rahtz, Tania M. Dickinson, and Loma Watts (Oxford, 1980), 81–142; Hodges, "State Formation and the Role of Trade in Middle Saxon England," *Social Organisation and Settlement*, eds. David R. Green, Colin Haselgrove, and Matthew Spriggs (Oxford, 1978), 439–54; Sawyer, *From Roman Britain to Norman England* (London, 1978); Dumville, "Kingship, Genealogies and King-Lists," *Early Medieval Kingship*, eds. Philip H. Sawyer and Ian N. Woods (Leeds, 1977b), 72–104; Wallace-Hadrill, *Early Germanic Kingship in England and on the Continent* (Oxford, 1971).
3. *The Gododdin of Aneirin*, trans. and ed. John T. Koch (Cardiff, 1997), xxxv–xli.

Chapter 25

1. Adamnan, *Life of Saint Columba, Founder of Hy (Iona)*, trans. and ed. William Reeves (Llanerch, rep. 1988), 2.36.
2. *Ibid*, 1.33. Considering the obvious transformations and additions to the Dal Riata genealogy, it is tempting to consider this, "robber," an expected description for a monk about a chieftain, to be the father of Fergus in the official Dal Riata history.
3. *Ibid*, 2.23.
4. Johnson, *Hengest, Gwrtheyrn, and the Chronology of Post-Roman Britain* (McFarland, 2014), 132–5.
5. A. Anderson, *Early Sources of Scottish History A.D. 500–1286* (Stamford, 1990), 83 fn. 2; M. Anderson, *Kings and Kingship in Early Scotland* (Edinburgh, 1980), 148–9; Bannerman, *Studies in the History of Dalriada* (Edinburgh, 1974), 1–2; Byrne, *Irish Kings and High-Kings* (London, rev. 2001), 110.
6. Adamnan, *Life of Saint Columba, Founder of Hy (Iona)*, trans. and ed. William Reeves (Llanerch, rep. 1988), 3.5.
7. *Trioedd Ynys Prydein: The Welsh Triads*, trans. and ed. Rachel Bromwich (Cardiff, rev. 1978), triads 29 and 54. He is called, "the Wily".

Chapter 26

1. Hamerow, *Rural Settlements and Society in Anglo-Saxon England* (Oxford, 2012).
2. Badon is in both British sources, is mentioned but not explored in Bede, and its effects seen in lower England with *The Anglo-Saxon Chronicle*.
3. Higham, "From Tribal Chieftains to Christian Kings," *The Anglo-Saxon World*, eds. Nicholas J. Higham and Martin J. Ryan (New Haven, 2013), 126–78.
4. One major hiccup a reader may have with this theory is Gildas' testimony, but a close look at his account suggests that the British fought raiders looking for food and supplies, not kings and their war-bands attempting any sort of conquest or even cattle raids.
5. Having no knowledge of the relations between villages the author must acknowledge that several warriors from each clan/war-band might have come to the battle. That possibility would have made it important islandwide without endangering all the kingdoms represented.
6. "Why farming matters: Wales," RSPB, retrieved November 2, 2015;, "Why farming matters: Scotland," RSPB, retrieved November 2, 2015;, "Why farming matters: North-

ern Ireland," RSPB, retrieved November 2, 2015;, "Why farming matters: England," RSPB, retrieved November 2, 2015.

7. Baillie, "Dendrochronology raises questions about the nature of the AD 536 dust-veil event," The Holocene 4.2 (Washington D.C., 1994), 212–7;, "Marking in Marker Dates: Towards and Archaeology with Historical Precision," WA 23.2 (Abingdon, 1991), 233–43.

8. *"Annales Cambriae," Nennius: British History and the Welsh Annals*, trans. and ed. John Morris (London, 1980), entry 547.

9. Wacher, *The Towns of Roman Britain* (Berkeley, 1974), 414–422; Russell, "Late Ancient and Medieval Population," *Transactions of the American Philosophical Society* 48.3 (Philadelphia, 1958), 71–99.

10. "The creation and early structure of the kingdom of Kent," *The Origins of the Anglo-Saxon Kingdoms*, ed. Stephen Bassett (Leicester, 1989), 55–74; N. Brown, *History and Climate Change: An Eurocentric Perspective* (Routledge, 2001), 94–5.

11. J. Davies, *Wales in the Early Middle Ages* (New York, 1982), 31.

Chapter 27

1. Frank M. Stenton is the classic example of this approach; Stenton, *Anglo-Saxon England* (Oxford, 1971). Though much maligned, one positive aspect of John Morris' contribution was that he surveyed each kingdom from their foundation into the Christian era; Morris, *The Age of Arthur* (London, 1976).

2. The best example is still Stephen Bassett (ed.) *The Origins of the Anglo-Saxon Kingdoms* (Leicester, 1989).

3. Over the passed thirty years Professor Higham has been the most active in this respect, with *An English empire* (Manchester, 1995) and *The Kingdom of Northumbria, A.D. 350–1100* (Stroud, 1993) in particular.

4. Chaney, *The Cult of Kingship in Anglo-Saxon England* (Manchester, 1970), 86–7.

5. Ibid, 12–17, 22, 55–6, 86, 113, 90, 94, 109, and 254.

6. de Vries, *Altgermanische Religiongeschichte* (Berlin, 1937), 32–43.

7. Chaney, *The Cult of Kingship in Anglo-Saxon England: The Transition from Paganism to Christianity* (Manchester, 1970), 15–17; G. Turville-Petre, *Myth and religion of the North: the religion of ancient Scandinavia* (London, 1964), 260–1; Kern, trans. Stanley B. Grimes, *Kingship and Law in the Middle Ages* (Oxford, 1939), 14; H. Chadwick, *Origins of the English Nation* (Cambridge, 1907), 303.

8. Marcellinus, *Res Gestae*, trans. John C. Rolfe (Cambridge, MA, 1971–72), 5.14, *Ynglingasaga*, and *Heimskringla*. The Norse saga materials are well beyond the purview of this book.

Chapter 28

1. Bede, *A History of the English Church and People*, trans. and ed. Leo Sherley-Price (Baltimore, 1955), 2.5.

2. Cerdic is a British name, the same as a later king of Elmet. Cerdic's son Cynric probably also had a British name. Ceawlin may or may not be British. All three characters were remembered as early Germanic leaders in the area.

3. Warriors lived on the king's generosity, finding their food and drink in his hall and being given women, silver, and armaments by him. This indebtedness, involving every aspect of their lives, generated an uncommon connection to the lord which grew stronger through years of living on his generosity.

4. *Historia Brittonum* and *The Anglo-Saxon Chronicle* do list four battles against Gwrtheyrn's kingdom.

5. *Historia Brittonum* says that Gwrtheyrn died in a castle sieged by his fellow Britons.

6. Brooks, Anglo-Saxon Myths: State and Church (London, 2000c), 40–1; Sims-Williams, "The settlement of England in Bede and the Chronicle," ASE 12 (London, 1983b), 35.

7. The initial work was done by Kirby ("Problems of early West Saxon history," EHR 80 (London, 1965), 10–29). Date-guessing was employed by the present author in *Gwrtheyrn, Hengest, and the Chronology of Post-Roman Britain* (Madison, 2014).

8. Dumville, "The West Saxon genaeological regnal list and the chronology of early Wessex," Peritia 4 (Galway, 1985), 21–66.

9. Kirby suggested that the early Wessex battles were designed to show one kingdom expanding in different directions under different kings, but a closer examination re-

veals the borders of the two or possibly three kingdoms that did exist in the last half of the sixth century; Kirby, "Problems of early West Saxon history," *EHR* 80 (London, 1965), 10–29.

10. At least as far back as the Dyrham notice, *The Anglo-Saxon Chronicle* may be recording historical battles. That particular notice says that three British kings—Coinmail, Condidan, and Farinmail—all fought. These names easily equate to Cynfail, Condilan, and Fernmael which the prestigious linguist Professor Kenneth Jackson thought might have come from a contemporary source (K. Jackson, *Language and History in Early Britain* (Edinburgh, 1953), 464–6 and 677). More recently, Sims-Williams has voiced uncertainty on how old the notice might be, suggesting that the Farinmail name is probably the oldest and would date to no earlier than 700 (Sims-Williams, "The Settlement of England in Bede and the Chronicle," *ASE* 12 (London, 1983b), 33–4.

11. Myres, "Romano-Saxon Pottery," *Dark-Age Britain: Studies Presented to E.T. Leeds*, ed. Donald B. Harden (London, 1956), 16–39. Gillam, "Romano-Saxon Pottery: an alternative explanation," *The End of Roman Britain*, ed. P. John Casey (London, 1979), 103–118; W. Roberts, *Romano-Saxon Pottery* (Oxford, 1982).

12. Brooks, *Anglo-Saxon Myths: State and Church 400–1066* (New York, 2003), 46–7; we cannot know the name of Eormenric's father as his career took place well before the historical horizon of perhaps 590–600.

13. Bede, *A History of the English Church and People*, trans. and ed. Leo Sherley-Price (Baltimore, 1955), 1.25.

14. *Ibid*, 15.1.

15. Brookes and Harrington, *The Kingdom and People of Kent, AD 400–1066: Their History and Archaeology* (Stroud, 2010), 46–7; Brooks, "The creation and early structure of the kingdom of Kent," *The Origins of the Anglo-Saxon Kingdoms*, ed. Stephen Bassett (Leicester, 1989), 55–74.

16. Mallory, *In Search of the Indo-Europeans* (London, 2005), 235.

17. J. Turville-Petre, "Hengest and Horsa," *SBVS* 14 (London, 1953–7), 273–90.

18. Professor Sims-Williams came to the same conclusion, suggesting that Hengest's late intrusion into the Kentish dynastic history explained the presence of a Jute in the Saxon kingdom; Sims-Williams, "The Settlement of England in Bede and the Chronicle," *ASE* 12 (London, 1983b), 22.

19. Bede, *A History of the English Church and People*, trans. and ed. Leo Sherley-Price (Baltimore, 1955), 2.5

20. Brooks suggests he had the same motivation with his use of the Octha/Ebissa campaign in Scotland; Brooks, *Anglo-Saxon Myths: State and Church 400–1066* (New York, 2003), 86.

21. Sims-Williams suggested he was the established founder of the Kentish dynasty and Hengest a late intruder, which would make sense if the traditional lineage was bolstered with a continental hero before being written down; Sims-Williams, "The Settlement of England in Bede and the Chronicle," *ASE* 12 (London, 1983b), 22.

22. J. Turville-Petre, "Hengest and Horsa," *SBVS* 14 (London, 1953–1957), 287. Turville-Petre called Æsc a Wessex substitute for Oisc, without explaining the linguistics. Whether or not there was originally such a connection, they hold the same position in the sources and the Kentish lineage.

23. *Ibid*, 273–90.

24. Brookes and Harrington, *The Kingdom and People of Kent, AD 400–1066: Their History and Archaeology* (Stroud, 2010), 71; S. Hawkes, "Anglo-Saxon Kent c. 425–725," *Archaeology in Kent to AD 1500*, ed. P.E. Leach (London, 1982), 70–4; Brooks, *Anglo-Saxon Myths: State and Church 400–1066* (New York, 2003), 52–3.

25. *The Anglo-Saxon Chronicle*, trans. George Norman Garmonsway (London, 1953), entry 568.

26. *Ibid*, entry 584.

27. This entry might have been a counterclaim to Kent's possession of the island—see below.

Chapter 29

1. As the name of the entire region and not a particular kingdom, "Bernician" could mean any Germanic chieftain from Northumbria.

2. *The Gododdin of Aneirin*, trans. and ed. John T. Koch (Cardiff, 1997), xiii–xxxiv.

3. *Ibid*, xii.

4. Johnson, *Hengest, Gwrtheyrn, and the Chronology of Post-Roman Britain* (McFarland, 2014), 144.

5. "*Historia Brittonum*," *Nennius: British History and the Welsh Annals*, trans. and ed. John Morris (London, 1980), ch. 63.
6. *Trioedd Ynys Prydein: The Welsh Triads*, trans. and ed. Rachel Bromwich (Cardiff, rev. 1978), Triad 30.
7. "*Historia Brittonum*," *Nennius: British History and the Welsh Annals*, trans. and ed. John Morris (London, 1980), ch. 61.
8. To be accurate, it is, "Eda Glinvawr" who is placed at Caer Greu. Traditionally this figure has been assumed to be a mistake for Adda because Ida is said to have died some twenty years earlier. However, as one of the benefits of the altered Bernician king-list was to extend the dynasty backward in time, the argument that Ida must have been dead by then is no longer valid. Ida may well have been a contemporary the battle. The author thinks that geography is a better approach. Ida is associated with Bamburgh deep inside Bernician territory, while the York of Peredur and Gwrgi was inside Deiran territory, and therefore any Bernician chieftain fighting them was likely much nearer the border.
9. Miller has already done a masterful overview of the subject. The approach taken here is largely based on her;, "The Dates of Deira," *ASE* 8 (London, 1979), 35–61.
10. Miller, "The Dates of Deira," *ASE* 8 (London, 1979), 42; Duddon, *Gregory the Great* (London, 1905), 156 fn. 3 and 196 fn. 1.
11. *The Anglo-Saxon Chronicle*, trans. George Norman Garmonsway (London, 1953).
12. The author's study on early Deiran kings showed that there were a number of equally plausible options regarding Ælle and Æthelric, including a theory that they were from two different dynasties; Johnson, *Hengest, Gwrtheyrn, and the Chronology of Post-Roman Britain* (McFarland, 2014), 146–7 and 219. Considering the official late sixth-century Bernician dynasty and its relationship with historical reality, two different dynasties seems even more likely.

Chapter 30

1. W. Davies, "Annals and the Origins of Mercia," *Mercian Studies*, ed. Ann Dornier (Leicester, 1977), 23; Yorke, "The Origins of Mercia," *Mercia: An Anglo-Saxon Kingdom in Europe*, eds. Michelle P. Brown and Carole A. Farr (New York, 2001), 18. All three scholars have hypothesized that a Wessex leader was conflated with an early Mercian king. Another possibility is that the Wessex leader was intentionally pulled into the official Mercian king-list, complete with his obit.
2. Clarke, *East Anglia* (London, 1963), 138–9.
3. Newton, *The Origins of Beowulf and the Pre-Viking Kingdom of East Anglia* (Cambridge, 1993), 112.
4. Higham, "East Anglia, Kingdom of," *The Blackwell Encyclopedia of Anglo-Saxon England*, eds. Michael Lapidge et al (London, 1999), 154–5.
5. Lapidge, "Kings of the East Angles," *The Blackwell Encyclopedia of Anglo-Saxon England*, ed. Michael Lapidge et al (London, 1999), 508–9. Lapidge approximates his obit at right around 616, the year he assumes his son Rædwald took the throne.
6. Higham, *An English Empire* (Manchester, 1995), 74–111.

Chapter 31

1. Most prominently, Koch has seen no linguistic issues with the connection; *The Gododdin of Aneirin*, trans. and ed. John T. Koch (Cardiff, 1997), l.
2. Morris, *Arthurian Period Sources 3: Persons* (Chichester, 1995), 162; Anderson, *Kings and Kingship in Early Scotland* (Edinburgh, 1980), 167.
3. *The Gododdin of Aneirin*, trans. and ed. John T. Koch (Cardiff, 1997), B^1.13 and A.9.
4. Bannerman, *Studies in the History of Dalriada* (Edinburgh, 1974), 92; Smyth, *Warlords and Holy Men: Scotland AD 80–1000* (Edinburgh, 1984), 70. Contra M. Anderson, *Kings and Kingship in Early Scotland* (Edinburgh, 1980), 154–5; Smyth, *Warlords and Holy Men: Scotland AD 80–1000* (Edinburgh, 1984), 79–80; *The Chronicle of Ireland*, trans. Thomas Charles-Edwards, vol. 1 (Liverpool, 2006), 146.
5. Fraser, *From Caledonia to Pictland: Scotland to 795* (Edinburgh, 2009), 204–5 and 250. Fraser argues that he was invented in the eighth century to strengthen the Dal Riata claims of Cenél nGartnait (descendants of Gartnait) to rule in Kintyre.

6. Smyth, *Warlords and Holy Men: Scotland AD 80–1000* (Edinburgh, 1984), 62–5 and table 2.

7. Bede, *A History of the English Church and People*, trans. and ed. Leo Sherley-Price (Baltimore, 1955), 2.5.

8. A. Anderson, *Early Sources of Scottish History A.D. 500–1286* (Stamford, 1990), 83 fn. 2; M. Anderson, *Kings and Kingship in Early Scotland* (Edinburgh, 1980), 94; Bannerman, *Studies in the History of Dalriada* (Edinburgh, 1974), 84–5, 91.

9. Adamnan, *Life of Saint Columba, Founder of Hy (Iona)*, trans. and ed. William Reeves (Llanerch, rep. 1988), 1.9; Bannerman, *Studies in the History of Dalriada* (Edinburgh, 1974), 85, 91–2.

10. The dynasty was called the Oiscingas, but that does not mean that Oisc was the founder. As has been explored above, it is very possible that Oisc's original name was Ansehis. Ansehis was a *foederati* chieftain who migrated to Britain in the late fourth century, at least a half century before the events of 441 and a century and a half before Kent could have formed into a kingdom.

11. Myres, "Romano-Saxon Pottery," *Dark-Age Britain: Studies Presented to E.T. Leeds*, ed. Donald B. Harden (London, 1956), 16–39; Gillam, "Romano-Saxon Pottery: an alternative explanation," *The End of Roman Britain*, ed. P. John Casey (London, 1979), 103–118; W. Roberts, *Romano-Saxon Pottery* (Oxford, 1982).

12. Wheeler, "Gildas' De Excidio Britanniae, Chapter 26," *EHR* 41 (London, 1926), 501–502; Brooks, "The creation and early structure of the kingdom of Kent," *The Origins of the Anglo-Saxon Kingdoms*, ed. Stephen Bassett (Leicester, 1989), 67; Johnson, *Hengest, Gwrtheyrn, and the Chronology of Post-Roman Britain* (McFarland, 2014), 77–8. Contra Harrison, *The Framework of Anglo-Saxon England to 900 A.D.* (Cambridge, 1976), 121–123.

13. Bede, *A History of the English Church and People*, trans. and ed. Leo Sherley-Price (Baltimore, 1955), 1.25.

14. *Ibid*, 2.3.

15. Johnson, *Hengest, Gwrtheyrn, and the Chronology of Post-Roman Britain* (McFarland, 2014), 144–5; see above for a summary.

16. Bede, *A History of the English Church and People*, trans. and ed. Leo Sherley-Price (Baltimore, 1955), 1.34.

17. Johnson, *Hengest, Gwrtheyrn, and the Chronology of Post-Roman Britain* (McFarland, 2014), 144.

18. *Ibid*, 205–6.

19. *The Gododdin of Aneirin*, trans. and ed. John T. Koch (Cardiff, 1997), xxv–xlii.

20. Higham, "King Edwin of the Deiri: rhetoric and the reality of power in early England," *Early Deira: Archaeological studies of the East Riding in the fourth to ninth centuries AD*, eds. Helen Geake and Jonathan Kenny (Oxford, 2000), 44.

21. Prestige seems to have attracted lesser kingdoms to pay "protection money" to larger kingdoms and forced the more powerful kingdoms to pay an outright tribute. It is possible if not probable that Æthelfrith collected tribute from Dal Riata after the battle. There is no record of this, but it makes no sense that he would not have taken advantage of his superiority there.

22. Kirby, *The Earliest English Kings* (London, 1992), 60–1.

23. The Irish Annals, *Annales Cambriae*, *The Anglo-Saxon Chronicle*, and *Historia Brittonum* give the range of dates 605–616. However, as the *Irish Annals* were not regularly interested in British affairs, *The Anglo-Saxon Chronicle* was written in the ninth century, and neither the Irish nor Wessex participated, their testimony is not as strong as Bede or *Annales Cambriae*. Bede may have written in 731 and *Annales Cambriae* some time after 795, but both Northumbria and several Welsh war-bands fought at Chester and Bede might have received accurate information from one of his northern sources while the Dyfed monks might have taken contemporary information from a monastery or an updated *Northern Memoranda*.

24. Stenton, *Anglo-Saxon England* (Oxford, 1971), 78.

25. Koch, "Æthelfrith," *Celtic Culture: A Historical Encylopedia*, ed. John T. Koch (Santa Barbara, 2006), 318.

26. Ziegler has suggested the massacre of the monks might have been part of a strategy to psychologically attack the Welsh before the attack. Bede believed it was retribution for not converting to Roman Christianity; Ziegler, "The Politics of Exile in Early Northumbria," *HA* 2 (St. John's, 1999), 10.

27. Plunkett, *Suffolk in Anglo-Saxon Times* (Stroud, 2005), 79.

28. Lapidge, *The Blackwell Encyclopaedia of Anglo-Saxon England* (London, 1999), 385.
29. Bede, *A History of the English Church and People*, trans. and ed. Leo Sherley-Price (Baltimore, 1955), 2.12.
30. Plunkett, *Suffolk in Anglo-Saxon Times* (Stroud, 2005), 76–8.
31. Bruce-Mitford, *Aspects of Anglo-Saxon Archaeology: Sutton Hoo and other discoveries* (London, 1974), 26, 33, and 73; Yorke, *Kings and Kingdoms of Early Anglo-Saxon England* (London, 2002), 59–60, 158.
32. Bede, eds. Judith McClure and Roger Collins (New York, 2008), 381 fn. 98.
33. Bruce-Mitford, *Aspects of Anglo-Saxon Archaeology: Sutton Hoo and other discoveries* (London, 1974), 3.
34. Kirby, *The Earliest English Kings* (London, 1992), 66.
35. Bede, *A History of the English Church and People*, trans. and ed. Leo Sherley-Price (Baltimore, 1955), 2.14; Higham, *The Kingdom of Northumbria, A.D. 350–1100* (Stroud, 1993), 112–113; Holdsworth, "Edwin," *The Blackwell Encyclopedia of Anglo-Saxon England* (London, 1999), 242–4.
36. Ó Cróinin, *Early Medieval Ireland, 400–1200* (London, 1995), 51–2; Byrne, *Irish Kings and High-Kings* (London, rev. 2001), 111. Fiachnae died in 626.
37. Bede, *A History of the English Church and People*, trans. and ed. Leo Sherley-Price (Baltimore, 1955), 4.23; Higham, *The Kingdom of Northumbria, A.D. 350–1100* (Stroud, 1993).84–7, 116.
38. Bede, *A History of the English Church and People*, trans. and ed. Leo Sherley-Price (Baltimore, 1955), 2.14.
39. Higham, *The Kingdom of Northumbria, A.D. 350–1100* (Stroud, 1993), 116; Stenton, *Anglo-Saxon England* (Oxford, 1971), 80–2.
40. Bede names Brocmail, Selyf's grandfather, even though the author and Dr. Miller before him have shown this is chronologically impossible; Johnson, *Hengest, Gwrtheyrn, and the Chronology of Post-Roman Britain* (McFarland, 2014), 138–9; Miller, "Date-guessing and pedigrees," *SC* 11 (Cardiff, 1976a), 96–109; *Cunedda, Cynan, Cadwallon, Cynddylan: Four Welsh Poems and Britain 383–655*, trans. and ed. John T. Koch (Cardiff, 2013), 109–111.
41. *Harleian 1* genealogy 1 and *Jesus College MS 20* genealogy 22.
42. Woolf, "Caedualla Rex Brittonum and the Passing of the Old North," *Northern History* 41.1 (Leeds, 2004), 5–24. His theory has not been well received due to a lack of supporting evidence and the invisible implications from Bede; Charles-Edwards, *Wales and the Britons 350–1064* (Oxford, 2013), 389–90; *Cunedda, Cynan, Cadwallon, Cynddylan: Four Welsh Poems and Britain 383–655*, trans. and ed. John T. Koch (Cardiff, 2013), 187.
43. Bede, *A History of the English Church and People*, trans. and ed. Leo Sherley-Price (Baltimore, 1955), 2.20.
44. "Cadwallon," ed. John T. Koch, *Celtic Culture: A Historical Encyclopedia* (Santa Barbara, 2006).
45. Bede, *A History of the English Church and People*, trans. and ed. Leo Sherley-Price (Baltimore, 1955), 3.1.
46. *Ibid*, 3.1.
47. Adamnan, *Life of Saint Columba, Founder of Hy (Iona)*, trans. and ed. William Reeves (Llanerch, rep. 1988), 1.1; Bede, *A History of the English Church and People*, trans. and ed. Leo Sherley-Price (Baltimore, 1955), 2.5.
48. Stancliffe, "Oswald, Most Holy and Most Victorious King of the Northumbrians," *Oswald: Northumbrian King to European Saint*, eds. Clare Stancliffe and Eric Cambridge (Stamford, 1995), 60.
49. Stancliffe, "Where was Oswald Killed?" *Oswald: Northumbrian King to European Saint*, eds. Clare Stancliffe and Eric Cambridge (Stamford, 1995b), 93.
50. Bede, *A History of the English Church and People*, trans. and ed. Leo Sherley-Price (Baltimore, 1955), 3.3 and 3.5.
51. Meaney, *A Gazetteer of Early Anglo-Saxon Burial Sites* (London, 1964); Fowler, "Anglian Settlement of the Derbyshire-Staffordshire Peak District," *Derbyshire Archaeological Journal* 74 (Derby, 1954), 134–51; Ozanne, "The Peak Dwellers," *Medieval Archaeology* 6–7 (Leeds, 1962–3), 15–52; Clough, Dornier, and Rutland, *Anglo-Saxon and Viking Leicestershire* (Leicester, 1975); Losco-Bradley and Wheeler., "Anglo-Saxon Settlement in the Trent Valley: Some Aspects," *Studies in Late Anglo-Saxon Settlement*, ed. Margaret L. Faull (Oxford, 1984), 101–114; Myres, *The English Settlements* (Oxford, 1986), 182–6; Brooks, *Anglo-Saxon Myths: Church and State, 400–1066* (New York, 2003), 66.

52. Ceorl may have been a joke on Mercia and not a personal name. It translates as "rustic"; Fleming, *Britain after Rome: The Fall and the Rise, 400 to 1070* (London, 2011), 111.
53. *Ibid*, 2.14.
54. Ziegler, "The Politics of Exile in Early Northumbria," HA 2 (St. John's, 1999), fn. 39.
55. Brooks has suggested that Creoda might have been the founder of a West Midlands kingship based on place-name evidence; Brooks, *Anglo-Saxon Myths: Church and State, 400–1066* (New York, 2003), 68–9.
56. Higham, "King Cearl, the Battle of Chester and the origins of Mercian," "Overkingship," Midland History 22 (Birmingham, 1992), 1–15.
57. Bede, *A History of the English Church and People*, trans. and ed. Leo Sherley-Price (Baltimore, 1955), 2.20.
58. "Historia Brittonum," *Nennius: British History and the Welsh Annals*, trans. and ed. John Morris (London, 1980), chapter 65.
59. Brooks, *Anglo-Saxon Myths: Church and State, 400–1066* (New York, 2003), 72–4.
60. Higham, *The Convert Kings: Power and Religious Affiliation in Early Anglo-Saxon England* (Manchester, 1997), 218–19.
61. Stancliffe, "Oswald, Most Holy and Most Victorious King of the Northumbrians," *Oswald: Northumbrian King to European Saint*, eds. Clare Stancliffe and Eric Cambridge (Stamford, 1995), 54; "The Politics of Exile in Early Northumbria," HA 2 (St. John's, 1999), fn. 39.
62. Kirby, *The Earliest English Kings* (London, 1992), 207, fn. 26.
63. Bede, *A History of the English Church and People*, trans. and ed. Leo Sherley-Price (Baltimore, 1955), 2.20
64. Kirby, *The Earliest English Kings* (London, 1992), 77.
65. Brooks, "The Formation of the Mercian Kingdom," *The Origins of the Anglo-Saxon Kingdoms*, ed. Stephen Bassett (Leicester, 1989), 165–7; Stancliffe, "Oswald, Most Holy and Most Victorious King of the Northumbrians," *Oswald: Northumbrian King to European Saint*, eds. Clare Stancliffe and Eric Cambridge (Stamford, 1995), 55–6.
66. Kirby, *The Earliest English Kings* (London, 1992), 57.
67. Higham, *The Convert Kings: Power and Religious Affiliation in Early Anglo-Saxon England* (Manchester, 1997), 240.
68. Brooks, "The Formation of the Mercian Kingdom," *The Origins of the Anglo-Saxon Kingdoms*, ed. Stephen Bassett (Leicester, 1989), 168.
69. Johnson, *Hengest, Gwrtheyrn, and the Chronology of Post-Roman Britain* (McFarland, 2014), 145. In the past several scholars have been reluctant to make the connection, but the present scholar's findings were unambiguous. Grimmer, "The Exogamous Marriages of Oswiu of Northumbria," HA 9 (St. John's, 2006), chapter 25; Kirby, *The Earliest English Kings* (London, 1992), 143; A. Williams, *Kingship and Government in Pre-Conquest England, c. 600–800* (Basingstoke, 1999), 18; Corning, "The Baptism of Edwin, king of Northumbria: A new analysis of the British tradition," Northern History 36 (Leeds, 2000), 11.
70. Bede, *A History of the English Church and People*, trans. and ed. Leo Sherley-Price (Baltimore, 1955), 3.6; *Annals of Ulster*, eds. Seán Mac Airt and Gearóid Mac Niocaill (Dublin, 1983), 650; Yorke, *Kings and Kingdoms of Early Anglo-Saxon England* (London, 1990), 78–9 and 105.
71. Kirby, *The Earliest English Kings* (London, 1992), 96.
72. Bede, *A History of the English Church and People*, trans. and ed. Leo Sherley-Price (Baltimore, 1955), 3.22; Higham, *The Convert Kings: Power and Religious Affiliation in Early Anglo-Saxon England* (Manchester, 1997), 249; Kirby, *The Earliest English Kings* (London, 1992), 97.
73. Bede, *A History of the English Church and People*, trans. and ed. Leo Sherley-Price (Baltimore, 1955), 3.24.
74. *Ibid*, 3.24.
75. Higham, *The Convert Kings: Power and Religious Affiliation in Early Anglo-Saxon England* (Manchester, 1997), 245–7; Kirby, *The Earliest English Kings* (London, 1992), 114. Kirby noted that Wulfhere married Eormenhild daughter of Eorcenberht, who was king of Kent and the only English ruler Oswiu had no influence over.
76. *Cunedda, Cynan, Cadwallon, Cynddylan: Four Welsh Poems and Britain 383–655*, trans. and ed. John T. Koch (Cardiff, 2013), 233–54; Brooks, "The Formation of the Mercian Kingdom," *The Origins of the Anglo-Saxon Kingdoms*, ed. Stephen Bassett (Leicester, 1989), 169.
77. Bede simply says that the kingdom lived in error for three years.

78. Bede, *A History of the English Church and People*, trans. and ed. Leo Sherley-Price (Baltimore, 1955), 2.15; a significantly later and less reliable historian, William of Malmesbury, claims he was Rædwald's stepson. There is no other record of that connection, however.
79. *The Anglo-Saxon Chronicle*, trans. and ed. Michael Swanton (London, 1997), 26. Yorke believes the exile began in 645 while Kirby and Plunkett argue for 648. Cenwalh would have needed to return to Wessex with Anna's aid by 651, when Penda forced Anna into exile; Yorke, *Kings and Kingdoms of Early Anglo-Saxon England* (London, 1990), 136; Kirby, *The Earliest English Kings* (London, 1992), 51; Plunkett, *Suffolk in Anglo-Saxon Times* (Stroud, 2005), 110.
80. Yorke, *Kings and Kingdoms of Early Anglo-Saxon England* (London, 1990), 62–3; Dumville, "Essex, Middle Anglia, and the Expansion of Mercia in the South-East Midlands," *The Origins of the Anglo-Saxon Kingdoms*, ed. Stephen Bassett (London, 1989a), 132.
81. Yorke, *Kings and Kingdoms of Early Anglo-Saxon England* (London, 1990), 65–6.
82. *Ibid*, 63 and 65.
83. *Ibid*, 70–1.
84. West, Scarfe, and Cramp, "Iken, St. Botolph, and the Coming of East Anglian Christianity," Proceedings of the Suffolk Institute of Archaeology 15 (Bury St Edmunds, 1984), 45.
85. For a discussion on Cwichelm please see Kirby, *The Earliest English Kings* (London, 1992), 51; Yorke, *Kings and Kingdoms of Early Anglo-Saxon England* (London, 1990), 143–4.
86. Johnson, *Hengest, Gwrtheyrn, and the Chronology of Post-Roman Britain* (McFarland, 2014), 150–2.
87. Yorke, *Kings and Kingdoms of Early Anglo-Saxon England* (London, 1990), 133–6 and 143–4; Kirby, *The Earliest English Kings* (London, 1992), 51.
88. Bede, *A History of the English Church and People*, trans. and ed. Leo Sherley-Price (Baltimore, 1955), 2.3.
89. Yorke, "The Kingdom of the East Saxons," *ASE* 14 (London, 1985), 18.
90. Yorke suggested they may have been his brothers Swithhelm and Swithfrith; Yorke, *Kings and Kingdoms of Early Anglo-Saxon England* (London, 1990), 48; York, "The Kingdom of the East Saxons," *ASE* 14 (London, 1985), 32.
91. Bede, *A History of the English Church and People*, trans. and ed. Leo Sherley-Price (Baltimore, 1955), 4.13; Yorke, *Wessex: Studies in the early history of Britain* (London, 1995), 59.

Chapter 32

1. Dumville, "The Floruit of St Patrick: Common and Less Common Ground," *Saint Patrick: A.D. 493–1993*, ed. David N. Dumville (Cambridge, 1993), 13–18.
2. Dumville, "Auxilius, Iserninus, Secundinus, and Benignus," *Saint Patrick: A.D. 493–1993*, ed. David N. Dumville (Cambridge, 1993), 89–105.
3. Fraser, *From Caledonia to Pictland: Scotland to 795* (Edinburgh, 2009), 68–93; Fraser, "Northumbrian Whithorn and the Making of St Ninian," *Innes Review* 53 (Edinbugh, 2002), 40–59; Clancy, "The Real St. Ninian," *Innes Review* 52 (Edinburgh, 2001), 1–28; Charles-Edwards, *Early Christian Ireland* (Cambridge, 2000), 291–3; "Gildas and Uinniau," *Gildas: New Approaches*, eds. David N. Dumville and Michael Lapidge (Woodbridge, 1984c), 207–214; Ó Riain, "Finnian or Winniau," *Irland und Europa. Die Kirche im Fruhmittelalter*, eds. Próinséas Ní Chatháin, Michael Richter, *Europa-Zentrum Tübingen* (Stuttgart, 1984), 407–14; "Finnio: A question of priority," *Indogermanica et Causica: Festschrift für Karl Horst Schmidt zum 65. Geburstad*, eds. Roland Bielmeier, Reinhard Stempel, and René Lansweert (New York, 1994), 407–14; "Finnio and Winniau: a return to the subject," *Ildanach Ildirech: a festschrift Proinsias MacCana*, eds. James Carey, John T. Koch, and Pierre-Yves Lambert (Andover, 1999), 187–202; *Feastdays of the saints: a history of Irish martyrologies* (Brussels, 2006).
4. Jocelyn, a monk of Furness: *The Life of Kentigern (Mungo)*, trans. Cynthia Whiddon Green (unpublished thesis, 1998), chapters 39–40.
5. Adamnan, *Life of Saint Columba, Founder of Hy (Iona)*, trans. and ed. William Reeves (Llanerch, rep. 1988), 1.16.
6. "Vita Cadoci," *Lives of the British Saints*, ed. Sabine Baring-Gould and John Fischer (Cardiff, 1907–13), chapter 18.

7. "*Historia Brittonum,*" *British history; and the Welsh Annals, History from the Sources 8,* trans. and ed. John Morris (London, 1980), chapters 32–5 and 47.

8. Neither ecclesiastics nor secular rulers are directly connected to the migration, but many *vitae* place contemporary ecclesiastics moving to Brittany. They also helped their followers by dealing with several Frankish kings according to the *vitae* and Gregory of Tours.

9. In fact most wealthy households had a study with its own small library stored in scrolls in a place called the *armaria*.

10. Charles-Edwards, *Wales and the Britons 350–1064* (Oxford, 2013), 632–7

11. "Bede's Native Sources for the *Historia Ecclesiastica*," *BJRL* 48 (London, 1965–1966), 341–371.

Chapter 33

1. Kirby, *The Earliest English Kings* (London, 1992), 67.

2. Corning, "The Baptism of Edwin, king of Northumbria: A new analysis of the British tradition," *Northern History* 36 (Leeds, 2000), 5–16.

Chapter 34

1. Rives, "Human Sacrifice among Pagans and Christians," JRS 85 (London, 1995), 85.

2. Hutton, *Blood and Mistletoe: The History of the Druids in Britain* (New Haven, 2009), 4–5, 17; N. Chadwick, *The Druids* (Cardiff, 1966), xviii, 28, and 91.

3. Caesar, *The Gallic Wars,* trans. Stanley Alexander Handford (Baltimore, 1951), 4.13, 6.13–18; Lucan, *Pharsalia,* trans. S.H. Braund (Oxford, 1992), 1.450–58; Suetonius, "Claudius," *De vita Caesarium,* trans. Philemon Holland, rev. Moses Hadas (New York, 1965), 25; Cicero, "Pro Fonteio," *Pro Milone. In Pisonem. Pro Scauro. Pro Fonteio. Pro Rabirio Postumo. Pro Marcello. Pro Ligario. Pro Rege Deiotaro,* trans. N.H. Watts. (Harvard, 1931); Cicero, *De Re Publica,* ed. J.E.G. Zetzel. (Cambridge, 1995); Diodorus Siculus, *Bibliotheca historicae,* 5.21–2; Diogenes Laërtius, *Lives of Eminent Philosophers,* ed. Tiziano Dorandi (Cambridge, 2013); Strabo, *The Geography,* 8 vols. trans. Horace Leonard Jones (New York, 1923), 4.4.4–5. Alexander Cornelius' *Polyhistor* also referred to druids as philosophers but we know about it only through paraphrases and quotes. Druids are also present in many Irish and Welsh stories.

4. For further reading on the druids please see Ronald Hutton, *Blood and Mistletoe: The History of the Druids in Britain* (New Haven, 2009).

5. Webster, *The Pagan Celts and their Gods under Rome* (London, 1986), 74–5; Irby-Massie, *Military Religion in Roman Britain* (Boston, 1999), 104.

6. Ross, *Pagan Celtic Britain* (London, 1967), 371.

7. Johnson, *Origins of Arthurian Romances* (McFarland, 2012), 101.

8. *Ibid,* 93–4.

9. They have been called the, "Young and Dying God". Father Time is often represented as being born on the first of the year and being an old man by the last day; they are the same concept.

10. *Trioedd Ynys Prydein: The Welsh Triads,* trans. and ed. Rachel Bromwich (Cardiff, rev. 1978), 240–2; *Mabinogion,* trans. Gwyn Jones and Thomas Jones (London, 1974), 37

11. " 'Preiddeu Annwn' and the figure of Taliesin," ed. and trans. Marged Haycock, SC 14/15 (Cardiff, 1984), ln. 14; *Mabinogion,* trans. Gwyn Jones and Thomas Jones (London, 1974), 226–7,

12. "Pa gur?," trans. Brynley Roberts, *Culhwch ac Olwen: An Edition and Study of the Earliest Arthurian Tale,* eds. Rachel Bromwich and D. Simon Evans (Cardiff, 1992), xxxv, ln. 21; *Mabinogion,* trans. Gwyn Jones and Thomas Jones (London, 1974), 135; *The Life of St. Samson of Dol,* trans. Thomas Taylor (Llanerch, rep. 1991), 26 and 27.

13. Johnson, *Origins of Arthurian Romances* (McFarland, 2012), 79–82.

14. *Ibid,* 75–136.

Bibliography

Abbreviations

AC	*Archaeologia Cambrensis*
AdB	*Annales de Bretagne*
Antiq	*Antiquity*
ASE	*Anglo-Saxon England*
BBCS	*Bulletin of the Board of Celtic Studies*
BJRL	*Bulletin of the John Rylands Library*
Brit	*Britannia*
CA	*Current Archaeology*
CMCS	*Cambridge/Cambrian Medieval Celtic Studies*
CQ	*Classical Quarterly*
CR	*Celtic Review*
EC	*Étude Celtique*
EHR	*English Historical Review*
HA	*The Heroic Age*
IEC	*Irish Ecclesiastical Record*
JRS	*Journal of Roman Studies*
NLW Journal	*National Library of Wales Journal*
PBA	*Publications of the British Academy*
RC	*Review Celtique*
RSPB	*Royal Society for the Protection of Birds*
SBVS	*Saga-Book of the Viking Saga*
SC	*Studia Celtica*
SE	*Sacris Erudiri*
TCWAAS	*Transactions of the Cumberland and Westmoreland Antiquarian and Archaeological Society*
TDGNAHS	*Transactions of the Dumfriesshire and Galloway Natural History and Antiquarian Society*
THSC	*Transactions of the Honourable Society of the Cymmrodorion*
WA	*World Archaeology*
WHR	*Welsh Historical Review*
ZDP	*Zeitschrift für Deutsche Philologie*
ZCP	*Zeitschrift für Celtische Philologie*

Bibliography

Primary Sources

Adamnan. *Life of Saint Columba, Founder of Hy (Iona)*. Ed. and trans. William Reeves (Llanerch, rep. 1988).
Alcuin. "De Pontificibus et Sanctis Ecclesiae Eboracensis Carmen." *The Historians of the Church of York*. Ed. James Raine (London, 1879–1894).
Aneirin. *Canu Aneirin*. Ed. Sir Ifor Williams (Cardiff, 1938).
Aneiren. *The Gododdin of Aneirin*. Ed. and trans. John T. Koch (Cardiff, 1997).
Aneirin. *The Gododdin: The Oldest Scottish Poem*. Ed. and trans. Kenneth H. Jackson (Edinburgh, 1969).
Aneirin. *Y Gododdin: Britain's Oldest Heroic Poem*. Ed. and trans. Alfred Owen Hughes Jarman (Llandysul, 1988).
The Anglo-Saxon Chronicle. Ed. and trans. Michael Swanton (London, 1997).
_____. Trans. George Norman Garmonsway (London, 1953).
"Annales Cambriae." Ed. and trans. John Morris. *Nennius: British History and the Welsh Annals* (London, 1980).
Annals of Clonmacnoise, Being Annals of Ireland from the Earliest Period to A.D. 1408. Translated into English A.D. 1627 by Conell Mageoghagan. Ed. Denis Murphy (Dublin, 1896).
Annals of Inisfallen (MS. Rawlinson B.503). Ed. and trans. Seán MacAirt (Dublin, 1951).
Annals of Tigernach. Ed. Whitley Stokes. RC 16 (Paris, 1895), 374–419.
_____. Ed. Whitley Stokes. RC 17 (Paris, 1896), 6–33, 119–263, 337–420, 458.
_____. Ed. Whitley Stokes. RC 18 (Paris, 1897), 9–59, 150–198, 267–303, 390–391.
Annals of Ulster. Ed. Seán Mac Airt, and Gearóid Mac Niocaill (Dublin, 1983).
The Anonymous History of Abbot Ceolfrith. Ed. and trans. David Hugh Farmer. *The Age of Bede* (Harmondsworth, rev. 1983), 211–230.
Bede. Eds. Judith McClure and Roger Collins (New York, 2008).
Bede. *Bedae Opera de Temporibus*. Ed. Charles Williams Jones (Cambridge, 1943).
Bede. *A History of the English Church and People*. Ed. and trans. Leo Sherley-Price (Baltimore, 1955).
Bede. *The Life of St. Cuthbert*. Trans. J.F. Webb. Ed. David H. Farmer. *The Age of Bede* (Harmondsworth, rev. 1983), 41–104.
Bede. *Lives of the Abbots of Wearmouth and Jarrow*. Ed. and trans. David H. Farmer. *The Age of Bede* (Harmondsworth, rev. 1983), 185–210.
Caesar, Julius Gaius. *The Gallic Wars*. Trans. Stanley Alexander Handford (Baltimore, 1951).
Canu Llywarch Hen. Ed. Sir Ifor Williams (Cardiff, 1960).
Chronica Minora I. Ed. Theodor Mommsen (Berlin, 1886), 515–660.
The Chronicle of Ireland. Trans. Thomas Charles-Edwards. Vol. 1 (Liverpool, 2006).
Cicero. *De Re Publica*. Ed. J.E.G. Zetzel (Cambridge, 1995).
_____. *Pro Milone. In Pisonem. Pro Scauro. Pro Fonteio. Pro Rabirio Postumo. Pro Marcello. Pro Ligario. Pro Rege Deiotaro*. Trans. N.H. Watts (Harvard, 1931).
Columbanus. *Le Pénitential de Saint Columban*. Ed. Jean Laporte (Tournai, 1958).
_____. *Sancti Columbanus Opera*. Trans., G.S.M. Walker. (Dublin, 1957).
Constantius. "Vitae Germani." *Bibliotheca Hagiographica Latina* (Brussels, 1898–1901).
Corpus Iuris Hibernici. Ed. David A. Binchy (Dublin, 1978).
Culhwch ac Olwen: An Edition and Study of the Oldest Arthurian Tale. Ed. Rachel Bromwich and D. Simon Evans (Cardiff, 1992).
Diogenes Laërtius. *Lives of Eminent Philosophers*. Ed. Tiziano Dorandi (Cambridge, 2013).

Early Welsh Saga Poetry. Ed. and trans. Jenny Rowland (Cambridge, 1990).
"The Expulsion of the Dessi." Ed. and trans. Kuno Meyer. *Y Cymmrodor* 14 (Cardiff, 1901), 101–35.
Gildas. *De Excidio Britanniae*. Trans. Michael Winterbottom (Chichester, 1978).
Gregory of Tours. *Gregory of Tours: The History of the Franks*. Ed. and trans. Lewis Thorpe (New York, 1974).
"Historia Brittonum." Ed. and trans. John Morris. *Nennius: British History and the Welsh Annals* (London, 1980).
The Law of Hywel Dda. Ed. and trans. Dafydd Jenkins (Llandysul, 1986).
"The Laws of Æthelberht." *The Laws of the Earliest English Kings*. Ed. and trans. Frederick L. Attenborough (Cambridge, 1922), 4–17.
"The Laws of Hlothere and Eadric." *The Laws of the Earliest English Kings*. Ed. and trans. Frederick L. Attenborough (Cambridge, 1922), 18–23.
"The Laws of Ine." *The Laws of the Earliest English Kings*. Ed. and trans. Frederick L. Attenborough (Cambridge, 1922), 36–61.
"The Laws of Wihtred." *The Laws of the Earliest English Kings*. Ed. and trans. Frederick L. Attenborough (Cambridge, 1922), 24–32.
The Life of Samson of Dol. Trans. Thomas Taylor (Llanerch, rep. 1991).
The Lives of St. Ninian and St. Kentigern. Ed. and trans. Alexander Penrose Forbes (Edinburgh, 1874).
Lives of the British Saints. Eds. Sabine Baring-Gould, and John Fischer (Cardiff, 1907–13).
Lives of the Welsh Saints. Trans., G.H. Doble. Ed. D. Simon Evans (Cardiff, 2015).
The Llandaff Charters. Ed. Wendy Davies (Aberystwyth, 1979).
Lucan. *Pharsalia*. Trans., S.H. Braund (Oxford, 1992).
Jocelyn, a Monk of Furness: The Life of Kentigern (Mungo). Trans. Cynthia Whiddon Green (unpublished thesis, 1998).
Mabinogion. Trans. Gwyn Jones, and Thomas Jones (London, 1974).
"Marwnad Cadwallon ap Cadfan." Trans. John T. Koch. *The Celtic Heroic Age: Literary Sources for Ancient Celtic Europe and Early Ireland and Wales*. Eds. John T. Koch, and John Carey (Malden, 1994), 351–3.
"Marwnad Cynddylan." Trans., John T. Koch. *The Celtic Heroic Age: Literary Sources for Ancient Celtic Europe and Early Ireland and Wales*. Eds. John T. Koch, and John Carey (Malden, 1994), 360–362.
"Moliant Cadwallon." Trans., John T. Koch. *The Celtic Heroic Age: Literary Sources for Ancient Celtic Europe and Early Ireland and Wales*. Eds. John T. Koch, and John Carey (Malden, 1994), 353–6.
A Monk of Rhuys and Caradoc of Llancarfan. *Two Lives of Gildas*. Trans. Hugh Williams (Llanerch, rep. 1990).
"Pa Gur." Trans., Brynley Roberts. Eds. Rachel Bromwich, and D. Simon Evans. *Culhwch ac Olwen: An Edition and Study of the Earliest Arthurian Tale* (Cardiff, 1992), xxxv.
Patrick. *The Works of St. Patrick*. Ed. Luwig Bieler (Westminster, 1953).
"The Poetry of Llywarch Hen." Trans. Patrick K. Ford. *The Celtic Heroic Age: Literary Sources for Ancient Celtic Europe and Early Ireland and Wales*. Eds. John T. Koch, and John Carey (Malden, 1994), 363–384.
Pomponius Mela. *Pomponius Mela's Description of the World*. Ed. Frank E. Romer (Ann Arbor, 1998).
Procopius. *Procopius*. Trans. Henry B. Dewing (London, rep. 1971).
Prosper of Aquitaine. *Prosperi Aquitani Opera*. Eds. P. Callens, and M. Gastaldo (Turnhout, 1972).
_____. *Prosperi Aquitani Opera*. Trans. Charles T. Huegelmeyer (Washington, 1962).

Stephanus, Eddius. *Eddius Stephanus: Life of Wilfrid*. Trans. James Francis Webb. Ed. David Hugh Farmer. *The Age of Bede* (Harmondsworth, rev. 1983), 105–184.
Strabo. *The Geography*. 8 vols. Trans. Horace Leonard Jones (New York, 1923).
Suetonius. *De Vita Caesarium*. Trans. Philemon Holland, rev., Moses Hadas (New York, 1965).
Taliesin. *Book of Taliesin*. Trans. John T. Koch, and John Carey. *The Celtic Heroic Age* (Malden, 1995).
_____. *Canu Taliesin*. Ed. Sir Ifor Williams (Cardiff, 1960).
_____. *Legendary Poems from the Book of Taliesin*. Ed. and trans. Marged Haycock (Cardiff, 2007).
Trioedd Ynys Prydein: The Welsh Triads. Ed. and trans. Rachel Bromwich (Cardiff, rev. 1978).
Two Lives of Saint Cuthbert: A Life by an Anonymous Monk of Lindisfarne and Bede's Prose Life. Ed. Bertram Colgrave (Cambridge, 1940).
Two of the Saxon Chronicles Parallel. Ed. and trans. Charles Plummer. 2 vols. (London, 1892–1899).
La Vie ancienne de Saint Samson de Dol. Ed. and trans. Piere Florent (Paris, 1997).
Vitae sanctorum Britanniae et genealogie. Ed. Arthur W. Wade-Evans (Cardiff, 1944).
The Welsh Life of David. Ed. D. Simon Evans (Cardiff, 1988).
Zosimus. *Zosimus: New History*. Trans. Ronald T. Ridley (Canberra, 1982).

Secondary Sources

Abel, Richard. *Lordship and Military Obligation in Anglo-Saxon England* (Los Angeles, 1988).
Abrams, Leslie, and James P. Carley. *The Archaeology and History of Glastonbury Abbey. Essays in Honour of the Ninetieth Birthday of C.A. Ralegh Radford* (Woodbridge, 1991).
Alcock, Leslie. *Arthur's Britain* (London, 1971).
Anderson, Alan Orr. *Early Sources of Scottish History A.D. 500–1286* (Stamford, 1990).
Anderson, Marjorie Ogilvie. *Kings and Kingship in Early Scotland* (Edinburgh, 1980).
Arnold, Christopher J. *An Archaeology of the Early Anglo-Saxon Kingdoms* (New York, 1988).
_____. "Social Evolution in Post-Roman Western Europe." *European Social Evolution*. Ed. John L. Bintliff (Bradford, 1984), 277–94.
_____. "Stress as a Factor in Social and Economic Change." *Ranking, Resource and Exchange*. Eds. A.Collin Renfrew, and Stephen Shennan (Cambridge, 1982), 124–31.
_____. "Wealth and Social Structure: A Matter of Life and Death." *Anglo-Saxon Cemetaries 1979*. Ed. Philip A. Rahtz, Tania M. Dickinson, and Loma Watts (Oxford, 1980), 81–142.
Baillie, Michael G.L. "Dendrochronology Raises Questions About the Nature of the Ad 536 Dust-Veil Event." *The Holocene* 4.2 (Washington, D.C., 1994), 212–7.
_____. "Marking in Marker Dates: Towards an Archaeology with Historical Precision." *World Archaeology* 23.2 (Abingdon, 1991), 233–43.
Bammesberger, Alfred, and Alfred Wollmann. *Britain: 400–600* (Heidelberg, 1990).
Bannerman, John. *Studies in the History of Dal Riata* (Edinburgh, 1974).
Bardy, Gustave. *Saint Germain d'Auxerre et son temps* (Auxerre, 1950), 89–108.
Barrett, Anthony. "Saint Germanus and the British Missions." *Brit* 40 (Stroud, 2009), 197–217.
Bartholomew, Philip. "Fifth-Century Facts." *Brit* 13 (Stroud, 1982), 261–70.
Bartrum, Peter S. "Some Studies in Early Welsh History." *TSC* (London, 1949), 279–302.

_____. *A Welsh Classical Dictionary: People in History and Legend Up to About 1000 A.D.* (Cardiff, 1993).
Bassett, Stephen. "In Search of the Origins of Anglo-Saxon Kingdoms." *The Origins of the Anglo-Saxon Kingdoms.* Ed. Stephen Bassett (Leicester, 1989), 3–27.
_____, ed. *The Origins of the Anglo-Saxon Kingdoms* (Leicester, 1989).
Berschin, Walter. "*Opus Deliberatum ac Perfectum*: Why Did the Venerable Bede Write a Second Prose Life of St. Cuthbert?" *St. Cuthbert, His Cult and His Community to AD 1200.* Eds. Gerald Bonner, David Rollason, and Clare Stancliffe (Woodbridge, 1989), 103–122.
Binchy, David A. "Celtic and Anglo-Saxon Kingship" (Oxford, 1970).
Bintliff, John L., ed. *European Social Evolution* (Bradford, 1984).
Birley, Anthony Richard. *The Roman Government of Britain* (Oxford, 2005).
Blair, John. "Frithuwold's Kingdom and the Origins of Surrey." *The Origins of the Anglo-Saxon Kingdoms.* Ed. Stephen Bassett (Leicester, 1989), 97–107.
Blair, Peter Hunter. "The Formation of the Mercian Kingdom." *The Origins of the Anglo-Saxon Kingdoms.* Ed. Stephen Bassett (Leicester, 1989), 159–170.
_____. *An Introduction to Anglo-Saxon England* (Cambridge, 1977).
Breeze, Andrew. "The Arthurian Battle of Badon and Braydon Forest, Wiltshire." *Journal of Literary Onomastics* 4.1 (Brockport, 2015), 20–30.
_____. "The Historical Arthur and Sixth-Century Scotland." *Northern History* 52.2 (Leeds, 2015), 158–81.
Bromwich, Rachel. "Concepts of Arthur." *SC* 10/11 (Cardiff, 1976), 163–181.
_____. "Dwy Chwedl a Thair Rhamant." *Y Traddodiad Rhyddiaith yn yr Oesoedd Canol.* Ed. Geraint Bowen (Llandysul, 1974), 143–175.
_____. "First Transmission from England to France." *The Arthur of the Welsh.* Eds. Rachel Bromwich, Brynley F. Roberts, and Alfred O.H. Jarman (Cardiff, 1991), 273–98.
_____. "The Tristan of the Welsh." *The Arthur of the Welsh.* Eds. Rachel Bromwich, Brynley F. Roberts, and Alfred O.H. Jarman (Cardiff, 1991), 209–28.
_____, and R. Brinley Jones, eds. *Astudiaethau ar yr Hengerdd* (Cardiff, 1978).
_____, and Alfred O.H. Jarman, and Brynley F. Roberts, eds. *The Arthur of the Welsh* (Cardiff, 1991).
_____, ed. *The Beginnings of Welsh Poetry: Studies by Sir Ifor Williams* (Cardiff, 2nd Ed. 1982).
Brooke, Christopher. *The Church and the Welsh Border in the Central Middle Ages* (Woodbridge, 1986).
Brookes, Stuart, and Sue Harrington. *The Kingdom and People of Kent, AD 400–1066: Their History and Archaeology* (Stroud, 2010).
Brooks, Nicholas. *Anglo-Saxon Myths: Church and State, 400–1066* (New York, 2003).
_____. *Bede and the English* (Jarrow, 2000).
_____. "Canterbury, Rome and the Construction of English Identity." *Early Medieval Rome and the Christian West: Essays in Honour of Donald A. Bullough.* Ed. Julia M.H. Smith (Boston, 2000a), 221–47.
_____. "The Creation and Early Structure of the Kingdom of Kent" *The Origins of the Anglo-Saxon Kingdoms.* Ed. Stephen Bassett (Leicester, 1989), 55–74.
_____. "The English Origin Myth." *Anglo-Saxon Myths: State and Church.* Ed. Nicholas Brooks (London, 2000c), 79–89.
_____. "The Formation of the Mercian Kingdom." *The Origins of the Anglo-Saxon Kingdoms.* Ed. Stephen Bassett (Leicester, 1989), 159–70.
Brouland, Marie Thérèse. "Peredur ab Efrawg." *Perceval-Parzival: Hier et aujourd'hui.* Eds. Danielle Buschinger, and Wolfgang Spiewok (Reineke, 1994), 59–70.

Brown, George Hardin. *A Companion to Bede* (Woodbridge, 2009).
Brown, Michelle P., and Carole A Farr, eds. *Mercia: An Anglo-Saxon Kingdom in Europe* (New York, 2001).
Brown, Neville. *History and Climate Change: An Eurocentric Perspective* (Routledge, 2001).
Bruce-Mitford, Rupert. *Aspects of Anglo-Saxon Archaeology: Sutton Hoo and Other Discoveries* (London, 1974).
Bruce, James Douglas. *The Evolution of Arthurian Romance, from the Beginnings Down to the Year 1300* (Gottingen, 1923).
Bugge, Robert. "Fertility Myth and Female Sovereignty in the Weddynge of Sir Gawen and Dame Ragnell." *CR* 39.2 (University Park, 2004), 198–218.
Bullock-Davies, Constance. *Professional Interpreters and the Matter of Britain* (Cardiff, 1966).
Burgess, Richard W. "The Dark Ages Return to Fifth-Century Britain: The 'Restored' Gallic Chronicle Exploded." *Brit* 21 (Stroud, 1990), 185–195.
Busby, Keith. *Gauvain in Old French Literature* (Amsterdam, 1980).
Buschinger, Danielle, and Michael Zink, eds. *Lancelot-Lanzelet: Hier et aujourd'hui* (Reineke, 1995).
Byrne, John Francis. *Irish Kings and High-Kings* (London, rev. 2001).
_____. "Seventh-Century Documents." IER 108 (Dublin, 1967), 164–82.
Cameron, Alan. *Claudian: Poetry and Propaganda at the Court of Hadrian* (Oxford, 1970).
Campbell, James. "The End of Roman Britain." *The Anglo-Saxons*. Eds. James Campbell, Eric John, and Patrick Wormald (London, 1982), 1–19.
_____. "The Lost Centuries 400–600." *The Anglo-Saxons*. Eds. James Campbell, Eric John, and Patrick Wormald (London, 1982), 20–54.
_____. "Rædwald." *Oxford Dictionary of National Biography* (Oxford, 2004). Web.
_____. "Bede's Reges and Principes" (Jarrow Lecture, 1979).
Campbell, James, ed. *The Anglo-Saxons* (London, 1982).
Campbell, James, Eric John, and Patrick Wormald. *The Anglo-Saxons* (London, 1982).
Campbell, Joseph. *The Hero with a Thousand Faces* (Princteon, 1949).
Carney, James. *Studies in Irish Literature and History* (Dublin, 1950).
Casey, P. John, ed. *The End of Roman Britain* (London, 1979).
Chadwick, Hector Munro. *Origins of the English Nation* (Cambridge, 1907).
_____. *Early Scotland: The Picts, the Scots, and the Welsh of Southern Scotland* (Cambridge, 1949).
Chadwick, Hector Munro, and Nora Kershaw Chadwick. *The Growth of Literature*. Vol 1 (Cambridge, 1932).
Chadwick, Nora Kershaw. *The Druids* (Cardiff, 1966).
_____. "Early Culture and Learning in North Wales." *Studies in the Early British Church*. Ed. Nora K. Chadwick (Cambridge, 1958), 29–120.
_____. *Poetry and Letters in Early Christian Gaul* (London, 1955).
Chadwick, Nora Kershaw, ed. *Celt and Saxon: Studies in the Early British Border* (Cambridge, 1963).
_____, ed. *Studies in Early British History* (Cambridge, 1954).
Chaney, William A. *The Cult of Kingship in Anglo-Saxon England: The Transition from Paganism to Christianity* (Manchester, 1970).
Charles-Edwards, Gifford. "Scribes of the Red Book of Hergest." *NLW Journal* 20 (1980), 246–56.
Charles-Edwards, Thomas Mawbray. "The Authenticity of the Gododdin: An Historian's View." Eds. Rachel Bromwich and R. Brinley Jones. *Astudiaethau ar yr Hengerdd* (Cardiff, 1978), 44–71.

_____. "The Date of the Four Branches of the *Mabinogi*." THSC (London, 1971), 263-98.
_____. *Early Irish and Welsh Kinship* (Oxford, 1993).
_____. *Early Christian Ireland* (Cambridge, 2000).
_____. *Wales and the Britons 350-1064* (Oxford, 2013).
Clancy, Thomas Owen. "The Real St Ninian." *Innes Review* 52 (Edinburgh, 2001), 1-28.
Clarke, Roy Rainbird. *East Anglia* (London, 1963).
Cleary, A. Simon Edward. *The Ending of Roman Britain* (London, 1989).
Clough, Timothy H. McK., Anne Dornier, and R. A. Rutland. *Anglo-Saxon and Viking Leicestershire* (Leicester, 1975).
Corning, Caitlin. "The Baptism of Edwin, King of Northumbria: A New Analysis of the British Tradition." *Northern History* 36 (Leeds, 2000), 5-16.
Crawford, Osberht Guy Stanthorpe. "Arthur and His Battles." *Antiq* 9 (Gloucester, 1935), 217-91.
Dalton, Ormonde Maddock. *The History of the Franks by Gregory of Tours*. 2 vols. (Oxford, 1927).
Dark, Kenneth Rainsbury. *Civitas to Kingdom: British Political Continuity 300-800* (Leicester, 1994).
_____. "St. Patrick's *Uillula* and the Fifth-Century Occupation of Romano-British Villas." *Saint Patrick: A.D. 493-1993*. Ed. David N. Dumville (Cambridge, 1993), 19-24.
_____. "A Sub-Roman Defense of Hadrian's Wall?" *Brit* 18 (Stroud, 1992), 111-120.
Davies, John. *A History of Wales* (New York, 1994).
Davies, Wendy. "Annals and the Origins of Mercia." *Mercian Studies*. Ed. Ann Dornier (Leicester, 1977), 17-29.
_____. *An Early Welsh Microcosm: Studies in the Llandaff Charters* (London, 1978).
_____. "Liber Landavensis: Its Construction and Credibility." *EHR* 88 (London, 1973), 335-342.
_____. "The Orthography of the Personal Names in the Charters of Liber Landevensis." *BBCS* 28 (Cardiff, 1980), 553-557.
_____. "Property Rights and Property Claims in Welsh 'Vitae' of the Eleventh Century." *Hagiographie, Cultures, et Sociétés IVe-XIIe Siécles*. Eds. Evelyne Patlagean and Pierre Riché (Paris, 1981), 515-533.
_____. *Wales in the Early Middle Ages* (New York, 1982).
DeGregorio, Scott, ed. *Innovation and Tradition in the Writings of the Venerable Bede* (Morgantown, 2006).
Dornier, Anne, ed. *Mercian Studies* (Leicester, 1977).
Drijvers, John Willem, and David Hunt. *The Late Roman World and Its Historians* (New York, 1999).
Drinkwater, John, ed. *Fifth-Century Gaul: A Crisis of Identity* (Cambridge, 2002).
Duddon, Frederick H. *Gregory the Great* (London, 1905).
Duine, François. "La Vie de S. Samson, à propos d'un ouvrage récent." *Annales de Bretagne* 28 (Paris, 1912-13), 332-56.
Dumville, David N. "Auxilius, Iserninus, Secundinus, and Benignus." *Saint Patrick: A.D. 493-1993*. Ed. David N. Dumville (Cambridge, 1993), 89-105.
_____. "The Chronology of De Excidio Britanniæ, Book I." *Gildas: New Approaches*. Eds., David N. Dumville and Michael Lapidge (Woodbridge, 1984b), 61-84.
_____. "Coroticus." *Saint Patrick: A.D. 493-1993*. Ed. David N. Dumville (Woodbridge, 1993), 107-116.
_____. "Early Welsh Poetry: Problems of Historicity." *Early Welsh Poetry: Studies in the Book of Aneirin*. Ed. Brynley F. Roberts (Aberystwyth, 1988), 1-16.
_____. "Essex, Middle Anglia, and the Expansion of Mercia in the South-East Midlands."

Ed. Stephen Bassett. *Origins of the Anglo-Saxon Kingdoms* (Leicester, 1989a), 123–40.

―――. "The Floruit of St Patrick—Common and Less Common Ground." *Saint Patrick: A.D. 493-1993*. Ed. David N. Dumville (Cambridge, 1993), 13–18.

―――. "*Historia Brittonum*: An Insular History from the Carolingian Age." *Historiographie im Frühen Mittelalter*. Ed. Anton Scharer and Georg Scheibelreitr (Munich, 1994), 406–34.

―――. "Gildas and Maelgwn: Problems of Dating." *Gildas: New Approaches*. Eds. David N. Dumville, and Michael Lapidge (Woodbridge, 1984a), 51–59.

―――. "Gildas and Uinniau." *Gildas: New Approaches*. Eds. David N. Dumville, and Michael Lapidge (Woodbridge, 1984c), 207–214.

―――. "Kingship, Genealogies and Regnal Lists." *Early Medieval Kingship*. Eds. Peter H. Sawyer, and Ian N. Wood (Leeds, 1977b), 72–104.

―――. "'Nennius' and the *Historia Brittonum*." *SC* 11 (Cardiff, 1976), 78–95.

―――. "On the North British Section of the *Historia Brittonum*." *WHR* 8 (Cardiff, 1977c), 345–354.

―――. *St Patrick: A.D. 493-1993* (Woodbridge, 1993).

―――. "Some Aspects of the Chronology of the *Historia Brittonum*." *BBCS* 25 (Cardiff, 1974), 439–445.

―――. "Sub-Roman Britain: History and Legend." *History* 62 (London, 1977a), 173–192.

―――. "*The Tribal Hidage*: An Introduction to Its Texts and Their Historicity." *The Origins of the Anglo-Saxon Kingdoms*. Ed. Stephen Bassett (Leicester, 1989b), 225–230.

―――. "The West Saxon Genaeological Regnal List and the Chronology of Early Wessex." *Peritia* 4 (Galway, 1985), 21–66.

Dumville, David N., and Michael Lapidge, eds. *Gildas: New Approaches* (Woodbridge, 1984).

Dundes, Alan, ed. *International Folkloristics: Classic Contributions by the Founders of Folklore* (Lanham, 1999).

Evison, Vera I., ed. *Angles, Jutes and Saxons* (Oxford, 1981).

Field, Peter J.C. "Gildas and the City of the Legions." *Ha* 1 (1999). Web.

Finberg, Herbert Patrick Reginald. "Anglo-Saxon England to 1042" Ed. Herbert P.R. Finberg. *The Agrarian History of England and Wales*. Vol. 1.2 (Cambridge, 1972).

Fleming, Robin. *Britain After Rome: The Fall and the Rise, 400 to 1070* (London, 2011).

Ford, Patrick K. *The Poetry of Llywarch Hen* (Berkeley, 1974).

Forsyth, Katherine. *Language in Pictland: The Case Against "Non-Indo-European Pictish"* (Utrecht, 1997).

Foster, Roy. *The Oxford Illustrated History of Ireland* (Oxford, 2001).

Foster, Sally M. *Picts, Gaels, and Scots: Early Historic Scotland* (London, 2004).

Fowler, Margaret. "Anglian Settlement of the Derbyshire-Staffordshire Peak District." *Derbyshire Archaeological Journal* 74 (Derby, 1954), 134–51.

Fraser, James E. *From Caledonia to Pictland: Scotland to 795* (Edinburgh, 2009).

―――. "Northumbrian Whithorn and the Making of St Ninian." *Innes Review* 53 (Edinbugh, 2002), 40–59.

Frere, Sheppard S. *Britannia. a History of Roman Britain* (London, 1967).

Fulk, Robert Dennis, Christopher M. Cain, and Rachel S. Anderson. *History of Old English Literature* (Malden, 2003).

Geake, Helen and Jonathan Kenny. *Early Deira: Archaeological Studies of the East Riding in the Fourth to Ninth Centuries AD* (Oxford, 2000).

Gillam, John P. "Romano-Saxon Pottery: An Alternative Explanation." Ed. P. John Casey. *The End of Roman Britain* (London, 1979), 103–118.

Goetinck, Glenys. *Peredur: A Study of Welsh Tradition in the Grail Legends* (Cardiff, 1975).
Goffart, Walter. *Barbarians and Romans 418–584. The Techniques of Accomodation* (Princeton, 1980).
_____. *The Narrators of Barbarian History (A.D. 550–800): Jordanes, Gregory of Tours, Bede, and Paul the Deacon* (Princeton, 1988).
Gowans, Linda. *Cei and the Arthurian Legend* (Cambridge, 1988).
Grimmer, Martin. "The Exogamous Marriages of Oswiu of Northumbria." *Ha* 9 (St. John's, 2006), chapters 1–32.
Grosjean, Paul. "Sur quelques exégetes irlandáis du VIIe siècle." *SE* 7 (Sint-Beggaplein, 1955), 67–98.
Gruffydd, R. Geraint. "Marwnad Cynddylan." *Bardos*. Ed. R. Geraint Gruffydd (Cardiff, 1982), 10–28.
Hamerow, Helena. *Rural Settlements and Society in Anglo-Saxon England* (Oxford, 2012).
Harden, Donald Benjamin, ed. *Dark-Age Britain: Studies Presented to E.T. Leeds* (London, 1956).
Harrison, Kenneth. *The Framework of Anglo-Saxon History to 900 A.D.* (Cambridge, 1976).
Hawkes, Charles Francis Christopher. "The South-East After the Romans: The Saxon Settlement." *The Saxon Shore*. Ed. Valerie A. Maxfield (Oxford, 1989), 78–95.
Hawkes, Sonia Chadwick. "Anglo-Saxon Kent C. 425–725." *Archaeology in Kent to AD 1500*. Ed. P.E. Leach (London, 1982), 64–78.
Haycock, Marged, ed. and trans. "'Preiddeu Annwn' and the Figure of Taliesin." *SC* 14/15 (Cardiff, 1984), 52–77.
Higham, Nicholas J. "East Anglia, Kingdom of." *The Blackwell Encyclopedia of Anglo-Saxon England*. Ed. Michael Lapidge et al. (London, 1999), 154–5.
_____. *The Convert Kings: Power and Religious Affiliation in Early Anglo-Saxon England* (Manchester, 1997).
_____. *An English Empire* (Manchester, 1995).
_____. "From Tribal Chieftains to Christian Kings." *The Anglo-Saxon World*. Eds. Nicholas J. Higham, and Martin J Ryan (New Haven, 2013), 126–178.
_____. "Gildas, Roman Walls and British Dykes." *CMCS* 22 (Cambridge, 1991), 1–14.
_____. *King Arthur: Mythmaking and History* (New York, 2002).
_____. "King Cearl, the Battle of Chester and the Origins of Mercian 'Overkingship.'" *Midland History* 22 (Birmingham, 1992), 1–15.
_____. "King Edwin of the Deiri: Rhetoric and the Reality of Power in Early England." *Early Deira: Archaeological Studies of the East Riding in the Fourth to Ninth Centuries AD*. Eds. Helen Geake and Jonathan Kenny (Oxford, 2000), 41–50.
_____. *The Kingdom of Northumbria, A.D. 350–1100* (Stroud, 1993).
_____. "Medieval 'Overlordship' in Wales: The Earliest Evidence." *WHR* 16 (London, 1992a), 145–159.
_____. *Rome, Britain and the Anglo-Saxons* (London, 1992b).
Higham, Nicholas J., and Martin J. Ryan. *The Anglo-Saxon World* (New Haven, 2013).
Hines, John. "Philology, Archaeology, and the adventus Saxonum vel Anglorum." *Britain: 400–600*. Eds. Alfred Bammesberger, and Alfred Wollmann (Heidelberg, 1990), 17–36.
Hodges, Richard. *Dark Age Economics: The Origins of Towns and Trade A.D. 600–1000* (London, 1982).
_____. "State Formation and the Role of Trade in Middle Saxon England." *Social Organisation and Settlement*. Eds. David R. Green, Colin Haselgrove, and Matthew Spriggs (Oxford, 1978), 439–54.

Hodgkin, Robert Howard. *A History of the Anglo-Saxons* (Oxford, 1935).
Holdsworth, Philip. "Edwin, King of Northumbria." *The Blackwell Encyclopedia of Anglo-Saxon England*. Ed. Michael Lapidge et al. (London, 1999), 242–4.
Hughes, Kathleen. "The Church in Irish Society, 400–800." *A New History of Ireland Vol I: Prehistoric and Early Ireland*. Ed. Dáibhí Ó Cróinín (Oxford, 2005), 301–29.
_____. *Early Christian Ireland: Introduction to the Sources* (New York, 1972).
_____. "The Welsh Latin Chronicles: *Annales Cambriae* and Related Texts." *PBA* 59 (London, 1975), 233–258.
Hutton, Ronald. *Blood and Mistletoe: The History of the Druids in Britain* (New Haven, 2009)
Huws, Daniel. "Llyfr Gwyn Rhydderch." *CMCS* 21 (Cambridge, 1991), 1–37.
_____. "Red Book of Hergest." *NLW* Journal 22 (Cardiff, 1981), 1–5.
Isaac, Graham R. "Cunedag." *BBCS* 38 (Cardiff, 1991), 100–1.
_____. "Mwynddawg Mwynfawr." *BBCS* 37 (Cardiff, 1990), 111–113.
Jackson, Anthony. *The Symbol Stones of Scotland* (Orkneys, 1984).
Jackson, Kenneth Hurlstone. "The Arthur of History." *Arthurian Literature in the Middle Ages*. Ed. Roger S. Loomis (Chicago, 1959), 1–11.
_____. "The Britons of Southern Scotland." *Antiquity* 29 (Gloucester, 1955), 77–88.
_____. "Edinburgh and the Anglian Occupation of Lothian." *The Anglo-Saxons: Studies in Some Aspects of Their History and Culture Presented to Bruce Dickens*. Ed. Peter Clemoes (London, 1959), 35–42.
_____. *Language and History in Early Britain* (Edinburgh, 1953).
_____. "On the Northern British Section in Nennius." *Celt and Saxon: Studies in the Early British Border*. Ed. Nora K. Chadwick (Cambridge, 1963), 20–62.
_____. "Once Again Arthur's Battles." *MP* 43 (Chicago, 1945), 44–57.
_____. "The Sources for the Life of St. Kentigern." *Studies in the Early British Church*. Ed. Nora K. Chadwick (Cambridge, 1958), 273–357.
Jackson, W.H., and Sylvia A. Ranawake. *The Tristan of the Germans* (Cardiff, 2000).
John, Eric. *Orbis Britanniae* (Leicester, 1966).
Johnson, Flint. *Evidence of Arthur: Fixing the Legendary King in Factual Place and Time* (McFarland, 2014).
_____. *Hengest, Gwrtheyrn, and the Chronology of Post-Roman Britain* (McFarland, 2014).
_____. *Origins of Arthurian Romances: Early Sources for the Legends of Tristan, the Grail and the Abduction of the Queen* (McFarland, 2012).
Jones, Charles W. *Saints' Lives and Chronicles in Early England* (Cornell, 1947 rep.1968).
Jones, Michael E., and John Casey. "The Gallic Chronicle Restored: A Chronology for the Anglo-Saxon Invasions and the End of Roman Britain."*Brittania* 19 (Stroud, 1978), 367–398.
Keevil, Graham D., David Collin Arthur Shotter, and Michael Robin McCarthy. "A Solidus of Valentinian 11 from Scotch Street, Carlisle."*Brittania* 20 (Stroud, 1989), 254–255.
Kelly, Douglas. "Chretien de Troyes." *The Arthur of the French: The Arthurian Legend in Medieval French and Occitan Literature*. Eds. Karen Pratt and Glynn Burgess (Cardiff, 2006).
Kelly, Fergus. *A Guide to Early Irish Law* (Dublin, 1988).
Kern, Fritz. Trans. Stanley B. Grimes. *Kingship and Law in the Middle Ages* (Oxford, 1939).
Kirby, David. "Bede and Northumbrian Chronology." *EHR* 78 (London, 1963), 514–527.
_____. "Bede's Native Sources for the Historia Ecclesiastica." *BJRL* 48 (London, 1965–1966), 341–371.

_____. "British Dynastic History in the Pre-Viking Period." *BBCS* 27 (Cardiff, 1976a), 81–114.
_____. *The Earliest English Kings* (London, 1992).
_____. "Hywel Dda: Anglophile?" *WHR* 8 (Cardiff, 1976b), 1–13.
_____. "Northumbria in the Time of Bede." *St. Wilfrid at Hexham*. Ed. David Kirby (Newcastle-upon-Tyne, 1974), 2–4.
_____. "Problems of Early West Saxon History." *EHR* 80 (London, 1965), 10–29.
_____. "Strathclyde and Cumbria: A Survey of Historical Development to 1092." *TCWAAS* 62 (Kendall, 1962), 71–92.
_____. "Vortigern." *BBCS* 23 (Cardiff, 1970), 37–59.
Koch, John T. "Cadwallon." Ed. John T. Koch. *Celtic Culture: A Historical Encylopedia* (Santa Barbara, 2006).
_____, ed. *Celtic Culture: A Historical Encyclopedia* (Santa Barbara, 2006).
_____. "Cerdic." Ed. John T. Koch. *Celtic Culture: A Historical Encylopedia* (Santa Barbara, 2006).
_____. *Cunedda, Cynan, Cadwallon, Cynddylan: Four Welsh Poems and Britain 383–655* (Cardiff, 2013).
_____. "Marwnad Cunedda a Diwedd y Brydain Rufeinig." *Yr Hen Iaith: Studies in Early Welsh*. Ed. Paul Russell (Cardiff, 2003), 171–97.
_____. "Thoughts on the Ur-Godoðin: Rethinking Aneirin and Mynyðawc Mwynvawr." *Language Sciences* 15.2 (Amsterdam, 1993), 81–9.
_____. "When Was Welsh Literature First Written Down?" *SC* 20/21 (Cardiff, 1985–86), 43–66.
Lapidge, Michael. *Columbanus; Studies on the Latin Writings* (New York, 1997).
_____. "Gildas' Education and the Latin Culture of Sub-Roman Britain." *Gildas: New Approaches*. Eds. David N. Dumville, and Michael Lapidge (Woodbridge, 1984), 27–50.
_____. "Kings of the East Angles." *The Blackwell Encyclopedia of Anglo-Saxon England*. Ed. Michael Lapidge, et al. (London, 1999), 508–9.
_____. "Rædwald." *The Blackwell Encyclopedia of Anglo-Saxon England*. Ed. Michael Lapidge, et al. (London, 1999), 385.
Lapidge, Michael et al. (Eds.) *The Blackwell Encyclopedia of Anglo-Saxon England* (London, 1999).
Laurie, Helen C.R. *Two Studies in Chrètien de Troyes* (Geneva, 1972).
Levison, Wilhelm. "Bischof Germanus von Auxerre und die Quellen zu seiner Geschichte." *Neues Archiv der Gesellschaft für Ältere Deutsche Geschichteskunde* 29 (Paris, 1903–1904), 95–175.
Lloyd, Sir John Edward. *A History of Wales: From the Earliest Times to the Edwardian Conquest* (London, 1912).
Loomis, Roger Sherman. *Arthurian Tradition and Chrétien* (New York, 1949).
_____. *Celtic Myth and Arthurian Romance* (New York, 1927).
_____. *The Grail: From Celtic Myth to Christian Symbol* (Cardiff, 1963).
_____. *Wales and the Arthurian Legend* (Cardiff, 1956).
Losco-Bradley, Stuart and H.M. Wheeler. "Anglo-Saxon Settlement in the Trent Valley: Some Aspects." *Studies in Late Anglo-Saxon Settlement*. Ed. Margaret L. Faull (Oxford, 1984), 101–114.
Loyn, Henry R. *The Governance of Anglo-Saxon England, 500–1087* (Stanford, 1984).
Lynch, Michael, ed. *The Oxford Companion to Scottish History* (Oxford, 2007).
MacQueen, John. "Yvain, Ewen, and Owein ap Urien." *TDGNAHS* 33 (Dumfries, 1956), 107–131.
_____. "A Reply to Professor Jackson." *TDGNAHS* 3rd series 36 (Dumfries, 1959), 175–83.

Mallory, James P. *In Search of the Europeans* (London, 2005).
Maxfield, Valerie A., ed. *The Saxon Shore* (Oxford, 1989).
McCarthy, Daniel, and Dáibhí Ó Cróinín. "The 'Lost' Irish 84-Year Easter Table Rediscovered." *Peritia* 6-7 (Galway, 1987), 227-42.
McCarthy, Daniel P. *The Irish Annals: Their Genesis, Evolution and History* (Chippenham, 2008).
McCarthy, Michael Robin. "Carlisle." *Current Archaeology* 116 (Friary, 1989), 368-372.
_____. *A Roman, Anglian and Medieval Site at Black Friar's Street, Carlisle* (Kendall, 1990), 368-372.
_____. "Thomas, Chadwick, and Post-Roman Britain." *The Early Church in Western Britain and Ireland*. Ed. Susan M. Pierce (Oxford, 1982), 241-256.
Meaney, Audrey L. *A Gazeteer of Early Anglo-Saxon Burial Sites* (London, 1964).
Mendelssohn, Ludwig. *Zosimi Comitiset Exadvocati Fisci Historia Nova* (Lipsiae, rep. 1963).
Miller, Molly. "Bede's Use of Gildas." *EHR* 90 (London, 1975a), 241-261.
_____. "The Commanders of Arthuret." *TCWAAS* 75 (Kendall, 1975c), 96-117.
_____. "Date-Guessing and Dyfed." *SC* 13 (Cardiff, 1978c), 33-61.
_____. "Date-Guessing and Pedigrees." *SC* 11 (Cardiff, 1976a), 96-109.
_____. "The Dates of Deira." *ASE* 8 (London, 1979), 35-61.
_____. "The Disputed Historical Horizon of the Pictish King-Lists." *BBCS* 28 (Cardiff, 1978d), 1-34.
_____. "Forms and Uses of Pedigrees." *THSC* (1978d), 195-206.
_____. "The Foundation Legend of Gwynedd in the Latin Texts." *BBCS* 27 (Cardiff, 1978a), 515-532.
_____. "Historicity and the Pedigrees of the Northcountrymen." *BBCS* 26 (Cardiff, 1975b), 255-280.
_____. "The Last British Entry in the 'Gallic Chronicles.'" *Brit* 9 (Stroud, 1978b), 315-318.
_____. "Relative and Absolute Publication Dates of Gildas' De Excidio in Medieval Scholarship." *BBCS* 26 (Cardiff, 1976b), 169-174.
_____. *Sicilian Colony Dates* (New York, 1970).
_____. "Stilicho's Pictish War."*Brittania* 6 (Stroud, 1975d), 141-145.
Mohrmann, Christine. *The Latin of St. Patrick: Four Lectures* (Dublin, 1961).
Moisl, Herman. "The Bernician Royal Dynasty and the Irish in the Seventh Century." *Peritia* 2 (Galway, 1983), 103-126.
Moore, Donald. *Irish Sea Province in Archaeology and History* (New York, 1970).
Morris, John. *The Age of Arthur* (London, 1973).
_____. *Arthurian Period Sources 3: Persons* (Chichester, 1995).
Murray, Margaret A. *The God of the Witches* (London, 1931).
Myres, John Nowell Linton. *Anglo-Saxon Pottery and the Settlement of England* (Oxford, 1969).
_____. *The English Settlements* (Oxford, 1986).
_____. "Pelagius and the End of Roman Britain." *The Journal of Roman Studies* 50 (London, 1960), 21-36.
_____. "Romano-Saxon Pottery." *Dark-Age Britain: Studies Presented to E.T. Leeds*. Ed. Donald B. Harden (London, 1956), 16-39.
Newton, Sam. *The Origins of Beowulf and the Pre-Viking Kingdom of East Anglia* (Cambridge, 1993).
Nutt, Alfred. *Studies on the Legend of the Holy Grail* (London, 1888).
Ó Corráin, Donnchadh. "Prehistoric and Early Christian Ireland." Ed. Roy Foster. *The Oxford Illustrated History of Ireland* (Oxford, 2001), 1-52.

Ó Cróinin, Dáibhí. *Early Medieval Ireland* (London, 1995).
_____. *A New History of Ireland Vol I: Prehistoric and Early Ireland* (Oxford, 2005).
O'Rahilly, Thomas F. *Early Irish History and Mythology* (Dublin, 1946).
_____. "On the Origin of the Names Érain and Ériu." *Ériu* 35 (Dublin, 1946b), 7–28.
Ó Riain, Pádraig. *Feastdays of the Saints: A History of Irish Martyrologies* (Brussels, 2006).
_____. "Finnian or Winniau." *Irland und Europa. Die Kirche im Frühmittelalter*. Eds. Próinséas Ní Chatháin, Michael Richter, Europa-Zentrum Tübingen (Stuttgart, 1984), 52–7.
_____. "Finnio: A Question of Priority." *Indogermanica et Causica: Festschrift für Karl Horst Schmidt Zum 65. Geburstad*. Eds. Roland Bielmeier, Reinhard Stempel, and René Lansweert (New York, 1994), 407–14.
_____. "Finnio and Winniau: A Return to the Subject." *Ildanach Ildirech: A Festschrift Proinsias MacCana*. Eds. James Carey, John T. Koch, and Pierre-Yves Lambert (Andover, 1999), 187–202.
Oliver, Lisi. *The Beginnings of English Law* (Toronto, 2002).
Olrik, Axel. "Epic Laws of Folk Narrative." *International Folkloristics: Classic Contributions by the Founders of Folklore*. Ed. Alan Dundes (Lanham, 1999), 83–105.
Owen, Morfydd E. "Y Cyfreithiau—(I) Natur Y Testanau." *Y Traddodiad Rhyddiaith yn yr Oesau Canol* (Cardiff, 1974), 197–8.
Oxanne, Audrey. "The Peak Dwellers." *Medieval Archaeology* 6–7 (Leeds, 1962–3), 15–52.
Padel, Oliver. "The Nature of Arthur." *CMCS* 27 (Cardiff, Summer 1994), 1–31.
Phillimore, Egerton. "The *Annales Cambriae* and Old-Welsh Genealogies from Harleian Ms. 3859." *Y Cymmrodor* 8 (Cardiff, 1888), 141–183.
Pierce, Susan M., ed. *The Early Church in Western Britain and Ireland* (Oxford, 1982).
Plunkett, Steven. *Suffolk in Anglo-Saxon Times* (Stroud, 2005).
Poole, Reginald L. *Chronicles and Annals* (Oxford, 1926).
Poulin, Jean-Claude. "Hagiographie et politique. La Première vie de S. Samson de Dol." *Francia* 5 (Paris, 1977), 1–26.
Pratt, Karen, and Glynn Burgess, eds. *The Arthur of the French: The Arthurian Legend in Medieval French and Occitan Literature* (Cardiff, 2006).
Price, Glanville, ed. *Languages in Britain and Ireland* (Oxford, 2000).
Price, Glanville. "Pictish." *Languages in Britain and Ireland*. Ed. Glanville Price (Oxford, 2000), 127–131.
Rahtz, Philip A., Tania M. Dickinson, and Loma Watts. *Anglo-Saxon Cemetaries 1979* (Oxford, 1980).
Reece, Richard. "The End of the City in Roman Britain." *The City in Late Antiquity*. Ed. John Rich (London, 1992), 136–44.
_____. "Town and Country: The End of Roman Britain." *World Archaeology* 12 (London, 1980), 77–92.
Renfew, A. Collin, and Stephen Shennan, eds. *Ranking, Resource and Exchange* (Cambridge, 1982).
Rich, John, ed. *The City in Late Antiquity* (London, 1992).
Richmond, Sir Ian, and Osberht Guy Stanhope Crawford, "The British Section of the Ravenna Cosmography." *Archaeologia Cambrensis* 93 (Cardiff, 1949), 1–50.
Rives, James. "Human Sacrifice Among Pagans and Christians." *Journal of Roman Studies* 85 (London, 1995), 65–85.
Roberts, Brynley F., ed. "Culhwch ac Olwen, the Triads, Saints' Lives." *The Arthur of the Welsh*. Eds., Rachel Bromwich, Alfred O.H. Jarman, and Brynley F. Roberts (Cardiff, 1991), 73–95.

_____. *Early Welsh Poetry: Studies in the Book of Aneirin* (Aberystwyth, 1988).
Roberts, William I. *Romano-Saxon Pottery* (Oxford, 1982).
Russell, J.C. "Late Ancient and Medieval Population." *Transactions of the American Philosophical Society* 48.3 (Philadelphia, 1958), 71–99.
Russell, Paul, ed. *Yr Hen Iaith: Studies in Early Welsh* (Cardiff, 2003).
Sawyer, Peter H., and Ian N. Wood, eds. *Early Medieval Kingship* (Leeds, 1977).
Sawyer, Peter H. *From Roman Britain to Norman England* (London, 1978).
Schaffner, Paul. "Britain's *Iudices*." *Gildas: New Approaches*. Eds. David N. Dumville, and Michael Lapidge (Woodbridge, 1984), 151–155.
Scharer, Anton, and Georg Scheibelreitr, eds. *Historiographie im Frühen Mittelalter* (Munich, 1994), 406–34.
Scharf, Ralf. "Germanus von auxerre—Chronologie seiner Vita." *Francia* 18.1 (Paris, 1991), 1–19.
Scull, Christopher. "Archaeology, Early Anglo-Saxon Society and the Origins of the Anglo-Saxon Kingdoms." *Anglo-Saxon Studies in Archaeology and History* 6 (Oxford, 1993), 65–82.
Selkirk, Andrew. "Birdoswald: Dark Age Halls in a Roman Fort." *Current Archaeology* 101 (Friary, 1986), 172–177.
_____. "Birdoswald: Dark Age Halls in a Roman Fort." *Current Archaeology* 116 (Friary, 1989), 288–91.
Sharpe, Richard. "Gildas as the Father of the Church." *Gildas: New Approaches*. Eds. David N. Dumville, and Michael Lapidge (Woodbridge, 1984), 193–205.
_____. "The Thriving of Dal Riata." *Kings, Clerics and Chronicles in Scotland 500–1297*. Ed. Simon Taylor (Dublin, 2000).
Sims-Williams, Patrick. "Gildas and the Anglo-Saxons." *CMCS* 6 (Cambridge, 1983a), 1–30.
_____. "The Settlement of England in Bede and the Chronicle." *ASE* 12 (London, 1983b), 1–41.
Sisam, Kenneth. "Anglo-Saxon Royal Genealogies." *PBA* 39 (London, 1953), 287–348.
Skene, William Forbes. *Arthur and the Britons in Wales and Scotland*. Ed. Derek Bryce (Lampeter, 1988).
Smith, Julia. M.H, ed. *Early Medieval Rome and the Christian West: Essays in Honour of Donald A. Bullough* (Boston, 2000).
Smyth, Alfred P. *Warlords and Holy Men: Scotland AD 80–1000* (London, 1984).
Snyder, Christopher A. *The World of King Arthur* (London, 2000).
Stafford, Pauline. *Queens, Concubines and Dowagers: The King's Wife in the Early Middle Ages* (Athens, GA, 1983).
Stancliffe, Clare. "Cuthbert and the Polarity Between Pastor and Solitary." *St. Cuthbert, His Cult and His Community to AD 1200*. Eds. Gerald Bonner, and Clare Stancliffe (Woodbridge, 1989), 21–44.
_____. "Oswald, Most Holy and Most Victorious King of the Northumbrians." *Oswald: Northumbrian King to European Saint*. Eds. Clare Stancliffe, and Eric Cambridge (Stamford, 1995), 33–83.
_____. *St. Martin and His Hagiographer: History and Miracle in Sulpicius Severus* (Oxford, 1983).
_____. "Where Was Oswald Killed?" *Oswald: Northumbrian King to European Saint*. Eds. Clare Stancliffe, and Eric Cambridge (Stamford, 1995b), 84–95.
Stancliffe, Clare, Gerald Bonner, and David Rollason, eds. *St. Cuthbert, His Cult and His Community to AD 1200* (Woodbridge, 1989), 103–115.
Stenton, Frank M. *Anglo-Saxon England* (Oxford, 1971).
_____. "The South-Western Element in the Old English Chronicle." *Essays in Medieval*

History Presented to Thomas Frederick Tout. Ed. A.G. Little and Sir Frederick Maurice Powicke (Manchester, 1925), 15-24.
Stokes, Whitley. *The Saltair na Rann. A Collection of Early Middle Irish Poems* (Oxford, 1883).
Strachan, John. "The Verbal System of the Saltair na Rann." *Transactions of the Philological Society* 42 (Hoboken, 1895), 1-76.
Sweet, Henry. "Some of the Sources of the Anglo-Saxon Chronicle." *Englische Studien* 2 (Leipzig, 1879), 310-312.
Taylor, Simon, ed. *Kings, Clerics and Chronicles in Scotland 500-1297* (Dublin, 2000).
_____. "Place Names." *The Oxford Companion to Scottish History.* Ed. Michael Lynch (Oxford, 2007).
Thacker, Alan. "Lindesfarne and the Origins of the Cult of St Cuthbert." *St. Cuthbert, His Cult and His Community to AD 1200.* Eds. Gerald Bonner, David Rollason, and Clare Stancliffe (Woodbridge, 1989), 103-122.
Thomas, Charles. *Christianity Up to About A.D. 500* (London, 1981).
Thompson, Edward A. "Britain, A.D. 406-410." *Brit* 8 (Stroud, 1977), 303-318.
_____. "Gildas and the History of Britain." *Brit* 10 (Stroud, 1979), 203-226.
_____. "Procopius on Brittia and Britannia." *Classical Quarterly* 30 (London, 1980), 498-507.
_____. *St Germanus of Auxerre and the End of Roman Britain* (Woodbridge, 1984).
_____. "St. Patrick and Coroticus." *JTS* 31 (London, 1980), 12-27.
_____. "Zosimus 6.10.2 and the Letters of Honorius." *CQ* 32 (London, 1982), 445-462.
Thornton, David E. "Dinogad." *Oxford Dictionary of National Biography* (Oxford, 2004). Web.
_____. "Mordaf Hael." *Oxford Dictionary of National Biography* (Oxford, 2004). Web.
Turville-Petre, Gabriel. *Myth and Religion of the North: The Religion of Ancient Scandinavia* (London, 1964).
Turville-Petre, Joan E. "Hengest and Horsa." *Saga-Book of the Viking Saga* 14 (London, 1953-7), 273-90.
Vansina, Jan. *Oral Tradition as History* (Madison, 1985).
de Vries, Jan. *Altgermanische Religiongeschichte* (Berlin, 1937), 32-43.
_____. "Die Ursprungssage der Sachsen." *Niedersächen Jarhbuch für Landesgeschichte* 31 (Berlin, 1959), 20-37.
Wacher, John S. *The Towns of Roman Britain* (Berkeley, 1974).
Wade-Evans, Arthur Wade. "Notes on the Excidium Britanniae: A Contribution Towards a Re-Statement of Early Saxo-Welsh History." *Celtic Review* 1 (Edinburgh, 1905), 289-95.
_____. "'The Ruin of Britannia': A Contribution Towards a Restatement [Sic] of Early Saxo-Welsh History." *Celtic Review* 2 (Edinburgh, 1906), 46-58 and 126-35.
Wallace-Hadrill, John Michael. *Early Germanic Kingship in England and on the Continent* (Oxford, 1971).
Ward-Perkins, Bryan. "Why Did the Anglo-Saxons Not Become More British." *EHR* 115 (Oxford, 2000), 513-33.
Watson, William J., and Simon Taylor. *The History of the Celtic Place-Names of Scotland* (Edinburgh, 2004).
Welch, Martin. "The Kingdom of the South Saxons: The Origins." *The Origins of the Anglo-Saxon Kingdoms.* Ed. Stephen Bassett (Leicester, 1989), 75-83.
Wells, Calvin. *Bones, Bodies and Disease* (London, 1964).
West, Martin Litchfield. *Indo-European Poetry and Myth* (Oxford, 2007).
West, S.E. Norman Scarfe, and R.J. Cramp. "Iken, St. Botolph, and the Coming of East

Anglian Christianity." *Proceedings of the Suffolk Institute of Archaeology* 15 (Bury St Edmunds, 1984), 279–301.
Weston, Jessie. *From Ritual to Romance* (London, 1920).
_____. *The Legend of Sir Gawain* (London, 1897).
_____. *The Quest of the Holy Grail* (London, 1913).
Wheeler, G. Henry. "Gildas' De Excidio Chapter 26." *EHR* 41 (London, 1926), 497–503.
White, Richard. "New Light on the Origins of the Kingdom of Gwynedd." *Studies in Old Welsh Poetry: Astudiaethau Ar Yr Hengerdd*. Eds. Rachel Bromwich and R. Brinley Jones (Cardiff, 1978), 350–5.
Whitelock, Dorothy. *English Historical Documents Vol. I. 500–1042* (London, 1968).
Williams, Anne, Alfred P. Smyth, and David P. Kirby. *A Biographical Dictionary of Dark Age Britain* (London, 1997).
Williams, Anne. *Kingship and Government in Pre-Conquest England, c. 500–1066* (Basingstoke, 1999).
Williams, Griffith John, and Evan John Jones. *Gramadegau'r Penceirddiaid* (Cardiff, 1934).
Williams, Hugh. *Gildae De Excidio Britanniae* (London, 1899).
Williams, Sir Ifor. *The Beginnings of Early Welsh Poetry*. Ed. Rachel Bromwich (Cardiff, 1972).
_____. *Hen Chwedlau* (Cardiff, 1949).
_____. "Marwnad Cynddylan." *BBCS* 6 (Cardiff, 1932), 134–141.
Williams, Nicholas J.A. "Llywarch Hen and the Finn Cycle." *Astudiaethau ar yr Hengerdd*. Eds. Rachel Bromwich and R. Brinley Jones (Cardiff, 1978), 234–265.
Woolf, Alex. "Caedualla Rex Brittonum and the Passing of the Old North." Northern History 41.1 (Leeds, 2004), 5–24.
___. "An Interpolation in the Text of the *De Excidio Britanniae* 23.3–4." Academia.edu.
Wood, Ian N. "Kings, Kingdoms and Consent." *Early Medieval Kingship*. Eds. Peter H. Sawyer, and Ian N. Wood (Leeds, 1977), 1–30.
_____. "The End of Roman Britain: Continental Evidence and Parallels." *Gildas: New Approaches*. Eds. David N. Dumville and Michael Lapidge (Woodbridge, 1984), 1–25.
_____. *The Most Holy Abbot Ceolfrid* (Jarrow, 1995).
_____. "Continuity or Calamity: The Constraints of Literary Models." Ed. John Drinkwater. *Fifth-Century Gaul: A Crisis of Identity* (Cambridge, 2002), 1–14.
"Why Farming Matters: England." RSPB. Retrieved November 2, 2015.
"Why Farming Matters: Northern Ireland." RSPB. Retrieved November 2, 2015.
"Why Farming Matters: Scotland." RSPB. Retrieved November 2, 2015.
"Why Farming Matters: Wales." RSPB. Retrieved November 2, 2015.
Wormald, Patrick. "Bede, the *Bretwaldas* and the Origins of the *Gens Anglorum*." Eds. Patrick Wormald, Donald Bullough, and Roger Collins. *Ideal and Reality in Frankish and Anglo-Saxon Society: Studies Presented to J.M. Wallace-Hadrill* (Oxford, 1983), 99–129.
_____. *The First Code of English Law* (Canterbury, 2005).
Wright, Neil. "Gildas's Geographical Perspective: Some Problems." *Gildas: New Approaches*. Eds. David N. Dumville and Michael Lapidge (Woodbridge, 1984), 85–105.
_____. "Gildas's Prose Style and Its Origins." *Gildas: New Approaches*. Eds. David N. Dumville and Michael Lapidge (Woodbridge, 1984), 107–128.
Yorke, Barbara. "The Jutes of Hampshire and Wight and the Origins of Wessex." *The Origins of the Anglo-Saxon Kingdoms*. Ed. Stephen Bassett (Leicester, 1989), 84–96.

_____. "The Kingdom of the East Saxons." *ASE* 14 (London, 1985), 1–30.
_____. *Kings and Kingdoms of Early Anglo-Saxon England* (London, 1990).
_____. "The Origins of Mercia." *Mercia: An Anglo-Saxon Kingdom in Europe*. Eds. Michelle P. Brown, and Carole A. Farr (New York, 2001), 1–19.
_____. *Wessex: Studies in the Early History of Britain* (London, 1995).
Ziegler, Michelle. "The Politics of Exile in Early Northumbria." *Ha* 2 (St. John's, 1999), 8–15.

Index

Aberffraw 106
Acha 179
Adda 167-9, 243
Adomnán 14 35, 184, 214, 220
Aed Brosc 110-11
Aed Sláine 33
Áedán 37-8, 149-50, 155, 175-9, 189, 198, 213, 220
Ælle 57, 143-4, 152-3, 158-9, 162, 169, 178, 181, 191, 213
Æthelberht 33-4, 50-2, 58-9, 112, 141, 153, 158-61, 163-4, 177-82, 188-9, 191, 196-7, 208, 213, 218, 230
Æthelburg 167, 182, 189, 198
Æthelfrith 135-6, 150, 153, 166-9, 176-83, 188, 191, 213, 244
Æthelhere 186-8
Æthelric 167-70, 179, 243
Æthelstan 139
Æthelthryth 188
Æthelwald 186, 191
Æthelwealh 191
Aetius 29-31, 84, 139, 212, 239
Aidan 167, 184
Aillil Molt 88
Alaric 5, 96
Alcock, Leslie 225, 237, 252
Aldfrith 36, 186
Alfred 2, 56, 59, 140, 217
Alhflæd 186, 198
Alhfrith 50, 59, 186-7, 220
Ambrosius 47-9, 55-6, 58, 100, 107-8, 205, 212
Aneirin 14, 32, 42, 58, 222-3, 226, 228, 230, 231, 233, 235, 237, 238, 239, 240, 242, 243, 244
Anglo-Saxon Chronicle 1-2, 7, 9-10, 14, 50, 56-8, 100, 128, 140, 142-4, 159-63, 169, 171, 178, 182, 185, 188, 210-1, 214, 217, 231, 239, 242-4, 247

Anna 185-6, 188-90, 213, 247
Annales Cambriae 2, 7, 9-10, 26, 29, 47-9, 55-6, 58, 109, 122, 127, 132, 182-3, 185, 217, 229, 231, 237-8, 241, 244
Annals of Clonmacnoise 33, 175-6, 217, 236
Annals of Innisfallen 175, 217, 236
Annals of Tigernach 175-6, 182, 184, 236
Annals of Ulster 175-6, 182, 217, 236
Ansehis 52, 105-6, 162, 207, 212, 244
Anthony the Great 36, 221
Antonine's Wall 30, 72, 215
Arfderydd, Battle of 127-8, 132-3, 144, 213
Argyll 68, 70, 74, 87
Armes Prydein 28
Arthur 2-3, 8, 11, 15, 31, 44-5
Athelstan 42, 54, 210, 218
Attila 16, 77, 82-4, 115, 204, 212
Augustine of Canterbury 33, 52, 158, 160, 168, 178, 189, 224
Augustine of Hippo 16, 19, 79, 200, 213

Badon 29, 47-8, 53, 95, 100, 107, 122-4, 132, 139, 151-2, 213, 237-8, 240
Baldred 38
Bangor 33, 36, 180, 198, 217
Bard 11, 28, 31-3, 43-48, 83, 95-101, 104, 106-7, 113, 115, 117-8, 123-4, 132, 140, 145, 156, 169, 206, 212, 215, 218, 220-1, 224, 229, 234, 236-7
Battle of Heavenfield 183-5, 188, 213
Battle of Woden's Barrow 190
Beandun, Battle of 190
Bede 1-2, 7-10, 14, 35, 41, 50-54, 56-59, 85, 100, 128, 139-40, 142-3, 158, 161-2, 166, 168-9, 172, 174, 176, 178, 180-1, 183-5, 195, 210, 212, 216, 218-9, 222, 227-8, 230-1, 235, 238-42, 244-8
Belatacudros 64, 102, 202-3
Belisarius 21, 223

268 Index

Berneich 28, 36, 57, 106, 233
Bertha 50, 177, 213
Black Book of Carmarthen 45, 109
Black Book of Chirk 42, 104, 238
Bragawt 98, 215
Bretwalda 43, 158-9, 162, 178, 181, 191, 215, 228, 239
British Heroic Age 96, 109, 235
Brude 90-1, 147, 174-5, 194, 201
Brychan 74, 102, 111
Brycheiniog 74, 87-8, 111

Cadafael 186-7
Cadell 40, 54, 108, 214, 220
Cadfan 181, 183
Cadwallon son of Cadfan 2, 28, 55, 96, 151, 181-7, 191
Cædwalla 183, 237
Caer Greu 167, 169, 243
Caesar, Julius 66, 202, 248
Camlann, Battle of 45, 55, 109, 122-3, 132
Canterbury 33, 52, 178, 207, 227, 230
Canu Heledd 41-2, 214, 217
Catraeth, Battle of 58, 104, 127-8, 133, 136-7, 144, 165-6, 213, 218, 233, 239
Cauponae 63, 215
Caw 91, 108-9, 233, 236
Cearl 181, 184-5, 246
Ceawlin 57, 143, 152-3, 158-60, 163-4, 169, 178, 190, 237, 241
Cenwealh 185-8, 190, 213
Ceol 190
Ceolfrith 41, 220
Cerdic 124, 152, 163, 182-3, 231, 237, 241
Ceredig 27, 103-4, 108, 110, 183, 220, 235
Ceretic 56
Cernunnos 202
Charles the Bald 54
Chester, Battle of 53, 132, 135, 180, 183, 85, 213, 244
Chrétien de Troyes 203, 222
Christianity 4, 15-6, 26-7, 37-8, 44, 53, 59, 65, 79-80, 156-7, 160, 162, 178, 180-2, 184, 186-8, 190-2, 194, 196-8, 200, 203, 206-8, 216, 218, 221, 228, 233-4, 241, 244, 247
Chronicle of Ireland 33, 214, 217, 243, 247
Cirencester, Battle of 190
Civitates 6, 70, 77, 85, 133
Claudian 14, 18, 224
Clovis 94
Clydno 104, 126
Clydog 42
Clydwyn 110
Cnebba 171
Code of Æthelberht 14, 33-4, 213, 218

Code of Hlothere and Eadric 14, 34, 214, 218
Code of Wihtred 34, 214, 218
Coel 104-5, 112, 145
Cogfry, Battle of 49, 213
Colgu 148
Columba 14, 35, 37, 74, 91, 147-50, 155, 175-6, 183-4, 189, 193-5, 213, 216, 220
Columbanus 14, 29, 36-7, 218
Comes 68, 215
Comgall 74, 111, 148
Conall Crandomna 37-8, 189, 220
Conchobar 45, 145
Conn Cétchathach 74
Connad Cerr 189
Connaught 189
Constantine 3, 5-6, 16, 21, 26, 30, 70, 77, 79-81, 85, 92-3, 119-20, 205, 212
Constantinople 19, 169
Constantius 6, 14, 20-1, 200, 213, 221, 224
Council of Carthage 16, 200, 212
Creoda son of Cynewald 171, 184, 246
Crida 171
Cú Chúlainn 45
Cuil Dremne, Battle of 147, 193
Culhwch ac Olwen 44, 90, 109, 124, 202, 214, 218, 223, 229, 233, 236, 237, 248
Cunedda 28, 101, 107-8, 110, 219, 233, 235
Cunomorus 128, 238
Currach 149, 215
Cutha 163-4, 178, 190
Cuthbert 36
Cuthwine 164, 190
Cuthwulf 164, 190
Cwichelm 182, 185, 190-1, 247
Cwœnburg 181, 184
Cynan Garwyn 2, 31, 134, 220
Cynddylan 37, 219
Cyneberht 52
Cyneburh 186
Cynegils 185, 190
Cynewald 171
Cynfelyn 104, 127, 131
Cyngen son of Cadell 40, 210, 220
Cynon 40, 210, 220

Dal Riata 35, 37-8, 68, 74, 87-9, 91, 111, 147-50, 155, 175-7, 180, 182-4, 186-7, 189, 191, 193-4, 198, 208, 220, 232, 240, 242-3
David 39, 55
De Excidio Britanniae 28-9, 31, 37, 52, 107, 112, 144, 194, 207, 209, 213, 218-9, 234-5, 239
Degsastan, Battle of 150, 177, 179-80, 213
Deira 53, 57, 59, 105-6, 133-7, 145, 168-70, 172, 179-81, 185-7, 191, 226, 243

Index

Dent 36, 134
Deorham, Battle of 190
Dewrarth 145
Din Eidyn 39, 127
Din Peledyr 127
Dinas Bran 40
Dinogad 133-4, 238
Domangart son of Nisse 111, 147
Domnall 148
Domnall Brecc 189
Druids 65, 201-2, 248
Druim Cett 148, 150, 213
Drystan son of Tallwch 102, 109, 236
Dunawt 132-4, 231
Dúnchad son of Conall 149, 176, 189
Dunpelder 39, 104
Dyfed 31, 54, 56, 74, 87-8, 107, 110-1, 139, 142, 183, 206, 208, 212-3, 223, 236, 244
Dyrham, Battle of 58-9, 160, 178, 182, 242

Eadbald 181-2, 188-9, 198
Eadfrith 36, 185
Eanflæd 189
Eanfrith 174, 176, 183-4, 187
East Anglia 57, 171-3, 180-2, 185-91, 197-8, 213, 243, 247
Easter Table 27, 29, 225, 235
Ecgfrith 188
Ecgric 185, 188, 198
Edwin 36-7, 48, 53, 56, 105, 179-85, 187-91, 198, 220, 244, 245, 246, 248
Einion Yrth 74, 106-7, 233, 236
Elidyr Mwynfar 126
Elisedd son of Gwylog 40-1, 220
Elmet 36, 56, 105, 126-7, 137, 167, 182-3, 213, 241
Eochaid Allmuir 74, 110
Eochaid Buide 189
Eochaid Mugmedon 86-7
Eochaid Muinremar 37
Eoganán son of Gabrán 149-50
Eorcenberht 197-9, 246
Eorpwald 187-8
Eowa 185
Epitoma Chronicon 19, 218
Erc 37, 148
Ernulf 34
Essex 57, 163-4, 178-81, 184, 187-191, 197-8, 207, 230
Eunapius 224
Eusebius 19, 218

Felix 188, 225
Fer 'n' Alban 14, 213, 220
Fflamddwyn 165
Fiacha Sroiptine 74, 86

Fiachnae 182, 245
Fionn macCumhail 122
Foederati 3, 16-18, 50, 67, 69, 71, 75, 81-5, 92-4, 100, 105, 114-5, 120, 138-9, 162, 196, 204-5, 207-9, 212, 215, 225, 234, 244
Fraomar 105, 212
Free Will 16, 19, 21, 79
Frithuwald 167-9

Gabrán 37, 74, 147-9, 176
Gai, Battle of 56
Gallic Chronicle of 511 6, 19, 81, 93-4, 200, 218, 223-4
Gallic Chronicle of 452 6, 19, 81, 93-4, 200, 218, 223-4
Garmon 54-5, 194, 214, 231
Gaul 5, 22, 36, 66, 82, 87, 94, 188, 224
Geoffrey of Monmouth 1, 4, 8, 10, 17, 45, 55, 102, 214, 219
Germanus of Auxerre 6, 19-20, 54-5, 80, 200, 210, 212, 214, 224, 231
Gildas 1-2, 7-10, 14, 19, 28-31, 37, 51-3, 55, 80, 85, 93, 100, 107-8, 114, 120, 124, 138-41, 151-2, 194-5, 200, 207, 209-11, 218-9, 231, 239, 240
Glamorgan 40, 214, 219
Glappa 167, 169
Gloucester 107-8, 128, 229, 237, 239
Gododdin 32, 39, 83, 101, 106, 125, 127, 131, 136-7, 144, 151, 165, 167, 216, 226
Grammaticus 29
Gregory 22, 36, 57, 144, 169, 197, 218
Gregory of Tours 14, 21-2, 213, 219, 228, 238, 248
Guitolin 107-8
Gwallog 31-2, 126-7, 134, 136, 145, 165, 170
Gwên 43
Gwenddoleu 127, 132-4
Gwent 31, 42, 210, 226
Gwladys 102, 108
Gwledyr 110
Gwrgi 127, 132-3, 167, 169, 213, 231, 243
Gwrthefyr 139-41, 230
Gwrtheyrn 3, 11-13, 38, 41, 46, 52, 54-55, 58, 107, 112-13, 125, 128, 138-43, 145, 158-9, 165, 190, 209-10, 220, 223, 228-36, 239, 241
Gwrwst Priodor 126
Gwynedd 28, 42, 54-6, 58, 74, 87-8, 101, 103, 106-8, 112, 124, 126-33, 136-7, 153, 174, 182-3, 186, 206, 210, 218-9, 223, 228, 231-3, 235-6, 239
Gwynllyw 102, 108

Hadrian's Wall 8, 26, 30, 68, 72, 81, 87, 102-3, 123-4

270　Index

Hatfield Chase, Battle of 37, 183, 185–6, 213
Heavenfield, Battle of 183–5, 188, 213
Hengest 3, 11–13, 38, 41, 46, 51–3, 55, 57–9, 106, 139–42, 145, 152, 158, 161–2, 165, 172, 197, 207–8, 210, 225, 230, 242
Herbert, Bishop 38–9
Hering 168, 177
Hidage 36
Historia Brittonum 1–2, 9, 13–14, 41, 44, 47–50, 53–4, 56–8, 4, 100, 105, 107–8, 110, 113, 122–3, 126, 133, 135–7, 139–40, 142, 144–5, 161, 165–8, 171, 174, 185, 210–11, 214, 219, 222, 236, 237, 241, 244
Historia Franconum 219
Historia Nova 19, 213
Historia Regum Britanniae 10, 45, 214, 219
Holy Grail 2–3, 80, 202, 222
Honorian Rescript 30, 212
Honorius 5–6, 20, 30, 77, 85, 92, 205, 231
Horsa 51, 53, 57, 106, 139, 161, 210, 225
Hrolf Kraki 145
Hueil 91, 102–3, 108–9
Hussa 135, 167–8
Hwicce 190–1
Hywel Dda 42, 54–6, 58, 139, 210, 214, 219, 228

Icel 171
Ida 57–8, 140, 145, 166–9, 237, 243
Iddeu 56
Idle, Battle of 176, 180–3, 213
Ine 34, 50, 219
Irish Annals 26, 32, 35, 55, 88, 175, 213, 217
Isidore's Chronicle 32, 55, 213, 217, 219
Iurminric 141–4, 159–60, 169–70

Jerome 19, 218
Jocelyn 38–9
Johan son of Conall 148
Jotun 156
Justinian Plague 21, 153, 194, 206, 213

Karvi 75, 216
Kent 7–8, 14–15, 33–4, 50–2, 55–6, 58, 105, 112–13, 128, 139, 141–2, 144–6, 158–63, 165, 170, 172, 177–81, 184, 187–9, 192, 196–8, 207–8, 210–1, 213, 218–19, 230
Kentigern 38–9, 102, 183, 194, 221
Kentish Source 7–8, 15, 47, 49–59, 128, 138–9, 141–2, 158, 161–2, 166, 178, 97, 210, 213, 219, 229–30

Laws of Hywel Dda 42, 54, 214, 219
Laws of Ine 14, 34, 214, 219
Lindesfarne 36, 126, 167–8, 238
Llandaff Charters 7, 40, 214, 219, 228

Lleudun 39, 102, 104
Llywarch Hen 42–4, 219–20
Lóegaire 87–8, 233
Lothian 38–9, 72, 81, 83, 102, 104, 111, 129, 137
Luguvalium 103

Magnus Maximus 68, 231
Mana 156–7, 197, 208, 216
Mansione 63, 216
Marcellinus, Ammianus 14, 18, 26, 67, 105, 212
Maredudd 55
Martin, St. 36, 203, 212
"Marwnad Cunedda" 28, 101, 219, 232–3, 235
"Marwnad Cynddylan" 2, 37, 41–2, 44, 219
Maserfelth, Battle of 37, 184–6, 189
Maximus 16, 30, 68–9, 106, 110, 212, 231
Medrawt 109–10
Mellitus, Bishop 191, 230
Mercia 11, 36–7, 41, 49, 53, 55, 124, 171–3, 181–2, 184–7, 189, 191–2, 197–8, 228, 230, 243, 246
Mervyn Frych 54
Middle Anglia 171–3, 185–6, 188, 198
Middlesex 163–4, 230
"Moliant Cadwallon" 2
Mons Graupius 72
Morgannwg 42, 210
Morgant 126
Muiredach Tírech 74, 86
Mutatione 63, 216
Myrddin 132, 213, 220, 238

Nechtan 175–6
Nechtanesmere, Battle of 49, 220
Nennius 1–2
Niall Noígíallach 74, 87–8, 92
Northern Memorandum 8, 15, 47–51, 53–9, 122, 157, 217, 219, 229–30, 237
Northern Uí Néill 189
Northumbria 7, 28, 36–9, 49–50, 52–3, 55, 58, 105–6, 135–7, 139, 141, 144–7, 150, 162, 165–71, 174, 176–7, 179–89, 191–2, 198, 207, 213, 219, 238, 242, 244
Nothhelm 51–2
Nudd Hael 126

Octha 52, 242
Odin 156–7
Oisc 52, 161–2, 242, 244
Olympiodorus of Thebes 20, 219, 224
Orric 52, 161–2
Oswald 37, 183–6, 189–91, 198
Oswine 185–6

Index

Oswiu 37, 49–50, 56, 59, 176, 83, 185–7, 191, 198, 207, 213, 229, 246
Owain son of Urien 8, 56, 134, 165

Padarn Peisrud 54, 106
Palladius 193, 212, 233
Pasgen 7, 134
Patrick, St. 14, 27–8, 47, 80, 87, 103–4, 193–4, 212, 220, 225, 233
Paul 189, 228, 257
Paulinus 167
Peada 185–7, 198, 213
Pelagians 6, 16, 19, 26, 79–80, 200–1, 205, 212, 218
Pelagius 16, 79, 200
"Pen Urien" 42–4, 200
Penda 37, 49, 55–6, 124, 171, 182–91, 198, 207, 213, 219, 226, 247
Pennawc 36
Peredur 3, 127, 132–3, 167, 169, 202–3, 213, 231, 243
Perym 36
Pictish Chronicle 34–5, 72–3, 90–1, 175–6, 214, 220
Pictland 11, 86–7, 90–1, 104, 108–9, 127, 147, 174–5, 177, 193, 220, 233
Pillar of Eliseg 40–1, 210, 214, 220
Port 163
Powys 41–3, 54–5, 58, 108, 127–8, 134, 139, 210, 219, 226
Predestination. 16, 21, 79, 200
Prophecy of Berchán 177, 220
Prosper of Aquitaine 14, 19, 193, 200, 217, 218
Ptolemy 71
Pybba 171, 184

Rædwald 172, 174, 176, 178, 180–3, 187–89, 191, 198, 243, 247
Ravenna Cosmography 23, 105, 162, 220
Rheged 44, 49, 167
Rhetor 29
Rhodri Mawr 40, 136, 139
Rhun son of Maelgwn 129, 131
Rhun son of Urien. 48–50, 56, 123, 229
Rhydderch 126–7, 136, 165, 170, 177, 194
Ricberht 188, 198
Ricula 163, 191
Rieinmellth 49, 186, 213, 229
Romanitas 3, 84, 95, 108, 216
Rome 3, 5–6, 13, 15–19, 25–6, 39, 41, 50, 61, 63–5, 67–75, 77, 79–86, 92–3, 96, 100, 103, 108, 110, 112, 114, 119–20, 124, 131, 181, 196–8, 00, 202, 204–7, 209, 212, 248
Rufinus' Chronicle 32, 212

Sæberht 163–4, 178, 181, 189, 191, 213
Sæward 191
Samson 14, 22–3, 80, 194, 213, 221, 225, 232, 248
Saxon Shore 68, 105, 232
Scriptorium 147, 216
Seaxburh 188–9
Seaxred 190–1
Selyf 31, 180, 183, 5
Senchus Fer n' Alban 37–8, 147–8, 220
Sidonius Apollonaris 14
Sigeberht 180, 187–8, 191, 198
Six Go Through the World 44, 223
Skop 11, 45–6, 96–7, 115–6, 145, 156, 167, 169, 216
Sledd 163, 191
Soemil 57, 105–6, 145, 169
Stephanus, Eddius 14, 41, 218, 228, 238
Stilicho 18, 84
Strathcarron, Battle of 189
Strathclyde 27, 38–9, 72, 81, 103–5, 111, 126, 137, 149–50, 167, 174, 176–7, 182, 189, 194, 206, 218, 226, 235
Stuf 163
Sulpicius Severus 36, 221
Superbus Tyrannus 52, 55, 100, 138, 140, 207, 209–10, 216, 225
Sussex 57, 145–6, 158–60, 162, 169–70, 184, 191, 231
Swithhelm 187, 191, 247
Symbol Stones 8, 223
Synod of Whitby 37, 53, 155, 187, 191, 208, 214

Tacitus 90–1, 232
Talhaearn 140, 210, 236–7
Taliesin 14, 28, 31–2, 42, 44, 48, 58, 101, 112–3, 126–7, 137, 165, 220, 229, 237
Talorcan 109, 176, 187
Täneü 39
Testudo 64, 216
Teulu 94, 118, 216
Theodoric 128, 135, 238
Theodosius the Elder 68, 212
Theodric 167–9
Tintagel 74, 87, 112
Tondberht 188
"Trawsganu Cynan Garwyn" 2, 31, 220
Tribal Hidage 7, 14, 36, 172, 213, 220
Trumhere 187
Tytila 172

Uí Néill 33, 189
Uinniau 37, 193
Urban 40, 214, 219
Urien 7–8, 31–2, 42–4, 47–50, 54, 56, 58,

101, 110, 112, 122–3, 125–7, 134–7, 144–6, 151–3, 165–8, 170, 179, 182, 187, 17, 220, 229, 231, 238
Uscfrea 189

Vita Cadoci 91, 102, 108, 111
Vita Carantoci 110, 220
Vita Columbae 175
Vita Cuthberti 14, 214, 221
Vita Germani 6, 14, 20–1, 75, 213, 231
Vita Gildae 90, 109, 217
Vita Gundleus 108
Vita Kentigerni 14, 38–9, 102, 132–3, 214, 221, 228
Vita Samsoni 14, 22–3, 202, 213, 221
Vita Wilfridi 14, 41, 134, 214, 218
Vortigern 52, 55, 57, 59, 107, 128, 139–43, 165, 201, 207–11, 230

Wallop, Battle of 107
Wehha 172
Welsh Triads 7–8, 14, 45, 102, 109, 127, 150, 167, 183, 221

Wessex 34, 56–7, 124, 145–6, 158–61, 163–4, 168, 170–2, 178, 182–4, 187–91, 211, 213, 217, 219, 230, 231, 241, 242, 243, 244, 247
West Saxon Genealogical Regnal List 159
Whitby, Synod of 37, 53, 155, 187, 191, 208, 214
Wihtgara 163
Wihtred 14, 34, 50, 214, 218
William the Conqueror 44–5
Winwæd, Battle of 37, 186, 188, 213
Woden's Barrow, Battle of 190
Wuffa 172
Wulfhere 187, 191, 246

Y Gododdin 2, 14, 32, 122, 124, 127, 133, 135–7, 145, 175, 218
Ystoria Taliesin 28

Zosimus 5, 14, 19–20, 30, 213, 219

www.ingramcontent.com/pod-product-compliance
Ingram Content Group UK Ltd.
Pitfield, Milton Keynes, MK11 3LW, UK
UKHW041930140426
5217IPUK00014B/402